MOTHERING A BODIED CURRICULUM
EMPLACEMENT, DESIRE, AFFECT

Edited by Stephanie Springgay and Debra Freedman

This collection of essays considers how notions of embodiment and mothering are related to curriculum theory and practices in education. Advancing a new understanding of the maternal body, it argues for a 'bodied curriculum' that attends to the relational, social, and ethical implications of 'being-with' other bodies differently, and to the different knowledges such bodily encounters produce.

The contributors to this volume argue that the prevailing silence about the maternal body in educational scholarship reinforces the binary split between domestic and public spaces, family life and work, one's own children and others' children, and women's roles as 'mothers' or 'others.' Providing an interdisciplinary perspective in which postmodern ideas about the body interact with those of learning and teaching, *Mothering a Bodied Curriculum* brings theory and practice together into an ever-evolving conversation.

STEPHANIE SPRINGGAY is an assistant professor in the Department of Curriculum, Teaching and Learning at the Ontario Institute for Studies in Education, University of Toronto.

DEBRA FREEDMAN is an instructor in the Department of Family Relations and Applied Nutrition at the University of Guelph.

EDITED BY STEPHANIE SPRINGGAY
AND DEBRA FREEDMAN

Mothering a Bodied Curriculum

- Book comes out of a post-structuralist perspective:

Emplacement, Desire, Affect   breaking open &
making it porous.

UNIVERSITY OF TORONTO PRESS

Toronto   Buffalo   London

© University of Toronto Press 2012
Toronto Buffalo London
www.utppublishing.com
Printed in Canada

ISBN 978-1-4426-4374-1 (cloth)
ISBN 978-1-4426-1227-3 (paper)

Printed on acid-free, 100% post-consumer recycled paper with vegetable-based inks.

Library and Archives Canada Cataloguing in Publication

Mothering a bodied curriculum : emplacement, desire, affect/edited by
Stephanie Springgay and Debra Freedman.

Includes bibliographical references.
ISBN 978-1-4426-4374-1 (bound).   ISBN 978-1-4426-1227-3 (pbk.)

1. Motherhood.   2. Motherhood–Social aspects.   3. Feminist theory.
4. Critical pedagogy.   I. Springgay, Stephanie   II. Freedman, Debra

HQ759.M883 2012   306.874'3   C2011-907278-5

This book has been published with the help of a grant from the Canadian
Federation for the Humanities and Social Sciences, through the Aid to
Scholarly Publications Program, using funds provided by the Social Sciences
and Humanities Research Council of Canada

University of Toronto Press acknowledges the financial assistance to its
publishing program of the Canada Council for the Arts and the Ontario Arts
Council.

  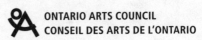

University of Toronto Press acknowledges the financial support for its
publishing activities of the Government of Canada through the Canada Book
Fund.

For Our Mothers

Contents

Acknowledgments

People are always surprised that mothering might be a topic of consideration for an academic text. Some nod in boredom as we talk about the relationships between curriculum, pedagogy, and the performance of mothering; others launch into their own stories about diaper rash, tantrums, the perils of finding daycare, and the feeding frenzies of teens. But these bored nods and frantic personal narratives are what fuels this collection of essays on mothering and education – for our lives as teachers are never wholly autonomous. They are always, already, woven and imbricated with other bodies and beings.

We are so grateful for the many 'doulas' we had on this journey towards publication. Thanks to University of Toronto Press – especially to Brittany Lavery and Virgil Duff. Brittany took over the reins of our project when Virgil retired – her help, insight, and guidance throughout the publication process has been much appreciated. Thanks also go to Shoshana Wasser and her team who helped us through the marketing process.

Thanks to our many colleagues who reviewed individual chapters; your insights and constructive comments helped complicate and strengthen our collective work. We also appreciate the three anonymous reviewers who reviewed our book manuscript in its entirety. Saskia Stille was a huge help in working on early edits of revised manuscripts and we were fortunate to have her assistance. This book is also indebted to Natalie Jolly's scholarship and vision on feminist mothering. We are so grateful for her insights and support of the project.

We express heartfelt gratitude to the authors of the individual chapters for their contributions and their patience throughout the long process of publication (similar to the last month of pregnancy, perhaps – full of expectation and uncertainty, along with random aches and unimaginable anxiety). This book has been a labour of love, one that has taken a very long time, and we are so glad you hung on until the end.

Once again we have edited a collection that neither Paras nor Koushik will claim to understand (or want to read). But without their support and the support from our children, Maurya, Liam, and Samuel this book would never have been realized. We also now know why Deb's mother used to hide in the bathroom with the door locked . . . sometimes mothers need space and quiet to collect their thoughts. We cannot express the gratitude enough to our own mothers – for their devotion to mothering and for the care they continue to provide our children. Thank you to everyone!

Guess it's time to go shoe shopping.

MOTHERING A BODIED CURRICULUM
EMPLACEMENT, DESIRE, AFFECT

Edited by Stephanie Springgay and Debra Freedman

Introduction: M/othering and a Minor Methodology

STEPHANIE SPRINGGAY AND DEBRA FREEDMAN

Mothering a Bodied Curriculum is a book that enacts curriculum theory as mothering. Interrogating curriculum theory as mothering is similar to what Patti Lather (2007) refers to as a 'double(d) movement that uses and troubles a category simultaneously' (p. 73). When curriculum theory and mothering collide, they disorient and disrupt one another, shattering assumptions and understandings. Lather compels us to consider a double(d) epistemology as incomprehensible, a process by which we make room for 'something else to come about' (p. 7).

The maternal subject and the act of mothering have been a focus of research across disciplines and in popular culture for more than three decades. In 1976, Adrienne Rich first published *Of Woman Born*, one of the earliest feminist texts on motherhood. Using a reflexive, open form of experimental writing, Rich's text refuses the simplifications of binary conventions by disrupting essentialized understandings of the maternal subject and mothering experiences. Susan Driver (2006), in writing about Rich's double(d) practice, suggests that Rich searches for 'ways to resist confinement in that symbolic space by disturbing it, perverting it, making trouble, seeking to exceed the boundary' (p. 113). Challenging representations of the mother as a passive and uniform subject, Rich thinks through the body, 'writing her desiring experiential body as a site of revision and improvisations, as a sensuous mode of interpretation, a performative enactment of maternal/daughterly self, putting out into the world gestures and words that make up new ways of being and thinking' (1976, p. 12). Rich's scholarship is important, we argue, for the ways that it takes up a corporeal, relational process: 'We are neither inner nor outer constructed; our skin is alive with signals, our lives and our deaths are inseparable from the release or blockage of our thinking bodies' (1976/1989, p. 284).

For the philosopher Merleau-Ponty (1962), how we perceive and understand the world is through our bodies. My body, as Merleau-Ponty describes it, 'is not a collection of adjacent organs but a synergic system, all of the functions of which are exercised and linked together in the general action of being in the world' (p. 234). Consciousness is not a purely mental phenomenon but a function of the integration of all of the senses, which is then related to past and future life events. Knowledge is not pre-existent in the world, but created through the tangible, dynamic, and intersubjective encounters of the body. This body is the subject of Madeleine Grumet's (1988) book *Bitter Milk*. Reconsidering the limiting effects of patriarchy on teachers' work, Grumet envisions women's experiences as positive sites of power, creativity, and aesthetics; she argues that the knowledge mothers have of reproduction and nurturance needs to become part of the 'epistemological systems and curricular forms that constitute the discourse and practice of public education' (p. 3). Like Rich, Grumet confronts hegemonic practices of reading and writing in the production of knowledge and the formation of the subject. Grumet asserts that when a text is viewed as a spectacle, the practice of reading and writing is external to our lived bodily experience. Rather, one should engage in the process of interpretation as a bodily performance, in which meaning is continually deferred, de-centred, and undone. This is similar to what Della Pollock (2007) calls 'performative writing,' where the reader is invited into 'a double-play.' For Pollock, reading and writing invites disorder and difference, displacing modernist notions of authenticity and authority with 'a subjectivity grounded in an ethics of error forecasting a politics of possibility' (p. 242). This is a form of reading, writing, thinking that is improvisational. It borders, Pollock claims, on the grotesque in that it risks error as a way to move towards what is possible. Moreover, this performative gesture dislodges the self from a knowing position to a self co-created in the writing process. To think of writing as performative is to think of mothering from a similar perspective – constituted in the spaces of relations, made and unmade through embodied experiences.

Although much of Western thought has celebrated the splitting of women's identity into 'mother' or 'other' – the perception that women cannot be both – rethinking mothering from the perspective of 'performativity' recognizes the relationality between mother and other

(Jeremiah, 2006). When mothering is conceived of as performative, it becomes an active practice de-stabilizing the notion that motherhood is passive and static. Performativity shifts our attention from motherhood as biological, selfless, and existing prior to culture, to a practice that is always incomplete, indeterminable, and vulnerable. Thus, mothering becomes a strategic site of political, economic, and cultural transformation. A performative understanding of mothering opens up the possibility of an ethical form of exchange between self and other in which the maternal subject is engaged in a relational process that is never complete and that demands reiteration.

Although the history of feminist scholarship on mothering has emphasized the knowing, sensing, dynamic body, contemporary popular culture continues to view the maternal body as a passive object surveilled, fetishized, and disempowered. For example, the image of the mother saturates our contemporary visual culture. However, this visibility does not increase a mother's freedom, but rather, reinforces 'greater cultural and ideological scrutiny of their bodies and activities' (Addison, Goodwin-Kelly, & Roth, 2009, p. 2). This scrutiny is external and internal. In the past decade mother-centred blogs, Websites, magazines, and books have proliferated, subjecting the maternal self to self-regulation. Moreover, these mother-generated texts construct a spectacle of mothering that is normative, white, heterosexual, and good. 'June Clever' has simply been replaced by a dishevelled, professional, mother who is able to scrutinize her own mothering skills in public through late night maternal blog confessions. Despite the limited visibility of mothers outside of heteronormative paradigms of the nuclear white family, the carefully constructed maternal image by the media during the 2008–2009 U.S. election season of Governor Sarah Palin, vice-presidential candidate and mother of five, reinforced the West's shaky tolerance and palatability of difference. The popular imaginary, we argue, devalues and debases the maternal subject while it simultaneously sanctifies the institution of motherhood, which according to Liss (2009) continues 'because notions of motherhood and femininity are still laden with assumptions of naturalness and passivity' (p. xviii).

The contemporary artist Monica Bock's installation 'Maternal Exposure (Don't Forget the Lunches)'[1] confronts the subtle and intimate ways that the daily ritual of mothering is subjected to public scrutiny. The piece consists of 418 lead sheet bags embossed with school and day camp lunch menus packed for two young children in the course of a year. In the installation space, the lead bags are spread across one-half of the floor in the order the original lunches were prepared. Inserted intermittently throughout the lead bags are 88 small lead sheet plaques that replace the lunch bags and announce sick days, snow days, holidays – days when no lunches had to be made. In the other half of the space are 428 cast glycerin soap bags, vulnerable counterparts to the protective yet poisonous lead bags. The intimacy, the disorderliness, and the delirious monotony of caring for one's children are rendered complex and double(d) in the installation, and they call into question the very notions of exposure and scrutiny.

Mindful of the scholarship, media images, and popular literature on the maternal, *Mothering a Bodied Curriculum* thinks against the limits of representation and interpretation of the maternal subject. Employing a double(d) gesture troubles existing meanings of mothering and simultaneously offers new understandings. Lather (2007) suggests that a double(d) reading 'intervenes in what it critiques by not only overturning the classical opposition but by a general displacement of the system' (p. 14). The doubling of mothering is not so much the act of making visible the invisible, as about 'troubling the very claims to represent' (p. 37). In other words, mothering is not about reclaiming the maternal or thinking the limits of curriculum theory, but about opening ourselves to the limit, to the unknowable, and to the incomprehensible.

The aim of this edited collection, thus, is not to reinscribe additional postmodern and/or post-structuralist ideas about the mother; rather, we turn to Rosi Braidotti's (2002/2006) feminist materialist theories of the body to engender an unworking of curriculum theory as mothering. In this introductory chapter, we disrupt Cartesian dualism by attending to the materiality and corporeality of the body. This is crucial for reconceptualizing a bodied curriculum because a materialist approach to the body takes on new definitions and understandings of the body outside of the mind/body debate. By *materiality* we mean the 'biological, molecular and material nature of the body and the perceptions within the brain/mind of that body' (Kennedy, 2004, p. 16). The body becomes enfleshed and emplaced, rendering it as an entity that is more than flesh and blood; it is an assemblage of intensities imbricated in space and time.

Furthermore, we situate this book within the post-reconceptualization of curriculum studies (Malewski, 2010) and a post-foundational, post-feminist methodology (Lather, 2007) by taking up Deleuze and Guattari's (1986) 'becoming minor.' We engage the minor in order to destabilize the autobiographical in both feminist research on mothering and in curriculum scholarship. The minor, according to Deleuze and Guattari, resists authorial power, and the role of interpretation in uncovering hidden meanings in a text. Thus, becoming minor moves us from discursive significations and representations, to assemblages of events and actions that are constituted in relations, and thus mothering and curriculum theory are capable of being considered performative.

The chapters in this book emerge out of diverse and polyvalent perspectives on mothering and curriculum theory. They intentionally disrupt any idea of commonality and, rather, through fragmentation, multiplicity, and messiness bring into relation the concepts of emplacement, desire, and affect. Working through the sites of curriculum theory as mothering enacts what Ellsworth (1997) calls 'coming up against stuck place after stuck place' (p. 9) in order to learn from the ruptures, refusals, and doublings. In particular, this book addresses the following questions:

- What are the intersections between curriculum studies and the maternal embodied subject?
- How do the experiences that attend to the practice of mothering challenge conventional ways of knowing, teaching, and learning?
- How does the maternal standpoint interact with other raced, sexed, classed, and disabled identities?
- What happens when mothers refuse to become the Other?

Materialist Feminist Theories of the Body

Western thought has inherited, from Cartesianism, an overreliance on categories such as mind/body, male/female, white/black, mother/other. This structuring of language has always privileged one term over the other with the secondary term being consumed within the primary. Despite the attention paid by feminist scholars to the secondary term, simply inverting the hierarchical placement continues to maintain the boundaries always, already present. As Elizabeth Grosz (1994) so aptly states, 'To reduce either the mind to the body or the body to the mind is to leave their interaction unexplained, explained away, impossible. Reductionism denies any interaction between mind and body for it focuses on the actions of either one of the binary terms at the expense of the other' (p. 7).

Grosz (1994) explains that there are three modes of conceptualizing the body that are based on Cartesianism. First is the biological, physical body, which takes into account medicalized, biologistic views that imply a continuity between man and animals; the concept of the human body being part of a natural order; and, as part of an organic system of interrelated parts. The second commonly held belief regards the body as a metaphor. In this perspective the body is a vessel or a tool for consciousness. This body becomes a passive object 'over which struggles between its "inhabitant" and others/exploiters may be possible' (p. 9). The body as a signifying medium is the third mode, and as such, it is through the body that the subject can express herself and through the body that she can receive, code, and translate the external world. Again, this mode presents a passive, neutralized body, which can be reduced to an object that is predictable and knowable.

To counter these dualistic frameworks, feminist theories of the body, while extremely varied, could be summarized as either focusing on sexual difference or on the social construction of gender. Although significant for the ways they develop alternative accounts of the agential body, corporeality remains neglected (Braidotti, 2002/2006). A materialist feminist conceptualization of the body considers the mind, brain, flesh-and-blood body in the ways we experience the world. The body is a multiplicity of processes, which are molecular, corporeal, and in assemblage with the cultural, the ideological, the libidinal, and the social (Kennedy, 2004). This notion of the body, as discontinuous, deterritorialized, and multiple is an attempt to reconceive of the body outside of binary oppositions. Drawing on Deleuze and Guattari's (1986) rhizomatic analysis, Grosz (1994) states, 'The body is regarded as neither a locus for a consciousness nor an organically determined entity; it is understood more in terms of what it can do, the things it can perform, the linkages it establishes, the transformations and becomings it undergoes, and the machinic connections it forms with other bodies, what it can link with, how it can proliferate its capacities' (p. 165). This is thinking outside the boundaries of Cartesian thought and requires a rethinking of the very foundations of thought itself, and a rethinking of the foundations of curriculum. A bodied understanding of curriculum opens up morphologies of embodiment to mutations, changes, and transformations, destabilizing knowledge. A materialist theory of becoming provides a way to think of curriculum theory as mothering and as a relational process, a site of inter-embodiment that shifts the figurations of maternal subjects and their ways of being in the world (Springgay, 2007, 2008; Springgay & Freedman, 2007, 2010).

Figurations enable us to examine curriculum theory as mothering outside of heteronormative reproductive logic. They de-centre representation and offer multilayered understandings of curriculum and mothering. Differing from metaphor, figurations are living maps, particular and specific accounts that 'defy the established modes of theoretical representation' (Braidotti, 2002/2006, p. 2).

To organize the different chapters in this book, we use the concept of *figuration* to create a relational map. Figurations enable us to consider chapters in relation to each other, not based on common elements nor interwoven metaphors or themes. Rather, figurations produce an alternative geography that deterritorializes and destabilizes certainties of knowing, and allows for a proliferation of micro or minor perspectives and understandings. Our three figurations are *emplacement, desire,* and *affect*.

Emplacement is the idea that the body, mind, and space are intertwined. Rather than the conjecture that the embodied subject is located in space, to be emplaced 'attends to the question of experience by accounting for the relationships between bodies, minds and the materiality and sensoriality of the environment' (Pink, 2009, p. 25). As opposed to Cartesian definitions of the body as a vessel, the body and space are imbricated and created simultaneously (Springgay, 2007, 2008). The chapters in this part of the book take up mothering as lived, situated practices that conceptualize difference outside the limits of representation. In order to think difference beyond binary opposition, where one term is always supplementary to the other, Deleuzian thinking affirms difference in terms of multiplicity or what Braidotti calls 'difference as the positivity of differences' (2002/2006, p. 71). These chapters posit a both-and relation. In the case of the mind-body dualism, both terms exist not as counter terms, nor in opposition to each other. Rather, 'one must pass by way of or through binaries, not in order to reproduce them but to find terms and modes that befuddle their operations, connections that demonstrate the impossibility of their binarization, terms, relations, and practices that link the binarily opposed terms' (Grosz, 1994, p. 181).

Deleuze and Guattari (1986) propose active and affirmative conceptions of desire. Although psychoanalysis relies on a notion of desire as a lack, *desire* according to Deleuze and Guattari is an 'actualization, a series of practices, bringing things together or separating them' (cited in Grosz, 1994, p. 165). This is a conception of desire that has to do with how bodies encounter other bodies and the linkages and assemblages produced through such encounters. Braidotti (2002/2006) refers to this as a network of becomings that enable non-pathological ways of expressing the intensities of experience and the body. Desire, however, does not entrench these multiplicities nor make them permanent. Like the chapters we have coupled in this part of the book, they are experiments, 'producing ever-new alignments, linkages, and connections, making things' (Grosz, 1994, p. 168). Desire thus, re-figures the notions of mothering and curriculum theory as creative, proliferating, and unpredictable events.

The final part of this volume is framed through the idea of affect. Although theories of embodiment have ruptured the expulsion of the body from consciousness, the sensing, emotional, and affective modes of existence and of knowing have continued to be excluded. Here the chapters examine the importance of affect in the production of knowledge, arguing that both mothering and curriculum need to attend to the smelliness, the repulsions, and the feelings of overwhelming joy that events produce. Feeling, thus, is not external to a subject but rather the subject is part of the feeling or affect. Brian Massumi (2002) writes that 'in feeling, being is *in* sensation' (p. 765, original emphasis). What is crucial about the way we have arranged these three figurations – emplacement, desire, and affect – is the importance that is placed on the fleshy, pulsating, dynamic, and active body. *Mothering a Bodied Curriculum* is, as such, a collection of essays that engenders a way of thinking about curriculum theory as mothering that makes possible new theories and actualizations of the body.

A Minor Methodology

The minor is a concept that deterritorializes the major; the major being dominant systems of signification and representation. The minor has no model; it is a becoming, a process. According to Simon O'Sullivan (2006), there are three characteristics to describing the minor. First, the minor involves a kind of stuttering, or what he refers to as a 'becoming stranger' (p. 70). The minor is not habitual; it is unfamiliar and inventive. Second, in the minor everything is political, meaning that the individuals who are imbricated by the minor are always linked to larger social spaces. Third, the minor is always collective. There is less emphasis on the autonomy of the individual, for instance, and more importance placed on the collective production of work and meaning. These characteristics provide a framework for thinking about curriculum as the 'collectivization of subjectivity and the calling forth of new kinds of community' (Nancy, 2000, p. 71), not based on common universal characteristics but on the coming together of difference in and as difference. Collectivity, in this sense, moves beyond comfortable understandings of individuality and knowledge production and, rather, foregrounds knowing as an inter-corporeal process.

We turn to the concept of the minor in an effort to tangle together the theories of the body that are central to this book and the very ways in which we imagine a methodology emerging out of our work. There is a compulsion in academic scholarship to structure research through com-mon frameworks or methodologies. When methodologies don't quite fit, scholars may choose to use a bricolage approach or, in some cases, to invent a new methodology. We struggled with framing this edited collection through the lineage of *currere*, autobiography, or arts-based research because the instant we brought the theories of this text into relation with these existing frameworks, our work no longer performed the becoming minoritarian that we felt was so important. Rather than completely disregard these existing methodologies and their relation-ships with curriculum theory, we chose to think of methodology as a minor practice, where a minor reading is not a counter-movement but 'a space surprised by difference into the performance of practices of not-knowing' (Lather, 2007, p. 7). A minor methodology is not a new methodology, with its own set of criteria or renderings; it is a way to unhinge the potential stasis of methodologies, the familiar, and the known. Engaging in a minor methodology means developing alterna-tive accounts of knowing, debating essentialist ideas that emplace the mother, and to demand complexity (Lather, 2007). Deleuze and Guat-tari (1986) would suggest that a minor methodology produces some-thing when some quality can be detached from its place and made to have a life of its own, to resonate, just for itself.

In terms of autobiography, feminist research has underscored the connection between the personal and the political, and the emphasis on women's experience as vital in the creation of gendered knowledge. Feminism has challenged the genre of autobiography, as unified, ob-jective, and transcendent, through a re-evaluation of autobiography in terms of subjectivity, knowledge and power, difference and collec-tive identity (Cosslett, Lury, & Summerfield, 2000). In addition, the increasing interdisciplinarity of scholarship has influenced what constitutes autobiographical work, which now includes oral narratives, contemporary art, curriculum vitas, fiction, dramatic plays, and graphic novels. The consideration of a variety of genres, we suggest, has challenged and contested the absence of women's writing and voices from the canons of autobiography and curriculum studies.

We admit, however, that understanding curriculum through autobiography is complex, ambiguous, and difficult (Wilson, 2002). These are uncertain, edgy spaces 'located at margins and boundaries, spaces of doubling, where "this or that" becomes "this and that," ambiguously, ambivalently – difficult places but nonetheless spaces of generative possibilities' (Aoki, 2003, p. 422). Yet, Petra Munro Hendry (2007) warns of the dangers of reducing narrative and autobiography to just method: 'We currently situate narrative within the metaphor of *research* and ultimately it is doomed to "methodology." Narrative has become reduced to methods, verification, validity, ways in which we as researchers can legitimate it as a means of research that tells us something about the world' (p. 497, original emphasis). Asking us to consider narrative outside the burden of explaining a life, Hendry (2007) contends that emphasis should be placed not on the stories that are told but on what the tellings of these stories *do*. If we reconsider autobiography through the minoritarian, then it 'works to connect up the different aspects of life, be they individual or social (or indeed non-human) so as to produce new lines of causality and new pathways of experimentation' (O'Sullivan, 2006, p. 74).

For Deleuze (1986) the process of becoming minor is parallel to writing. Trinh T. Minh-ha (1989) describes this process: 'To write is to become. Not to become a writer (or a poet), but to become, intransitively. Not when writing adopts established keynotes or policy, but when it traces for itself lines of evasion' (p. 19). The stuttering that takes place in the minor, or what Lather (2007) refers to as a 'double(d) science,' where one writes against authoritative voice and certainty, is a 'process of unsettling binarism, linearity and other sedimented unitary habits. Writing is about transiting in in-between space, cultivating transversality and mutations' (Braidotti, 2002/2006, p. 94). Writing about curriculum theory as mothering, which is what each of the authors in this collection engage with, is a creative rather than reactive project. Thus, the minor, we contend moves us towards an affirmation of life's potentialities.

As one engages with our figurations, one needs to learn to stutter, to hesitate, and to double back through the deterritorializations offered in each chapter, to write your own minor becomings. The minor, we contend, refuses interpretation and representation, and thus, any minor methodology performs new cartographies, emplacing one's self with and outside the texts and stresses the importance of desire and affective interconnections.

Mothering a Bodied Curriculum

Mothering a Bodied Curriculum: Emplacement, Desire, and Affect extends and simultaneously reconfigures our previous scholarship on the body and curriculum (see Springgay & Freedman, 2007). Arguing that a bodied curriculum is necessary when conceiving of a relational, social, and ethical way of being-with bodies in difference, this edited collection is vital for the ways that the body needs to be reconsidered, reconfigured, and deterritorialized in curriculum theory. A bodied curriculum, we contend, is embedded in the doubling that Lather (2007) calls for: 'a double task that works the necessary tensions that structure feminist methodology as fertile ground for the production of new practices' (p. 76).

The bifurcation of the mother as Other continues in contemporary discourses and representations of mothering despite the decades of feminist scholarship on motherhood that continue to underwrite a certain passiveness and assumption of innate goodness and nurturing capacities. On the other extreme the mother is unruly, all too visible, and obscene. Such paradoxical understandings continue to objectify, consume, and regulate mothering, negating the corporeality of mothering and knowing. For example, quite recently the maternity wing of the Women's College Hospital in Toronto was closed. The mothers and babies were shuffled north to the state-of-the-art Sunnybrook Hospital, out of the risky core of the urban centre, where they had been living for years, in close proximity to immigrants, crime, and homelessness. As one drove north on Bayview Avenue, for months before the closure, signs announced, 'The babies are coming home' signalling the very ideology that mothering, the body, and curriculum requires an intervention from outside; that it needs to be disciplined, managed, and taken control of. Mothering was a threat to the civilized order of the city, and it needed to be civilized through modern medicalization, only offered in a new hospital facility. In the popular press, Women's College Hospital was described as a cramped and crumbling mess, in which the maternity wing was insufficiently capable of providing necessary maternal care. In the interest of 'health,' mothers were transferred to an $18 million addition located at Sunnybrook Hospital. Despite the potential 'gains' for birthing moms, like jacuzzis, large screen TVs, and roomier accommodations akin to a five-star hotel, the move signifies mothering as an illness system focused on treatment and the institutionalization of life processes such as birthing. We acknowledge that this book is not a vehicle for debating hospital reform, however, we use this as an example of the continued pathologization of mothering and the body in a highly technologized consumerist society.

Likewise, in contrast to a reductionist approach to curriculum theory, this collection 'proliferates' to use Malewski's (2010) term. Curriculum theory as mothering engenders a creative and experimental way of thinking about teaching and learning, of which aesthetics becomes part of the contingent process of thinking. The concept of aesthetics under modernist or dualistic discourse is premised on notions of beauty, taste, and judgment. For a work of art to be understood as beautiful, it has had to adhere to a specific form – the use of tone, line, space, and colour – which could then be manipulated through stylistic devices such as repetition, proportion, etc. Thus, form was a significant element in determining the beauty of an artwork and connected to transcendent notions of goodness and morality. When we turn aesthetics to the work of the minor, beauty (or, in this case, mothering) is no longer consistent with goodness but to feelings of sensation, duration, movement, and intensity. This is an aesthetic premised on the materiality of the body emplacing us in the world, responding and resonating through desire and affect with matter around us. Dislodging curriculum as a fixed, authoritative form, we contend, requires that we think of curriculum as an aesthetic process. Curriculum theory as mothering is the capacity to dwell at the limit, to enlarge the universe by enabling its potential to be otherwise, and to be figured as unknowable.

Note

1 http://monicabock.com

References

Addison, H., Goodwin-Kelly, M.K., & Roth, E. (Eds.). (2009). *Motherhood misconceived: Representing the maternal in film.* New York: State University of New York Press.

Aoki, T. (2003). Locating living pedagogy in teacher research: Five metonymic moments. Reprinted in E. Hasbe-Ludt & W. Hurren (Eds.), *Curriculum intertext: Place/language/pedagogy* (pp. 2–6). New York: Peter Lang.

Braidotti, R. (2002/2006). *Metamorphoses: Towards a materialist theory of becoming*. Cambridge, MA: Polity.

Cosslett, T., Lury, C., & Summerfield, P. (2000). *Feminist autobiography*. New York: Routledge.

Deleuze, G., & Guattari, F. (1986). *Kafka: Towards a minor literature*. Minneapolis, MN: University of Minnesota Press.

Driver, S. (2006). Reading Adrienne Rich's *Of Woman Born* as a queer feminist daughter. *Journal of the Association for Research on Mothering, 8* (1&2), 109–122.

Ellsworth, E. (1997). *Teaching positions*. New York: Teachers College Press.

Grosz, E. (1994). *Volatile bodies: Toward a corporeal feminism*. Bloomington, IN: Indiana University Press.

Grumet, M.R. (1988). *Bitter milk: Women and teaching*. Amherst, MA: University of Massachusetts Press.

Hendry, P.M. (2007). The future of narrative. *Qualitative Inquiry, 13* (4), 487–498.

Jeremiah, E. (2006). Motherhood to mothering and beyond: Maternity in recent feminist thought. *Journal of the Association for Research on Mothering, 8* (1/2), 21–33.

Kennedy, B. (2004). *Deleuze and cinema: The aesthetics of sensation*. Edinburgh: Edinburgh University Press.

Lather, P. (2007). *Getting lost: Feminist efforts toward a double(d) science*. Albany, NY: State University of New York Press.

Liss, A. (2009). *Feminist art and the maternal*. Minneapolis, MN: University of Minnesota Press.

Malewski, E. (2010). Introduction. In E. Malewski (Ed.). *Curriculum studies handbook: The next moment* (pp. 1–39). New York: Routledge.

Massumi, B. (2002). *Parables for the virtual: Movement, affect, sensation*. Durham, NC: Duke University Press.

Merleau-Ponty, M. (1962). *Phenomenology of perception*. New York: Routledge.

Minh-ha,T.T. (1989). Woman native other: Writing postcoloniality and feminism. Bloomington, IN: Indiana University Press.

Nancy, J.L. (2000). *Of being singular plural*. Stanford, CA: Stanford University Press.

O'Sullivan, S. (2006). *Art encounters: Deleuze and Guattari. Thoughts beyond representation*. London: Palgrave.

Pink, S. (2009). *Doing sensory ethnography*. Thousand Oaks, CA: Sage.

Pollock, D. (2007). The performative 'I.' *Cultural Studies Critical Methodologies, 7* (3), 239–255.

Rich, A. (1976). *Of woman born: Motherhood as Experience and Institution.* New York: Norton.

Springgay, S. (2007). Nurse-in: Breastfeeding and a/r/tographical research. In M. Cahnmann & R. Siegesmund (Eds.), *Arts-based research in education: Foundations for Practice* (pp. 137–140). New York: Routledge.

Springgay, S. (2008). *Body knowledge and curriculum: Pedagogies of touch in youth and visual culture.* New York: Peter Lang.

Springgay, S., & Freedman, D. (2007). Introduction: On touching and a bodied curriculum. In S. Springgay & D. Freedman (Eds.), *Curriculum and the cultural body* (pp. xvii–xxvii). New York: Peter Lang.

Springgay, S., & Freedman, D. (2010). Breasted bodies as pedagogies of excess: Towards a materialist theory of becoming mother. In J. Sandlin, B. Shultz, & J. Burdick (Eds.), *Handbook of public pedagogy* (pp. 351–365). New York: Routledge.

Wilson, S. (2002). Collecting rocks, leaves, and seeds: A journey through loss. *Educational Insights, 7* (1). Available: http://www.csci.educ.ubc.ca/publication/insights/v07n01/contextualexplorations/wilson/

PART 1

Emplacement

1 Consuming M/otherhood: Pedagogical Regimes of Truth in Parental Consumerism

JAKE BURDICK AND JONEL THALLER

Throughout the twentieth century, feminist theorists and writers have focused on the function of patriarchy in the reduction of women's lives into a specific, essentialized set of roles (see, e.g., Ehrenreich & English, 2005; Friedan, 2000). Frequently, feminist discourse (particularly in the second and third waves of feminism) worked to address the objectification of women via the gross over-sexualization of the feminine body, the disproportionate presence and (de)valuation of women in the workplace, and the persistent argument regarding women's reproductive rights. This final point has been typically associated with the abortion debate; however, scholars have also begun to address the ways in which pregnancy and birth have also been *colonized* by the discourse and practices of the medical industry (Bryant, Porter, Tracy, & Sullivan, 2007; Ehrenreich & English, 2005; Jolly, 2007; Ponte, 2007; Zadoroznyj, 2001). Some authors cite the increase in elective caesarian birth (Ponte, 2007; Jolly, 2007), the dominance of medical *authority* in decision making about birth, and the pathologizing of the pregnant body as *sick* and in need of scientific/medical intervention as signalling the loss of women's agency in one of the most profound experiences of womanhood itself (Jolly, 2007; Bryant et al., 2007; Ehrenreich & English, 2005). While, as Jolly has articulated, the twentieth century saw these medical and scientific communities emerge as the established authorities on pregnancy and birth, a strand of potential resistance manifested itself in the growing *natural* childbirth movement (including home birth, midwifery, and homeopathic techniques). Perhaps as a testament to this, associations of doulas, midwives, and naturopathic practitioners, as well as other formal organizations have enjoyed strong membership and are experiencing increasing presence in the dialogue about natural birth and naturalistic child raising (see, e.g., Weiner, 1994).

Current practices around birthing largely fall into two ideological categories: those that support the dominant medical model, as evidenced by the growing number of elective caesarian deliveries and the pathologizing of pregnancy, and the increasingly prevalent *natural* birth movement, which emphasizes vaginal delivery and women's control of the birthing process (Bryant et al., 2007; Jolly, 2007; Zadoroznyj, 2001). Along with this bifurcation, a wide spectrum of birthing products and services exists, with extremes ranging from what Jolly has called the privatized 'celebrity caesarian' to the specialized, inflatable birthing tubs used in at-home, water deliveries. In step with the kind of corporate marketing efforts that characterize much of the American discursive landscape, each side of the divide utilizes powerful pedagogies of doubt and fear to sell its model of *good* birthing, *good* care, and ultimately *good* parenting, points largely constructed in opposition to the other side's position. These market-based discourses frequently serve interests that cohere less with human well-being than they do with furthering an organizational profit motive.

Lake and Epstein's 2008 documentary *The Business of Being Born* (Slotnick, Netto, & Epstein) might be viewed as a high-water mark for the natural birthing movement. Through several interviews, video recordings of natural birth, and testimonies, the filmmakers offer their audience both a critical perspective on the medical community's construction of birthing and a strong endorsement for a return to the *natural* experience of childbirth. In short, the film reiterates that women still have a choice in their birthing experience. A qualitative study of birthing choices in Australia (Bryant et al., 2007) suggested that the rhetoric of choice is also used by the medical industry to promote caesarian birth: choice of an exact birth time, of a dedicated medical staff, and of a *safer*, less *messy* birth experience. Bryant et al. posited that capitalizing on this notion of choice marks the entry of neo-liberal ideology – the relegation of autonomy and agency to practices that further a market economy – into the medical community/industry. Although the title of Lake and Epstein's film was likely meant as a critique of the corporatization of the medical model, it is difficult to see either side of the birthing debate as completely free from the notion of *business*. Rather, many elements of the natural childbirthing and naturalistic child-rearing movement have become braided into the nascent *green* consumerism movement of the late 2000s, a market space in which the ideal of returning to a more 'natural' eco-friendly lifestyle is achieved via *responsible* product purchasing (rather than the cessation of consumptive practices). Choice, then, in both of these competing discourses becomes about a certain way of *consuming* childbirth – of aligning oneself to a predetermined set of practices, behaviours, and products that constitute either the medical or the naturalistic parent. Lost beneath this discourse are the needs, material conditions, and ability of the mother (and father) to decide how to navigate the uncertainty of parenthood. Instead, both positions on birthing are implicated in the production of a specialized, valuated construct of parental identity, complete with its own performative criteria for operating within a *good/bad* parenting binary and a deeply embodied, classed, gendered, and ultimately deficit-producing species of desire.

Stories, Bodies, and Parenting

In this chapter, we seek to illustrate how elements of the growing naturalistic parenting movement, despite its espoused commitment to women's choice and empowerment, have worked to construct a commodified, rigid notion of parenthood and parent identity. This identification is transmitted and reconstructed through what Klein (2002) calls 'lifestyle branding,' a form of marketing in which the brand's symbolic capital takes precedence over the actual worth or use-value of the product itself (Aldridge, 2003). Accordingly, representations of the naturalistic mother or father are generated, in no small part, by a description of the kinds of products parents buy and the ways in which those products are to be consumed within the larger culture. To provide examples of this commodified identity, as well as its links to a highly specific kind of class-based distinction (Bourdieu, 2000), we reviewed recent issues of *Mothering: Natural Family Living*, a widely read magazine that claims a commitment to natural childbirth and naturalistic parenting, as well as the marketing material available via the magazine's Website, specifically noting the ways in which the magazine's authors promote/reinforce the development of a certain consumptive, classed identity in their writing. Finally, using a theoretical construct based on the work of Bourdieu (2000) and Gore (1992), we suggest the ways in which this (re)production of identity acts as a public pedagogy of consumer desire – manipulating ideological constructions of distinction, choice, and fear as means to promote consumers of this particular *brand* (Klein, 2002; Aldridge, 2003) of parenthood.

Additionally, we intersperse the chapter with short, autoethnographic vignettes in which we hope to convey how our local stories of parenthood illustrate the experience of being caught between the dominant public pedagogies of birthing and child-rearing offered by both medical and naturalistic positions. By including this narrative aspect of the chapter, we hope to construct our inquiry as a means of posing questions to our readers rather than offering them some form of authoritative meaning and direct evaluation. Accordingly, the stories are not meant to serve the purpose of triangulation or as a means of exposing researcher bias, and the purpose of this text is not to produce a kind of reconstituted certainty around birth and parenthood. We merely hope to raise what we feel are important questions around the pedagogical import of consumerism within birthing practices, as well as to communicate our own deeply felt ambivalence, uncertainty, and occasional self-betrayal in our decisions as parents caught between powerful regimes of identity.

Tasting the Consumer/d Parent

For our analysis, we reviewed six recent issues of *Mothering* magazine, which began publication in 1976 and describes itself as 'the birthplace of the natural family lifestyle' (*Media Kit*, 2008). We selected this magazine for its wide readership and national visibility as a marker of naturalistic mothering. The magazine devotes much of each issue to *discussions* of alternative, naturalistic motherhood practices and products, as well as a considerable amount of advertising (a total of 133 ads in the 104-page March–April 2008 issue alone) for these products. The magazine's Website (www.mothering.com) provides potential advertisers with a 'media kit' consisting of descriptions of the magazine's goals and purpose and demographic data regarding the magazine's readership, described as 'young, responsive, highly educated, affluent, and well-informed' women and men, who are concerned with 'environmental and health values . . . reflected in the high-quality food, and personal care and natural products they purchase for themselves and their families' (*Media Kit*, p. 4). Demographic data support this description. The average reader of *Mothering* magazine has an annual household income of $92,500, nearly twice the 2004 U.S. median household income (U.S. Census, 2006); 44% have graduate degrees; and 79% purchase natural or organic food at least weekly. Considering that a vast majority of mothers are excluded from these demographics, this positioning seems at odds with the overall ideology of empowerment forwarded by the naturalistic mothering movement.

One way of understanding the kind of consumerism promoted by *Mothering* magazine is evidenced in Bourdieu's (2000) relation of *taste* and *distinction* in consumer choices. The kinds of tastes we form towards a particular object or image are largely determined by what Bourdieu (1977) names our *habitus*, the embodied structure that guides, and in some ways prefigures, our relationship to the world. Habitus is produced as part of bodies at a very early stage in our lives and is wholly linked to the social environment in which we are raised, including the general socioeconomic class of that environment. In Bourdieu's framework, *taste* is a bodied response to sociological experience, involving both delight and disgust: we desire certain objects for what they are as much as for what they are not, and the pedagogy of advertising helps us to understand the semiotic meaning inherent in a particular product as well as how that meaning is positioned in relation to our habitus.

The consumptive identity invoked in *Mothering* magazine, the naturalistic parent, operates not necessarily as a point of departure from the greater discourse surrounding women's bodies and the patriarchal ideology from which that discourse stems. Rather, as a marketing tool, the notion of a woman's choice and ownership of her own body loses its standing as a radical proposition – it is simply an appropriately piquant point of distinction aimed at a rigorously predetermined demographic. Many of the commodity alternatives to status quo parenting practices only serve as points of distinction in the economy of signifiers that represent mothering. Collectively, these commodities construct a prescriptive practice of consuming motherhood that, despite their condemnation of the medical and social construction of the feminine body, still only offer a different set of a priori representations created independently of a woman's experience of her own pregnant body and parenting competence. In essence, they create the space for her to occupy, however ill the fit.

It's 2003, just a few weeks after the birth of my first child, my son, and I am coming home from work. My wife is in the bathroom, crying, but I can't hear her over the mechanical whirr of her breast pump. She's crying because my son has yet to latch on correctly (he never will), because her breasts have been engorged with milk for days, and because she spends the 20 or so hours of her time awake either in pain or locked away in the bathroom, alone save the white noise of the pump. We'd talked to the lactation consultant at the hospital earlier in the week and shared e-mails with a representative from La Leche League. They both told my wife that she wasn't doing it right and to keep trying. Meanwhile, she's locked in the bathroom, absent from her own life, from her new baby, desperate to give our child the natural nutrition he deserves. Afraid to do anything else, I urge her to continue on this way.

To explicate Bourdieu's (1977, 2000) constructs of distinction and habitus to current consumer practices, it is also necessary to theorize how changes occur in consumptive meanings over time, as well as the ways in which consumers learn to read and reproduce these signs. To address this issue, we need to understand consumerism, advertising, and brand identification as forms of public pedagogy (Hoeschsmann, 2007) that work across the body, aligning products to the particular distinction of a target demographic, and educating that demographic towards this economy of representation. The medical community's use of this form of pedagogy is widely criticized by feminist scholars working on the subject of birth (e.g. Jolly, 2007; Brady et al., 2007), yet the marketplace for alternative practices of naturalistic mothering has been structured in a similar pedagogical fashion.

Targeting formal sites of education and educational research, Gore (1992) uses Foucault's notion of *regimes of truth* to discuss the ways in which both dominant and resistant pedagogies operate as colonizing, totalizing discourses. In short, she claims that both the cultural pedagogy of domination and the critical and feminist responses to that domination take on a maieutic character, one that subtly forces students to inhabit a particularized identity and set of practices in order to correctly act, speak, and think. Gore states, 'Feminists can become "good" and "true" women/feminists only through particular ethical and intellectual practices, not simply by the fact of being women' (p. 125). Gore ultimately suggests that to be engaged in truly reflexive critical practice, we need to r/eject notions of *correct* feminism and *correct* social criticism or we simply reinvent domination with a new vocabulary. The 'social logic of consumption' (Baudrillard, 1970), and the constraints its semiotic economy places on identity construction in terms of both the dominant medical and the naturalistic views of birthing, also work to promote the very species of problematic pedagogy that Gore critiques. Whereas the influence of the medical community and its symbolic authority is well documented in research on birthing choices (Jolly, 2007;

Brady et al., 2007; Zadoroznyj, 2001), a notable silence surrounds naturalistic parenting's consumerist aspect.

> During the first six months of my daughter's life, I am relieved every time
> she wakes up from a nap or nighttime sleep. Try as I might, I can't erase
> the threat of SIDS from my mind. I try to cure my anxiety with research.
> Was I doing all I could? One school of thought blamed flame-retardant
> chemicals for crib death. Exorbitantly expensive organic mattresses were
> the cure. I spend several days, lose several hours, scouring the Internet
> for an affordable organic mattress. In the end, I decide we just can't afford
> it, and I compromise by buying organic crib sheets instead. I convince
> myself that I'm making the right decision, but I still feel uneasy when the
> sheets come in the mail. Maybe I had just compromised my daughter's
> life to save $300. If she doesn't wake up one day, I'm sure it will be my
> fault.

Parenthood, Consumption, and Pedagogy

A sample of articles within *Mothering* magazine aptly exemplifies
Bourdieu's (1977, 2000) theory of distinction and Gore's (1992) depiction of critical pedagogy's double bind. An article titled 'The ABCs of
Going Cloth' (Gawlik, 2008) provides information and a detailed buy-
er's guide for cloth diapers, predicated on three separate rationales for
going cloth: budget, environment, and the baby's comfort. The author
recommends purchasing at least 30 cloth diapers to maintain a manageable washing schedule (washing diapers every three and a half
days). With a minimum cost of $6 a piece in the recommended brands
(and a maximum of $40), the initial investment for cloth diapers is ap-
proximately $180 dollars. Further, mothers making this consumptive
choice must have the extra time to do two loads of diaper laundry per
week. These factors suggest the kind of class distinction defined by the
magazine's *Media Kit* (2008). In most working-class families, both parents work full-time, presenting difficulty in taking the requisite time
to wash cloth diapers and in finding a child care provider willing to
manage the cloth diaper process. Ostensibly, then, the ability to be a
good mother and responsible global citizen – signifiers of naturalistic
mothering heavily advocated in *Mothering* – depends largely on one's
social standing and material/cultural capital.

The rhetoric of responsible global citizenry and, by extension, responsible parenting also manifests in an article titled 'Fresh First

Foods' (Lair, 2008), in which the author advocates the use of locally grown, organic produce for homemade baby foods in order to benefit the local economy and reduce global oil and gas consumption. However, beyond this moral dictate, a distinction of taste and class dependent upon a mother's time and access is indelibly present in the issues we reviewed. Baby food (home)made from local and organic produce, for example, was described as fresher, more palatable, and 'in tune with Mother Nature' (p. 86). Jarred food, in contrast, was billed as dull, bland, and composed of empty calories, a default for mothers who lack the time or resources to join a food co-op, visit the local farmers' market (assuming there is one), and prepare their own baby food.

A distinction of taste and class was also present in an article titled 'Small Hands, Big Art' (Van't Hul, 2007), which provides tips for hosting a toddler art party. In this article, the author details her own love of art and, in regard to her daughter, asserts that 'laying a strong artistic and creative foundation now will serve her well in the future . . . to help provide her with a mind that can think creatively, one that can give her access to, and an appreciation of, the amazing world of art' (p. 45). To build this foundation, the author advises, 'It's important to have a dedicated art space . . . and ready access to a variety of art materials' (p. 45). The author describes the art materials she purchases as 'inexpensive,' yet the list of materials is extensive: a variety of paints, brushes, markers, crayons, and paper, as well as an easel, a portfolio, mats, and frames. The author further details meeting with her friends and their children on a Wednesday morning for the art party, allowing the children an opportunity to create art while the moms 'hang out and chat' (p. 44). The leisure and aesthetic described in this article are also present in the types of toys promoted in 'Santa's Workshop Rediscovered' (Walsh, 2007), where parents are encouraged to 'get back to the artisanal and simple roots of holiday gift giving' by purchasing toys described as 'enchanting' and of 'heirloom quality' (p. 88). The dolls showcased in this article, and crafted of only natural and organic materials, range in price from $60 to $110, with the exception of a pocket-sized doll priced at $30.

In contrast to this piece is an article that initially seems to promote consumer activism. In 'Ban the Bags' (Walker, 2008), the author criticizes a common trend in hospitals of providing new mothers with 'discharge bags' filled with trial samples of various products. The article contains an image of the kinds of products one might find in a discharge bag, including infant formula powder, nursing pads, nursing-aid bottles, diapers, pacifiers, and information on breastfeeding. The author takes a stance and tone not unlike that forwarded by several critics of the incursion of marketing and product placement into educational environments (e.g., Molnar, 2004), stating that 'formula companies know that when a trusted physician, nurse, or hospital hands a new mother a discharge bag containing a sample of formula, the mother will assume that the brand is sanctioned by the health-care provider' and that 'brand loyalty means big bucks for the formula manufacturer over the long term' (Walker, 2008, p. 74). Although this article seems to advocate for a powerful kind of activism in the face of the corporate intrusion into hospitals, the argument is made within a magazine that, a mere 20 pages later, endorses the purchase of $90 diaper bags and $20 baby powder.

The emphasis in these articles is on the alignment towards a specific kind of consumption, one that resists the status quo and moves towards a more naturalistic experience of motherhood, one that comes at a cost of time and labour that many North American women simply cannot afford. Moreover, the issues we reviewed did not offer alternatives to address the possible financial and time constraints that might affect individuals living below the $92,500/year income claimed by the *Media Kit* (2008). Still, these articles operate from the premise that the more *natural* a product is, the better it is for a child. Although we would agree that benefits are to be gained from the kind of products *Mothering* endorses, naturalistic mothering must be regarded as a construct rooted in a certain perception of what nature *is* and *means*. Simply, our understanding of nature is already embedded in the habitus (Bourdieu, 1977), filtered through the lens of culture. The conception of a natural practice of mothering is a piecemeal, constructed simulacra, one predicated on an indictment of the *un-natural* practices of Other(ed) women. Even more divisive, however, is the posture of the construct of naturalistic mothering as *good* mothering, and the necessary implication of its inverse: *artificial/bad* mothering. What constitutes a good mother in the logic of *Mothering* magazine presupposes a kind of class distinction and a level of cultural and material capital commensurate with the ability to provide your child with the comfort and safety of naturalistic living. This logic suggests that women living in lower-class conditions or women who might simply be unaware of the consumer options available to them implicitly, but absolutely, give their children a lower quality existence.

We are in our birthing class with our midwife who has plastic babies and knitted uterus replicas, and she's excitedly showing us how birthing ought to be. Throughout the room I see couples nodding their heads in rhythm with her argument. They marvel at the capability of the female body as the midwife sketches it out on flip charts and projects it onto the bumpy stucco wall. Our pregnant peers shake their heads at the horrors of the medical machine, its chemicals, its technologies, its devaluation of the woman, its violence against the newborn. I shake my head, too. I nod and bob and laugh at the right moments, but I can't stop the guilt from spreading through me. Jonel and I are the only students here who already have a child, and we had him at the hospital with the chemicals and the technology and the incorrect birthing position and the episiotomy and the rough clinical handling. We told the group all of this during class introductions. While I am shaking and nodding my head in concert, I listen to my classmates demand how people could allow this to happen to the women they love? . . . to their own children? I'm hoping they weren't paying attention when we introduced ourselves. And I'm wondering just how badly we might have hurt our little boy.

M/othering: An Embodied Fiction

Our purpose is not to pit these narratives against one another and derive yet another correct version of the parenting narrative to further cement a troubling binary. As parents ourselves, we have shared experiences that reside within both regimes. We have also inhabited areas yet to be claimed by either narrative. Our first child was born in a hospital with several forms of medical intervention. He was also exclusively formula fed from the time he was 6 weeks old. Our second child was born at home in the presence of a midwife and has been, more or less, exclusively breastfed until introduced to solid foods, many of which were organic and locally grown. Accordingly, our intent is to describe the limitations imposed upon parents by the existence of dominating narratives and to examine whose purposes they ultimately serve.

The available discourse within *Mothering* magazine suggests that the revolutionary space of women's empowerment via control of their bodies is available only to those women who meet a certain capability for and disposition towards the products and lifestyle sold between its pages. This consumerist strand of the naturalistic mothering movement reproduces the problematic history of second-wave feminism, constructing a prescriptive image of motherhood and parenting that is all but closed to women and families who do not possess the requisite means to achieve it. However, within *Mothering*, readers regularly express their gratitude to the editors in the form of 'love letters' printed within the 'your letters' section of the magazine, suggesting that parents have found information, inspiration, and solace within these pages. The problem, then, lies within the construct of naturalistic parenting as a grand narrative and a brand identity that includes or excludes families based on their parenting and lifestyle choices, as well as their socioeconomic status. The opportunity for an honest dialogue about parenting and its challenges is lost to a set of predetermined criteria. In this discourse, a mother encounters the challenge of telling her story without that story becoming the organizing principle of her every action related to child rearing, the maintenance of her family and home, and her feelings about herself as a parent.

> I decide to let my daughter cry at night because my body can no longer accept the many months of sleep deprivation forced upon it. When my daughter cries, I cry with her, but I refuse to give into her late night demands. The book said the crying would only last a few nights, but my child seems particularly stubborn, or maybe she can just sense that I'm close to giving in. But, I don't. Later, when she is sleep-trained, I'm finally getting more of the sleep I need, but I still feel guilty that I let her cry. It's a topic – like religion or politics – that I wouldn't dare discuss with people I didn't know very well. Some would offer empathy and support; others might call me out on my cruelty. No mother wants to hear her baby cry, but there are limits to what one body can take.

Gore (1992) observed a pervasive sense of hopelessness under pedagogical regimes of truth. She asks, 'What is one to do when one accepts that no practices or discourses are inherently liberating or oppressive, that our most liberatory intentions have no guaranteed effects?' (p. 137). As we seek the best for our children in the competing discourses of parenting, we often lose sight of what is ultimately at stake beyond these pedagogies – the well-being of the mother herself. Instead, under the weight of the greater discourse on parenthood, mothers long to possess their own birthing/parenting story, one that is more or less complete. The task of creating such a narrative, one that is sanitized and certain, can only be described as impossible. No doubt, women will begin to see themselves as inadequate mothers, especially if the story they tell does not match the cultural scripts available to them or if the body they experience does not feel like the one described on the page. From a social welfare perspective, Featherstone (1999) argues that this false narrative of parenthood – that one should always feel comfortable within his or her parenting identity – can be dangerous, especially when parents are afraid to admit their concerns or ask for help. Featherstone describes ambivalence, as well as powerful love-hate emotions and the blurring of body boundaries, as central to parenting. She notes that, even as children grow and develop, parents are part of a developmental process. Still, notions of good and bad parenting render the expression of these experiences unacceptable, much less marketable.

In order to transgress the dominant narratives of consumption, we suggest that motherhood must be recast as its own strong narrative. Artist and psychoanalysis scholar Bracha Ettinger (2006) offers a potential means of escaping the regimes (Gore, 1992) that delineate and delimit the possibilities of women's bodies and narratives. Ettinger attempts to locate a space for forming identities, narratives of the self, beyond the characteristic phallocentrism and symbolic violence of most psychoanalytical theory. To this end, she offers the notion of a 'matrixial borderspace' that operates from the physical actuality and metaphoric construction of the womb. In this space, subjects are produced in the relational, emergent act of cohabiting a single body in the experience of pregnancy. Ettinger relates this space as a site of feminine discourse that exists beyond the reach of patriarchal symbolization, noting that 'the matrix – "womb" in Latin – as a major signifier gives an approximate sense of this originary difference that is always already in the feminine, laboring and evolving through it' (p. 183). Taken psychosocially, Ettinger's borderspace locates resistance to the notion of colonization as metaphorically linked to the pregnant body itself, a space that, once reclaimed – offers women (and in a metaphoric sense, men) the ability to define or undefine themselves without the demands of the pedagogies we have described in this chapter bearing upon them. With this ability, women literally and figuratively begin to feel the curricula of otherness within their own bodies. They experience the production of self and other not as part of a process of rending and alienation, but as part of the act of simply becoming.

Using the concepts Ettinger (2006) forwards as a theoretical backdrop, we argue for a pedagogical approach that transcends consumer desire and its undergirding of classist values and judgment. The fields

we represent as scholars (education and social work) both offer critical space in which we might interrupt the market's encroachment into
the naturalistic mothering movement and begin to reconnect with that
movement's original, still-espoused, aims and purposes – women's
agency in birthing and experiences of motherhood. From the point of
view of education, in the broad sense of the term, formal health curricula might offer suggestions for more healthful, naturalistic approaches
to pregnancy and childbirth that are not rooted in the conspicuous consumption of a particularized set of (expensive) products. Further, in
feminist classroom discourse, students might engage in the kinds of
analyses we have undertaken in this chapter, questioning the intended
audience of parenting literature and popular messages to ascertain the
underlying class scripts, implicit aims, and prefigured identities that
this discourse offers. From the social welfare point of view, clinicians
must have the courage to explore the origins of their own notions of
good parenting and note that these distinctions, as well as those set forth
in popular culture and government welfare agencies, are class based.
Failure to accept the act of parenting as complex, contradictory, and
cultural can result in a serious disconnect between parents who need
assistance and those who can assist them.

These interventions, in either discipline, must work to de-centre the
primacy of either regime to uncover the logic of consumption and distinction that lies beneath and offer women's own phenomenological
counter-stories to the *oughts* and *shoulds* of the consumerist drive. In
this space, men and women might engage in the discussions that ven-
ues like *Mothering* magazine cannot support. The actual experience of
parenthood – and the small, local pedagogies that parenting enacts –
might be repositioned to transgress the ubiquitous voice of the market and to recast the imperfect body as its own strong narrative of the
self-in-emergence. Our stories and analyses in this chapter have been
an attempt for us to explore our own borderspaces, our own tensions
of being and becoming, as well as the pressures that have shaped our
stories to preconceived ends. By doing so, we sought to problematize
the narratives and images offered to us by the dominant discourse of
parenthood and, thus, offer space for others to do the same.

References

Aldridge, A. (2003). *Consumption*. Cambridge, MA: Polity Press.
Baudrillard, J. (1970). *The consumer society*. London: Sage.

Bourdieu, P. (1977). *Outline of a theory of practice*. New York: Cambridge University Press.

Bourdieu, P. (2000). The aesthetic sense as the sense of distinction. In J.B. Schor & D.B. Holt (Eds.), *The consumer society reader* (pp. 205–211). New York: New Press. (Original work published 1979).

Bryant, J., Porter, M., Tracy, S.K., & Sullivan, E.A. (2007). Caesarian birth: Consumption, safety, order, and good mothering. *Social Science & Medicine, 65*, 1192–1201.

Ehrenreich, B., & English, D. (2005). *For her own good*. New York: Anchor Books.

Ettinger, B.L. (2006). *The matrixial borderspace*. Minneapolis, MN: University of Minnesota Press.

Featherstone, B. (1999). Taking mothering seriously: The implications for child protection. *Child and Family Social Work, 4*, 43–53.

Friedan, B. (2000). The sexual sell. In J.B. Schor & D.B. Holt (Eds.), *The consumer society reader* (pp. 26–46). New York: New Press.

Gawlik, E. (2008, March–April). The ABCs of going cloth. *Mothering: Natural family living, 147*, 52–57.

Gore, J. (1992). *The struggle for pedagogies*. New York: Routledge.

Hoeschsmann, M. (2007). Advertising pedagogy: Teaching and learning consumption. In S. Steinberg & D. Macedo (Eds.), *Media literacy: A reader* (pp. 653–666). New York: Peter Lang.

Jolly, N. (2007). Cesarean, celebrity, and childbirth: Students encounter modern birth and the question of female embodiment. In S. Springgay & D. Freedman, (Eds.), *Curriculum and the cultural body* (pp. 175–187). New York: Peter Lang.

Klein, N. (2002). *No logo: No space, no choice, no jobs*. New York: Picador.

Lair, C. (2008, March–April). Fresh foods first. *Mothering: Natural family living, 147*, 82–87.

Media Kit. (2008). Retrieved 17 April 2008, from http://www.mothering.com/sections/advertising/media-kit-2008.pdf.

Molnar, A. (2004). *School commercialism*. New York: Routledge.

Ponte, W. (2007, September–October). Caesarian birth in a culture of fear. *Mothering: Natural family living, 144*, 49–63.

Slotnik, A. (Producer), Netto, P. (Producer), & Epstein, A. (Producer/Director). (2008). *The business of being born*. [Motion picture]. New York: Barranca Productions.

U.S. Census. (2006). Two-Year-Average Median Household Income by State: 2004–2006. Retrieved 29 April 2008, from http://www.census.gov/hhes/www/income/income06/statemhi2.html.

Van't Hul, J. (2007, July–August). Small hands, big art. *Mothering: Natural family living*, 143, 42–47.

Walker, M. (2008, March–April). Ban the bags. *Mothering: Natural family living*, 147, 72–81.

Walsh, C. (2007, November–December). Santa's workshop rediscovered. *Mothering: Natural family living*, 145, 88–91.

Weiner, L.Y. (1994). Reconstructing motherhood: The La Leche League in postwar America. *Journal of American History*, *80* (4), 1357–1381.

Zadoroznyj, M. (2001). Birth and the 'reflexive consumer': Trust, risk and medical dominance in obstetric encounters. *Journal of Sociology, 37* (2), 117–139.

2 Pregnant Pedagogy

JULIE GARLEN MAUDLIN

When I discovered in 2003 that I would be adding another child to the two I was already raising while teaching full-time and pursuing a doctoral degree, I found myself thinking about how this unexpected pregnancy would impact me as a teacher and a researcher. I had just begun to feel confident in my role as a budding scholar when suddenly I found myself in this awkward, 'delicate' position. In spite of what I had learned about unstable, shifting postmodern identities, I found myself in a circumstance intimately tied to my physical condition. This experience, coupled with my previous history as a young mother and graduate student, prompted me to consider what I began to perceive as the disembodiment of curriculum, a situation in which the contexts of physical bodies, *corporealities*, as I term them, seem virtually absent from the high-stakes content-focused curriculum, so much so that a pregnant body seemed out of place in the 'sterile' school environment. This was particularly concerning for me, having gestated during all three of my formal higher education experiences as an undergraduate, graduate, and doctoral student, because I recognized that this experience must have had some impact on my actions and perceptions as a student and educator-in-training. Upon re-examining my own theories about curriculum that had emerged through the course of my studies, I discovered important parallels with the pregnancies that had shaped the landscape of my educational development. In doing so, I came to understand the experience of pregnancy as a powerful conceptual lens through which we can imagine the possibilities of an embodied curriculum.

Theorizing the Pregnant Body

The initial theoretical dissonance I experienced as a result of my condition led me to re-examine the notion of the biological body in the context of postmodern discourse. Postmodernism, with its 'incredulity toward metanarratives,' as Lyotard (1989) describes it, has problematized the notions of fixed unities, destabilizing identity and the notion that the body could exist as a distinct biological construct, separate from and unaffected by the cultural context in which it has emerged. Postmodern thought across the disciplines allowed us to understand that being or identity is not rooted in or inherent to the body, but constructed through sociocultural interactions. Thus, our bodies become texts, to be read, interpreted, shaped, and discursively constructed. As a text, situated within language and representation, the body as simply a biological organism resistant to cultural influence does not exist.

The postmodern subject position recognizes the relationship between body and language, and thus, human experience. With the rejection of a nature/culture binary, we remove the body from one side of a false dichotomy, and situate it within a complex, fluid system, making it difficult to locate any substantive 'self.' If the body does not exist independently of culture, and we have to dissolve the notion that there is no distinct 'nature,' then we are no longer responsible for explaining how nature and culture work together, and we are left with the question of whether the body can really be said to 'be' at all. As Peter McLaren (1988) points out, rarely in all the discourse of 'bodies without organs, shadow bodies which are merely discursive fictions, or fractured bodies composed of solitary links along a signifying chain' do we ever find bodies and/or subjects 'who bleed, who suffer, who feel pain, who possess the critical capacity to make political choices, and who have the moral courage to carry these choices out' (p. 57).

Here, I share Gail Weiss's (2003) sentiment about the predicament that this ontological indifference creates: 'While I, too, accept the notion that the body can and should be viewed as a text, I am also concerned about the ethical implications of such a position, implications that are rarely acknowledged and, for that very reason, all the more urgent to consider' (p. 25). It is dangerous to assume that we could understand the body outside of our cultural contexts, but we also take a risk by totally eliminating *any* notion of the physical because we are left without a way to understand phenomena, such as illness and injury, which seem to *us* to *be* physical. Perhaps this could explain how it is that we have often failed to include disability in our criticisms of identity, because as, Holmes (2003) notes, 'Disability reminds us of that which is most personal (and thus shameful) in the intellectual life, that which is not aesthetic or abstract. This same body is also what is least personal, most generically human – that which we in academia hope to surpass with distinctive and irreplaceable creations that usually celebrate our minds' (p. x).

However, if we are to remain incredulous, as Lyotard suggests, we must not allow postmodernism itself to become a nihilistic metanarrative by constructing the body as *either* a discursive fiction *or* a distinct biological organism. Even Derrida (quoted in Kearney & Ricoeur, 1984), who announced the 'death' of the subject, admits that it does, indeed, exist: 'I have never said that the subject should be dispensed with. Only that it should be deconstructed. To deconstruct the subject does not mean to deny its existence. There are subjects, operations, or effects of subjectivity. That is an incontrovertible fact. To acknowledge this does not mean, however, that the subject is what it says it is. The subject is not some meta-linguistic presence; it is always inscribed in language. My work does not, therefore, destroy the subject; it simply tries to resituate it' (p. 125). Similarly, if we intend to use postmodern/ post-structural as a connector rather than a divider, we can resituate the body without denying the physical existence of the flesh. We can see the body, as Lennard Davis (1995) asserts, as 'a way of organizing through the realm of the sense the variations and modalities of physical existence as they are embodied into being through a larger social/ political Matrix' (p. 14). This understanding of the body allows us to talk about the body without erasing the significance of its physical substance. The body becomes, then, what McLaren (1995) terms, the 'point d'appui,' the point at which we find the 'dialectical reinitiation of meaning and desire' (p. 63). LeCourt (2004) puts it yet another way: 'The body, that is, experiences and enacts culture as more than a discursive relation, but rather as a confluence of meaning, desire, and affect literally written into the flesh. We learn our identities in discursive relations that mediate experience; we perceive our bodies in their material relation to the world via such discursively constructed identities' (p. 19). To understand the body in this way allows us to bring the body back into academic discourse in a way that is meaningful and creates a space in which we can begin to develop an embodied paradigm that is not inconsistent with postmodern sentiments.

We can begin the process of constructing such a paradigm by rethinking the body in theory. We need to resist the temptation to employ postmodernism in writing the physical body out of discursive subjectivity. We can appreciate the fleeting quality of our culturally constructed identities without losing sight of bodies that gestate, lactate, bleed, and break. We have to recognize not only the ways that we discursively construct our bodies but how our bodies participate in language games through initiation and response, sometimes without our permission. To do so requires that we 'get over' our biological insecurities, our fears of confronting the frailty of human flesh. Davis's (2002) notion of 'dismodernism,' provides us with a valuable alternative. From this framework and the biological necessities of gestation emerge a family of pedagogical practices that might help us imagine new ways to embody, complicate, re-member, and re-vise curricula to make public education more personal and meaningful for all students.

Davis (2002) suggests that we can reimagine the body in theory by expanding our thinking from postmodernism to what he calls 'dismodernism,' a rethinking of our understanding of postmodern identity through disability. Davis (1995) also observes that disability is unique in that it is historically linked to the categories of oppression most visible in academic discourse: race, gender, and sexuality. These transgressive bodies were faultily but powerfully constructed through pathological categories of disability. Thus, by studying the ways that disability has been constructed, we can explore 'how all groups, based on physical traits or markings, are selected for disablement by a larger system of regulation and signification' (Davis, 2002, p. 29).

Davis argues that, considering the initial construction of race, gender, and sexuality, as well as the vast assortment of 'conditions' (blindness, amputation, obesity, disfigurement, diabetes, attention deficit disorder, Asperger's, learning disability, and so on) that are included under the category, disability presents us with a 'malleable view of the human body and identity' (p. 26). Thus, Davis's notion of 'dismodernism' helps us understand how power has operated to construct the inequality of particular bodies, and the importance of the recognition that human bodies cannot and should not be standardized: 'The dismodern era ushers in the concept that difference is what all of us have in common. That identity is not fixed but malleable. That technology is not separate but part of the body. That dependence, not individual interdependence, is the rule. There is no single clockmaker who made the uniform clock of the human body. The watchword of dismodernism could be: Form follows dysfunction' (p. 27). The notion of dismodernism helps to bring the body into discourse in a way that recognizes the 'magic of human variability,' the unity in difference, and the fiction of 'normalcy.' Davis's expansion of the postmodern subject allows us to bring the body into discourse in a meaningful way while maintaining our understanding of the physical body as inseparable from its discursive social, cultural, and educational contexts.

Situating the Pregnant Body

Recognizing the fiction of normalcy and the role our bodies play as the nexus of our social/cultural/technological interactions can also help us resituate the body within the curriculum. The bodies of teachers and students are knowing-bodies existing both in the classroom and in the world. These inquiring bodies are our nexus for knowing the world and interacting with others; we cannot act on the teacher or the student without also acting on the body because the body is always already inscribed in language, written into the curriculum in more or less damaging ways. The disembodied curriculum is one that fails to 'see' the body, one that writes the body into the margins in order to accomplish its educational goals.

An embodied curriculum is one that 'sees' the body, one that brings the body fully into the learning process to act as the vinculum drawn over social/cultural/technological interactions within and beyond the classroom. An embodied curriculum draws us into intimacy with the sensual, unruly, unpredictable, desirous body; it is a curriculum that recognizes the connections 'between materiality and the psychic world, between social and cultural conditions and circumstances, between desires and pleasures, as well as disappointments,' and 'undermines "orderly" teacher-student relations' (Levy, 2000, p. 83). It's difficult to imagine a more intimate, 'connected' experience than pregnancy, a condition once believed so provocative that it was banned from educational institutions and discourse. However, it is precisely the kind of metaphor that we need to move curriculum beyond the sterility and isolation of traditional practices. Based on my own experiences, I believe that pregnancy is a powerful conceptual lens through which we can imagine the possibilities of an embodied curriculum.

Pregnancy implies 'life in-process,' a connected, intimate, generative process of development that seems conceptually distant from typical content-focused curricula. The knowledge-centred focus of our test-focused educational culture suggests that learning is a process of disengaging the brain from the physical body, but pregnancy serves as a reminder that our bodies are always already part of the way we engage in curricula, because its visibility forces us to recognize the body in a way that we would not do otherwise. Pregnant pedagogy, then, refers back to the embodied subject and the larger contexts from which it is inseparable. The physical state of pregnancy can be considered as occurring within the convergence of meaning, desire, and affect.

The idea that pregnancy is an evocative medium for the reconceptualization of curriculum is not intended to privilege this particular route to motherhood or to suggest that biology is a necessary component in reinterpreting curriculum in a meaningful way. Other forms of motherhood, such as adoption and surrogacy, might provoke a different conversation but are no less meaningful metaphors for those who have experienced them. Furthermore, I would not suggest that every woman who has experienced gestation might relate to the embodied practices I describe here. Rather, I will use this particular interpretation to illustrate that, in order to realize the potential of embodied pedagogy, we must examine our own bodily experiences and use them to inform our educational philosophies.

The embodied curriculum and the pedagogical practices that serve to bring it to fruition, like the culturally/socially/technologically embedded pregnant body, are connected, responsive, meaningful, personal, multiplex. In honouring the variability of bodies and contexts, I would not venture to offer a prescriptive framework for engaging in pregnant pedagogies, but these practices most resonate with my understanding of embodied pedagogy. Like the 'corporealities' from which they emerge, they are not conceptually distinct; they bleed into and from one another, and they could be expressed in many different ways depending on the particular context in which they emerge. Although, for me, these practices emerge from a postmodern theoretical framework, they are not altogether unlike many of the 'best practices' that appear in much educational literature, such as Scherer's (2009) recent collection of articles on *Engaging the Whole Child*. Furthermore, there are numerous empirical studies that might serve to validate the methodologies they imply. For example, parallels can be seen between the kind of instructional inquiry embodied practices demand and the assertions of Paulus, Woodside, and Ziegler (2008), who recognize qualitative research as evolving, emergent, collaborative, and dialogic. Similarly, James, Dunning, Connolly, and Elliott (2007) reveal the positive impact of collaborative, reflective practice on school success, while Kalliola, Nakari, and Pesonen (2006) provide theoretical and empirical evidence for the use of dialogue to promote positive organizational change. Finally, the findings of Brandes and Crowson (2009) reveal how isolation from and lack of understanding of our bodies and others, specifically disabled bodies, can impact teachers' abilities to enable their diverse students to become productive and independent members of society. While these and countless other studies exist to provide empirical support for the pedagogical practices described here, the primary purpose is not to seek out statistically verified strategies, but instead to theorize through the experience of pregnancy an embodied process of teacher decision making that recognizes both the significance of curriculum theory as well as the merit of exemplary instructional practices.

Disclosure

Donna LeCourt (2004) observes that 'theory does not begin in the academy; it begins in everyday interactions and reactions. It begins in autobiography' (p. 1). This process of disclosure is important to pregnant pedagogy because it is a way of purposefully bringing our bodies, our inquiring subjectivities, into the classroom. When I became pregnant with my third child, I struggled with how and when to share this information with my 9- and 10-year-old students, and, inevitably, I waited until hiding the pregnancy was no longer an option. Before sharing this with my students, I felt awkward about the changes that were taking place in my body unbeknownst to them, and I wondered about the changes they themselves were experiencing but unable to share. I was also reminded of my experience as a pregnant college senior, when my professors no longer called on me to answer questions, as if the hormonal changes had robbed me of my senses, a situation I wished that I had been able to understand and articulate at age 22. In this way, I found I shared a connection to those who have had to explain how various physical disabilities impacted their work as students and as teachers. While examining the body through the perceptual lens of disability, I came across a dialogue between three scholars with disabilities who, each new term, anticipated the moment when they would 'disclose' their disabilities to their university students. I wondered, if we all walk into the classrooms with different needs, desires, identities, and varying abilities and disabilities, why don't we feel the need to offer a similar 'confession'? If we think of our bodies in Davis's (2002) 'dismodern' terms, and we accept that 'form follows dysfunction,' then we can see how disclosure can undermine the isolating and alienating fiction of normalcy and bring us into a more intimate relationship with ourselves and others.

However, because we are accustomed to relegating our corporealities to the margins of educational environments, such disclosure does not come naturally. Brueggemann and Moddelmog, who term this 'coming out pedagogy' (2003), observe that 'this act of naming our invisible and supposedly private identities can seem to turn the classroom away from knowledge and toward intimacy, and this can be troubling for both our students and ourselves because we have been conditioned to see the classroom as only an intellectual space' (p. 213). Yet, this process of 'coming out,' of confessing our particular embodied subjectivities, serves to deconstruct the boundaries we have created to confine the body in the traditional school curriculum. The process becomes even more meaningful when it becomes a continual process rather than a single moment: 'Within this perspective, our coming out is not so much a functional disclosure as it is an embodied performance' (p. 213). This embodied performance allows teachers and students to resituate identity within an understanding of both oppressive and enabling relationships. In this way, the ongoing dialogue of disclosure becomes 'a bidirectional process of communication in which we and our students must do more than simply encounter a "secret": We and they must relate to it. That relationship is sometimes comforting, sometimes discomforting, and sometimes both at once' (p. 213).

Teachers can facilitate this process of disclosure by inviting students to share the needs, desires, interests, and assumptions that they bring into the classroom. They can encourage students to question their assumptions about the learning experience, and they can use techniques such as journaling, questionnaires, and autobiographical essays to establish the importance of individual circumstances and promote understanding and empathy. Such tasks can allow students to explore the ways in which habits, interests, and physical conditions, as well as emotional and pyschological needs, impact the way that they learn. Even young children can engage in dialogue about personal and physical characteristics that may impact their experience in the classroom. Most importantly, the teachers themselves must engage in the same process of sharing and disclosing and be responsive to the disclosures of the students by recognizing their role in shaping instructional practice.

Lability

Although pregnancies do tend to progress through fairly predictable trimesters of development, every woman experiences those stages in different ways, and individual responses are far from predictable. Therefore, the process of disclosure is perpetuated through another element of reflexive practice: *lability*, an openness to change and spontaneity. I choose to use this term because its meanings are rooted in the body: In biochemistry, labile means easily repositioned, as, for example, a labile nitric oxide molecule. In a psychiatric context, labile refers to emotional instability, freely expressed and easily aroused emotions and uncontrolled moods. I take great pleasure in adopting this term, often used by medical professionals to describe the mood swings experienced by menstruating, pregnant, and menopausal women, and presenting it as a positive trait of reflexive pedagogy. Freedom of emotional expression, instability, and spontaneity are all vital elements of our being open to the new ways of teaching and learning that emerge from our deepened explorations of our subjectivities.

Once we have begun to participate in the process of disclosure, our particular needs and desires can inform and shape the curriculum so that we avoid privileging certain bodies and ways of knowing. However, the traditional structures that guide school improvement – schedules, grading and promotion policies, assessments, and outwardly imposed expert 'interventions' – are not often conducive to a responsive, collaborative curriculum, and they generally operate under paradigms of efficiency and control. As Eisner (2005) asserts, 'For U.S. schools, the speed of reaching the destination is considered a virtue: The brighter students are the faster students' (p. 17). Education becomes not something to evoke pleasure and fulfilment (like a satisfying meal) but another rebarbative chore that must be accomplished in order to move on to more important things (like waste management). Consider the traditional model of curriculum proposed by Bobbitt (1918) nearly a century ago in *The Curriculum:* 'These will show the abilities, attitudes, habits, appreciations and forms of knowledge that men need. These will be the objectives of the curriculum. They will be numerous, definite and particularized. The curriculum will then be that series of experiences which children and youth must have by way of obtaining those objectives' (p. 42). This canonical view of curriculum, from which Tyler's (1949) authoritative *Basic Principles of Curriculum and Instruction* emerged, could very well describe the state-mandated models now in use, which leave little room for flexible, sensitive instruction that addresses the needs and desires of particular bodies.

Embracing lability in the classroom means being open to circumstances that may impact instructional strategies on a day-to-day basis. This does not suggest the complete absence of planned lessons, rules, or routines. Rather, it requires a level of flexibility when responding to the needs of students and embracing the 'teachable moments' that can occur spontaneously. In order for teachers to be responsive to students, the process of disclosure must be perpetuated throughout the learning experience so that students feel free to express at anytime their needs, desires, and interests, and pedagogical practices can be revised frequently to reflect the changing circumstances of students. Currently, many teachers are not given the discretion to make day-to-day decisions about the strategies, content, and resources that are most appropriate for their particular students at any specific time. Scripted curricula, mandated textbooks, and standardized assessments limit teachers' ability to establish responsive pedagogical practices. For teachers to become comfortable with this level of flexibility, they must be trusted to make instructional decisions based on the relationships and connections they have built with their students.

Dialogue

To create spaces for disclosure and flexibility and, thus, risk, we have to re-evaluate our embedded perceptions of teaching and learning through critical dialogue. The symbiotic relationship between mother and fetus is indicative of the kind of meaningful, personal exchange that does not value the contribution of one individual over another. If we accept the body as inscribed in language, then embodied pedagogy must involve engaging in meaningful, personal discourse. As Reynolds (2003) suggests, 'a curriculum should allow both teacher and student to develop a critical, caring, compassionate conversation rather than treat human beings as objects to be manipulated by prescribed and pre-fashioned technical rationales that reduce human beings to mere raw material' (p. 43). Peter Trifonas (2005) explains that discourse is important because it is the 'medium through which students can practice the critical power to interrogate concepts for the sake of learning more about the self while keeping in mind the exploitation or alienation that may arise when knowledge claims are taken to be absolute and not interpretations to be enriched by the creative adding of the difference of experience to a rational possibility' (p. 159).

Dialogue creates passages from which to negotiate the complexities of embodied subjectivity, and asks teachers and students to reconsider knowledge claims through an understanding of difference. Dialogue gives way to critical pedagogy, which 'allows, indeed encourages, students and teachers together to confront the real problems of their existence and relationships . . . When students confront the real problems of their existence they will soon also be faced with their own oppression' (Grundy, 1987, p. 105). Critical dialogue opens up the curriculum to possibility, contradiction, and difference. Students can then begin to interrogate the ways that regulation and signification operate to 'castigate difference in the everyday conditions that house the living realm of our aspirations as students and teachers' (Trifonas, 2005, p. 159).

Like disclosure, dialogue does not necessarily emerge easily when both teachers and students are accustomed to a passive, top-down, standardized curriculum. Engaging in critical dialogue calls our identities and beliefs into question, which Delpit (1988) says, 'is not easy. It is painful as well, because it means turning yourself inside out, giving up your sense of who you are, and being willing to see yourself in the unflattering light of another's angry gaze. It is not easy, but it is the only way to learn what it might feel like to be someone else and the only way to start the dialogue' (p. 297). By starting the dialogue, we engage our bodies in the learning process and the active, collaborative transformation of our inquiring subjectivities.

Gestation involves a unique form of collaboration whereby the fetus is physically dependent on the mother to provide the environment for growth, but also develops independently through processes that are totally beyond her control. In the same way, embodied curricula require the teacher to foster the environment in which students can develop according to their own needs, interests, and desires. By continually disclosing and building connections through our discursive 'secrets,' and engaging in critical dialogue, teachers and students can work together, operating jointly to construct a classroom curriculum that is meaningful and personal – embodied. Kohn (2005) calls this collaborative model a *working with* approach rather than a *doing to* strategy. Rather than imposing the mandated curriculum on students through a set of prescribed practices laid out neatly by a textbook, curriculum standards become a part of our disclosure as teachers: we expose them to the students and engage them in constructing learning experiences that can reach the needs and desires they have disclosed to us. All of the constraints and mandates that are imposed on us – performance standards, pacing guides, textbooks, assessments – as well as our own needs and desires as experienced educators, are brought into the dialogue so that these limits can become part of the critical conversation.

In the same way that we name our subjective identities through disclosure, we name the mandates, exposing them and making them transparent so that they become a part of the ongoing dialogue about how and why and what we learn. Teachers who embrace dialogue must be willing not only to engage their students in these conversations, but to actively listen and respond. Meaningful dialogue must go beyond calling on students for answers and asking them to mirror what we model. Rather, we must provide opportunities and really hear what students have to say and meaningfully respond, even if, and perhaps, especially if, we find ourselves in disagreement. Such conversations, whether in the form of one-on-one, small group, or even large group discussions, perpetuate the disclosure process and inform the labile curriculum. Like the co-evolving body/culture/technology complex, we work through our rhizomatic connections to 'cooperate' in constructing the curriculum, enacting new social relations, and laying bare the power relations that create inequality along the way. Through consistent and ongoing dialogue, the curriculum (even a standardized one) can be revisited, reimagined, and reconstructed to meet the meet the needs of our knowing-bodies.

Discomfort

Anyone who has experienced pregnancy knows that gestation, although miraculous and awe-inspiring, is nonetheless often awkward and uncomfortable. Aside from the physical pain associated with pregnancy and birth, we often find ourselves subject to a level of bodily scrutiny that can be quite embarrassing. Once our pregnancies become visible, the overt product of our sexuality is on constant display, and suddenly strangers believe they have received licence to strike up conversations and actually physically touch our bodies. Similarly, the process of continual disclosure and dialogue opens up the curriculum to a level of intimacy and interdependence that can be disconcerting, which leads us to the pedagogical necessity of discomfort. Embodied pedagogy requires us to constantly move out of our comfort zones to unearth the private and the passionate, which have long been silenced by the traditional school curriculum. Yet, it is through such discomfort that we can confront the contradictions of our corporealities, interrogate normalcy and disability, and accept and embrace difference in order to construct a reflexive curriculum.

This discomfiting dialogue is a transformative space from which we can explore our own subjectivities and call into question the dominant values that typically frame teaching and learning, which Boler and Zembylas (2003) describe as 'pedagogy of discomfort.' Through this process, students and teachers work together to recognize and problematize 'the deeply embedded emotional dimensions that frame and shape daily habits, routines, and unconscious complicity with hegemony (p. 111). Pedagogy of discomfort purposefully attends to affective perception and embodied knowing in order to expose the ways we perform and hypostatize the prevailing norms and assumptions of traditional educational habits and routines. As Boler and Zembylas explain, 'By closely examining emotional reactions and responses – what we call emotional stances – one begins to identify unconscious privileges as well as invisible ways in which one complies with dominant ideology' (p. 111).

Engaging in embodied curricula requires that we bring our whole selves, our physiological as well as our psychological beings, more fully into the classrooms so that we can learn to accept and appreciate difference, as uncomfortable as that may be. As Brueggemann and Moddelmog (2003) submit, 'This approach to coming out makes our classrooms places of comfort and discomfort because it encourages our students and us to share our stories, to investigate our identities, and to name our passions' (p. 216). Teachers and students must initiate this process of 'fleshing out' our stories, identities, and passions because it does not emerge effortlessly from an educational culture of standardization and sterility. This initiation can be difficult, as Martha Stoddard Holmes describes of her own experience of exposing bodies in the classroom: 'The classroom bodies were all under scrutiny, even when the class talked about bodies, disabilities, or differences as concepts. Many discussions were unintentionally painful in their association with the bodies the discussants lived in outside of the classroom, bodies that were stared at, rejected, obstructed from access to bathrooms and classrooms, diagnosed and classified, loved for the wrong reasons, photographed, written about, beaten, as well as treated kindly, loved, soothed and delighted' (Freedman & Holmes, 2003, p. 5). While self-exposure can unearth powerful emotions in a classroom of adults, such a process may emerge with less difficulty for children who have not yet experienced a lifetime of affective repression. We can begin this dialogue even with very young children (and we do this in preschool) by helping them name their thoughts, feelings, emotions, and experiences, but this process needs to continue into adulthood. Perhaps, if we engage children in this dialogue of disclosure as they grow, we can help them resist the oppression and hegemony that has left so many of us feeling lost and distant.

Embracing the practice of discomfort requires us as teachers to move beyond those practices and habits with which we are familiar and exhibit openness to change. We must be willing to question our own assumptions about teaching and learning, and particularly our dispositions towards and expectations for students so that we can maintain an awareness of how they influence instructional decisions. We may feel uncertain about letting go of the authoritative role of the teacher as primary purveyor of knowledge, but this state of disequilibrium is necessary if we hope to realize a 'working-with' approach to teaching. Openly validating the contributions of students by recognizing the merit of verbal and written feedback, adopting dynamic instructional strategies that are responsive to the changing particularities of students, and allowing for unexpected and perhaps even unpleasant dialogue can help to bring our corporealities into the curriculum. Such an engagement in critical, reflexive practice asks teachers to radically re-evaluate their traditional roles as technicians of a standardized curriculum and offer themselves up to pedagogies of difference, responsiveness, and uncertainty. Thus, classrooms where discomfort is embraced as transformative become 'spaces of intellectual and personal discovery as we explore the ways in which identity can ground and trouble us and seek to understand how we come to know what we think we know about ourselves and others' (Brueggemann & Moddelmog, 2003, p. 216).

Towards Pregnant Pedagogies

It is one thing to imagine embodied curricula through pregnancy, but the theory is barren if it does not generate action. My own pedagogical experiences are continually changing, as I seek ways to bring the elements I have explored here – disclosure, lability, dialogue, and discomfort – more fully into my practice as a teacher-educator. Practice, like pregnancy itself, is 'life in-process,' in a constant state of change, and each term begins a new cycle of growing in an understanding of embodied practice, so that I am perpetually reinventing and re-examining my attempts to engage my students in meaningful, critical ways. Some cycles are more fruitful than others. However, I do find that, by articulating these qualities as commitments, I am able to reflect on the extent to which I am engaging in embodied pedagogy. In turn, I hope to influence the pedagogical commitments of the pre-service and practising educators who populate my classes.

The elements described here, while not comprehensive or rigidly defined, are some of the ways that I envision pregnant pedagogies emerging from the rhetorical morass of 'no child *left*' standards, sanctions, and accountability. As Fuller (2007) so aptly notes, 'In this brave new world of childhood, the aim is to raise youngsters' test scores not long after they shed [their] diapers' (p. xi). For over a decade, this world has been at the centre of government educational policy throughout North America. Perhaps, in such a context, it is logically untenable to envision a future in which different schools construct and adopt different learning goals and standards that are meaningful and personal for their particular knowing-bodies, but that does not give us licence to abandon embodied pedagogy altogether. Rather, I believe that in the current climate of high-stakes minimum competency accountability, it is more important than ever that we seek ways to bring public education into the realm of the intimate, the personal, the pleasurable, the affective. We must do this if we hope to make the marginalizing, categorizing, alienating, dehumanizing institution that public education has become into something generative, liberating, meaningful, and promising.

References

Bobbitt, F. (1918). *The curriculum*. Manchester, NH: Ayer.

Boler, M., & Zembylas, M. 2003. Discomforting truths: The emotional terrain of understanding difference. In P. Trifonas (Ed.), *Pedagogies of difference*, pp. 110–136. New York: Routledge.

Brandes, J., & Crowson, H. (2009). Predicting dispositions toward inclusion of students with disabilities: The role of conservative ideology and discomfort with disability. *Social Psychology of Education, 12* (2), 271–289.

Brueggemann, B., Garland-Thomson, R., & Kleege, G. (2005). What her body taught (or, teaching about and with a disability: A conversation. *Feminist Studies, 31* (1), 13–33.

Brueggemann, B., & Moddelmog, D. (2003). Coming out pedagogy. In D. Freedman & M.S. Holmes (Eds.), *The teacher's body: Embodiment, authority, and identity in the academy,* pp. 209–234. Albany, NY: State University of New York Press.

Davis, L.J. (1995). *Enforcing normalcy: Disability, deafness and the body.* London: Verso.

Davis, L.J. (2002). *Bending over backwards: Disability, dismodernism, and other difficult positions.* New York: New York University Press.

Delpit, L.D. (1988). The silenced dialogue: Power and pedagogy in educating other people's children. *Harvard Educational Review, 58* (3), 280–298.

Eisner, E. (2005). Back to whole. *Educational Leadership, 63* (1), 14–18.

Freedman, D., & Holmes, M.S. (Eds.). (2003). *The teacher's body: Embodiment, authority, and identity in the academy.* Albany, NY: State University of New York Press.

Fuller, B. (2007). *Standardized childhood: The political and cultural struggle over early education.* Stanford, CA: Stanford University Press.

Grundy, S. (1987). *Curriculum: Product or praxis?* New York: Falmer Press.

Holmes, M.S. (2003). *Fictions of affliction: Physical disability in Victorian culture.* Ann Arbor, MI: University of Michigan Press.

James, C.R., Dunning, G., Connolly, M., & Elliott, T. (2007). Collaborative practice: A model of successful working in schools. *Journal of Educational Administration, 45* (5), 541–555.

Kalliola, S., Nakari, R., & Pesonen, I. (2006). Learning to make changes: Democratic dialogue in action. *Journal of Workplace Learning, 18* (7–8), 464–477.

Kearney, R., & Ricoeur, P. (1984). *Dialogues with contemporary continental thinkers.* Manchester: Manchester University Press.

Kohn, A. (2005). Unconditional teaching. *Educational Leadership, 63* (1), 20–24.

LeCourt, D. (2004). *Identity matters: Schooling the student body in academic discourse.* Albany, NY: State University of New York Press.

Levy, B. (2000). Pedagogy: Incomplete, unrequited. In C. O'Farrell, D. Meadmore, E. McWilliam, & C. Synes (Eds.), *Taught bodies,* pp. 81–90. New York: Peter Lang.

Lyotard, J.-F. (1989). *The postmodern condition: A report on knowledge.* Minneapolis, MN: University of Minnesota Press.

McLaren, P. (1988). Schooling the postmodern body: Critical pedagogy and the politics of enfleshment. *Journal of Education, 170* (3), 53–83.

McLaren, P. (1995) Schooling the postmodern body: Critical pedagogy and the politics of enfleshment. In P. McLaren (Ed.), *Critical pedagogy and predatory culture:Oppositional politics in a postmodern era*, pp. 58–84. New York: Routledge.

Paulus, T., Woodside, M., & Ziegler, M. (2008). Extending the conversation: Quality research as dialogic collaborative process. *Qualitative Report, 13* (2), 226–243.

Reynolds, W.M. (2003). *Curriculum: A river runs through it.* New York: Peter Lang.

Scherer, M. (2009). *Engaging the whole child: Reflections on best practices in learning, teaching, and leadership.* Alexandria, VA: ASCD.

Trifonas, P. (2005) Postmodernism, poststructuralism, and difference. *Journal of Curriculum Theorizing, 20* (1), 151–163.

Tyler, R. (1949). *Basic principles of curriculum and instruction.* Chicago, IL: University of Chicago Press.

Weiss, G. (2003). The body as a narrative horizon. In J.J. Cohen & G. Weiss (Eds.), *Thinking the limits of the body,* pp. 25–38. Albany, NY: State University of New York Press.

3 M/othering Midst Tensioned Spaces: Towards Theorizing Home Schooling as a Bodied Curriculum

DIANE WATT

We're all familiar with popular images of homeschoolers in America: Extreme fundamentalist families gathering for a morning prayer and Bible study. Tired mothers teaching in front of a chalkboard after late nights of preparing lesson plans, or perhaps stumbling recklessly through unfamiliar subject matter they are not qualified to teach. Lonely, friendless children sitting at home, wistfully dreaming of an exciting, lively social life at school . . . isolated little misfits tragically unaware that an outside world even exists.

Gathercole, 2005, p. 1

As a mother who temporarily opted out of my career as a public school teacher so my children could opt out of institutional schooling, my negotiation of dominant discourses related to mothering and home schooling is ongoing. Although home schooling has become more mainstream over the past 25 years, this alternative form of education and the mothers associated with it remain poorly understood (Basham, Merrifield, & Hepburn, 2007; Davies & Aurini, 2003; Isenberg, 2007; Stevens, 2003). A call for papers on mothering and a bodied curriculum provoked this inquiry into the 15 years my children and I spent learning together outside of school. We exchanged what are widely considered necessary components of schooling – a sequenced curriculum, peer groupings, competition, standards, testing, grades, and rigid schedules – for a saner life in the embodied here-and-now, challenging many assumptions about education. As mother-educator, I felt close and deeply attuned to the bodies and minds of my children and to the possibilities of 'curriculum improvisations' (Aoki, 1990). Relationality was at the heart of our educational practice, for learning emerged from our being together – mother and children – in the context of everyday life. We abandoned the confines of the classroom to live and learn in the wider community and in our own back yard. At the same time, my decision to educate my children in these ways was fraught with struggle and contradiction. Although I was deeply committed to and passionate about our unconventional lifestyle, I also felt ambivalence within my maternal body and mind.

I would like to engage some of the tensions surrounding mothering and home education through the lens of postmodern feminism and curriculum theory, towards theorizing home schooling as a bodied curriculum. Springgay and Freedman's (2007) notion of a bodied curriculum resonates compellingly with my sense of how my family lived and learned outside of school. Springgay (2008a, 2008b) calls for an ethics of embodiment for education, which encompasses ways of knowing that are not only cognitive, but relational and intercorporeal, where learning is a relation and not an object. Whereas traditional schooling focuses largely on curriculum as content, our live(d) experiences generated much of our curriculum (Aoki, 1993), including forms of feminist knowledge not often admitted into institutional education.

Before looking at the nature of my practice to theorize it as a bodied curriculum, I review the academic literature on home education. I then situate my experiences as a home schooling mother midst some of the tensions within broader discursive contexts. Given my contention that mothering and home schooling constitute relational practices, to ignore the discursive spaces in which these intertwined practices unfold would be to understate the complexity surrounding both the maternal body and home education. Although a single chapter provides only a cursory introduction to these topics, it may nonetheless open curriculum theorizing to new possibilities.

Un/naming My Educational Practice

Given that language is an important site of struggle, the term *home schooling* must be interrogated for what it says and what it leaves unsaid about the range of educational practices that fall under this label. Priesnitz (2008) explains that this term is commonly used by families to describe their unique educational contexts. However, as Wyatt (2008) asserts, home schooling is difficult to label and define because the practice is so diverse. He finds the descriptor, 'home school' misleading because it implies that families are 'doing school at home' when, in fact, they often draw upon a wide array of material and human resources and learn in an amazing variety of contexts (Watt, 2003). In one Canadian study, Van Pelt (2003) found the average home schooled child is regularly involved in eight activities outside the home. Although families often start out with planned lessons based on structured teaching materials, research indicates that few maintain such a rigid routine (Thomas & Pattison, 2007), as learning tends to become more informal (Thomas, 1998). Despite these issues, I reluctantly use *home schooling* as an umbrella term that 'applies to a variety of ways of obtaining an education with the help of one's family outside of formal institutions' (Wyatt, 2008 p. 5). In addition, this is the label most familiar to the general public and the professional educational community.

At the same time, new language has evolved, which suggests the multiple ways in which families view their practice. Some adopt 'home-based education,' to indicate they are not 'doing school' at home, but this label still suggests learning takes place mostly at home. Holt (1982, 1989), an educator and early home school advocate, coined the term 'unschooling' to highlight an outright rejection of the assumptions underlying schooling. Priesnitz (2008) uses 'life learning' to describe what she and her family do. She explains that 'this helps to uncouple the concepts of learning and schooling,' and for her, it illustrates 'what getting an education is all about' (p. 10). To highlight the postmodern theoretical spaces I engage in this inquiry, I propose mothering and home schooling be re/thought as 'doing curriculum mother/wise.'[1] This expression dislodges fixed meanings associated with modernist discourses, and leaves mothering, home education, and curriculum infinitely open to difference.

A Different Kind of Education: Research on Home Schooling

Although it remains controversial, home education has continued to grow and gain acceptance over the past decade (Basham et al., 2007; Cooper, 2005; Davies & Aurini, 2003; Gaither, 2008; Isenberg, 2007; Wyatt, 2008). Concerns expressed by the public and the professional educational community, particularly regarding issues of socialization, academic achievement, and parent-as-teacher qualifications, have mostly been laid to rest (Basham et al., 2007; Gaither, 2008; Ray, 2005; Thomas & Pattison, 2007; Van Pelt, 2003). The number of children

being educated outside of school is small compared with the general
school population (estimates are around 2 million in the United States
and 90,000 in Canada), yet many argue the home schooling movement
can influence the larger educational system (Basham et al., 2007; Bauman, 2002; Meighan, 1995; Thomas & Pattison, 2007). Some researchers and practitioners conclude that home education challenges some
basic assumptions about education (Bahsam et al., 2007; Bauman,
2002; Meghan, 1995; Priesnitz, 2000), and this inquiry supports that
assertion.

The home schooling movement emerged out of the anti-establish-
ment counterculture of the 1960s and 1970s, but the most prominent
home schooling lobby in the United States has historically been aligned
with conservative, evangelical Christian families (Gaither, 2008; Stevens, 2003; Wyatt, 2008). This helps to explain some of the stereotypical assumptions about home educating families, often assumed to be
either 'move-to-the-country anarchist goat-herders, or right-wing Bible
thumpers' (Ray, 2005, p. 1). More recent studies suggest that home
schoolers are actually a much more heterogeneous group than previously thought (Brabant, Bordon, & Jutras, 2003; Ray, 2005; Gaither,
2008; Taylor, 2005; Wyatt, 2008). Rothermel (2003) observes that 'home
educators share remarkably little in common beyond the fact that
they home educate' (p. 83), and asserts that the classifications used to
describe them are 'simplistic and misleading' (p. 74). Stevens (2003)
agrees these families come from different sectors in society and have
pursued their interests in contextually specific ways, noting that 'one
would be hard pressed to find a social movement peopled by a wider
spectrum of faiths and philosophies' (pp. 4–5). Gaither (2008) finds
home education is now being practised by so many different people
for so many different reasons it no longer makes sense to speak of it as
a single movement.

Much scholarly research compares home schooled children with
their school peers. Many home educators object to this because they
do not consider it worthwhile to compare home schooling 'success'
against measures and categories designed to rate institutionalized
education (Kaseman & Kaseman, 1991). Many forms of knowledge,
which parents emphasize in their children's education, are not assess-
able through standardized testing (Welner & Welner, 1999). Learning
outside of school is a completely different endeavour from institutional schooling. Raising children who are able to think critically and
direct their own learning is a primary goal for many parents (Hern,

2003; Arai, 1999); they don't believe this happens in school where curriculum content and the learning process are dictated by educational professionals.

Having said this, the academic literature tells us little about what home educating families actually *do,* and what kinds of knowledge they value. Parents have written about their experiences (e.g., Chicoine, 2008; Ellis, 2008; Home Education Magazine; Priesnitz, 2008; Schenwar, 2008), and although valuable, these anecdotal accounts have not been a focus of scholarly inquiry. Although a few studies consider how parents educate their children outside of school (Apostoleris, 2000; Cai, Reeve, & Robinson, 2002; Thomas, 1998; Thomas & Pattison, 2007; Watt, 2003), these only begin to engage with larger issues in the field of home-based education. Recently, researchers have focused more attention on the nature of family relationships, perhaps because this is one of the main reasons parents give for home schooling (Brabant et al., 2003; Mullady, 2006; Thomas & Pattison, 2007; Wyatt, 2008). Some consider what they are doing to be 'a total change in lifestyle . . . a more flexible and easy-going approach to life' (Neuman & Aviram, 2003, 132). Medlin (2000) finds many parents choose this option not for academic reasons, 'but to surround their children with the kind of nurturing atmosphere that will support their development' (p. 119). However, professional educators and researchers know little about what these learning environments look like.

In addition, I have been unable to locate any research on home school learning undertaken from postmodern feminist theoretical perspectives. Bodies in general, and maternal bodies in particular, remain absent from the academic literature, even though women most often carry out the day-to-day work of home educating (Stevens, 2003; Wyatt, 2008). Stevens confirms that in the secular home school literature 'mother can be hard to find' (2003, p. 88). He attributes the absence of mothers to the emphasis many place on child-centred pedagogy. In Holt's (1982, 1989) vision of unschooling – to which many home schoolers subscribe – teaching becomes largely a passive enterprise, for learning is assumed to be taking place 'all the time' (1989). Stevens (2003) asserts that unschooling pedagogy 'tends to make parents disappear' (p. 88), and the emphasis on children to the exclusion of parents has significant consequences. The focus on children tends 'to feminize the work in practice' (p. 89); but just because mother is rhetorically invisible does not erase her material presence. Indeed, she is present, facilitating learning by providing resources and creating a nurturing environment. Similarly, her partner is also invisible, although earning the income needed to support the household. Stevens argues that by not being explicit about the roles of each parent, the home schooling project becomes women's work by default. He compares this to conventional households, 'where not talking about the housework usually means that women do more of it' (p. 89). Likewise, he explains 'not talking about home-school divisions of labor means more of the work goes to the mom' (p. 89). For these reasons and others, mothers (and fathers or partners) should be brought explicitly into the research and discourse on home schooling.

Given that women often take primary responsibility for educating their children outside of school, it is remarkable how little scholarly work exists on home schooling from feminist perspectives. Indeed, research has devoted scant attention to the subjectivities and lived experiences of home schooling mothers. As well, many of the studies that have been conducted have been quantitative, with few in-depth, qualitative accounts. This focus may be due to an initial preoccupation with how well home educated children fare academically as a group and a perceived need to provide hard data to support these claims. The nature of learning in-between children and mothers educating outside of school is unknown to the professional educational community, despite this being a potentially rich site from which to theorize feminism, pedagogy, and curriculum. This may, in part, be explained by the reality that home schooling is a private, intimate practice where flexible schedules and curricula are common. Scholars have noted the difficulties outsiders face in attempting to gain access to these settings (Thomas, 1998; Watt, 2003). Auto/ethno/graphic inquiries undertaken by home schooling mothers themselves could provide a valuable contribution to the research literature.

The Im/possibilities of Auto/ethno/graphic Inquiry

Auto/ethno/graphy merges self-representation with cultural critique (Russell, 1998) to challenge mainstream knowledge. Foregrounding the multiple nature of selfhood (Reed-Danahay, 1997), it becomes a vehicle 'for challenging imposed forms of identity' (Russell, 1998, 2). Drawing upon my personal experiences and my own complex entanglement in language, I intervene into the history of binary thought. Rereading and reworking some of the discourses that circulate around practices of mothering and home education, I theorize what it might mean to 'do curriculum other/wise.' Following curriculum theorist, Ted Aoki (1996), Morawski and Palulis (2009) place slashes between the *auto*, the *ethno*, and the *graphy* to emphasize the doublings – the need for educators to dwell in the spaces in-between. The self is situated in culture, and the cultural is in the self; the scholar writes *about* culture and also *re/produces* culture through language. Experience is 'out of reach of language and discourse and on the borderlines of consciousness and awareness' (Denzin, 1997, p. 61). However, we may tentatively re/present a life and its meanings as told in narrative, for this is 'the realm of lived experience that is recoverable' (p. 61), although the original meaning of a told experience is not recoverable. 'There are only retellings,' which 'become new expressions of the experience' (p. 61). As Munro Hendry (2007) suggests, our stories are 'the tales through which we constitute our identities' (p. 495), but we cannot fully step outside of ourselves to study ourselves. Theorizing auto/ethno/graphic narratives only offers clues into what official stories hide and may suggest ways to disrupt the status quo. In Aokian (1993) terms, this is a matter of 'experiencing differences in kind in the tension between the master stories and the daily stories' (p. 211). Grumet (2001) suggests we write narratives that pose questions about our experiences in the world and invite readers to join us in the examination of the complex issues that are evoked. How might one woman's stories of mothering and home schooling complicate both the maternal and curriculum theorizing?

Home Schooling M/other as Walking Contradiction

Although my life as home schooling mother was extremely gratifying, and I benefited in innumerable ways, I was not immune from a nagging sense of ambivalence. On the one hand, I considered myself to be an educator who wanted something different for my family other than what the official school system could offer. By refusing conventional schooling, I felt as radical as some of the educational theorists who legitimized my practice (e.g., Illich, 1972; Gatto, 1992; Priesnitz, 1987, 2000; Holt, 1982, 1989). I considered my decision subversive, rebellious, courageous – going against the grain. On the other hand, temporarily putting my career on hold to spend this time with my children seemed 'strangely traditional' (Ellis, 2008), a betrayal of feminist values. Was my decision to home school radical, traditional, both, or neither – and who decides?

When I became a mother in 1989, popular narratives of second-wave liberal feminism had been critical of the role that mothering played in women's oppression. Motherhood was and continues to be seen by some as an obstacle to success in the outside world (Featherstone, 1997; Hirshman, 2007). Richards (2008) argues that even though the feminist project has attempted to promote parenting as a valuable practice deserving of more recognition in society, all these years later it is 'debatable whether feminism is yet free enough of the surrounding culture to respect women who choose to be full-time mothers' (p. 32). In any case, I resisted those elements of the feminist movement that measured a woman's worth in terms her work outside home and family. My children would only be young for a short time, and I responded accordingly. At the same time, staying out of the paid workforce meant foregoing a second income, social status, and career advancement. No matter what decision I made, my situation as a mother was inherently complex, difficult, and confusing. As Kinser (2008a) observes, 'we do motherwork in tension' (p. 4). Contrary to what the label 'full-time mother' might imply, during the years I took off from my career I was involved in many pursuits besides mothering and home educating.

The binary thinking that organizes a mother's possibilities into 'work' and 'home' seriously limits the maternal body. Our decisions and lives are much more complicated than what popular discourses admit (e.g., the 'Mommy Wars'; Belkin, 2003; Hansen, 2006). As Richards (2008) writes, 'To work or not work is *not* the question' (p. 15; original emphasis). Whose interests are served by perpetuating the myth that we must determine 'once and for all what will win out: working or staying home' (p. 15)? Richards advises women to be inspired by their own unique approaches to parenting and to celebrate 'the unique links between motherhood and feminism, rather than bemoan which is a better or more admirable choice' (p. 11). In my own case, I was convinced that with experience and determination unwanted doubts and tensions would somehow be resolved. Although I endlessly sought stability and certainty in mothering and home schooling, these never did materialize. Feminist theorists are now calling for a more dynamic understanding of mothering (O'Reilly, 2008; Reichert Powell, 2008; Springgay & Freedman, 2009). By bringing the slash into mothering we 'accentuate the activity of movement and the in-between' (Springgay, 2008a, p. 6) of mother and other. Springgay suggests that 'un/folding with the slash allows the term to reverberate, to flicker, and to be in a constant state of movement' (p. 6). Rather than conceiving of 'home schooling mother' as a pre-given identity subject to the category-maintenance work of humanist binary thought, mothering as performance becomes an ongoing, generative practice continuously produced as we mother and do curriculum other/wise with our children outside of school.

Dis/locating S/m/othering and Isolation

Among the most enduring stereotypes associated with home schooling mothers are those relating to issues surrounding the physical proximity of the maternal body to the bodies of her children. Just how close is *too close*? Within the intimate context of a family, where bodies are physically and emotionally close, relationships may thrive. However, does not such closeness also risk becoming too intense, smothering? A related concern is that children who do not attend school will be isolated from the 'real world.' In addition, mothers who spend so much time with their children may be accused of an extreme version of 'intensive mothering' (Hayes, 1996) – a discourse that imposes impossible standards of 'sacrificial motherhood' (O'Reilly, 2004) on women. Negotiating mothering identities in this thorny discursive terrain is challenging.

Regarding the issue of isolation, Dewey (1938, as cited in Lines, 2001) bemoaned the fact that school had been artificially 'set apart' from society and had become 'so isolated from the ordinary conditions and motives of life' that it was 'the one place in the world where it is most difficult to get experience' (p. 2). Schools face a major challenge in trying to connect the real world to curriculum, and little provision is made to welcome the embodied knowledge children bring to the learning situation. Although home educated children may seem isolated, and families have been charged with 'cocooning' (Apple, 2000) – children may actually be kept out of school so they might live more fully in their communities. Many value the meaningful learning that takes place through experience and interaction with a wide variety of people – the knowledge created in-between bodies in live(d) situations (Aoki, 1993).

The decision to home school is often much more than a rejection of the school system: it is an alternative lifestyle (Neuman & Aviram, 2003). Where schooling is preoccupied with preparing students for an imaginary future – standardized tests, the next grade level, university entrance, a job – many want their children's lives to be situated fully in the present. Noddings (2003) believes 'happiness should be an aim of education, and a good education should contribute significantly to personal and collective happiness' (p. 1), both present and future. Home schooling mother, Gaye Chicoine (2008), wonders what is so wrong with allowing your kids to enjoy their lives? Chicoine's curriculum goes beyond academics and instrumentalism. Her openness to present moments, her focus on learning with her children, and her emphasis on life skills, community, and family relationships expands curriculum discourses. Could thinking about mothering and home education as bodied, relational practices dedicated to living well disrupt s/mothering?

Finally, as long as home schooling mothers are viewed as living in a perpetual state of personal sacrifice, we fail to appreciate the worth they attach to their practice. Women make sacrifices and may feel overwhelmed and exhausted, but don't women who work full-time outside the home also often feel this way (Hochschild, 2003)? What is less known is that some home educators see themselves 'as sitting right at the heart of real social change, not just personal accomplishment' (Hern, 2003, p. 146). Civic-minded mothers may choose home education precisely because of their concern for community and making the world a better place. They consider themselves social activists, and raising their children outside of institutionalized schooling is important to their vision for the future. For example, flexible schedules permit home educators to become involved in community service. One family I know actively participates in a turtle conservation program and often makes appeals to other families for help when needed. Charities and community organizations increasingly recognize the home schooling community as a valuable resource to count on, and mothers bring valuable skills and expertise to these contexts (Watt, 2005). In my experience, mothers who do curriculum other/wise are unlikely to see their own lives uniquely in terms of providing for the needs of their children. They create spaces for their personal dreams and commitments as well.

Third-Wave Feminist Discourses: Embracing a More Complicated Maternal Body

Third-wave feminist discourses, which draw from postmodern theoretical spaces, posit mothering as a practice of multiplicity (Kinser, 2008a, 2008b; Richards, 2008; Springgay & Freedman, 2007). In postmodern discourse, mothering is not passive or static, but performative (Butler, 1993). From this perspective, dwelling midst tensioned spaces opens up mothers who do curriculum other/wise to infinite possibilities. Kinser (2008a) suggests a need to confront the inconsistency and ambivalence in our lives and identities, to face the irresolvable messiness of mothering. In other words, 'the frictions that emerge are tensions to be lived with rather than problems to be resolved' (p. 11). Richards (2008) similarly suggests that 'feminism is a process, not a conclusion' (p. 12), and it is a 'mistaken idea that certain choices are more feminist than others' (p. 18). As mothers, we might 'continue to courageously explore the irresolvable tensions of feminism and the family' (Kinser, 2008b, p. 138). Conceptualizing mothering as difference may disrupt assumptions about maternal bodies situated in a stubbornly binary world.

Home Schooling as Postmodern Curriculum

I now turn to a consideration of my home schooling practice from postmodern theoretical perspectives to consider what this alternative form of education might have to offer the broader system. Schools struggle within the confines of the efficiency and accountability movement, where students and teachers labour under the weight of prescribed curricula tightly binding bodies to standards and measurement. Given this state of affairs, educators and researchers might look to home educators to gain a greater sense of the vast potential of postmodern visions of curriculum. Although they may not label their practices in these terms, many home educators are creating the conditions under which postmodern curricula may flourish.

How did my own home schooling practice constitute a postmodern curriculum? First, we lived and learned in an environment that I would characterize as an open system (Doll, 1993, 2008) with a high degree of flexibility. Educating outside of an institution permits families to gain more control over how they live their lives, which in turn, opens possibilities for curriculum to be done differently. Doll (2008) uses words such as 'dynamic, emergent, transformative, and nonlinear' (p. 8) to describe postmodern approaches to education, and my own practice was indeed in a perpetual state of fluctuation. I made constant adjustments according to what I felt was optimal for my children at any given time, and I tried to remain emotionally 'attuned' (Aoki, 1990) to the material situation and to whatever my children might be communicating, either through words or their bodied actions. For Ahmed (2004), 'to be emotional is to have one's judgment affected: it is to be reactive rather than active, dependent rather than anonymous' (p. 3). Furthermore, ours might be conceptualized as an opportunistic curriculum, open to the potentiality of whatever or whoever might appear on the scene of our daily lives. Without the constraints of rigid schedules or physical confinement to particular locations, we were able to move in whatever directions we wished if an interest or a need was provoked. Our curriculum was negotiated in the spaces in-between what Aoki (1991) refers to as curriculum-as-plan and curriculum-as-lived, with emphasis on the latter. We did slog through math textbooks, try out spelling programs, and complete social studies units, but we readily abandoned anything that was no longer working for us. We were not bound to any curriculum, and together we negotiated what, when, where, how, and with whom we would learn, as we went along.

As a home schooling mother, curriculum was very much a matter of 'being orientated [sic] to others, to touch, to reflect, and to dwell with others relationally' (Springgay & Freedman, 2009, p. 25). It emerged from our lived situation – out of our bodied interactions with others and the material world. We did not regularly 'cover' any particular, pre-given curriculum in linear, sequential fashion; nor were we limited to the spaces of our home. Rather, the flexibility of our situation allowed us to open our bodies and minds to the abundance of the world around us (Jardine, Friesen, & Clifford, 2006). Jardine (2008) contends that education should embody 'a sense of plenitude' (p. 1), and by avoiding 'the panics of schooling' (p. 1) we tried to seek out what we felt were worthwhile knowledge and activities that we might 'while' over. We had time and space to connect to one another and to our surroundings. This approach to curriculum necessarily implicates emotional, sensual, and cognitive processes. Learning became intrinsically desired, not forced upon our bodies by invisible, outside forces. It emerged out of our everyday, lived experiences, and was therefore meaningful to us. Although I was always bringing new ideas, activities, and people into our realm, I was unable to predict what might spark an interest or where it might lead. Much of what took place was child-initiated, spontaneous, messy, circuitous, emotional, impossible to measure, haphazard. The institutionalized educational system seriously questions the ability of children to learn in these ways. The texture, locations, and time of our curriculum were very different from what can be offered in more closed learning contexts. An indefinable excess emerged during the learning which often eluded words. When we value and create spaces for more open, embodied, relational visions of curriculum – which I conceptualize as doing curriculum mother/wise – we decentrer the prescribed, one-size-fits-all, standards-based model.

Traditional pedagogy and curriculum attempt a transparent, univocal, transmission of a body of information, understood as the content or signifieds of a discipline (Ulmer, 1985). This fixed content – presented as 'truth' – is simplified and doled out one concept at a time in mind-numbing linear fashion, as children 'progress' from one grade to another. Students must accept what they do within the institution as the-learning-that-matters-most. To make sure they do, they and their teachers are held accountable through never-ending evaluation procedures – a norming and normalizing affair. In spite of the odds against them, many educators vigorously resist school as a predominantly closed system dedicated to reproduction rather than possibility – a system that largely fails to recognize and accommodate difference. Some parents educate their children outside of school because they reject the mastery of knowledge discourse and the exclusions it incurs. They are searching for a different, more ethical relation with knowing and with otherness. Immersed in humanist discourses, they struggle to practise curriculum other/wise, a situation in which, following Jacques Derrida (1968), knowledge and identity become an openness to what is to come.

Informal Learning and Conversation as Bodied Practices

Gaither (2008) might refer to our curriculum as eclectic. As stated, we learned in a wide variety of contexts, with many different people, with a mixture of curricula. Other studies with home schooling families similarly find a wide variety of types of learning and curricula present (Meighan, 1995; Thomas, 1998; Watt, 2003). Thomas notes that a great deal of the learning was incidental, often arising from and reinforced by the numerous parent-child conversations that are common in these settings. He explains that children and parents are often not even aware of the extent of the learning taking place, as it naturally emerges in the context of everyday activities. Smith (2006) contends that informal learning is often 'shaped by conversation' (p. 15). Experience may be enlarged, expanded, questioned, and felt more deeply in the embodied situations in which conversation takes place. Children learning in home education settings spend their days with responsive adults who are usually willing to share and discuss whatever comes up. Conversation is the medium through which identities and knowledge are continuously negotiated, and therefore deeply implicated in a bodied curriculum.

Springgay (2008a) theorizes a 'pedagogy of corporeal generosity for education,' which encourages 'interpersonal, affective relations' (p. 122). Within the intimate context of a home schooling family, a mother's (or father's) responsiveness and availability to engage in multiple, spontaneous conversations and interactions with her children throughout the day may exemplify corporeal generosity in practice. Indeed, rethinking mothering and home schooling as doing curriculum m/other/wise may open up exciting new possibilities for theorizing a bodied curriculum. We might ask ourselves how the mothers and young people involved in this alternative form of education might actually be creating 'passages out of and away from the stasis of the historical present' (Pinar, 2004, p. 39).

Note

1 This expression is inspired by a British home schooling parent support group, who call their organization, Education Otherwise. This name was taken from the wording in the British Education Act, which states children may receive an education 'either by regular attendance at school *or otherwise*' (Rothermel, 2003, p. 74).

References

Ahmed, S. (2004). *The cultural politics of emotion*. London: Routledge.

Aoki, T. (1990). Sonare and videre: A story, three echoes and a lingering note. In W.F. Pinar & R.L. Irwin (Eds.), (2005) *Curriculum in a new key: The collected works of Ted T. Aoki* (pp. 367–376). Mahwah, NJ: Lawrence Erlbaum. (Hereafter: *The collected works*).

Aoki, T. (1991). Teaching as in-dwelling between two curriculum worlds. In *The collected works* (pp. 159–166).

Aoki, T. (1993). Legitimating lived curriculum: Toward a curricular landscape of multiplicity. In *The collected works* (pp. 199–215).

Aoki, T. (1996). Imaginaries of 'East and West': Slippery curricular signifiers in education. In *The collected works* (pp. 313–319).

Apostoleris, N.H. (2000). Children's love of learning: Home schooling and intrinsic motivation for learning. *Dissertation Abstracts International, 61* (3). (ERIC Documentation Reproduction Service No. AAI9964473).

Apple, M.W. (2000). The cultural politics of home schooling. *Peabody Journal of Education, 75*, 256–271.

Arai, A.B. (1999). Homeschooling and the redefinition of citizenship. *Education Policy Analysis Archives.* Retrieved 7 July 2002, from http://apaa.asu.edu/epaa/v2n27.html.

Basham, P., Merrifield, J., & Hepburn, C.R. (2007). *Home schooling: From the extreme to the mainstream* (2nd ed.). Vancouver: Fraser Institute.

Bauman, K.J. (2002). Home schooling in the United States: Trends and characteristics. *Education Policy Analysis Archives,10.* Retrieved 10 July 2002, from http://epaa.asu/edu/epaa/v10n26.html.

Belkin, L. (2003, 26 October). The opt-out revolution. *New York Times.* [Online.] Retrieved 20 February 2009, from http://www.nytimes.com/2003/10/26/magazine/26WOMEN.html?pagewanted=1.

Brabant, C., Bordon, S., & Jutras, F. (2003). Home education in Quebec: Family first. *Evaluation and Research in Education, 17* (1&2), 112–131.

Butler, J. (1993). *Bodies that matter: On the discursive limits of 'sex.'* New York: Routledge.

Cai, Y., Reeve, J., & Robinson, D.T. (2002). Home school and teaching style: Comparing the motivating styles of home school and public school teachers. *Journal of Educational Psychology, 94*, 372–380.

Chicoine, G. (2008). *Living dreams.* Wakefield, QC: Ed & Gaye Chicoine.

Cooper, B.C. (2005). Preface: An introduction to home schooling. In B.C. Cooper (Ed.), *Home schooling in full view: A reader* (pp. ix–xix). Greenwich, CT: Information Age Publishing.

Davies, S., & Aurini, J. (2003). Homeschooling and Canadian educational politics: Rights, pluralism and pedagogical individualism. *Evaluation and Research in Education, 17*, 63–73.

Denzin, (1997). *Interpretive ethnography: Ethnographic practices for the 21st century.* Thousand Oaks, CA: Sage.

Derrida, J. (1968). Différance. (A. Bass, Trans., 1982). *Jacques Derrida: Margins of philosophy* (pp. 1–28). Chicago, IL: University of Chicago Press.

Doll, W.E. Jr. (1993). *A post-modern perspective on curriculum.* New York: Teachers College Press.

Doll, W.E. Jr. (2008). Looking back to the future: A recursive retrospective. *Journal of the Canadian Association for Curriculum Studies, 6*, 3–20.

Education Otherwise. Retrieved 10 March 2009, from http://www.education-otherwise.org.

Ellis, B. (2008, March–April). Won't get schooled again. *Briarpatch Magazine.* Retrieved 30 November 2008, from http://www.briarpatchmagazine.com/2008/03/01/wont-get-schooled-again/Oct1/08.

Featherstone, B. (1997). Introduction: The Western family in crisis. In W. Holloway & B. Featherstone (Eds.), *Mothering and ambivalence* (pp. 1–16). New York: Routledge.

Gaither, M. (2008). *Homeschool: An American history.* New York: Palgrave Macmillan.

Gathercole, R. (2005, July–August). Homeschooling's true colors. *Mothering: Natural family living.* Retrieved 20 November 2008, from http://www.mothering.com/articles/growing_child/education/homeschoolings-true-colors.html.

Gatto, J.T. (1992). *Dumbing us down: The hidden curriculum of compulsory schooling.* Philadelphia, PA: New Society Publishers.

Grumet, M.R. (2001). Autobiography: The mixed genre of private and public. In D.H. Holdstein & D. Bleich (Eds.), *Personal effects: The social character of scholarly writing* (pp. 165–177). Logan, UT: Utah State University Press.

Hansen, S. (2006, 27 June). Firing another volley in the 'Mommy Wars.' *Times.* Retrieved 20 February 2009, from http://www.calendarlive.com/books/cl-ethirshman27june,27,0,1452053.story?coll.

Hayes, S. (1996). *The cultural contractions of motherhood.* New Haven, CT: Yale University Press.

Hern, M. (2003). *Field day: Getting society out of school.* Vancouver: New Star Books.

Hern, M. (Ed.). (2008). *Everywhere all the time: A new deschooling reader.* Oakland, CA: AK Press.

Hirshman, L.R. (2007). *Get to work: A manifesto for women of the world.* New York: Penguin.

Hochschild, A. (2003). *The second shift.* Toronto: Penguin.

Holt, J. (1982). *Teach your own: A hopeful path for education.* New York: Delta.

Holt, J. (1989). *Learning all the time.* Toronto: Addison-Wesley.

Home Education Magazine. Retrieved 6 February 2009, from http://www.homeedmag.com/HEM/issueindex.html.

Illich, I. (1972). *Deschooling society.* New York: Harper Row.

Isenberg, E.J. (2007). What have we learned about homeschooling? *Peabody Journal of Education, 82,* 387–409.

Jardine, D.W. (2008). On the while of things. *Journal of the American Association for the Advancement of Curriculum Studies, 4,* 1–16.

Jardine, D.W., Friesen, S., & Clifford, P. (2006). *Curriculum in abundance.* Mahwah, NJ: Lawrence Erlbaum.

Kaseman, L., & Kaseman, S. (1991). Does homeschooling research help homeschooling? *Home Education Magazine.* Retrieved 17 October 2003, from http://www.home-ed-magazine.com/INF/FREE/free_rsrch.htm.

Kinser, A.E. (2008a). Thinking about and going about mothering in the third wave. In A.E. Kinser (Éd.), *Mothering in the third wave* (pp. 1–16). Toronto: Demeter Press.

Kinser, A.E. (2008b). Mothering as relational consciousness. In A. O'Reilly (Ed.), *Feminist mothering* (pp. 123–142). Albany, NY: State University of New York Press.

Lines, P.M. (2001). Homeschooling. *Eric Digest.* Retrieved 15 July 2011, from http://eric.uoregon.edu/publications/digests/digest151.html.

Medlin, R.G. (2000). Home schooling and the question of socialization. *Peabody Journal of Education, 75,* 107–123.

Meighan, R. (1995). Home-based education effectiveness research and some of its implications. *Educational Review, 47,* 275–287.

Morawski, C.M., & Palulis, P. (2009). Auto/ethno/graphies as teaching lives: An aesthetics of difference. *Journal of Curriculum Theorizing, 25,* 3–21.

Mullady, A.M. (2006). *Beyond stereotypes: Stories of home school families.* Doctoral dissertation, Arizona State University.

Munro Hendry, P. (2007). The future of narrative. *Qualitative Inquiry, 13,* 487–498.

Neuman, A., & Aviram, A. (2003). Homeschooling as a fundamental change in lifestyle. *Evaluation and Research in Education, 7,* 132–143.

Noddings, N. (2003). *Happiness and education.* New York: Cambridge University Press.

O'Reilly, A. (Ed.). (2004). *Mother matters: Motherhood as discourse and practice.* Toronto: Association for Research on Mothering.

O'Reilly, A. (2008). Introduction. In A. O'Reilly (Ed.), *Feminist mothering* (pp. 1–24). Albany, NY: State University of New York Press.

Pinar, W.F. (2004). *What is curriculum theory?* Mahwah, NJ: Lawrence Erlbaum.

Priesntiz, W. (1987). *School free: The homeschooling handbook.* St George, ON: Alternate Press.

Priesnitz, W. (2000). *Challenging assumptions in education.* St George, ON: Alternate Press.

Priesnitz, W. (Ed.). (2008). *Life learning: Lessons from the educational frontier.* St George, ON: Alternate Press.

Ray, B.D. (2001). Research in focus: Homeschooling in Canada. *Education Canada, 4,* 28–31.

Ray, B.D. (2005). A homeschool research story. In B.C. Cooper (Ed.), *Home schooling in full view: A reader* (pp. 1–20). Greenwich, CT: Information Age Publishing.

Reed-Danahay, D.E. (1997). *Auto/ethnography: Rewriting the self and the social.* Oxford: Berg.

Reichert Powell, P. (2008). Balancing act: Discourses of feminism, motherhood, and activism. In A. O'Reilly (Ed.), *Feminist mothering* (pp. 257–272). Albany, NY: State University of New York Press.

Richards, A. (2008). *Opting in: Having a child without losing yourself.* New York: Farrar, Straus & Giroux.

Rothermel, P. (2003). Can we classify motives for home education? *Evaluation and Research in Education, 17,* 74–89.

Russell, C. (1998). *Autoethnography: Journeys of the self.* Retrieved 11 January 2005, from http://www.haussite.net/haus.0/SCRIPT/txt2001/01/russel_X.HTML.

Schenwar, M. (2008). Learning curve: Radical 'unschooling' moms are changing the stay-at-home landscape. *Bitch Magazine.* Retrieved 1 March 2009, from http://www.bitchmagazine.org/articles/learninging-curve.

Smith, M.K. (2006). Beyond the curriculum: Fostering associational life in schools. In Z. Bekerman, N.C. Burbules, & D. Silberman-Keller (Eds.), *Learning in places: The informal education reader* (pp. 9–34). New York: Peter Lang.

Springgay, S. (2008a). *Body knowledge and curriculum: Pedagogies of touch in youth and visual culture.* New York: Peter Lang.

Springgay, S. (2008b). An ethics of embodiment, civic engagement and A/R/tography: Ways of becoming nomadic in art, research and teaching. *Educational Insights, 12.* Retrieved 15 November 2008, from http://www.ccfi.educ.ubc.ca/publication/Insights/v12n2/articles/springgay/index.html.

Springgay, S., & Freedman, D. (Eds). (2007). *Curriculum and the cultural body.* New York: Peter Lang.

Springgay, S., & Freedman, D. (2009). Mothering a bodied curriculum: Sleeping with cake and other touchable encounters. *Journal of Curriculum Theorizing, 25,* 25–37.

Stevens, M.L. (2003). *Kingdom of children: Culture and controversy in the homeschooling movement.* Princeton, NJ: Princeton University Press.

Taylor, V.L. (2005). Behind the trend: Increases in homeschooling among African-American families. In B.C. Cooper (Ed.), *Home schooling in full view: A reader* (pp. 121–134). Greenwich, CT: Information Age Publishing.

Thomas, A. (1998). *Educating children at home.* London: Cassell Education.

Thomas, A., & Pattison, H. (2007). *How children learn at home.* London: Continuum.

Ulmer, G.L. (1985). *Applied grammatology: Post(e)-pedagogy from Jacques Derrida to Joseph Beuys.* Baltimore, MD: Johns Hopkins University Press.

Van Pelt, D. (2003). *Home education in Canada.* London, ON: Canadian Centre for Home Education.

Watt, D.P. (2003). *A different kind of education: One family's perceptions of learning outside of school.* Paper presented at the American Educational Research Association, Montreal, May 2005.

Watt, D.P. (2005). *Opting out of school, opting out of society?* Unpublished paper written in doctoral course, 'Experience and Education,' University of Ottawa.

Welner, K.M., & Welner, K.G. (1999). Contextualizing homeschooling data: A response to Rudner. *Education Policy Analysis Archives, 7,* 1–13.

Wyatt, G. (2008). *Family ties: Relationships, socialization, and home schooling.* Toronto: University Press of America.

4 The Mindful Materfessor: M/othering Bodies of Difference in Education

LEAH C. FOWLER

For those of us whose profession is academic study, maintaining a critical (if variable) distance between our work and the society in which it occurs remains an obligation.

– W. Pinar, 'The Worldliness of a Cosmopolitan Education'

A bodied curriculum asserts that knowledge is corporeal; it is produced in and through touch – mothering our own becoming.

– J. Springgay & D. Freedman, 'Mothering a Bodied Curriculum'

There is an urgent need to move to new ways of working in education. Those new ways need to be more physically, relationally, politically, pedagogically, and intellectually *mindful*. Through research and experience rooted in pre-service teacher education, curriculum studies, narrative case study, autobiography, autoethnography, Buddhist psychology, and mindfulness texts, I explore the concept of a more humane and restorative approach to education and to *being*. That begins with bringing the body along with the brain, and being capable of empathy, learning, and mindfulness.

If materfessors, especially women scholars in education and other 'impossible professions' (Britzman, 2009), can embody and perform human curricula with a commitment to healthy diversity in learning beneficial ways of being without reinscribing hegemonic patterns within educational institutions, more people can participate in reading the word and reading the world (Freire & Macedo, 1987) in a generative, inclusive way. Dwelling well together in communities of difference is more possible with literacies of a nurturing embodied, mindful brain and wise heart as we engage in learning and living. Among such literacies of a mindful, embodied scholar working towards a restorative curriculum amid uncertainty, I explore the question here: What would a human/e curriculum look like in practice?

Certainly, an integrated embodied personal and professional persona that perdures over all encounters would be necessary to authentic engagement in education. We foster our students' *selfable*[1] individual personal agency in this engagement, within an abiding compassionate presence, mutual respect, and intelligent relational focus and care.[2] There would be an absence of inappropriate 'doing for or to' (matronizing arising from the proverbial excuse of 'for your own good'),[3] absence of resentment or ill will, absence of over-directive commentary, absence of the need to be *in power*. There is a responsibility to help people with access to full participation, assistance to remove barriers to knowledge getting, resource or skill acquisition, and attribute development, even if there is an unacknowledged discomfort that *they* might learn or *get* as much as *we* have. There is an obligation to share generosity of scholarship. There is also a professional ethic to witness, walk with, and respect students, and all people, as they are, without derision, criticism, or asserting relations of power. Any utterance about someone should be able to be repeated with the person present.

Any encounter with people can further development of generative knowledge, skill, or attribute in their mind, body, or spirit. Mothering, mindful, embodied materfessors may be able to use their power, privilege, expertise, and hard-won experiences in new ways to reduce barriers to access at the education table; they may use them to support deep study about what matters most and sustains, and contribute to the demographic commonweal.

The Mindful Brain

The outermost membrane of the *meninges* that cover the brain and spinal cord is the *dura mater,* and the innermost membrane covering the brain and spinal cord is called the *pia mater*. 'Hard mother' and 'tender mother' literally surround our brains – protecting, encompassing, sheltering, with space, without interference, without actually being part of the brain or spinal cord. I am moved by this positive metaphor for the materfessor (maternal embodied professor) attentive to the needs of self, familiar, and other. One case I am familiar with involves supervisory work with pre-service teachers in school practica, but the implications for professional practice, indeed, for living well, abide underneath a humane curriculum.

A central part of the *mindful* brain is the *prefrontal cortex*, that part that is capable of reflection. Siegel (2007) suggests that educators can be seen as '"neurosculptors" of our future' (p. 260) and refers to this part of the brain's education as the '"cortex humanitas," which is the "neural hub of our humanity." In addition to reflection being a part of our prefrontal heritage, this integrative region also supports relationships and resilience, perhaps giving us a fifth and sixth "R" of basic education' (p. 261).

Also key from Siegel's (2007) work, for the *materfessor,* is the concept of learning *mindsight.* Since education is a central part of children's (and later, adult) development, it makes sense to move towards 'mindsight, our capacity to sense the mind in ourselves, and in others, and move away from mindlessness' (p. 261), in school and in life.

Working narratively, I am interested in the following questions: How does a materfessor supervising pre-service student teachers navigate encountered and lived places of rupture and possibility? How do I learn not to matronize students and experienced teachers by my own expectation, power, and privilege? How shall I attend to embodied practices of being present with all encountered? How does one embody support, curiosity, engagement, and challenge to promote growth and well-being in a complex and ever-changing educational matrix?

The watchful attunement of a skilful mother-professor also can inform how we reflect and shape actions of self and others in educational enterprises: Being mindful can alter the brain's neuroplastic ability to create flexibility and self-observation, empathy, and morality (Doidge, 2007; Siegel, 2007).[4] As embodied materfessors, in this difficult world, it is time to go back to the school of our bodies, the curriculum of breath, conversation, and dwelling together with as many mothers as possible. We can wean ourselves from received wisdoms of hegemony and patriarchy with their entrenched and harmful modes of engagement: war, colonizing, profiteering; even head-butting sports and human commodification are unskilful metaphors for relationships between self, other, and Earth. We need to wean ourselves from a diet of greed, excessive growth, and gendered competition. A mature diet with more non-harming virtues such as deliberate cultivation of care and the spontaneous integrity of the awakened heart can be the 'foundation for radical change. It means that we carry ourselves with truthfulness, integrity, passion, and purpose in all we do. This is the powerful, even fierce force that ennobles individuals and inspires social justice and equality worldwide. Just as a life of virtue brings happiness, it also packs a punch' (Kornfield, 2008, pp. 332–333).

I The M/othering Teacher: An Autoethnographic Narrative Thought Experiment

As I enter the main doors of Good Heart Elementary, she is in the hall again, the second grader, down by the classroom where I am headed. I wave. She pokes her head back over the threshold and yells: 'Hey, Mr Student Teacher: your Doctor Teacher is here.' She holds out her hand to shake mine, and says, 'Hi, he's doing pretty good so far. He is ready for you with his lessons 'n stuff, all nice in that binder on that desk. I think he'll be a good teacher – he's a keeper. His name is hard to say though – long.'

I smile, shake her extended hand, and inquire about the reason she is out in the hall. She laughs cheerfully in her raspy voice: 'I talk too much and forget to listen when it's the same again, and it stops people from doing their work – hey, Mister Student Teacher, can I come back? I'll be quiet now.' And we both go in to watch my student teach.

Another second grader, a boy sitting near where I sit with evaluation sheets laid out on the back desk, says to me, 'Are you Mr Student Teacher's Mom?'

My Hall Girl interrupts and corrects him, 'NO. Duh! She's Student Teacher's professor from the university. She's watching 'im this morning. She a learning doctor.'

He hears, but keeps his gaze on me to test what he just heard, 'Do you have kids?'

'None of my own,' I answer, 'You?'

'No.' And we both laugh.

I become aware again that I am a pedagogic mother, not a biological mother. I reflect on being *in loco marentis*,[5] how I speak with a sense of protective care as that stand-in-day-time parent: 'my kids,' 'my boys,' 'my Hall Girl.' This care can manifest itself when children, students, and colleagues experience the cognitive and affective dissonance of encountering 'other.' Awareness of what is unknown jump-starts ceaseless movement between known and unknown (Greene, 1973), competence and challenge, Self and Other. Although disequilibrium is fundamental to learning, it requires pedagogical care, timeliness, and authenticity to supply increasingly complex 'nutrients' that equip neural pathways for difficult worlds.

Professional practice field placement is particularly fertile ground between theory and practice for students, mentors, and supervising professors alike. It constitutes a third space where opportunity exists to expand the capacity to nurture a generative curriculum of difference. A starting point is conscious embodiment in the present moment.

Optimally, the approach of the teacher educator, *materfessor*,[6] is experienced and strategic with a mindful brain, and a wise heart, able to allow space for what may develop and be learned and become embodied. In that 'space between,' questions occur: What is essential, what is new, what is difficult, what can be changed, and what can be let go? Student teaching is one space to embody the profession of teaching. And bodies learn to teach as much as the mind and emotions.

Like new mothers, new teachers especially get fatigued, need extra naps, and get sick from exhaustion and exposure to new microbes. Habits change: eating, sleeping, activities, what is needed for next day. Living patterns morph, and bodies begin to live into teaching. Self-care, balance, and compassion are necessary for a positive professional life to be sustained. The artful *how* and *why* insist themselves in education and in life. Both understanding along with misunderstanding, and pleasure along with pain in teaching are part of the auto/biographical mentoring project of pre-practice students. In all learning, corporeal knowledge is deep: 'Within this fathom-long body and mind is found all of the teachings' (Buddha, in Kornfield, 2008, p. 110).

One of the questions about *how* to teach concerns educators not replicating male practices labelled *patronizing* (Weiler, 1994). Those unfortunate habits tend to interfere with maturation and autonomy, infantilize people's identity and experience, prolong dependence, foster unequal relationships, and inculcate resentment and discouragement. Let women professors – materfessors – *not* do that.

What non-matronizing materfessors of all genders *can* do is to situate themselves among all the narratives of those with whom we work: I am a teacher education professor in a small comprehensive liberal arts university in western Canada. Our students perform at least three increasingly long practica in schools (half in rural schools, and half in urban schools). I teach theory classes about literacy, curriculum, and pedagogy, and then follow my (!)[7] students to schools to supervise their teaching. While in those schools, I-not-a-mother, participate *in loco marentis*.

I also serve on boards of governors, work in professorial offices, classrooms, buildings, and paths where twenty-first-century dark-edged learning (with its carnal knowledge of the wars and rampages of the twentieth century) calls for the wiser heart, more mindful, loving brain, and watchful attunement of a skilful mother. Individuating too far from our mothers may not be skilful in human development and maturation. North Americans, especially, need to put down the gun, drug, money, resentment, debt, poverty, politics, and refusal-to-know-what-we-really-are-doing practices. For survival, citizens and schools must cradle differences differently so that children can grow towards a sustainable global village that is live-able in specific and local contexts of breathing beings. This means staying embodied and monitoring a refusal to know difficulty and other lacks in educational courage.

People live their professional lives amid these contemporary and corporeal realities. By situation and research interest, I work with pre-service teachers, and also mature teachers, some themselves at per-sonal, professional, and existential risk of illness, withdrawal, distress, and failure in teaching. My research includes questions about how those hard classrooms can become home to all who attend,[8] and how bodied women perform well there *in loco marentis*. Remarkable change and challenge have shaped the past few years of teaching: economic downturn, immigration, increasing identification of students with learning difficulties, retirement of experienced leaders and adminis-trators, and new contempt by multimedia-savvy-elementary-school students (Arafeh & Levin, 2002). Authority no longer comes with the titular position of teacher: it is negotiated in relational, social, ethical, material, and corporeal flux. Concepts of expertise are often evaluated in terms of at-hand-media-skills rather than knowledge, unwarranted confidence rather than sustained gratification of developing wisdom.

Instructional and relational scaffolding become more complex in these circumstances: teachers are faced continually with bridging learner realities from where they are to where more equitable life op-portunities exist. Supervising in classrooms, as I do, opens inquiry about multiples identities and practices of teachers everywhere. And what *do* evaluating professors/materfessors of pre-service education students and administrators notice? Like many of my colleagues across the planet in roles of observing student teachers, I notice communi-cation skills, instructional knowledge, relationships, and authentic, en-gaged learning. I also notice classroom management, leadership, and professional attributes. Stewards of young, vulnerable populations must be in possession of themselves so that children safely may explore new knowledge and skills.

Most of all, as a supervising materfessor, I notice a relational literacy in balance with self, other, and the world.⁹ If there is a contiguous, coherent, ethical, and responsive mode of being as *model* and mentor, then usually the professional knowledge, skills, curriculum, and instruction can be learned by would-be teachers. The adult Mother can nurture this kind of mindful spirit-and-bodied becoming, learning, and emerging.

As described in *Bitter Milk* (Grumet, 1988), intelligent, courageous, strategic mother-educators can build restorative consciousness in the learning spirit. With decreasing resources, damaged and discouraged teachers, and poor ecological practices, a new ethic of performative, relational, and *intracultural* (as well as intercultural) mindfulness is an essential inner literacy for educators that offers courage and enables authentic participation in caring for and about the wounded world.

At this rural school, I observe again my student's manner, talk, being, and relationships a few days into his second practicum. He is a Science major, a young Canadian-immigrant Muslim newcomer from another continent, placed in a white, rural, prairie, elementary school. I am an English and Biology major, a Canadian-born middle-aged White woman working with Buddhist affinities of mind. We are both aware of differences between us (culture, gender, religion, social class, economic strata, sexual orientation) and have spoken about them in theory classes. Here, theories give way to a common focus on the practicalities, strategies, and needs of his current teaching placement. Yes, certainly I notice if his units are planned in his subject area, and if planned lessons of appropriate scope and sequence are in place. But as we all know, lessons planned are not lessons lived. In vivo, I am attentive to how he establishes engagement, interest, trust, and productive work amid noise and unfamiliar terrain. It is important to know how he navigates unpredictable, indeterminate, incomplete, even potentially dangerous interstices of school life. I am curious how he engages what is clearly Other for him. The day I am there, students are patient with him and behave well, so they must like him. If they didn't, they and I know, they have the power to take him down in front of me. That they support him and cooperate in front of the evaluating-me tell me much good about his work already.

I am more than old enough to be this adult student's mother. We have studied together in several classes in preparation for these times where theory meets practice in the crucible of the classroom. We respect each other even though we have actively disagreed: as a professor, I have spoken sharply to him about my perceptions of his seeming sexism, judgment, disapproval, and reaffirmed the right of others to have dissenting views (including his own), and he has told me off and argued beyond politeness. At this first formal visit to the school to watch him teach, neither of us knows if he will 'make it' as a teacher. Wariness of each other would be true at this beginning point in his practicum.

In our post-lesson conference, a Grade 2 student interrupts our talk and pats my student's plaid-flannel-shirted arm. She asks for assistance with the clasp on her lunch bucket. He rightly leaves our conversation and shows her how to open and close it. He watches her practise twice, and she goes away content with her new adeptness at accessing lunch.

He shakes his head and we both laugh. I ask, 'Did you ever imagine being here, doing this?'

'Women do this automatically,' he says. 'Mothers just know this stuff.'

Instead of reacting to what could be regarded as another sexist comment, I refuse a simple binary of yes/no and sit with his comment. He provoked me to think again: How much mothering *is* there in a schoolteacher's work and how much teaching is there in mothering? The body of the teaching-mothering person requires resilience during the early, sustained, and late hours of the visible and invisible work that attends both teaching and parenting. The sheer physical stamina of being on the feet all day, buffeted by numerous careless or unskilled bodies nudging, bumping, clinging – all these require attention, safety, care, and recognition. No routines can prevent unpredictable self-organizing chaos all day long. Structures in place, oh yes, but anything could happen in a teacher's or parent's daily world. The best one can do is pay unceasing intelligent attention with a wise heart and mindful brain, as do effective teaching mothers.

From two stances, those of a wise heart and loving mindful brain, I argue for the need to wean twentieth-century pedagogical didactic selves from habituated (and potentially) harmful educational practices, and to approach knowledge and curriculum studies and theory with generative, new embodied professional awareness. Curricula nourished by wise hearts and mindful brains resonate as needful for psychic survival. Those qualities characterized in positive child rearing are also effective, even necessary, in educational development to sustain growth and make viable human meaning, being, and thriving.

In the information age, different, post-agrarian, post-industrial, post-war knowledges, Mothering can ameliorate rote, unskilful practices to wean us all from non-viable, static forms of being. No longer can we buy everything on credit, dispose of massive material waste and food, gobble energy, abuse our bodies and each other, and distract ourselves from poverty, war, mental illness, and daily basic needs of a global population. Education is an obvious and natural site for this per/formative, disrupting, ethical, relational work to learn new ways to engage the curricula and each other.

Bio-physiologically, weaning is the process of gradually introducing an infant to its adult diet while withdrawing the supply of its mother's milk. What, in terms of (reconceptualist) curriculum and education, should the adult diet be?[10] This question is the practical form of the perennial curriculum question: What knowledge is of most worth for the next generation in schools, in the whole world? The answers (global and personal) differ from those of the past century.

> Towards the end of our post-teaching session of talking about the observed lesson and plans ahead for the next week, two boys from class interrupt us. They sidle up right and left of the student teacher's body and stand close, bumping his arms as he is seated. They ask him to settle an argument started on the playground. He smiles, stands, puts a hand on each of their shoulders and says, 'Set up three chairs in a circle. I will be there in a minute. I am just finishing talking to Dr Fowler.'
>
> They look startled and ask him if he is sick. He laughs and says, 'No, she is a doctor of learning, my teacher and supervisor.' They regard me as one says to the other, 'I told you she wasn't his mom.' We all laugh, I shake hands with my student, assure him of his clear and positive direction in learning to teach, and say if he continues in this thoughtful mentoring way with students, no doubt he will pass this practicum, and make a very good mothering educative presence wherever he teaches.

Trust and Empathy – Abiding Bodies and Performative Kindness

In loco marentis, amid teaching and supervising pre-service teachers, I remain drawn to the concept of a quantum teaching self (Fowler, 2006) physically and bio-dynamically, both matter and energy moving through space and time. That kind of flexible embodied being fits with the quantum classroom that Fleener (2002) suggests in her 'Transformational Crossings.' Educators can use the energy of noise, chaos, irrelevancy, uncertainty, anomalies, and complexity to cultivate an embodied, grounded being as both stranger/other or familiar, being that cultivates a spaciousness of heart and mind that allows us to let go without falling apart, allows possibility and a fresh heart every day. Professionally, we learn to breathe and stay present in both great difference and shared experience, using language and narrative to discover how to live well together, to nurture learning.

Pedagogically, attuned mothers have a capacity, when appropriate for those they have been 'caring' for, to let go of attachment to outcomes, to develop competence in living with dissonance, and to continue being generative in unpredictability. Such attunement fosters trust and empathy: 'The trust or distrust a child feels for a teacher, a voter for a politician, a lover for a partner, a reader for a writer, will markedly affect the kind and degree of attention brought to the details of what she is told, . . . what is sufficiently significant to be remembered and integrated with lived experience. Trust affects how one person connects with another person, text, discourse, and the meaning she makes of it' (Donawa, 1999, p. 46).

For advice about tools, psychologies, and practices that develop trust and are useful in coping and living well in such times, many theorists and educators are interested in questions and answers held within Buddhist psychology – insight, awareness, attunement, attention to breath, heart, spirit, mind (Kornfield, 2008; Santorelli, 1999; Siegel, 2007). The compassion associated with Buddhism may be an appropriate response to suffering in education. Maybe education work could focus more on 'holding the world in kindness [and in studying the] psychology of compassion that arises from our interconnections with all beings' (Kornfield, 2008, p. 16).

The interconnected energies of trust and empathy that anchor Mothering and embodied attentiveness open doors to a more compassionate conceptualizing of curriculum. Ruddick (1989) tells us that 'attention is akin to the capacity for empathy.' Empathy liberates the moral imagination: '[Empathy] invites metaphor and narrative: it illuminates meaning-making; it constructs relational ties that link public and private discourse . . . Empathy is relational, not contractual . . . The empathic insight so necessary [to nurturing relationships] is also crucial to the emotionally literate teacher, scientist, scholar or administrator' (Donawa, 1999, p. 142),

An empathic grounding to curricula encourages teaching mothers to engage with 'a range of approaches and purposes of women who are involved in teaching in order to illustrate aspects of necessarily varied and changed conceptions of feminist pedagogies and curriculum as well as theorizing and research processes' (Miller, 2005, p. 37). Such enlarged thinking functions to 'break silences that have constrained conceptions of ourselves as students, as teachers, as curriculum creators . . . by attending to and challenging the gendered discourses, relationships, and structures that infuse our taken-for-granted yet always power-inflected [binary] notions of public and private, self and other, male and female, the knower and the known' (Miller, 2005, p. 17).

The Wise Heart

Mindfulness of the body allows us to live fully. It brings healing, wisdom, and freedom.

– J. Kornfield, *The Wise Heart*

The teaching body is a public text for all to read (Freedman & Holmes, 2003), and the need for embodied mindfulness is great in teachers. But how do we cultivate such physical mindfulness in being and in professional practice? Supervising pre-service teachers entails transporting my literal body through the classroom door: that act alone alters what is being lived, so I need to be mindful of it as a text and what may be 'read' there. When I am ill, troubled, or have friends or family dying, I notice that being present and fully attentive to what is literal and at hand grounds me. Without all the usual inner narratives, memories, and imagination playing full-time, in mortal difficulty, there is a sharp awareness and immediacy to relationship and to being alive. Life clutter falls away and when there is so little time, attention to that which matters most emerges. Such sharp awareness enhances the experience of being alive, rekindles the capacity to learn what is essential.

The qualities that educators develop in such experiences are those strengths and abilities needed most for the demands, needs, and loneliness of the long-distance teacher. When many people must face the mortal wall, beauty, love, poetry, nature, and music seem to have a heightened place in perception and consciousness. At difficult times in life, we can learn to become our best selves to nourish pure, rare moments with those we love who will soon be gone. There is a limited and mortal quality to teaching, just as there is to parenting. And our children/our students are always soon gone: we have so little time with one another. So, what if we always brought our most focused, immediate mindful selves every day to the teaching project? This is a critical, some would say even palliative, time in education; perhaps mindful materfessors can model that care-full embodiment for student teachers.

For many years, I have been studying difficulty in teaching and the effects on the teaching self of prolonged periods of distress, both personal and professional; I have also studied restorative ways of returning to wholeness and health. While researching the concept of mindfulness in teaching amid difficulty and change in *A Curriculum of Difficulty* (Fowler, 2006), I also honour those engaged in the essential and compelling work of education, who continue to endure, reinvent, and re-enter freshly reconstructed each term, each class, each year, with all its challenges, pleasures, struggles, satisfactions, griefs, and inspirations.

Re-understanding the meaning of teaching and curriculum, being a resilient, reflective professional, requires that we be always beginning again, with our own *inner student teacher* and *supervisor selves*. The reiterative rhythms of what Buddhists term *beginner's mind* increase authenticity and capacity for self-government, knowledge, and skilful choices. We learn to be present and trustworthy with our students, without bias, inappropriate judgment, or unrealistic goals: 'The depth and personal substance of our connections enables us to give and accept help without the burdening attachments of power or value judgment: we move . . . seamlessly from a noisy cacophony of lively disagreement . . . to strong sensitive support in more intractable dilemmas' (Donawa, 1999, p. 148).

Teachers do need support: many North American studies report that close to one-half of new teachers quit the profession within 4 years, and the attrition rate of teachers is increasing (Dickson, 2006; Boe et al., 2002; Hellsten, Ebanks, and Lei, 2008), but many Mothers do stay, for the educational benefit of children, young adults, and communities. I am most concerned with those *stalwarts* who abide in the teaching profession in a generative way. Teaching is not for the faint of heart.

Perhaps because so many teachers are women, mothers, they have a higher-than-healthy tolerance for chaos and being taken for granted; many do not have even an office at work. Few have agency about their working lives, choice of colleagues or administrators, or control about curriculum content or the methods they use. It is more difficult to live with a wise heart and loving, mindful brain in these (worsening) conditions, but the more difficult the circumstances, the deeper the need for mindfulness as restorative practice. Everywhere, all over the world, teachers work long hours at unremarkable salaries to care for, nurture, and teach young people safely, help them study what they need, prepare them for work, and provide opportunities for meaningful experiences along the way. We live by clocks, bells, and buzzers that have little to do with readiness or a more natural flux of educational enterprises. Taken together, the affective and social dissonance produced in school spaces is staggering.

Teachers do this kind of in/visible and essential work daily. They sometimes are taunted for being mediocre intellectuals who *whine* (!) about class size, contact hours, and inappropriate curriculum (often set by publishers from other regions who know little of students' needs or of local contexts and communities). But most of the teachers that I encounter strive continually and reflectively to be the best possible educators they can be. They themselves continually learn, adapt, accommodate, and remain mindful of their central human tasks. I write for these stewards of young people, to provoke, inspire, and make visible the invisible work of teaching. I think the measure of a community can be known in its quality of education, especially amid difficulty and perpetual change.

If I only had an hour or a day to talk with anyone about what I have learned in 30 years of teaching and education, it would be about relationships: active ethics, informed concern, commitment to ease suffering and facilitate equality, abiding non-violence, and sentient awareness of self and other. It would be about how we can use our hearts mindfully and our brains wisely to effect personal, social, and communal justice. By mindful attentiveness to Other, it is more possible to develop openness, curiosity, communication, and critical courage in students and their teachers: Courage interests me – when we have it, when we don't, and how we make the decision to be brave or cowardly. We have created a world where most children live in some form of war, and I write about them to try to do honour to their strength and courage. I have learned there is no such thing as 'other people's children' (Deborah Ellis, discussed in Leggett, 2005, p. 17).

Like Ellis and other authors of children's and young adult literature, I and other educational theorists (Chambers, 2006, 2007, 2008; Lewis &

Tupper, 2009; Pinar, 2009) speak of new literacies for this hostile world: relational, ecological, participatory, sustainable literacies that enact equanimity without demanding constant change, consumption, and acquisition. We want literacies that can nurture, calm, respond, and connect in human-paced days and gentle nights, with music, safety, laughter, family (however defined): those basics so far from reach for so many of our children and selves, cities, and citizens. Feminist research and curriculum studies theory about teaching praxis provide deeper understanding of the nature, structure, and function of being *teacher*.

From these two stances of wise heart and mindful brain, the central curriculum we all teach, consciously or unconsciously, is our own particularity of being, along with whatever our society determines is of most worth. In action, this double stance of materfessors employs narrative, relational, and hermeneutic literacies that can be useful when confronted with the needs of women and children. Recently, during discussion of a motion to approve the building of a daycare centre on a university campus, an opposing board member said to me: 'Why do you care? You are not a mother; you don't have children of your own. It is not the business of the university to run daycare.' It was an opportunity to teach about the need to attend to mothers in public office with language, interpretive tools, and embodied ground of my own (Chambers, 2008).[11]

The North American teaching demographic is aging. Experienced teachers are *at risk* as much as their students, burned out, longing to become unencumbered with the 'stuff' of a teaching life. More than ever, a healthy and thriving teaching population is needed, with active, intelligent, healthy minds, hearts, spirits, and psychologies. Productive teacher educators perhaps can *trouble* current practices to reduce the suffering of future teachers who might otherwise crash and burn in isolation in alienating school rooms and offices, trying to last from school holiday to the next professional development day, just hanging on, *until*.

Living well with never-finished, always-changing work, and having minimum power with maximum responsibility, requires a persistent attentiveness and attunement to what is called for in the moment. School and institutional life can lull us into a dangerous inattention, risking missed opportunities, and giving us life-grief for what might have been.

Insight and mindfulness can make it possible to really see what is going on, really listen to what is being said, notice the struggles and happiness, desires and griefs, tears and laughter, heavy demands and Herculean social work, *without* being taken from ourselves, and *without* being exhausted by continually being too little for too many.

What if we are fine as we are? In any given moment, we are doing the best we can. 'I couldn't be better,' says Buddhist educator, Sylvia Boorstein with the subtext *'If I could be better, I would.'* In the stillness of mindful insight, perhaps even existential suffering itself can be eased by noticing simply what *is*, without having to rescue, judge, or fix it, but rather, invite new modes of engagement with teaching. If *we* can travel lightly in our daily journeys, materfessors can be committed, attuned, and truthfully aware of what transpires in daily lives in the education enterprise.

> As I enter the main doors of Good Heart Elementary for the many-eth time, she is in the hall, that second grader, this time just inside the classroom door where I am headed. I wave as I approach. She pokes her head back into the room and says, 'Mr Student Teacher: your Doctor Teacher is here.' She turns around, holds out her hand to shake mine, as is our ritual, and says, 'Hi, he's doing good. He is ready for you with all his stuff in that big binder on his desk. He is a good teacher – a keeper. I know his name now. I learned a lot from him. Guess he passed, 'cause you hugged him. Gonna miss 'im. Gonna miss you, teacher doctor lady.'

What matters most now in a humane curriculum of embodied learning? My answers for now include well-being for all sentient beings insofar as possible. Desiring to hear all the stories, study in all disciplines, and maintain wise, caring relationships. What sustains me and the place I inhabit in this curriculum? Knowing. Loving relationships. Selfability. Absence of fear, shame, anger. Presence of love, friendship, care. Working well. Authentic attention. Wakeful active practice. The inner cathedral and library of language and story mattering inside my consciousness. Trusting appropriately and being trustworthy. Truth. Justice. Healing. Laughter and play. Creativity, respect, insight, compassion, freedom, dignity. Story, study, and care of bodymindspirit. Each item in the list above is a tiny universe of complexity and patternicity. And all these matter, so for materfessors, learning embodied heartfulness and cultivating a mindful brain is essential to moving towards wisdom.

Notes

1 By selfable, I do not mean selfish or narcissistic, but appropriately possessing mature knowledge about oneself with its needs, strengths, foibles, and fit in relationship and community; responsible for one's thoughts, feelings, and actions without projecting onto others or requiring extra work from others to sustain existence, work, and love; able with self-control, sentient, aware, reflective, responsive, and willing to participate equitably in life and society.

2 See Smith (2004) for a good introduction to Nel Noddings who wrote so much about care and education.

3 See Alice Miller's book by the same name (1983/2002).

4 Neuroplasticity is central to the new brain research about changes in the brain from experience, reading, and thinking. Cognitive work of education literally changes our brain structure. Doidge (2007) and Siegel (2007) are two good places to start on this subject in readable language for the general public.

5 As a certified teacher, I can step in at any time as a legal teacher as the reasonable adult in charge, responsible for (under legal age) students of a public school classroom as per legal contract of most teaching boards: contractually teachers are known to be *in loco parentis*, and I play on this term with *in loco marentis*.

6 *Materfessor* is a playful term I invent to connote female professor in mentoring or supervisory roles within an academic post-secondary education institution, an expert teacher in authority of female gender. Fessor is an American colloquial shortening of professor. Pro from the Latin = on behalf of, and mater from the Latin: mother, origin, source. I also use *in loca marentis* – as feminist play with *in loco parentis*, the contract and covenant of public teachers of education.

7 I catch myself at pre-reflective, habituated language here!

8 By hard, I mean many students with too many learning needs, too extreme shifting power relations (where in the past some may have relied on mere titular or 'expert as teacher' or 'adult person in charge here' control), too rapid technological or curricular change, or incompatible infrastructure or administrative change experienced negatively (especially by established teachers once known to be 'good teachers' who now cannot cope with or even accommodate the daily realities of multiple languages, agendas, ideologies, and contexts).

9 The capacity to *read the word* and *read the world* (Freire & Macedo, 1987). Also in terms of Canadian curriculum documents and syllabi, knowledge, skills, and erudite attributes in use of thought and language arts, including reading, writing, speaking, listening, viewing, and visually representing.

10 Research the bodies of work by William F. Pinar and Madeleine Grumet, for example.
11 The motion to approve the building of the daycare centre ultimately passed, I am happy to say, and many children and parent-students are benefiting from it as I make these final revisions.

References

Arafeh, S., & Levin, D. (2002). *The digital disconnect: The widening gap between Internet-savvy students and their schools.* Washington, DC: Pew Research Center.
Boe, E. (2006). The chronic and increasing shortage of fully certified teachers in special and general education. *Journal for Exceptional Children, 72* (4), 443–460.
Boorstein, S. (2008). *Happiness is an inside job: Practicing for a joyful life.* New York: Ballantyne Books.
Britzman, D. (2009). The very thought of education: Psychoanalysis and the impossible professions. *Journal of American Psychoanalytical Associations, 58,* 611–614.
Chambers, C. (2006). 'The land is the best teacher I ever had': Places as pedagogy for precarious times. *Journal of Curriculum Theorizing, 22* (3), 27–37.
Chambers, C. (2007). *On spelling and other illiteracies.* Paper presented at the Canadian Association for Curriculum Studies and Language and Literacy Researchers of Canada Joint CSSE Pre-Conference.
Chambers, C. (2008). Where are we? Finding common ground in a curriculum of place. *Journal of the Canadian Association for Curriculum Studies, 6* (2), 113–128.
Dickson, E. (2006). Disability standards for education: And the obligation of reasonable adjustment. *Australia and New Zealand Journal of law and Education, 11* (2), 23–42.
Doidge, N. (2007). *The brain that changes itself: Stories of personal triumph from the frontiers of brain science.* London: Penguin.
Donawa, W. (1999). *A rebel band of friends: Understanding through women's narratives of friendship, identity, and moral agency.* Unpublished dissertation, University of Victoria, Victoria, BC.
Fleener, J. (2002). *Curriculum dynamics: Recreating heart.* New York: Peter Lang.
Fowler, L.C. (2006). *A curriculum of difficulty: Narrative research and the practice of teaching.* New York: Peter Lang.
Freedman, D.P., & Holmes, M.S. (Eds.). (2003). *The teacher's body: Embodiment, authority, and identity in the academy.* Albany, NY: State University of New York Press.

Freire, P., & Macedo, D.P. (1987). *Literacy: Reading the word and the world.* Westport,CT: Greenwood.

Greene, M. (1973). *Teacher as stranger.* Belmont, CA: Wadsworth.

Grumet, M. (1988). *Bitter milk.* Boston, MA: University of Massachusetts Press.

Hellsten, L, Prytula, M, Ebanks, A, & Lai, H. (2009). Teacher induction: Exploring beginning teacher mentorship. *Canadian Journal of Education, 32* (4), 703–733.

Kornfield, J. (2008). *The wise heart: A guide to the universal teachings of Buddhist psychology.* New York: Bantam.

Leggett, K. (2005). Deborah Ellis. *Children's literature: Independent information and reviews.* http://www.childrenslit.com/childrenslit/mai_ellis_deborah.html.

Lewis, P., &. Tupper, J. (Eds.). (2009). *Challenges bequeathed: Taking up the challenges of Dwayne Huebner.* Rotterdam: Sense Publishing.

Miller, J. (2005). *Sounds of silence breaking: Woman, autobiography, curriculum.* New York: Peter Lang.

Pinar, W.F. (2009). *The worldliness of a cosmopolitan education: Passionate lives in public service.* London: Routledge.

Ruddick, S. (1989). *Maternal thinking: Towards a politics of peace.* New York: Ballantine.

Santorelli, S. (1999). *Heal thyself: Lessons on mindfulness in medicine.* New York: Bell Tower.

Siegel, D. (2007). *The mindful brain: Reflection and attunement in the cultivation of well-being.* New York: Norton.

Smith, M. (2004). Nel Noddings, the ethics of care and education, the encyclopedia of informal education. Retrieved from www.infed.org/thinkers/noddings.htm.

Springgay, S., & Freedman, D. (2009). Mothering a bodied curriculum: Sleeping with cake and other touchable encounters. *Journal of Curriculum Theorizing, 25* (2), 25–37.

Weiler, K. (1994). Freire and a feminist pedagogy of difference. In P. McLaren & C. Lankshear, (Eds.), *Politics of liberation: Paths from Freire* (pp. 12–40). New York: Routledge.

5 Relational Teaching and Mothers with Disabilities: Bridging the Public/Private, Dependency/Nurturance Divides

CLAUDIA MALACRIDA

In her discussion of the challenges that (mostly) female teachers face in providing caring, interdependent, and nurturing pedagogy, Madeleine Grumet describes tensions that arise from the competing goals of women teachers as professionals who must prepare children for a public and independent world and as women whose learned qualities of nurturance and protection are undervalued and constrained within masculinist and objectivist educational environments. In this instance, teachers are challenged to sustain their socialized, gendered qualities of caring and nurturance within a culture that values independence, autonomy, and competition. A second conflict arises in struggles over 'whose children' schoolchildren really are; teachers can also feel ambivalent about usurping the mothering role from children's actual mothers while at the same time undermining those mothers' relationships of interdependency with their children. In short, teachers as agents of institutional socialization, and as vectors into the public and independent world of school and work, operate in ways that go against their own socialization as nurturers and that also are in opposition to the mothering that other women do (Grumet, 1988).

Another element in the mother-teacher dilemma is that the role of mothers in their children's educational lives is a difficult, yet critical one; mothers are disproportionately the ones to whom educators address concerns regarding children, in part, because mothers are more likely to be the at-home or available parent, but also because mothers continue to be seen as the 'first' and most 'naturally responsible' parent in children's lives. On the one hand, mothers are responsible for nurturing their children in an increasingly strident climate of high maternal expectations (Choi, Baker, & Tree, 2005), and on the other, they are held liable when their children experience difficulties or troubles (Swift, 1995). Mothers thus are potentially their children's advocates and champions with the schools and the individuals who are seen to be responsible for their children's difficulties (if not necessarily their accomplishments) by their children's teachers and school administrators. These tensions can become even more complicated when the mother involved is a woman with disabilities, since mothers with disabilities face their own dilemmas of dependency and interdependency and are often themselves in need of advocacy. As I have argued elsewhere, mothers with disabilities face a double bind of being seen as dependent, inadequate, and infantile while at the same time being charged with the responsibility of achieving increasingly high standards of what Elizabeth Hays (1996) has termed 'intensive mothering'(Malacrida, 2007, 2009a). Likewise, because parenting with a disability is often viewed from a 'deficit model,' where challenges are seen as incompetency rather than simply as problems to be dealt with, disabled mothers are frequently judged as inadequate or even harmful to their children simply because these mothers are dealing with disability (Newman, 2002; Swain & Cameron, 2003).

Disabled women face challenges in the private sphere because of increased vulnerability to violence; heightened rates of sole parenthood; physical, mental, or emotional challenges to providing care as a result of their conditions; and inadequate support from policies and programs that fail to accommodate their disabilities or their mothering roles (Asch, Rousso, & Jefferies, 2001; Blackford, 1993; Malacrida, 2009b). In the public sphere, they are likely to experience poor educational and occupational opportunities, poverty, inadequate and inaccessible housing, and lack of social support; all of these can impinge on their capacity to provide care to their children (Malacrida, 2010). Mothers with disabilities may experience challenges in presenting themselves as 'good enough' mothers to teachers and helping professionals because of the stigma of poverty, inadequate housing, social isolation, and vulnerability to abuse and violence that are all too frequently attached to disability (McConnell & Llewellyn, 2000; Mosoff, 1997; Swain & Cameron, 2003). In turn, this can mean that mothers with disabilities are liable to negative evaluations of their parenting capacity by educators that, at a minimum, pose challenges to parent-teacher communication and collaboration and that, in the extreme, can be deleterious to their family life.

Disability and motherhood is an important issue; 11% of all American families are headed by one or two parents with disabilities (Kirshbaum & Olkin, 2002). In addition to the structural challenges faced by disabled mothers, outlined above, mothers with disabilities face disability discrimination in the form of stigmatizing public perceptions of them as inadequate or inappropriate in the role of parents. For example, helping professionals often discourage women with disabilities from becoming pregnant, expressing concerns that they will not be competent mothers and reflecting eugenic worries that their disabilities might be passed on to their children (Gerodetti, 2003). These perceptions about incompetence are even more likely if the parents have intellectual disabilities, mental health problems, or profound mobility limitations (Booth & Booth, 1998; Mosoff, 1997). It is possible to speculate that mothers with disabilities may not be seen by teachers as 'naturally' engaging in the nurturing, responsible actions that other mothers accomplish because educators also may believe that women with disabilities are neither appropriate nor adequate to the task of mothering. When such disability discrimination enters into parent-teacher relations, it can mean that disabled mothers may not be included as adults in their children's schooling, and they may find it difficult to be taken seriously by their children's teachers and accommodated in their children's schools.

The Study

This chapter draws on qualitative interviews with 39 U.K. and 43 Canadian mothers with physical, mental health, cognitive, and sensory impairments, which were collected in the context of a broader project involving mothers with disabilities in Canada and the United Kingdom. The research utilizes a feminist, narrative analysis, with the understanding that women are best able to tell us about the aspects of the social world that make their lives difficult. I ask women to tell me their stories of interactions with policy, official programs, neighbours, family, and the institutions meant to assist them. Included among those institutions mentioned by the mothers are, of course, the schools that these women's children attend. As noted earlier, despite shifts in parental roles, mothers in modern Western societies continue to be idealized as 'natural' caregivers for children, who are held completely responsible for the good and bad that befalls their children (Hays, 1996). They are also liable for the moral reproduction of society through the nurturing of physically, emotionally, and morally healthy children (Knowles, 1996; Ladd-Taylor & Umansky, 1998). Thus, we can assume that mothers are likely to be the responsible parents when it comes to dealings with their children's schools. That being said, many mothers mentioned that, despite this cultural expectation and role of mothers, they actually felt themselves excluded in dealings with their children's teachers and school officials, as will be seen.

In their interviews, the women identified three primary axes that were problematic in their interactions with educators. The first relates to disability discrimination in the form of negative assumptions about disabled women as mothers; the second, and most common, concerns accommodation and accessibility broadly defined; and the third hinges on a lack of understanding about disabled mothers' embedded and embodied relations of care. In a fourth axis, mothers also poignantly described educators who transcended the tensions between mothers and teachers, public and private, and independence and dependency to provide compassionate and connected care for women and their children.

Disability Discrimination and Lack of Acknowledgment

Many people only see disabled people in terms of dependency, incompetence, or deficit, and the mothers in this study often described interactions with educators that conveyed such perceptions. Several mothers worried, as Canadian mother Karen Gomes (all names are pseudonyms), who has muscular dystrophy said, about 'the stigma attached to having somebody who's a bit different in the family.' Like U.K. mother Cathy Cairns, who has cerebral palsy, they described not being acknowledged by their children's teachers. Cathy explained:

> [My daughter's] teacher didn't take me seriously . . . Often, this particular teacher would turn away from me and carry on talking to another parent . . . and I actually walked in front of her and said, 'I'm sorry, I'm talking to you. Please listen to me.' And she looked at me as if for the first time and actually saw me and said, 'Oh, I'm sorry, yes, what were you saying?' . . . but I had to do that to make her understand that I'm saying things because they're important and they involve my children. I'm not just twittering away about nothing!

It's hard to know whether these interactions occurred because of simple disability discrimination, where people with disabilities are often perceived as discomforting or disgusting, or whether the teacher dismissed Cathy's approaches because she assumed that a woman with disabilities could not have responsible and important things to say about her child's education; either way, it is clear that Cathy felt she had to struggle to be acknowledged by her child's teacher.

Indeed, the mothers' worries about not being seen as responsible adults in their children's lives often prove to be realistic. In a similar way to several other wheelchair users in the study, Danielle Smith, who has multiple sclerosis, described how teachers minimized her mothering role:

> When we would go to the school, they would tend to talk to Graham [my husband] as a parent rather than me. So things like going for school meetings, they were always inaccessible, always upstairs or something like that. And they always used to say, 'Well, the father's here, he can come up.'

In this story, it is clear that, because of his non-disabled status, the father was 'promoted' to 'first parent.' I am, of course, not arguing here that fathers should not be treated as equal partners in their children's development. I am, however, arguing that in our current culture this is typically *not* the case unless the mother is not acknowledged as a competent, caring, responsible adult.

Educators' assumptions that mothers with disabilities are incompetent were particularly evident for mothers with intellectual or mental health issues. Often, the women described communications that were in language that they did not understand. More problematically, they described communications that bypassed them altogether, indicating an assumption that such women either would not or could not act as responsible parents to their children. An example of this can be found in the story told by Canadian mother Monika Petrenko, who has learning disabilities and is deaf. She said:

> They used to just get in touch with his [her ex-husband's] parents and never told me anything that was going on.

This was a particularly troublesome choice because, although Monika was the legal custodial parent following the breakup with her husband, the parents-in-law (who were not disabled people) were able to maintain the authority with the school, insisting that they were the 'proper' parents to Monika's two children and that they should handle school-parent interactions. This situation was extremely deleterious for Monika and for her children; because of long-standing hostilities between Monika and her parents-in-law, notices and homework information got filtered through the in-laws and were not passed on to Monika. Eventually, this led the school to suspect Monika of being a neglectful and hostile parent, and they referred her and her children to child welfare. With the help of a third-party social worker/advocate (who attended Monika's interview with me and verified this woeful tale, since Monika wanted to tell her story, but remains suspicious of well-intentioned middle-classed professionals like myself) things eventually were sorted out, and Monika has retained custody of her children and has a new, more clear line of communication with the school. However, at one point, it seemed quite plausible that Monika's child custody was under threat, simply because of these miscommunications. It is also fair to assume that at least part of the explanation for the ease with which Monika's in-laws were able to convince teachers and school administrators that they were the 'proper' people to handle the children's issues lay in little more than a presumption that Monika could and would not be a competent partner in her children's education.

In another example of how teachers can sideline mothers in their children's educational development, U.K. single mother Hazel Smith, who had a stroke, resulting in depression, memory loss, and poor speech, described how her daughter was tested and coded for dyslexia. She recalled:

> They phoned me up out of the blue and said, 'Oh, we've tested Bethany and she's dyslexic. Have you got any questions?' and I was sort of taken aback. I took a friend who's a retired head teacher to school with me for a meeting and first thing was how I didn't think that you could test a child without a parent's consent. Nobody ever took the time out to explain things to me.

In Hazel's story, it is difficult to see the struggle for ascendency over the care of the child that can happen between teachers and mothers that Grumet imagines; instead, in this and the other narratives described above, the struggle is non-existent. The educators have already taken over the children's care, and they have written these mothers out of their children's lives, despite that these women *are* actively nurturing their children in relations of care.

Failure to Accommodate Disability

The second and most common concern that was expressed by almost all of the mothers concerned very broad barriers to accommodation and accessibility. Of course, many of these barriers concerned physical accessibility, and it was sobering that over half of the women with physical disabilities in this study described children's schools that were physically inaccessible. Although this meant that parents were not included in events like parent-teacher meetings and resulted perhaps in even more difficult mother-teacher relations than with other parents, it also meant that mothers were excluded from their children's lives on a regular basis. Chelsea McAdams, a Canadian single mother of two living with a spinal cord injury, said:

> You know, I want to come in and volunteer, come to my kids' Christmas parties, do that sort of thing and have that interaction. I want to see how they are when they're there. You know, just regular parents things.

The 'regular parent things' that mothers with physical disabilities worried about included regular communication with their children's teachers, but also things like picking young children up from class for appointments, bringing children's projects to and from classrooms, and casually meeting with the teacher, other parents, and their children's friends. In short, lack of physical accommodation not only had the potential to contribute to mothers' poor relationships with teachers, but also with their community members, their children, and their children's social networks. Indeed, mothers with all kinds of disabilities, both visible and invisible, complained consistently about social isolation in all aspects of their parenting lives, and it seems that while schools could play an important role in integrating these women into community life and decreasing disability stigma, this golden opportunity has all too frequently been missed.

Physical inaccessibility is a prime example of how schools as patriarchal and public-sphere institutions can deny the intentions of both teachers and mothers, as Grumet intimates. Some mothers described teachers who made extra efforts to include the women, and how those efforts often worked in contradictory ways, actually highlighting disabled women's differences from other parents. Canadian mother Yvonne Jameson, who has myasthenia gravis and uses a wheelchair, described some of the ironies of her daughter's school's efforts at inclusion:

> I've not been able to attend school performances because there are no, there's no ramp in. Unless I'm willing to go through the humiliation of being carried in, which I've done. And then you get to be put in an obscure angle where you can't see anything anyway and sit alone, which is, you know, classic. And everybody gets to stare at you because you're off to one side. I've bummed my way up stairs, flights of stairs – I mean when I was well enough to – and you arrive sweating and breathless. And the real burden is that I would end up trying to make *them* feel comfortable with *me!*

In instances like Yvonne describes, where teachers and administrators are not willing or able to work through the system to have fundamental architectural changes made, their efforts to bridge the school and home can fall flat and may even cause more problems than they presume to fix. In Yvonne's case, as with several of the other mothers, rather than accept the humiliations of this kind of 'inclusion,' they chose to remain outside of this aspect of their children's lives. It is important to note that these decisions came with much difficulty for these women, and carried a price for the children involved and the mother-child relationship. Yvonne described how school plays and Christmas pageants ended up not only as a moment of exclusion for her, but evolved into a source of friction between herself and her daughter, whom she says, "felt abandoned, I guess, and basically threw a fit" when her mother decided to forego the humiliation and stay home.

Another barrier to accessibility concerned lack of access to the educational and communicative process itself. This was particularly problematic in both Canada and the United Kingdom for mothers with intellectual disabilities, brain injuries, or sensory disabilities. Dianne Holmes is blind, as is her husband. She described her frustrations with access to information about her children's schooling:

> We went to the school and said, 'What we need from you, or what would help us out is if anything that came home from school, whether it be Polly's homework notices or anything, that it comes home in large print, or electronically, because my husband can access that stuff.' They said 'Oh, yeah, yeah, yeah.' They all gave lip-service to being able to help us

out, or wanting to. And they sent newsletters to Mike electronically, and
that has been it.

In a similar vein, mothers with intellectual disabilities who asked for
plain language or simple verbal versions of handouts, notices, and
homework instructions described ongoing frustrations in obtaining
those materials in accessible formats. These barriers, ironically, occa-
sionally had negative implications for the children and for the mothers,
who were not seen as active partners in their children's schooling.

This was particularly difficult when children were struggling with
their own issues, as was the case for several mothers who had learning
disabilities and whose children also had learning or behavioural problems at school. Unless such mothers had personal advocates, they often
found themselves failing to make the grade as parents, missing deadlines, not helping their children to complete homework assignments,
and generally remaining out of the loop of their children's school lives.
Carly Grossman has dyslexia and mobility issues because of Crohn's
disease, and her son has recently been diagnosed with mild learning
disabilities. She described how being assigned an out-of-school advocate has helped her:

> The agency gave me the worker, and she's been a godsend ever since . . . She
> went to the school with me, to the counsellors and that lady that did the
> test, and she was able to tell me properly what they were saying. Because
> it was all mumble jumble to me. And then, with her being beside me, I
> was able to get it out to the teacher that I can't read. Please don't send
> homework home with me. He gets flustered. I get flustered, then we're
> screaming at each other, then I'm upset, then my Crohn's is upset, I'm in
> bed in pain for a week, and everything goes sideways.

In Carly's comments, we begin to understand how the lives of women
with disabilities are embedded in multiple relationships of care and
dependency, and that this can further complicate relationships between mothers and teachers. Teachers, if they are to make connections with such mothers, have not only to work through their own
ambivalence about disability and the mother-teacher relationship, but
they also need to work through multiple levels of public/private interaction. This can mean dealing with local or provincial authorities
for building improvements, or it can require interacting with social
workers in a way that is not exclusionary or punitive to mothers with

disability challenges; either way, it means taking these women's challenges as important and legitimate and being creative in finding ways to meet their needs.

Disabled Mothers' Embodied and Embedded Relations of Care

Women with disabilities often have embodied challenges that make their relationships of care more difficult than those of other women. Some women with physical disabilities may find themselves hospitalized for routine or acute care, disrupting their children's home lives. Other mothers with disabilities may experience profound shifts in capacity. For example, mothers with muscular dystrophy can experience continuing changes in their needs and capacities; mothers with multiple sclerosis can experience shifts such that one year they are dealing with blindness and immobility, and the next year they are able to walk and see, but experience, instead, severe vertigo and memory loss. Obviously, it is not always easy for educators to accommodate such shifts in family needs; however, it was also clear from mothers' stories that not all educators were keen to make those efforts at all. Single parent and stroke survivor Hilary Stephens elaborated:

> [My daughter] struggles in school, because if I'm in the hospital or things, her reading doesn't get done, her spelling doesn't get done. She doesn't get that support. But I feel that at the time then the school should be picking up that Mom's not around so this needs to be done. I've spoken more than once with her teacher when these things have come up, but I can't seem to get through.

Hilary's story highlights another aspect of the tensions between teachers and mothers with disabilities. Because mothers are necessary contributors to their children's education, when they are bypassed as co-educators, it is their children who pay the price. For Hilary's daughter, who is very bright, that price amounted to little more than late assignments, some conflicts with her teacher, and perhaps some minor learning gaps. However, for children facing their own challenges, the price can be more serious problems with classroom learning and discipline.

Even when there are not changes in mothers' situations, the disjunctures between mothers' embodied capacities and their children's' educational attainments can play out in varied ways. Mothers with learning disabilities may have difficulties helping with written home-work, for example, if not provided with tailored and appropriate sup-port from the children's teachers. Challenges may also play out in ways that are difficult to anticipate, requiring teachers to be closely in touch with mothers and children, and open to understanding the world from the family's perspective. For example, Canadian mother Rachel Jones, who has a degenerative neuromuscular disease, noted that all four of her children have struggled with physical education in school, which has, in turn, affected their social inclusion:

> You know, my kids never got out to the park with me very much, or played in sports with me, so they're behind. They've struggled to catch up with their peers, and that's something I think their teachers have never been able to understand – how my disability has played a role in their lives.

In Rachel's account, we begin to see how mothers, teachers, and chil-dren's lives and work are interconnected, and how taking these in-terconnections into account is crucial to good pedagogy, particularly when the mother has a disability.

Discussion: Transcending the Tensions, Achieving Connection

In the above sections, I outlined some of the difficulties that disabled mothers experienced relating to disability discrimination, accessi-bility issues, and a failure to take disabled mothers' embedded and embodied relations of care into account. However, it is important to note that some educators do manage to navigate the tensions be-tween mothers and teachers, public and private, and independence and nurturance.

Mavis Wilson is a U.K. mother with Crohn's disease and related mo-bility issues. Her daughter's school bus was scheduled to pick her up at 7:40 in the morning for a 9:15 start. For Mavis, this meant getting up at 5:30 'because my first hour of the day is spent on the loo.' Then, with the pain that attends Crohn's-related arthritis, it would be a long, slow struggle to get her daughter Amy ready for school. When she explained this dilemma to the school,

> what they actually did is they arranged for a coach to come back and pick her up at 9 o'clock.

Even more impressive, when they learned that Amy, who has ADHD, is a child who if left unescorted at the roadside is likely to run away, they made further changes. Mavis explained:

> All the other kids on the coach you've got to go up to the coach and meet them. Because Amy will do a runner if you're sitting out there waiting, and because they know I can't chase after her, they've agreed that the escort will actually bring her right down to the front door and back again. So that really helps.

In this situation, the school, rather than seeing this mother as incompetent, has instead, chosen to see the issue as a problem simply solved and as an issue of shared pedagogy that extends beyond the classroom. And truly, this is not a solution that demands much extra effort on the part of the system, although undoubtedly it was a solution that occurred at least, in part, because the school was able to work within a bureaucracy that was supportive rather than obstructive. As Mavis speculated, 'Our school is a good one, and the Local Education Authority in our area is well-heeled.' This combination – of resources and willingness – has made a profound difference for Mavis and her family.

Resources are often a necessary component in extending relational pedagogy to disabled mothers and their children. Mothers who are deaf require interpreters for school plays and teacher meetings, and this is expensive; ramps, elevators, and wide doorways are costly to install; and organizing an extra bus run for an overly active child and her physically challenged mother is not cheap. Nevertheless, many of the gestures that bridge the tensions between educators and mothers with disabilities rely on an ethos of responsibility and care rather than an uncaring or underfunded institutional bureaucracy. In many cases, it can be as simple as relaxing the rules. U.K. mother Kate Wyckstrom has fibromyalgia, and she described how being permitted to park in the staff lot and use the staff lounge to wait for her daughter rather than struggle to pick her daughter up from class,

> just made all the difference for me – and because I wasn't exhausted, we actually started getting her homework done!

Bridging the divide occurs through building connections into teacher-mother interactions. Canadian mother Madeleine Lane and her 14-year-old son both sustained severe brain injuries from a motor

vehicle accident several years ago. For Madeleine, this resulted in severe memory loss, challenges in organizing her and her son's life, and
bouts of depression; for her son, this has meant behavioural challenges
and anger management issues. In our interview, Madeleine spoke mov-
ingly about a school meeting in which she struggled to present her family's challenges. The teacher stopped the conversation and said:

> 'I want you to know that I understand this more than you might expect.'
> And I'm thinking, 'Ya, ya, ya. That's what they all say.' And she went on
> to say how her brother had sustained a brain injury falling off a mountain,
> he was a climber. And she had been through the full recovery and been by
> his side as her parents kinda bailed on him . . . This was just such a huge
> blessing.

In this teacher's response, we see that her own relationships of dependency informed her care for the mother; by seeing Madeleine as a person, and drawing on her own experience, this teacher reached across
the divides to provide connection and support to a struggling mother.

In her exquisite treatise on the relationship between femininity,
equality, and dependency, Eva Feder Kittay (1999) offers a fruitful alternative to the often adversarial relationships that can occur between
those who provide care and those who are cared for. In Kittay's model,
we can see hope for ways to enrich the often punitive relationships between teachers as vectors to independence and the public sphere, and
disabled mothers as caregivers and women who also need care. She
describes those who deal with disabled persons as *dependency workers*,
emphasizing that such work must take individual variations in capacity into account and treat these variations as valuable. Teachers must
learn to do this as well. The challenges facing disabled mothers and
their children extend beyond the classroom and into the community,
fluctuate routinely with changing embodied circumstances, and are
embedded in complicated relations of care. Teachers, despite their ambivalence about dependency and nurturance, tensions over mothers'
roles in children's education, and their own disability prejudices, have
the potential to build capacity for disabled women and their families by
valuing difference rather than seeing it as deficit. Clearly, in the stories
mothers tell of compassion and insight from some of their children's
educators, we can see that such relational pedagogy is not only possible, but is enriching to children, mothers, and the educators who embody it.

References

Asch, A., Rousso, H., & Jefferies, T. (2001). Beyond pedestals: The lives of girls and women with disabilities. In H. Rousso & M.L. Wehmeyer (Eds.), *Double jeopardy: Addressing gender equity in special education* (pp. 13–48). Albany, NY: State University of New York Press.

Blackford, K.A. (1993). Erasing mothers with disabilities through Canadian family-related policy. *Disability, Handicap & Society, 8* (3), 281–294.

Booth, T., & Booth, W. (1998). The myth of the upside down family. In T. Booth & W. Booth (Eds.), *Growing up with parents who have learning difficulties* (pp. 146–168). London: Routledge.

Choi, P.H., Baker, S., & Tree, J. (2005). Supermom, superwife, super every-thing: Performing femininity in the transition to motherhood. *Journal of Reproductive and Infant Psychology, 23* (2), 167–180.

Gerodetti, N. (2003). *'Disabling' femininities and eugenics: Sexuality, disability and citizenship in modern Switzerland.* Lausanne: University of Lausanne.

Grumet, M.R. (1988). *Bitter milk: Women and teaching.* Amherst, MA: University of Massachusetts Press.

Hays, S. (1996). *The cultural contradictions of motherhood.* New Haven, CT: Yale University Press.

Kirshbaum, M., & Olkin, R. (2002). Parents with physical, systemic, or visual disabilities. *Sexuality and Disability, 20* (1), 65–80.

Kittay, E.F. (1999). *Love's labor: Essays on women, equality and dependency.* New York: Routledge.

Knowles, C. (1996). *Family boundaries: The invention of normality and dangerousness.* Peterborough, ON: Broadview Press.

Ladd-Taylor, M., & Umansky, L. (1998). *'Bad' mothers: The politics of blame in twentieth-century America.* New York: New York University Press.

Malacrida, C. (2007). Negotiating the dependency/nurturance tightrope: Dilemmas of disabled motherhood. *Canadian Review of Sociology, 144* (4), 469–493.

Malacrida, C. (2009a). Performing motherhood in a disablist world: Dilemmas of motherhood, femininity and disability. *International Journal of Qualitative Studies in Education, 23* (1), 99–117.

Malacrida, C. (2009b). Services for mothers with disabilities: Surveillance, gender struggles and infantilization. In G. Katsas (Ed.), *Sociology in a changing world* (pp. 271–282). Athens, GA: Athens Institute for Education and Research.

Malacrida, C. (2010). Parents with disabilities. In D. Cheal (Ed.), *Canadian families today: New perspectives* (pp. 213–233). Toronto: Oxford University Press.

102   Claudia Malacrida

McConnell, D., & Llewellyn, G. (2000). Disability and discrimination in statutory child protection proceedings. *Disability & Society, 15* (6), 883–895.

Mosoff, J. (1997). 'A jury dressed in medical white and judicial black': Mothers with mental health histories in child welfare and custody. In S.B. Boyd (Ed.), *Challenging the public private/ divide: Feminism, law and public policy* (pp. 227–252). Toronto: University of Toronto Press.

Newman, T. (2002). 'Young carers' and disabled parents: Time for a change of direction? *Disability & Society, 17* (6), 613–625.

Swain, P.A., & Cameron, N. (2003). 'Good enough parenting': Parental disability and child protection. *Disability & Society, 18* (2), 165–177.

Swift, K. (1995). *Manufacturing 'bad mothers': A critical perspective on child neglect.* Toronto: University of Toronto Press.

6 E-Mail from a Digital Daddy: A Conversation with My (Future) Child in an Age of Digital (Communication) Technology

B. STEPHEN CARPENTER II

From: Steve Carpenter <bscarpenterii@gmail.com>
Date: Thur, 15 Jan 2009 10:27:07-0600
To: B Stephen Carpenter II <bscarpenterii@mobile.me>
Subject: Face to face interface

For now, I must send these e-mails to myself. I must stand-in for you; take your place until you can take up/stand up/speak up for yourself. In talking to myself I am talking to you and by talking to you this way, I am helping myself to better know you and me. Thank you for talking with me. I guess I am trying to work out, for the time being, a better sense of what we mean to each other.

Our shared autobiographical imagining has been helpful for me so far. I hope that one day, you/I will understand what these talks meant to me. I hope that we will always be able to communicate with each other, whether mediated through digital devices or not. I am a bit 'old school' in some respects – more 1.0 than 2.0 some might say – and prefer face-to-face interface. For now, these e-mail exchanges will have to do.
Love,
Papa

My wife and I recently learned that we were expecting our first child. As I began the process of preparing for the birth of our child and our future lives together, I was forced to confront the complexities of identity – most specifically racial, cultural, ethnic, gender, and linguistic – that lie ahead for the new addition to our family. At the time I started writing this chapter, my wife and I lived in Texas, a part of the United States that is geographically removed from both sets of our parents, siblings, their families, and our extended families, and thus we must rely on e-mail, video conferencing (Skype), and text/instant messaging (IM) to remain in contact with our large and growing family. These digital communication technologies enable us to maintain and strengthen our relationships with our own parents and families, both verbally and visually. My parents and most of my family live in the mid-Atlantic region of the United States. My wife's family lives in Tunisia, overseas on another continent. We visit with her parents, siblings, and extended family less frequently than with my own, given the geographical distance and thus we rely even more so on digital communication technologies to 'stay in touch' and maintain our relationships with the ones we love in North Africa. Our telephone conversations, video chats, Facebook postings, and IMs are double- and triple-coded conversations that merge English, French, and Arabic.

Last year, we began preparing to include our child into this digitized, intercultural, multilinguistic family. Perhaps more easily than my wife and I entered our current digital lives, our child will simply be a 'digital native' (Prensky, 2001), a being born into a digital world. My use of the term *digital world* here refers to a lifestyle that includes access to, use of, and challenges that result from the use of digital technology (by choice and otherwise) on a daily basis. I imagine my daughter will grow up with a more comfortable sense of the complex relationships among these aspects of her daily life in the face of digitial communication technology, identity, and her body than her parents currently have with theirs. But as I imagine such a future, I also acknowledge my/our own privilege to access such technologies and the large numbers of fathers and daughters around the world who do not or cannot face such 'problems' by virtue of how they are situated with respect to the 'digital divide' (Bolt & Crawford, 2000) – once conceived as a matter of digital 'haves and have nots' in terms of access but that has since evolved to have other social, gendered, racial, economic, and political aspects.

Other scholars have taken up reviews of the scholarship on the realities of the 'digital divide' as they relate to international issues, globalization, and education (Bolt & Crawford, 2000; Dolby & Rahman, 2008), and doing so in-depth here is beyond my intentions for this work. The lack of a substantive review of that literature here should not be read as an attempt to pass over the importance of this scholarship or the issues these scholars address. As a matter of fact, the work of these scholars is an explicit reminder for me to consider the identity and subjectivity of my future daughter and myself within my musings here, and I am fully aware that any discussion of a so-called digital age is only an issue for a portion of the world's population, let alone all North Americans.

Not unlike Richardson's (2008) fears that, as they grow older, his own pre-teen son and daughter will not 'be Googled well' – that is, seen in a favourable light as a result of less than impressive hits from a Web search of their names – by admissions officers, potential employers, and life partners, in part, my conversation with my future daughter is directly tied to my own uncertainties about what current and future uses of digital technology have in store for my daughter and for others in relationship to her and her identity. For more than a decade, scholars interested in the influences and affordances of digital technology have warned of unintended consequences and problems inherent in the increasing use and expectations of the medium. This work has laid the groundwork for critical perspectives on 'the digital age' with respect to social, cultural, political, economic, and educational concerns. For example, Burbles and Callister (2000) point to important social, cultural, and economic aspects related to access to digital technology by financially challenged communities and the implications for education. Similarly, Bolt and Crawford (2000) considered current and future challenges resulting from the increased attention to computer technology and the social, economic, and educational lives of children in North America but, more specifically, in the United States. Although lauded for being some of the earliest responses to an inevitable digital future, these works have been criticized as being limited in the depths of their criticism of the 'digital divide' and their consideration of social, political, and economic challenges that educators and others would face as a result of digital technology. I am aware that any discussion or labelling of a 'digital age' is problematic, in that it supposes an existence for a larger group based on the specific situation of a few. I am fully conscious that the age in which I live (and my daughter will enter into) is a digital one for us, and I do not wish to impose such a lifestyle or expectations on others.

In this chapter, I engage a form of autobiographical inquiry through which I muse about a future relationship between my daughter and myself with/because of digital technology as opposed to lived experiences between us, past or present. I do not intend for my use of the term *globalization* here to be considered as having a singular or concise definition, but rather as Bloland (2005) suggests, its meaning depends on what is being emphasized. That is, for some, 'globalization involves the flow of money, goods, people, information, knowledge, technology, and culture, as well as disease and terror, across a networked world' (p. 127). Because I do not wish to imply that globalization has only positive effects nor to reify class and national privilege to the detriment of others, I acknowledge the concept of globalization as 'complex in its implications, ambiguous in its in meaning, and fraught with political conflict' (p. 127).

In short, this chapter is a musing on my future role as a father in the age of digital technology, visual culture, and globalization. In part, this chapter affords me an opportunity to point to and question some of my own blind spots – what cannot be seen, is not seen, or is unable to be seen – with my own increased use of digital communication technologies. This chapter is also a brief presentation of my speculations about and preparations for the relationship that I imagine will develop between my child and myself within this context. Although this chapter is written in a linear, sequential format, it is at the same time a multilayered and complex autobiographical narrative in which I consider issues of identity, language, culture, race, gender, and society with respect to myself and my future child, as manifested in digital communication technologies and digital visual culture. Through a series of e-mail messages I composed and sent to myself – both actual and constructed for this work – the chapter revolves around my reflections on and preparations for ways in which digital communication technologies and their affordances might work towards constructing, informing, resisting, and encouraging the relationship I will develop with my child and how our identities are currently assumed/presumed for us through such technologies in television advertisements, YouTube videos, and other forms of digital visual culture (Nakamura, 2008). That is, the underlying intention is my own consideration of how digital communication and visual culture construct a normative image for my child's life and my relationship to her.

I recognize that a relatively small number of the total population of the world has daily access to the kinds of technologies I discuss in this imagining, and that the pros and cons of how these technologies inform parent-child relationships are not matters of concern for all parents. Further, because I identify as an upper middle-class, heterosexual, North American, Muslim, male of mixed race and ethnicity, I do not wish to project or predetermine the ways in which my future daughter will construct and present her own subjectivity with respect to class, sexuality, gender, ethnicity, religion, and race. As Mirzoeff (2009) notes, 'Race, class and gender were inextricably linked in a classificatory system that insisted that these categories be visible, as white European scientists viewed and attempted to control Black African bodies' (pp. 155–156). Similarly, I sense that because of the linguistic (English, Arabic, and French) and visible (skin and hair colour and facial features) markers I assume she will possess, given these qualities in her parents, I know my daughter's body will constantly serve as a reminder of colonized peoples, power struggles, and assumed gender roles. My interest in what follows is in how she will construct her own self-image and navigate the assumptions she encounters about who she is/should be viewed through digital communication technology and visual culture.

Before I continue, I must acknowledge this musing for what it is – a masked self-reflection about myself as a future father. That is, through this speculation about our daughter and who she might become, I consider indirectly who I might be as a parent within this relationship. As I anticipate her birth, I am occupied with questions and uncertainties about myself in my new role. Questions I pose about how our daughter will develop her sense of self in the context of digital communication technology are really questions I am asking myself about what it will mean to be her father. But there are other questions, too. Am I too old? Am I up to this challenge? How will I know how to be who she needs me to be? How will I know how to be a good father? How will I navigate the line between spoiling her and making her life comfortable? How will I present my racial, ethnic, linguistic, religious, and other identities to her? How will I frame my views on economic disparities and social justice? I am already imagining how I will position myself – literally and metaphorically – with respect to these and other questions, well aware that everything I do and say is potentially an educational experience. As the eldest son of four boys, I witnessed daily how my parents interacted with their sons. I know I will draw upon these memories in my ongoing evolution as our daughter's father.

From: Steve Carpenter <bscarpenterii@gmail.com>
Date: Wed, 18 Feb 2009 14:40:22-0600
To: B Stephen Carpenter II <bscarpenterii@mobile.me>
Subject: Musing about a/musing with you

Your kicking is how I am interfacing with you at the moment. I wonder about taking my first image of you with my iPhone and sending that image to eagerly awaiting family and friends. I have received similar images and e-mails from family and friends. Waiting my turn to return the favor has been tough. I often find myself telling people who ask about your due date, 'I cannot wait to meet her.' This is the case; I am very much looking forward to meeting you. I am looking forward to showing and sharing with you the wonders of this world. I am also trying to make sense of who you will be and what this world will mean to/for you and your development as a person, a young girl, a woman. The world you enter will be one in which you will take for granted such technologies like Skype, Facebook, and IM. How will these become part of you and you part of them? How will they shape who you will become? How will these technologies help the two of us know each other better, stay in touch, and 'communicate as father and daughter'? What will it be like the first time I put my iPhone into your tiny hands? What will it look like when your little hands first touch the smooth screen and tap on the rounded-corner apps buttons? What apps will you and I find most entertaining? I am looking forward to meeting you.

Love,
Papa

The series of e-mails that comprise much of this chapter are a means through which I can connect with my daughter prior to her birth through a form of digital communication technology I use daily. I cannot imagine not using this technology to communicate with her when she is old enough to type letters on a keyboard, although such text-based e-mail communication might be outdated by the time she is ready to use it. Video and audio e-mail may be the preferred mode at that point. I imagine mobile phones functioning like digital video recorders and enabling users to video-conference with each other in real time and store such messages in the in-box of their mobile devices. My own iPhone is replete with images and audio recordings of my family and friends. Their bodies are trapped, preserved, and admired within its confines. I also realize that although I am writing e-mails to my daughter, I could just as well be chatting, blogging, IMing, Twittering, Facebooking, YouTubing, or Myspacing with her, too. These technologies and social networks will change, evolve, fade from grace, and give way to other forms of communication. For those who have access, what will not change is the central premise and service they provide users; the digital substitution for interpersonal relationships of physical bodies. I am fully conscious of the complexities of the 'digital divide' and my existence among the affordances of these technologies is also the case for only a small fraction of the world's population who access and use them on a daily basis. As Ishaq (2001) underscored a decade ago, 'Today, there is virtually no technological constraint preventing access . . . The constraint, therefore, is purely financial' (n.p.) and imposed primarily by national policies, political struggles, and economic conditions. In fact, while visiting my future daughter's grandparents in the large urban centre of Tunis, just as is the case in small college towns in North America or other parts of the world, we are sometimes unable to access the Internet because of limitations set by service providers and other systems of power rather than by our inability to open our laptops.

From: Booker Stephen Carpenter, II <bscarpenterii@me.com>
Subject: Baby OC
Date: March 04, 2009 08:24:46 AM CDT
To: bscarpenterii@me.com <bscarpenterii@me.com>

Today your mother and I have an appointment to see Dr Bonds. We are eagerly awaiting your arrival ten weeks from now. Your due date is May 12. I know what it means to wait for people to arrive on an airplane or a train, but a due date is not exactly like an arrival time on a ticket. I know what it feels like to wait at the gate to see a familiar face come down the hallway after disembarking from a plane, but I do not have your face in my memory; I only have your face as I imagine it to be. I am sure I will recognize you once I see you.

Love,
Papa

B Stephen Carpenter II

Sent from my iPhone

I have been an avid television viewer since my early childhood. My mother proudly tells the story of how she and I waited for weeks for the first episode of *Sesame Street* to air in the fall of 1969. Now, as an adult, I spend hours after dinner with my wife, reclined on the couch in the living room with our Sony Bravia in front of us presenting a seemingly non-stop line of sit-coms, police and law dramas, late night talk shows, and cooking or travel shows, while we each pound away on our respective laptops, attempting to keep up with e-mail or some other work-related deadline. On the television show *Without a Trace* one night we viewed one of the characters using Skype on her computer as a baby monitor interfaced with another. The teenage characters on other shows such as *Modern Family* and *The Good Wife* also use video conferencing to communicate with one another. These technologies are featured prominently, almost as digital characters within the storylines; they symbolically enable the characters to exist within a contemporary context where such modes of communication have replaced fixed-line telephone conversation. I wonder about when we will do the same with our daughter, seeing as how we use Skype and iChat to communicate regularly with her future grandparents, uncles, aunts, cousins, and friends.

Although I acknowledge the affordances and self-imposed concerns my access to this technology enables me, I must also admit that viewing the faces and bodies of loved ones on a computer screen, watching them move, and hearing their voices is now common practice for us. It was oddly similar for us to first see our daughter's face and body as visual representations on a computer screen through the digital technology of ultrasound well before she was born. As parents, we first knew her visually as a digitally represented body; of course, my wife had a far deeper and more intimate, biological relationship with our daughter and her body for many months prior. Through the ultrasound technology we listened to our daughter's heartbeat and watched her tiny black and white pixilated body move every now and again on a small computer screen. From that point on, we had an 'image' of her, provided by/through/because of digital technology; an image that we had to reconcile among our own individual, joint, and social preconceptions of how daughters and girls should look and be seen.

Henry Jenkins and his son Henry G. Jenkins IV (2006) offer us a nice example of an exchange between father and child. They present a dialogic essay inspired by the father's work related to media violence. Their chapter is an attempt to explore how television shows that depict violence 'might enable conversations about (and across) generational differences . . . Discussing television characters can encourage a process of introspection and speculation, which often opens up fresh ways of thinking and talking together. Sometimes you can hide behind the characters; sometimes they can help you find ways to bring thoughts and feelings into the open' (p. 228). In my own writing, I have argued in favour of using interpretations and discussions of television sit-com episodes as rich pedagogical sites (Sourdot & Carpenter, 2009). I now imagine having conversations with my future daughter similar to those between Jenkins, the father, and Jenkins, the son. I hope that our conversations will include interpretations with critical aspects as well; aspects that encourage careful considerations of technological devices and the systems in which they are used to promote images and expectations of gender, class, and social status. I want my daughter to be aware that her family lives with technologies that are neither accessible nor desirable to everyone, whether they are interested in them or not. In no way would I want my conversations with my daughter to function as an 'othering' of parents and children who do not have this same relationship with digital communication technology. The pervasive interface of digital technology in my life is merely a means to describe my life at this point in history.

I am well aware that television commercials can serve as catalysts for discussions about issues of gender, race, sexuality, stereotypes, and identity, all key aspects of contemporary visual culture (Mirzoeff, 2009). A popular T-mobile telephone company commercial offers such an example (see http://www.youtube.com/watch?v=-3cnbW8LSNk). The commercial is part of T-mobile's add campaign for 'who is in your five,' a reference to the user's five 'favourite people' which translates into a short list of the user's five most frequently called contacts. The commercial depicts a mother, father, daughter, and son sitting at the kitchen table. Apparently, the children have recently received their first mobile telephones. The mother asks, 'So, did you two kids pick your five yet?' The daughter responds with the names of five girls. The son recites the same five names and exclaims, 'Your friends are hot.' The daughter pleads with the parents to 'do something' about the brother's sexist and invasive response. The father suggests to the daughter, 'Maybe you should have uglier friends.' The mother nods in agreement.

Viewers of this commercial implicitly learn that the objectification of girls by boys is an acceptable practice, condoned by both parents through verbal and silent approval. Will my wife and I contribute to this hidden curriculum of objectification with our daughter, facilitated through the features of her mobile phone and its 'family plan'? While I know we have no plans to encourage our daughter to be a submissive object of the male gaze or to facilitate such an image of her based on the material goods she desires and needs, I am certain she will encounter numerous challenges as she negotiates the politics of being a teenage consumer and an inhabitant of various cultural, social, and national spaces (Maira & Soep, 2004). I wonder in what ways will the technology in our lives serve as means to inform the social identity of our daughter, intended or not.

From: Booker Stephen Carpenter, II <bscarpenterii@me.com>
Subject: Color my world
Date: April 2, 2009 12:29:02 AM CDT
To: bscarpenterii@me.com <bscarpenterii@me.com>

So, I have been thinking aloud about your cultural and racial identity. For some reason I had not thought much about it to this point, but lately it has remained a constant thought in my mind. I find this a bit unusual seeing as how so much of what I seem to be working on these days has to do with race, culture, and identity politics. As best as I can figure, you will be both an African American and an American African.

I like thinking of you as a North African North American.

Love,
Papa

Worldwide, the growth of Internet users is constantly changing (Barboza, 2008). Yet, while the realities I describe here are realities for me and my soon-to-be daughter, I realize using the term *the digital age* or an *age of digital communication* risks naming a current time period for everyone based on a limited world view and social, cultural, and political framework in which I see my own life. Further, I realize the problem I am setting up by even considering a worldwide or global context because of the potential to both set up the concept of globalization as a singular force rather than a complex array of definitions and interactions, and assume the existence of a globalized context/world at the risk of privileging my own act of naming above and perhaps to the exclusion of other forms of naming/knowing the world. Terms such as *globalized world* or *a global context* wrongly imply a uniform quality that disregards particular aspects of how local cultures and societies function within and outside of others and a politics of naming that implies only certain (self-identified) groups have the power or right to determine who is part of such a global world and who is not (Sintos Coloma, 2009). I see the increased international interest in virtual worlds as an interesting location to examine practices of naming and assumptions of the uniformity of visual identities.

Since 2007 I have used the online three-dimensional virtual world of Second Life (http://www.secondlife.com) to explore pedagogical possibilities for learning, teaching, and interpreting visual culture and curriculum. Within Second Life, like other virtual worlds and online massive multi-user games, each user creates an avatar, a digital representation within the virtual world that serves as the user's proxy. Users can change the sex, body shape, colour, size, and other visual attributes of their avatars by selecting options on a menu. Identity constructed in these ways is not fixed in relation to visual appearance. In this light, the facility with which users are in control of the visual representation of their avatars in Second Life opens a space to explore how identity is constructed, interpreted, manipulated, and represented.

One day shortly after logging in to Second Life, a flurry of banter started from some of the members of one of the groups to which I belong. Sometimes these exchanges are quite interesting and filled with information about upcoming meetings, talks, or events. Other times, these exchanges are simply discussions among members of the group who use the group IM feature as a way to stay in touch. These exchanges make me think about how people used to use telephone party lines to listen in to conversations between other people. In these instances, I try not to 'listen in' but this time, this day, I could not resist. One user, through the online virtual identity of his avatar was seeking digital representations of skin for his students' avatars for a course assignment. (In what follows, I have changed the names of the avatars to protect their virtual identities and the actual identities of their users.)

[12:32] Professor Avatar: Hi folks – my students are doing an in-world gender/race change assignment and though I have a lot of skins, I don't have a single MALE black skin or shape (and I've got mostly white girls in my class switching to black males). Does anyone have any they could send to me? Thanks!

[12:32] Avatar One: do you need a real skin or will demos do?

[12:32] Avatar Two: I'm sure one of the default Linden avs is a black male.

[12:33] Avatar Three: I'm on USDLC Star island now and they have some.

[12:33] Avatar Four: where do you find high-end female white skins for free?

[12:33] Professor Avatar: a demo will do, thanks!

[12:34] Avatar Five: also check for african-american groups.

[12:34] Professor Avatar: do you have a location for USDLC?

[12:34] Avatar One: lol high end and free are oxymorons.

[12:34] Professor Avatar: yeah, but I want them to change, not create a whole new avatar – they've been in already for almost two months.

[12:34] Avatar Four: hey never know how about not free.

[12:34] Avatar Six: NCI might have one in their freebie packs.

[12:35] Avatar One: or Soul.

[12:35] Avatar Four: ok ty.

[12:35] Avatar One: Platinum Africa also.

[12:35] Avatar One: and if demos will do go to Ebony and Ivory.

[12:35] Avatar One: and Ebony and Ivory.

[12:35] Professor Avatar: Ok – good suggestions, thanks; I thought I'd see if any of you just happened to have any in your inventory that were copyable.

[12:35] Avatar Six: http://slurl.com/secondlife/Kuula/55/168/29.

[12:36] Professor Avatar: ok, thanks!

[12:36] Avatar One: my alt has a few but I don't think they copy.

[12:36] Avatar One: and the freebie place where I got them no longer exists.

This exchange brought to mind the various ways in which the identity of our daughter as a mixed-race North African North American Arab American Muslim girl will be presented, represented, interpreted, and stereotyped through various online forms and formats. How easily will she be able to become her own avatar and change her skin or 'pass' as Arab or American or African American when it is most convenient to do so? How will her actual skin be interpreted by the T.S.A. as she goes through airport security and has her passport swiped and read digitally? How will her body be scanned by digital cameras and monitors and optically by human eyes? How will her skin be read and viewed by others through digital technology? I can only imagine how her identity, or those with which she might identify, can and will be critiqued on Websites or indirectly through avatars (Nakamura, 2008) made accessible online in the future as she comes to know herself. She will have to come to terms with her layered identity as mediated through digital technology, and adopt a most likely identity of a 'global soul' (Dolby & Rizvi, 2008), comfortably negotiating various international sites physically, linguistically, socially, and digitally, as she examines critically the global cultural economy (Kenway & Bullen, 2008).

What seems clear to me about my daughter's future identity and its mediation through digital technology is that her North American subjectivity will take a decentred role among the total number of Internet consumers and producers worldwide. At some point during the summer of 2008, the China Internet Network Information Center in Beijing announced the number of Internet users in China had reached approximately 253 million (Barboza, 2008). This number was about only 19% of the total Chinese population but larger than the number of estimated users in the United States, at about 70% of the population. Barboza (2008) also noted that such an increase in Internet use creates political challenges and opportunities for government leaders and private citizens. In the process of coming to terms with her layered identity through online content, my daughter will have a greater and greater chance of seeing herself in juxtaposition with more and more users who live outside of her physical home in North America.

From: Booker Stephen Carpenter, II <bscarpenterii@me.com>
Subject: We are always in relation to technology
Date: April 17, 2009 08:07:05 PM CDT
To: bscarpenterii@me.com <bscarpenterii@me.com>

As I write this, your mother is lying on the sofa, with her small laptop computer propped on a pillow. Your due date is less than a month away and your mother has been placed on bed rest for the remainder of the pregnancy. Among her constant companions have been her Blackberry and her Acer computer with which she stays in touch with family, colleagues, students and friends. Your little body is warm and cozy in close proximity with these devices. These devices will be considered ancient by the time you are old enough to use them for your own communication with other people. As I watch your mother sending e-mails, IMs and talking with your aunts, uncles, cousins and grandparents on Skype, I cannot help but think about how these devices and technologies are so close to you physically but so far away at the same time. I imagine your first video-conference with your grandparents overseas – the first time perhaps you see and recognize another person, or even yourself, through digitally mediated technology.

I wonder about your first text message on your first mobile phone. What will it say? What will that machine look like? What will you look like using it? Will you be a Blackberry or an iPhone kid? Will these be out of style when you are ready for such technology? I am looking forward to reading what you send and hearing your voice in my head as you read your message to me the way people do in television sit-coms.

Love,
Papa

B Stephen Carpenter II
_____
Sent from my iPhone

For me, part of the anticipation of the birth of our daughter was my image of the future – our future – with this little girl in my life. At once, the relationship with my wife – physical, emotional, interpersonal, and otherwise – would soon change and a new relationship with a new person would begin, and continue into the future. In some sense, I was imagining in a proleptic space (Slattery, 2006), as my past and future merged into the present. But these imaginings about three people together were taking place with only the visual evidence of two bodies; the third body always implied visibly within the form of her mother. Above I noted, 'I cannot help but think about how these devices and technologies are so close to you physically but so far away at the same time.' This reality is a way of life for numbers of people around the world who actually create such devices for less than a living wage but yet are unable to purchase them, own them, and use them to stay in touch with their own families. I admit my own access to the devices and networks that make them accessible at the risk of overlooking the realities of the lives of other people. One size does not fit all.

Another ritualized aspect of the anticipation of our daughter's birth emerged through the decision-making process of selecting her name. Several months prior to her due date, my wife and I constructed a list of potential names that I kept on my iPhone. We solicited suggestions from friends and family members, and made our own contributions. We decided early on that our child would have a double last name to signify her life as the embodied relationship of her parents. In this light, I typed each potential name on the list as a complete name – first name, middle name, last name, last name – as a means for us to imagine her through written form before actually seeing her in a physical one. Each week prior to her birth, we deleted a name from the electronic list, a process that continued until the day we finally made our selection, in the hospital. Finally, we selected her name from our final list of candidates on the day we were discharged from the hospital; I held my iPhone in my hands, and my wife held our daughter's tiny body in her arms.

This same phone, referred to as both a smart phone and a mobile device, serves as a surrogate for my own sight, hearing, voice, and memory. In the months after her birth, it has become the primary means through which I have captured still images of our daughter's body and through which I have shared these images with friends and family, either by simply revealing the screen of the phone to another person or by sending an IM or e-mail with a digital photograph attachment. I have used the audio recording app on my phone to capture the sounds of her crying, and I listen to these brief recordings periodically. These digitized audio recordings, coupled with the digital images of her on the same phone, enable me to recall my daughter's body mediated through my prosthetic mechanized senses. Interestingly, these same digital communication technologies will enable her, as they do currently numerous workers across the globe, to participate as part of a transnational labour force engaged in the 'virtual migration' (Aneesh, 2006) of data and information rather than bodies from homes to worksites. Her cultural identity might take the form of a 'transcultural' subjectivity (Mirzoeff, 2009), a 'hybrid product of networks' (p. 41), built of linguistic, national, racial, geographical, and other connections facilitated by the digital communication technologies she uses and encounters.

From: Booker Stephen Carpenter, II <bscarpenterii@me.com>
Subject: Sitting waiting for you
Date: April 22, 2009 10:08:12 AM CDT
To: bscarpenterii@me.com <bscarpenterii@me.com>

Well, you are full of surprises little one.

Yesterday we had your week 37 check up. Dr Bonds said we should plan to induce labor next Friday. Then, at 2:00 a.m. you changed the plans. So now I am sitting in LDR5 and your mother is in the bed with an epidural, feeling 'comfortably numb' as you make your slow descent and prepare for your grand exit/entrance. We are surrounded by technology beeping and counting and measuring and monitoring your little body and your mother's body. Your mother and I are using our respective Blackberry and iPhone to cancel meetings or IM students and colleagues of our absences today – we are careful not to reveal the surprise of your arrival prior to your due date.

Your mother has switched to her iPod, listening to some soothing tunes as the contractions continue to remind and prepare us both for you.

Ok, I have to go. I look forward to meeting you later today, kid.

Love,
Papa

B Stephen Carpenter II

Sent from my iPhone

Resting beneath the surface of my thoughts about our daughter are considerations about the degree to which digital communication and visual culture will function as normative images for her. Who do these technologies expect her to be? What expectations do I have for her because of the current state of our digitally mediated existence? Similarly, in considering *technoculture* – interdisciplinary scholarship and politics of the intersection of technology and cultural studies – During (2005) warned, 'No one knows exactly where it is heading or indeed exactly what it is' (p. 137). I would like to think that our daughter will become whoever she chooses to be, but I know no matter how strong she is as a young girl or woman, she will always be constructed in relationship to the technologies she uses, the ways others use that technology in relationship to her, and the social, cultural, economic, and political systems that encourage or inhibit such use. Will she be a Mac or a PC? Perhaps she will be a Linux or Open Source kid. Will she be iPhone or Blackberry; or Droid, or something else? In some ways, the technology she uses will say more to others about who she is than who she is will have to say about her technology. Whoever our daughter chooses to become, I hope she might live at some level as a *cyberflaneur* (Kenway & Bullen, 2008) and use 'information and communications technologies (ICTs) as tools for inquiry and digital technologies for the production of visual and written commentary and critique' (p. 24). Again, like Kenway and Bullen (2008), I am aware that there are current and future daughters who 'do not have ready, adequate, or ongoing access to ICTs' (p. 24).

My digitally enhanced relationship with our daughter started before she could even use it. I listened to her digitized heartbeat. I saw her grainy pixilated black and white body in the doctor's office computer screen. On my PowerMac I read about the most efficient techniques to swaddle her little body based on results of a Google search. Through fluid and skin, she listened to music on my iPhone downloaded from iTunes. Her mother's pregnant body was the focus of Skype video conferences with both sets of grandparents, text messages sent and received on mobile phones, and photographs sent and received as e-mail attachments and uploaded on my MobileMe site. Our daughter was surrounded by technology, defined by it, stimulated by it, and measured by it, even before she could use it or recognize it.

But in all of this musing, I am left with numerous ongoing questions. When do digitally enhanced relationships begin? How do digital technologies work towards the construction of relationships between parents and children? How are the identities of parents and children informed by digital technologies, at what cost, and for what gain? How will I negotiate a digitally mediated relationship with my daughter? How does digital communication and visual culture construct a normative image for my child's life and my relationship to her? I am certain that answers to these questions are not fixed and will not be easy to identify. I am certain that our daughter will be 'born digital' (Prensky, 2001), surrounded by a digitally mediated and enhanced world, able to speak 'the digital language of computers, video games and the Internet' (p. 1) as if they were extentions of her own body.

Certainly, this musing could be extended further to challenge through lenses such as anti-colonial and post-colonial and feminist views on the intersections of globalization, subjectivity, and digital communication technologies. Perhaps my daughter, as I imagine her to be/come in her day-to-day role as combination cyberflaneur, global soul, and transcultural being, will critically consider her engagements with digital communication technology and act accordingly with more facility and depth than her father has here. I am eager to explore questions and critical readings of our digitally mediated relationship further in the future, a (digital) future that now includes our daughter, Ranya.

From: Booker Stephen Carpenter, II <bscarpenterii@me.com>
Subject: Epilogue
Date: August 22, 2010 12:39:12 AM CDT
To: bscarpenterii@me.com <bscarpenterii@me.com>

My dear Ranya,
I have wanted to write this e-mail to you for some time but have not found words until now. Your entire lifetime has passed since I last wrote

to you. As I revisit our conversation, this message is by far the most difficult – perhaps because I am now writing to you as someone I know
rather than someone I imagine I know. We have just returned from a
wonderful visit with your grandparents, aunts, uncles, and cousins in
Tunisia – this is in fact your third trip to North Africa. You seem to be
comfortable being pushed in your stroller through long corridors and
waiting areas in airport terminals by parents weighted down with carry-
on baggage. You have already passed through airport security about two
dozen times. Digital cameras, monitors, metal detectors and human eyes
have scanned you. You have had your passport swiped and read digitally. Homeland Security, border guards, customs officials and *la douane*
have ordered us to remove your shoes and have tested your bottles for
your/our security.

Over the past 16 months, some of the questions I posed previously still
linger, yet others now seem less important. I am still not certain about how
the technology in our lives will serve specifically as means to inform your
social, racial, cultural, religious, or gendered identities, however I now
know more about your life as a digital native. You are a veteran at Skype
and respond to that odd cartoon-like swooping sound whenever the laptop cover and application open. Several times each week, you sit on my
lap or dance around the living room as we Skype with the grandparents in
North Africa and North America. You recognize them on the laptop screen
and display selected toys by holding them up near the camera. You know
how to open my iPhone and navigate the interface by sliding your tiny
index finger across the smooth touch screen. I like to peer over your shoulder as you hold it in your two little hands, shifting its orientation, tapping
buttons and keyboard keys with your thumbs, and periodically sending
e-mails or making international phone calls without my knowledge. In
fact, your tiny fingers created your first drawings on my iPhone using the
Brushes app several weeks before your mother and I invested in analog
crayons and paper. Like my early viewings and memories of Grover on
Sesame Street, you have taken a keen interest in Elmo through DVDs and
videos we access online. And I am amazed that you already know how to
navigate among the three remote controls we have in the living room, one
each for the DVD, DVR, and Sony Bravia television.

While I know that you have access to these technologies as an inherent
part of your life, I feel I must work to ensure that you develop a critical awareness that access to these technologies is not equally available to
most citizens of the world due to politics and economics. Your mother
and I hope one day you will realize that your family on both sides of the

Atlantic Ocean currently lives with technologies that are neither accessible nor desirable to everyone, and that not all parents and children have this same relationship with digital communication technology. We also hope you come to realize that humans are in fact capable of existing without these digital technologies.

I am still left with numerous ongoing questions about our digitally enhanced relationship and how it will be constructed and evolve; how our identities as parent and child will be informed by digital technologies, at what cost and for what gain; and, how we will negotiate our digitally mediated relationship. I am still not sure how easily you will be able to become your own avatar, 'change' your skin, and 'pass' as Arab or American or African American. I am not certain how you will construct your own self-image in light of the waiting negative assumptions and expectations you will face as a mixed-race North African North American Arab American American Arab Muslim girl as seen through digital communication technology and visual culture. I cannot yet state for sure how the identity politics that surround visual re/presentations of other mixed race, mixed ethnicity, multilingual, trans-continental selves/others like Barack Obama [mixed race president of the United States], Keith Ellison [Muslim member of the U.S. House of Representatives], Rima Fakih [Arab and Muslim Miss USA] for example – as portrayed through digital communication technologies and visual culture – will work toward the construction of normative images of your life and our relationship. What I can say for sure is that your mother and I will do our best to provide you with an environment that encourages critical reflection so that you might develop your own sense of who you are and what that means, in all of its complexity.

As I write these final lines of this e-mail to you, I am reminded of the pervasive presence of digital communication technology in our lives. Thank you for allowing me to identify and question some of my own blind spots with respect to these technologies and the roles they might play in the construction of our lives together. Thank you for allowing me to engage in this digitally mediated, quasi-epistolary self-reflexive project.

So, as I reflect on the lingering questions – questions about you but also about what it will mean to be your father – I still do not know for sure what these technologies expect you/us to be. What seems clearer to me now is that I may not have made explicit my awareness that being your parent would not merely be a matter of simply nestling into a fixed identity. I knew then – and know more fully now – that I never aspired to become some/other person who would perform a prescribed role of parent, but rather I hope to continuously live in a critically conscious state of always becoming your father.

Love,
Papa

B Stephen Carpenter II
_____
Sent from my iPad

References

Aneesh, A. (2006). *Virtual migration: The programming of globalization*. Durham, NC: Duke University Press.

Barboza, D. (2008, 26 July). China surpasses U.S. in number of internet users. *New York Times*. Retrieved from http://www.nytimes.com.

Bloland, H.G. (2005). Whatever happened to postmodernism in higher education? No requiem in the new millennium. *Journal of Higher Education, 76* (2), 121–151.

Bolt, D., & Crawford, R. (2000). *Digital divide: Computers and our children's future*. New York: TV Books.

Burbules, N.C., & Callister Jr, T.A. (2000). *Watch IT: The risks and promises of information technology for education*. Boulder, CO: Westview Press.

Dolby N., & Rahman A. (2008). Research in international education. *Review of Educational Research, 78* (3), 676–726.

Dolby, N., & Rizvi, F. (Eds.). (2008). *Youth moves: Identities and education in global perspective*. London: Routledge.

During, S. (2005). *Cultural studies: A critical introduction*. London: Routledge.

Ishaq, A. (2001). On the global digital divide. *Finance and Developement, 38* (3), n.p.

Jenkins, H., & Jenkins, H.G. (2006). The monsters next door: A father-son dialogue about Buffy, moral panic, and generational differences. In H. Jenkins, *Fans, bloggers, and gamers: Exploring participatory culture* (pp. 226–247). New York: New York University Press.

Kenway, J., & Bullen, E. (2008). The global cultural economy and the young cyberflâneur: A pedagogy for global citizenship. In N. Dolby & F. Rizvi (Eds.), *Youth moves: Identities and education in global perspective* (pp. 17–32). New York: Routledge.

Maira, S., & Soep, E. (Eds.). (2004). *Youthscapes: The popular, the national, the global*. Philadelphia, PA: University of Pennsylvania Press.

Mirzoeff, N. (2009). *An introduction to visual culture.* (2nd ed.). New York: Routledge.

Nakamura, L. (2008). *Digitizing race: Visual culture of the internet.* Minneapolis, MN: University of Minnesota Press.

Prensky, M. (2001). Digital natives, digital immigrants. *On the Horizon, 9* (5). Retrieved from http://www.marcprensky.com/writing/Prensky%20-%20Digital%20Natives,%20Digital%20Immigrants%20-%20Part1.pdf.

Richardson, W. (2008). Footprints in the digital age. *Educational Leadership, 66* (3), 16–19.

Sintos Coloma, R. (Ed). (2009). *Postcolonial challenges in education.* New York: Peter Lang.

Slattery, P. (2006). *Curriculum development in the postmodern era.* (2nd ed.). New York: Routledge.

Sourdot, L.A., & Carpenter, B.S. (2009). (Over)turning the tables: Aliens in America as a curriculum of identity construction and (multi)cultural violence. *Journal of Cultural Research in Art Education, 27,* 107–121.

7 *Harriet's House:* Mothering Other People's Children

TARA GOLDSTEIN

Harriet's House (Goldstein, 2010) is an ethnographic play in which a mother and her three daughters negotiate the challenges and politics of transnational/transracial adoption in a same-sex family.[1] It was produced for the first time on July 2, 3, and 4, 2010, at Hart House Theatre at the University of Toronto as part of the Toronto Pride Festival. The script is based on stories, ideas, and opinions gathered from written personal narratives by members of adoptive families and from interviews with them. The richness of ethnographic playwriting comes from three sources: the research from which a play script is created, the reading or performance of the play, and the conversations that take place after the reading or performance. In these follow-up conversations, research participants and other readers or audience members have input about the conclusions of the research. The incorporation of audience input into ongoing revisions of a play provides an opportunity for mutual analysis, and helps researcher-playwrights create more collaborative relationships between themselves, their research participants, and the communities to which their research participants belong.

Scholarly and personal narrative accounts of transnational/transracial adoption suggest that it is a complex, political, and contested practice that raises many questions and issues for adoptive parents and their children. For example, anthropologist Patricia Turner Strong (2001) writes that transnational/transracial adoption is at once 'an act of violence and an act of love, an excruciating rupture and a generous incorporation, an appropriation of valued resources and a constitution of personal ties' (p. 471). Recent writing from the 'new adoption studies,' that is, work written by adoptees themselves (Armstrong &

Slaytor, 2002; Bishoff & Rankin, 1997; Clement, 1998; Klatzin, 1999; Lee, 2005; Register, 2005; Robinson, 2002; Trenka, 2005, 2009; Trenka, Oparah, & Shin, 2006), understands transnational/transracial adoption as 'the intimate face of colonization, racism, militarism, imperialism, and globalization,' and directs attention to the need for long-term solutions that address the root causes leading to children of colour being removed from their families and/or surrendered for adoption (Trenka, Oparah, & Shin 2006, p. 7). Writing from the new adoption studies also describes adoptees' experiences of racism, isolation, abuse, depression, addiction, and alienation which indicates that adoption across boundaries of race, nation, and culture can exact emotional and spiritual costs (pp. 4–5). Finally, writing from the new adoption studies demonstrates the ways in which transnational/transracial adoptees have been able to negotiate a variety of tensions within their adoptive families, rebuild connections to communities and families of origin, make productive meaning of their adoption, and create new identities based on their life experiences (p. 4).

Teachers, adoption support workers, and child and youth workers have much to learn from the transnational/transracial adoptive families they work with (Raible, 2006). *Harriet's House* is aimed at creating opportunities for teachers and other professionals to engage in such learning within the particular context of a same-sex family. In their groundbreaking anthology *Outsiders Within: Writing on Transracial Adoption*, editors Trenka, Oparah, and Shin (2006) identify a pressing need for new writing about the experiences of transnational/transracial adoptees raised by gay and lesbian parents. In staging a story of mothering 'Other people's children' (Delpit, 1995),[2] *Harriet's House* attempts to challenge the binary split between family life and classroom life described in the introduction of this anthology. In doing so, it attempts to create opportunities for thinking about both the mothering of Other people's children in the private space of an adoptive same-sex family and the teaching of Other people's children in the public space of a classroom.

This chapter begins with a synopsis and several scenes from the play that focus on the ways Harriet and her daughters Luisa, Ana, and Clare live out and negotiate the politics of transnational adoption in their family life. These scenes about mothering and daughtering across cultural, linguistic, and national borders have something to say to teachers and other professionals who are teaching and working across borders, and they are discussed in a commentary that follows.[3]

Harriet's House

Harriet's House begins in the middle of a heated argument between Harriet and her 17-year-old-adopted daughter Luisa. The daughter wants to go back to Colombia and work in the orphanage where she spent three years of her life but needs Harriet's permission to do so. Harriet, who wants Luisa to attend university the following January, refuses to give her permission to go. This is not the first time that Luisa and Harriet have been in a heated argument. They've been arguing from the time that Luisa and her younger sister Ana first came to live with Harriet in Toronto. Luisa took care of Ana at the orphanage before Harriet and her former husband Jonathon adopted them at the ages of 7 and 10. It was difficult for Luisa to completely give up mothering Ana, and in the end, both Harriet and Luisa had to learn to share their parenting of Ana. The argument between Harriet and Luisa ends when Harriet reluctantly gives Luisa permission to return to Colombia to work at the orphanage on the condition that she promises to begin university in the fall.

At the same time as Harriet is getting ready to send Luisa off to Colombia, she is getting ready to come out as a lesbian to Ana and Clare, her third, biological, daughter. Jonathon and Harriet divorced several years ago, and when Harriet began dating again, she discovered she preferred the company of women to the company of men. She is now in a relationship with a woman named Marty who wants Harriet to come out. But Harriet wants to wait until Luisa leaves for Colombia before coming out to her daughters and friends. Luisa leaves after Christmas, and Harriet comes out to Ana and Clare, and her close friend Anita. Anita is the founder of the international adoption agency that Harriet and Jonathon worked with when they adopted Luisa and Ana. Although Ana and Clare embrace Marty as Harriet's new partner, Anita does not, and the friendship between Harriet and Anita dissolves. Harriet knows she has to come out to Luisa, as well, but after the hurt of Anita's rejection, she keeps putting it off.

At the end of the summer, Luisa reluctantly returns to Harriet's house to attend university just as she had promised. Unfortunately, Harriet never did find the right moment to come out to Luisa while she was away. When the news comes out unexpectedly, Luisa is upset. Heartbroken that she still hasn't found out what happened to her birth mother, and angry that Harriet didn't tell her about Marty sooner, Luisa reneges on her promise to go to university and returns to Bogotá to continue her search.

The second part of the play takes place 7 months after the first part. Harriet has been diagnosed with breast cancer and has just finished chemotherapy. She decides to travel to Bogotá with Marty, Ana, and Clare and ask Luisa to come back Toronto. When Harriet and her family arrive in Bogotá, they find out that Luisa and Ana's birth mother died very soon after she left her daughters at the orphanage. For the last year and a half, Luisa's purpose has been to find her mother. Having lost that purpose, she's at a loss as to what to do next. Before coming to Bogotá, Clare led a fundraising campaign at her school to raise money for the orphanage, and she has come to Colombia with a $10,000 cheque. Clare proposes beginning a second campaign to raise money for a community health clinic. Harriet suggests Luisa come back to Toronto to raise money and spend some time with her family. She tells Luisa that her sisters need her. After talking with Ana, Luisa decides to return to Toronto. The play ends with Harriet and Marty deciding to get married to give their same-sex adoptive family social and legal legitimacy, illustrating once again, the complexities of living and loving in a same-sex, adoptive family.

Scene 6

(Set in Toronto: Luisa wants Ana to return with her to Colombia)
(Harriet's kitchen. Ana and Luisa are at the island drying dishes, pots, and pans. The music fades.)
LUISA: *Estas cambiada.* ('You're different,' in a fundamental way.')
ANA: You think?
LUISA: *Y no para bien* ('And not in a good way.')
(ANA SHRUGS HER SHOULDERS.)
YA NO HABLAS ESPAÑOL. ('You don't speak Spanish anymore.')
ANA: So what?
LUISA: *Es nuestro idioma.* ('It's our language.')
ANA: Speak Spanish with Clare. She can count up to a thousand now.
LUISA: *¡ Caramba muchacha!* ['Jesus, girl'!] *No quiero hablar español con* Clare. *Lo quiero hablar contigo.* ('I don't want to speak Spanish with Clare. I want to speak Spanish with you.')
(Ana shrugs her shoulders.)
Quiero que no lo tierdas. ('I don't want you to lose it.')

ANA: You've been home for less than twenty-four hours and already you're bossing me around. I don't need it here.

LUISA: *Aquí no vas a pasar toda la vida.* ('You're not going to be here all your life.')

ANA: *(Grounded)* Yes, I am.

LUISA: *(Switches to English)* No, you aren't. You're going to go back some-day.

ANA: How do you know?

LUISA: You're going to be curious.

ANA: About what?

LUISA: About how people in Colombia live. What our culture's like, what our music's like.

ANA: *(Puts down the dish/pot she's dried)* I know what Colombian music's like. I've heard it. Lots of times.

(She takes her dishtowel and snaps it against Luisa's backside playfully. It doesn't hurt.)

LUISA: Ow!

(She takes her dishtowel and tries to snap it against Ana's backside, but Ana moves away too quickly. Ana laughs.) There's more to Colombian music than Shakira, you know.

ANA: *(Picks up another pot, still grounded)* I like Shakira.

LUISA: *(Excited)* You need to hear some *Reggaetón.*

ANA: Shakira sings *Reggaetón.*

(She begins to sing 'Hips Don't Lie' from Shakira's Oral Fixation CD.)

LUISA: I mean real *Reggaetón. (Puts down the pot she's dried)* I want you to come back with me next summer.

ANA: I already have plans.

LUISA: What plans?

ANA: *(Puts down the pot she's dried and picks up a third one)* I'm going to work at Brian's camp.

LUISA: Brian, Brian, Brian. All I hear about is Brian. *(Beat)* He's the reason you don't speak Spanish anymore. He's the reason you act white.

ANA: You're behind, I've done four you've done one.

LUISA: *(Picks up a pan/dish)* Three. You've done three. *(Beat)* Don't you want to meet her?

ANA: Who?

LUISA: Our *Mamá.*

ANA: *(Puts down the dried pot and picks up another one and waves it in Luisa's face)* I'm way ahead of you. We should get the dishes done before Harriet gets back. Are you going to help?

LUISA: Where is she?

ANA: She's at the doctor. She told you.

LUISA: *(Starts drying again)* We have to find out what happened to her.

ANA: Harriet?

LUISA: No. Our *Mamá.*

ANA: If you haven't found out by now, she's probably dead.

LUISA: But there's no record of her death in our files. The Sisters looked.

ANA: So?

LUISA: So, there's a chance that she's still alive. And that one day I'll find her and we'll get a chance to meet her.

ANA: I don't need to meet her.

LUISA: I don't believe you. *(Puts down the pot)* You look just like her.

ANA: *(Suddenly angry)* Even if I do look like her, I'd never act like her. Every single thing inside of me comes from living here. In this family. In this country. *(Raises her voice)* If you want to go back to Colombia, go! You want to look for a woman who left us and who is probably dead, go! Go look for her. But I'm staying here.

(Harriet enters.)

HARRIET: What's going on?

LUISA: Nothing.

HARRIET: *(To Ana)* Why are you shouting?

ANA: She made me mad.

HARRIET: *(Light)* Just like old times.

LUISA: All I did was ask her to come to Colombia with me next summer and she freaked out.

ANA: I didn't freak out.

LUISA: Yes, you did.

(Puts down the pot she's drying, picks up another one)

ANA: *(Angry)* No, I didn't. I told you that I'm not going because I've got other plans. You just can't take no for an answer.

HARRIET: *(To Ana)* You don't want to go?

ANA: *(Trying to be calm)* No.

HARRIET: *(Trying to buffer the tension)* Well, there's no rush. Most of the other Global kids don't go back until they finish high school. You have plenty of time.

LUISA: *(Exasperated, puts the pot down with a bang)* You shouldn't try and influence her that way.

HARRIET: I wasn't trying to influence her. I just said there's no rush.

LUISA: Yes, there is a rush. She's not speaking Spanish anymore. She's losing it. *(Accusatory)* She's being robbed of our heritage.

HARRIET: And that's my fault?!

(CLARE, who has been standing in the doorway quietly enters.)

LUISA: She doesn't have a chance to practice. She spends all her time with Brian. She doesn't see any of the Globals anymore. Clare says you didn't go to Seder and you haven't been to any of the events since Passover. What's that about?

HARRIET: *(Worried now)* That's a long story . . . Let me make some tea and we can –

CLARE: I can do it.

HARRIET: No, that's okay, honey. I'll do it.

LUISA: What happened?

ANA: It's because of Marty.

LUISA: Marty? Who's Marty?

HARRIET: You remember my friend Marty. From school?

ANA: She's my new hockey coach.

CLARE: And she's Harriet's –

HARRIET: Clare, honey, could you go next door and ask to borrow some milk for the tea? We're all out.

CLARE: Okay. Luisa, do you want to come with me?

LUISA: No. You go. I'll stay here.

CLARE: Okay. ¡hasta luego!

(Clare leaves.)

LUISA: So what's the problem with Marty? Anita doesn't like her?

HARRIET: Anita has never even met her.

LUISA: So then why – ?

HARRIET: Marty's gay.

LUISA: So?

HARRIET: *(Brave, defiant)* And so am I. She's my partner now and Anita doesn't approve.

(There's a second or two of silence while Luisa absorbs the news.)

LUISA: She's your partner?

(Harriet nods.)

You're with a woman?

(Harriet nods.)

Why didn't you tell me? I called every Sunday. You could have said something!

HARRIET: I wanted to . . . but you were so full of stories of what you were doing in Colombia . . . they seemed more interesting than my . . . I don't know. I should've told you. I'm sorry.

LUISA: Sorry's not good enough.

HARRIET: Sorry's what I have to offer.

ANA: There's nothing to be sorry about. Marty's great. Everyone likes her. I like her, Clare likes her. She's even got Clare coming to our games.

LUISA: Are you planning on moving in together?

HARRIET: Someday.

LUISA: Someday soon?

HARRIET: I don't know. Maybe

LUISA: With Ana and Clare still living here?

HARRIET: Maybe. Why not?

ANA: Marty's great!

LUISA: Sshh.

ANA: Don't sshh me! This isn't Colombia. I'm not one of your orphans who you can sshh.

LUISA: *(Ignores Ana, to Harriet)* I don't think she should move in here.

HARRIET: Well, it's not your decision to make.

LUISA: Fine. I'm not staying anyway.

HARRIET: You made a promise that you'd go back to school if I let you go to Bogotá. You promised to give it a year. All your registration material is sitting here, waiting for you. I want you back to school next week. Just like you promised.

LUISA: I don't care about what you want or don't want. I'm done listening to you. I'm done hearing what you want me to do and not do. I'm 18 now and I am going to do what I want. I'm not interested in going back to school. There's only one thing I'm interested in. Finding out what happened to my real mother.

(Luisa leaves. Ana and Harriet look at each other in dismay and then Ana goes over to give Harriet a hug.)

HARRIET: What am I going to do about your sister?

ANA: What can you do? You have to let her go.

Scene 10

(Bogotá: Ana and Luisa discuss Harriet's request that Luisa return to Toronto)
(Outside an orphanage in Bogotá. Afternoon. Luisa and Ana are sitting on a bench.)

ANA: Everything is so much smaller.

LUISA: Yeah. I thought so too when I first got here.

ANA: The blackboard was bigger. The window.

LUISA: The bookshelf near the door.

ANA: It's really hot here.

LUISA: You get used to it.

ANA: It's hard to breathe.

LUISA: Take slower breaths.

(Ana slows down her breathing.)

And drink some water. That will help.

(Ana drinks some water.)

I'M GLAD YOU'RE HERE.

(Ana drinks some more water.)

ANA: I feel like I might pass out.

LUISA: You're probably dehydrated. Keep drinking. But sip it slowly.

(Ana sips some more water.)

SO DID YOU REMEMBER ANY OF THE SISTERS?

ANA: *(Soft)* All of them.

(She sips some more water.)

LUISA: Me too. I remembered all of them. It's incredible what they've done here with so little money.

(Ana sips some more water.)

ANA: Everyone here's so poor.

LUISA: I know.

ANA: Do you ever think about what would have happened if we had stayed here?

LUISA: Yes.

ANA: We would've had nothing.

LUISA: We'd be out working.

ANA: Doing what?

LUISA: I don't know. A few of the girls work in the orphanage. Cooking meals, doing laundry. Because I finished high school and can speak and write English, I'm allowed to teach. Lots of the girls go out and clean people's houses.

ANA: I'd hate that.

LUISA: It's safer than working in the sex trade. Lots of poor girls do that.

(Ana is shocked and is silent for a few seconds.)

Ana: Do you ever feel guilty?

LUISA; THAT WE GOT TO LEAVE AND OTHERS DIDN'T?

ANA: *(Takes a sip of water)* Yeah.

LUISA: No. What I feel is mad. Our *Mamá* didn't have to die. People don't have to die of pneumonia. If she hadn't been so poor she would've seen a doctor and gotten antibiotics. And she wouldn't have had to leave her two little girls in an orphanage to be adopted by a family who lived a world away from everything they knew and loved.

ANA: I feel guilty.

LUISA: Feeling guilty doesn't help anyone. Or change anything. I want to change things.

ANA: How?

LUISA: I don't know yet.

ANA: Are you coming back with us?

LUISA: Maybe.

ANA: Whose room would you sleep in?

(She drinks some water.)

Luisa: I don't know. My old room I guess.

ANA: You mean *our* old room. Which is my room now.

LUISA: *(Hurt)* You want me to share with Clare?

ANA: That depends.

LUISA: On what?

ANA: *(Takes another sip of water)* If you're coming back as my sister or my mother.

LUISA: What's that supposed to mean?

ANA: It means I don't want to have two mothers again. You and Harriet. I like having just one. Harriet.

LUISA: Harriet said you and Clare needed me.

ANA: We do. It's awful hearing Harriet throw up after chemo. I hate it. So does Clare. And it'll be better if you're home. But not if you're always mad at me for not speaking Spanish. And not if you're not nice to Brian.

LUISA: *(Sighs and rolls her eyes)* Brian. *(Beat)* You know, I was really glad to see her.

ANA: Who?

LUISA: Harriet. I missed her. A lot.

ANA: You should tell her.

Scene 11

(TORONTO: Luisa wants Harriet to reconcile with Anita)

(Harriet's kitchen. Luisa and Anita are sitting at the island stuffing Global Family newsletters into envelopes.)

Anita: *(Upset)* I didn't know.

LUISA: *(Surprised)* How could you not know?

ANITA: I don't know. I was busy. We stopped talking …

LUISA: None of the other Globals said anything?

ANITA: No. They must not know either.

LUISA: *(Angry)* How is it that none of the Globals know that Harriet has breast cancer? Did everyone cut her off?

ANITA: *(Defensive)* We didn't cut her off. She cut *us* off!

LUISA: Did you ever try to call her after that disagreement about Seder?

ANITA: Of course. *(Beat)* Once or twice.

LUISA: *(Angry)* Once or twice! You were close friends. She was the one who hosted all those Global Family parties. Why didn't you try harder?

ANITA: *(Defensive)* How hard did you try? You're the one who took off to Colombia when you found out about …

LUISA: Marty.

ANITA: Marty. What kind of name is that for a woman?

LUISA: I didn't leave because of Marty. I left to find my mother. And I didn't stop speaking to her. I spoke to her every Sunday. Just like before.

ANITA: And did you tell the Sisters all about your mother's new girlfriend?

LUISA: *(Hesitates, then)* No.

ANITA: It's not so easy, is it?

LUISA: But I didn't cut her off and I came back when she needed me.

ANITA: *(Sincere)* And I'm sure she's very glad to have you home.

LUISA: You need to apologize.

ANITA: What?

LUISA: We still don't know if they got it all. Or if the cancer will come back. If it does, we'll need help from you and the other Globals. You need to apologize so you can become friends again.

ANITA: I tried calling. She never returned my calls.

LUISA: She says you rejected her.

ANITA: I didn't reject her.

LUISA: Well, she thinks you did.

ANITA: Well, that's her problem. Tell me about you. Have you started fund-raising?

LUISA: *(Decides to allow Anita to change the topic for the moment)* I'm strategizing. I went to see the people at the Stephen Lewis Foundation. They raise money to support AIDS orphans in Africa.

ANITA: I know what they do.

LUISA: I like their philosophy. *(Careful, trying to avoid an argument)* They think that one of the best ways to help children is to support the orphanages in a way that allows them to stay in their own countries.

ANITA: *(Annoyed)* I hate all that talk about how bad it is to take children out of their country, out of their culture. They live in an orphanage, for God's sake. They have no culture.

LUISA: You know that's not true. Ana and I learned to read and write Spanish in the orphanage. We sang songs, played games. When we came here, we lost a lot of that.

ANITA: You can't tell me that growing up in an orphanage is better than growing up in a family.

LUISA: I know.

(There's an awkward silence.)

Anita: So how long are you planning to stay?

LUISA: I'm not sure. I'm thinking of going back to school. Marty says I should use the privileged middle-class life Harriet gave me to go to medical school so I can set up the clinic we're building.

ANITA: *(Annoyed again)* She didn't just give you a 'privileged middle-class life.' She gave you and Ana a loving home. A family. She gave you a mother!

LUISA: We didn't need a mother. We already had one.

ANITA: No you didn't. Your mother had died.

LUISA: But we didn't know she died. To us, she was still alive. And because she was alive in my mind, Harriet could never be my mother. She was just a woman, a very nice woman, who was taking care of Ana and me in a country far, far away from home until we were old enough to take care of ourselves and find our real mother. I never wanted to be Harriet's daughter. All I ever wanted was to go back to Bogotá so I could find my own mother and be her daughter.

ANITA: *(Angry)* I don't understand you.

LUISA: Well, Marty does.

ANITA: Is that so?

LUISA: Marty says it doesn't matter that I never wanted to be Harriet's daughter. What matters is that when Harriet needed me, I came back. That's what daughters do.

(Anita doesn't respond.)

   And that's what good friends do. She needs you back.

(Anita takes a look at her watch.)

Anita: What time did you say she was coming back?

LUISA: Five.

ANITA: And she knows I'm here.

LUISA: She knows.

ANITA: And she'll be happy to see me.

LUISA: If you apologize.

ANITA: It's been such a long time. What do I say?

LUISA: Hi. It's good to see you. I'm sorry you've been sick.

ANITA: You make it sound so easy.

(Offstage, Harriet and Marty are talking and are about to enter. Harriet is still wearing a bandana that covers her bald head.)

Anita: *(Looks at her watch)* She's early!

(Harriet and Marty enter carrying grocery bags.)

Luisa: *(Gets up)* Hi. Let me help you. *(Takes the bags from Harriet)* Marty, this is Anita Levinson from Global Family.

MARTY: Hi.

ANITA: *(Too loud)* Hello. *(Softer)* Hello.

LUISA: We're stuffing newsletters.

HARRIET: Just like old times.

ANITA: Hi. It's good to see you. I'm sorry you've been sick.

HARRIET: *(Guarded)* Thank you. *(To Luisa)* There are more bags in the car.

LUISA: I'll help Marty bring them in.

HARRIET: Thanks.

(Harriet sits down. Marty and Luisa leave. Anita tears up. Harriet stares at her.)

Anita: I'm sorry. It's such a shock. To see you so pale, with that *schmatte* on your head.

HARRIET: I didn't want a wig. They're too hot.

(Anita nods.)

So.

ANITA: So.

HARRIET: I'm really pissed off at you.

ANITA: *(More vulnerable than angry)* I'm really pissed off at you.

HARRIET: What?

ANITA: You never returned my calls.

HARRIET: You never apologized. I'm waiting for an apology.

ANITA: For what? Not inviting you to the Seder? That was over a year ago.

HARRIET: For deserting me. And the girls. Just when we needed you most.

ANITA: You put me in a terrible position.

HARRIET: What?

ANITA: You made me choose between you and the agency.

HARRIET: That's ridiculous.

ANITA: If I condoned your relationship with Marty and the Sisters in Colombia had found out, they would have cut us off. They would have found
another agency to work with.

HARRIET: Bullshit.

ANITA: Easy for you to say.

HARRIET: We visited the Sisters. All of us. As a family. They met Marty and
they liked her. No one cut us off.

ANITA: They liked her?

HARRIET: Of course they liked her. They admired her. She's the one who kept our family grounded during the surgery, through the chemo. After you abandoned us. *(Beat) (Raw with anger, sadness, regret, loss)* The irony would have been funny if it hadn't hurt so fucking much. The same woman who has dedicated her life to finding homes and families for abandoned children, abandoned one of the families she helped create.

ANITA: *(Shocked, then)* I'm sorry. I'm very sorry.

HARRIET: All right, then.

ANITA: *(Reaches out her hand)* Let's start again. Tell me about Marty.

Commentary

On Language Maintenance and Language Loss

At the beginning of Scene 6 Luisa wants Ana to speak Spanish with her. Ana refuses and tells Luisa to speak Spanish with Clare. It is Clare, Harriet's youngest Toronto-born, English-speaking daughter who wants to speak Spanish with her oldest adopted sister so that she can create an intimate relationship with her.[4] But it's not Clare that Luisa wants to Spanish with, it's Ana. She is worried that Ana is losing her ability to speak Spanish, and as a result is losing an emotional connection to the country they were born in, a country to which Luisa plans to return and make a life in. But Ana, who has important emotional connections in Toronto, for example, with her English-speaking boyfriend Brian, isn't as connected to Colombia as Luisa is. During Luisa's first trip back to Colombia, the family also lost contact with their 'global family,' a community of other transnational adoptive families in Toronto, when Anita rejected Harriet's new same-sex partner Marty. As a result, Ana hasn't recently connected to other adopted children from Colombia. This, too, has played a role in her investment (Norton, 1995) in English rather than Spanish. Angry at her sister's refusal to speak Spanish, Luisa accuses Ana of acting white and Harriet of robbing Ana of her heritage. Harriet insists that Ana's preference to speak English is not her fault.

The politics of language use and language choice in bilingual families and bilingual classrooms are complex and can be difficult to manage (Baker, 2000; Goldstein, 2003, chapters 2 and 3). Family members can hold different emotional and social investments in the languages that are spoken in the family causing linguistic tension and conflict.

Mothers and teachers living and working in multilingual environments need a sophisticated understanding of language use if they
are to support children in managing and maintaining strong family/
community ties across linguistic differences. Adoption researchers
and writers have demonstrated that many adopted adolescents, like
Luisa, go through a development stage of wanting to explore their
roots, and adoptive parents need to prepare for this moment in their
children's lives (Register, 2005). Providing children with opportunities to develop fluency in the language of their birth countries is
central to this preparation. In her second memoir *Fugitive Visons: An
Adoptee's Return to Korea,* Korean adoptee Jane Joeng Trenka (2009)
writes powerfully about the emotional consequences of not being
able to speak the language of her birth country as well as she speaks
English:

> Transnational is supposed to look like choices, is supposed to look like
> breaking boundaries, is supposed to look like freedom . . . Transnationalism
> is not supposed to look like sisters trying to rebuild their relationship after
> being unwillingly separated, families struggling to talk to each other . . . In a
> country where 'American' is used synonymously with 'white,' my inability
> to speak fluent Korean combined with my inability to be white is a defor-
> mity. I am a sort of monster, a mix of the familiar with the terribly unex-
> pected, alike a fish with a human face or a chicken that barks. (pp.109–110)

On Crafting Identity and Making Useful Meaning of Adoption

Like adolescent children living in non-adoptive families, transna-
tional/transracial adoptees use their adolescent years to begin crafting a set of identities or a set of identifications that they will continue
to hone and develop as adults. In addition to beginning this identity
work, they also begin the hard work of making useful meaning of
their adoption (Register, 2005). At the end of Scene 10, Ana asks Luisa
if she feels guilty that they were able to leave the orphanage when
other children were not. Luisa responds by telling Ana that feeling
guilty doesn't help anyone or change anything. She wants to change
things. Although at the moment Luisa isn't sure how she wants to
change things, she is sure that she wants to return to Bogotá and intervene against the poverty that killed her mother. To fulfil this desire (a
desire that reflects the call from adult adoptees for long-term solutions

that address the root causes leading to children being surrendered for adoption), Luisa begins to craft a transnational identity of a border crosser. In Scene 11, she tells Anita that she's thinking of going to university in Toronto and use the 'privileged middle-class life' Harriet gave her to go to medical school so she can set up the community health clinic she and Clare hope to build. At this point, the reader/ audience can imagine Luisa becoming a doctor without borders, an identity or identification that has grown out of her experience as a child living in a transnational adoptive family. The crafting of such an identity is a creative act that resists the pressure children of transnational adoptive families sometimes feel to assimilate to the culture of their adoptive countries, a pressure that some writers understand as an act of violence (Turner Strong, 2001; Register, 2005; Trenka, 2009). Importantly, Luisa has the support of her adoptive family in creating a life that brings her back to Colombia to change things.

On Homophobia

In Scene 11, Luisa is angry that none of the 'Globals' seem to know that Harriet has breast cancer, and have not provided Harriet, Ana, or Clare any support. The 'Globals' are the members of Global Family, Anita's social and support group of transnational/transracial adoptive families. Before Anita rejected Harriet's new relationship with Marty, Harriet had been a major contributor to the group's activities. She hosted all the Global Family parties that kept their adopted children and youth from Colombia connected to each other and to their cultural and linguistic heritage. When Luisa asks Anita why she didn't try harder to reconnect with Harriet after their disagreement about the Seder (Anita wouldn't invite Marty to her annual Global Family Seder and Harriet wouldn't go without Marty), Anita becomes defensive and notes that Luisa was also concerned about what the Sisters at the orphanage would think of Harriet's new same-sex family life. However, Anita's worry had different consequences for Harriet's family than Luisa's worry. Whereas Luisa stayed connected to her adoptive mother and her sisters, Anita's worry broke up the long-standing relationship she had with Harriet, Ana, and Clare. And in breaking off her relationship with Harriet's family, Anita disconnected them from the Global Family community that had been established to support adoptive families. When Harriet directly confronts Anita about her abandonment of her family, Anita offers an apology, which Harriet accepts. The reader/audience anticipates that the friends will try to recalibrate the relationship they once had, but are left wondering if things will ever be the same between the two of them. The reader/audience is also provoked to think about how unprepared Anita was to deal with the changes in Harriet's transnational/transracial adoptive family, how difficult it is for Harriet to challenge Anita's homophobia, and what Anita's homophobic withdrawal from Harriet's family cost them. While Harriet's same-sex transnational/transracial adoptive family needs to deal with the same complex issues as heterosexual transnational/transracial adoptive families, they also have to deal with the extra trauma of homophobia. As intersectionality theory (e.g., Crenshaw, 1991; Collins, 1990; Nakano-Glenn, 2000; Kumashiro & Mc-Cready, 2006) explains, the family's experience of linguistic conflict, Luisa's need to return to Colombia, Anita's homophobic rejection of Marty – which results in the alienation of Harriet's family from other adoptive families – and Anita's fear of homophobia in Colombia do not act independently of each other. They all inter-relate. They all intersect, creating an intersection of multiple issues for Harriet's family to work through.

Conclusion

Harriet's House is the first of two plays about I've written about Harriet's family. It focuses on Harriet's eldest adopted daughter Luisa, her experience of growing up in a transnational/transracial adoptive same-sex family, and the way she begins to make useful meaning of her adoption. A second play, *Ana's Shadow* (2011), focuses on Ana, Harriet's middle adopted daughter. As a set, the plays attempt to present the multiple and intersecting issues, perspectives, and experiences that emerge for transnational/transracial adoptive same-sex families and those who work with them. In doing so, the plays aim to link writing in the new adoption studies to pedagogical work in critical teacher education and critical social work studies. Reading an ethnographic script aloud or watching a performance of one of the plays allows readers and audience members to enter into the perspectives of a variety of characters who take a variety of stances on different issues and experiences around transnational/transracial adoption. Such an entrée provides them with an opportunity become aware of their own stances, and to reconsider these stances in light of the characters' experiences, experiences that in many cases, they have not had themselves.

Notes

1 In the introduction to their anthology *Outsiders Within: Writing on Transracial Adoption*, Trenka, Oparah, and Shin (2006) explain that many people who have been described in the adoption literature as 'intercountry' or 'international' or 'transnational' have begun to redefine themselves as 'transracial' adoptees. This redefinition emphasizes the ways adoptees feel they have been racialized throughout their lives, and works to highlight the connections between adoptees of colour who have been adopted domestically and adoptees who have been adopted internationally. In this chapter, I use the term *transnational/transracial* to describe adoptees to emphasize this moment of redefinition in the new adoption studies.

2 The phrase 'Other people's children' was coined by educator Lisa Delpit (1995) and refers to children of colour who have experienced cultural conflict and racism in schools staffed by large numbers of white, middle-class teachers. When white, middle-class teachers teach children from communities that are culturally different from their own, they teach 'Other people's children.'

3 A copy of the entire script is available from T-space, the University of Toronto's Research Repository, which can be accessed on web with the following address: https://tspace.library.utoronto.ca/. For a larger discussion of research-informed theatre and the writing and production of *Harriet's House* see Goldstein (in press).

4 For a discussion of language choice and its importance to relationship building see Goldstein (2003, chapter 1).

References

Armstrong, S., & Slaytor, P. (Eds.). (2002). *The colour of difference: Journeys in transracial adoption.* Sydney, Australia: Federation Press.

Baker, C. (2000). *A parents and teachers guide to bilingualism.* (2nd ed.). Clevedon, England: Multilingual Matters.

Bishoff, T., & Rankin, J. (Eds.). (1997). *Seeds from a silent tree: An anthology by Korean adoptees.* Glendale, CA: Pandal Press.

Clement, T.P. (1998). *Dust of the streets: The unforgotten war.* Bloomfield, IN: Truepeny.

Collins, P.H. (1990/2000). *Black feminist thought: Knowledge, consciousness and the politics of empowerment.* New York: Routledge.

Crenshaw, K. (1991). Mapping the margins: Intersectionality, identity politics and violence against women of colour. *Stanford Law Review, 43,* 1241–1252, 1262–1265.

Delpit, L. (1995). *Other people's children: Cultural conflict in the classroom*. New York: New Press.

Goldstein, T. (in press) *Staging Harriet's House: Writing and producing research-informed theatre*. New York: Peter Lang.

Goldstein, T. (2003). *Teaching and learning in a multilingual school: Choices, risks and dilemmas*. With contributions by Gordon Pon and Judith Ngan. Mahwah, NJ: Lawrence Erlbaum.

Goldstein, T. (2010). *Harriet's House*. Unpublished playscript.

Klatzin, A. (1999). *A passage to the heart: Writings from families with children from China*. St Paul, MN: Yeong & Yeong.

Lee, M.M. (2005). *Somebody's daughter: A novel*. Boston, MA: Beacon Press.

McCready, L., & Kumashiro, K. K. (2006). Race, sexuality, and education. In H.R. Milner & E.W. Ross (Eds.), *Race, ethnicity and education*, vol. 3, *Racial identity in education* (pp. 131–144). Westport, CT: Praeger.

Nakano-Glenn, E. (2000). The social construction and institutionalization of gender and race. In J.L.M.M. Ferree & B.B. Hess (Eds.), *Revisioning gender* (pp. 3–43). Thousand Oaks, CA: Sage.

Norton Peirce, B. (1995). Social identity, investment, and language learning. *TESOL Quarterly, 29* (1), 9–31.

Raible, J. (2006). Lifelong impact, enduring need. In J.J. Trenka, J.C. Oparah, & S.Y. Shin (Eds.), *Outsiders within: Writing on transracial adoption* (pp.179–188). Cambridge, MA: South End Press.

Register, C. (2005). *Beyond good intentions: A mother reflects on raising internationally adopted children*. St Paul, MN: Yeong & Yeong.

Robinson, K. (2002). *A single square picture: A Korean adoptee's search for her roots*. Berkeley, CA: Berkeley Publishing Group.

Trenka, J.J. (2005). *The language of blood*. St Paul, MN: Borealis Books.

Trenka, J.J. (2009). *Fugitive visions: An adoptee's return to Korea*. St Paul, MN: Graywolf Press.

Trenka, J.J., Oparah, J.C., & Shin, S.Y. (Eds.). (2006). *Outsiders within: Writing on transracial adoption*. Cambridge, MA: South End Press.

Turner Strong, P. (2001). To forget their tongue, their name, and their whole relation. In S. Franklin & S. McKinnon (Eds.), *Relative values: Reconfiguring kinship studies* (pp. 468–493). Durham, NC: Duke University Press.

PART 2

Desire

8 Living as/through Revolt: Judaism, Circumcision, and M/othering

DEBRA FREEDMAN

In this chapter, I explore mothering through the Jewish tradition of male circumcision. Through analysis of my memories concerning the decision of whether or not to have my son circumcised, I consider what it means to become a Jewish mother; what it means to mark the body as a sign of belonging to a community; what it means to question universals; and, what it means to get mired in complexities, multiplicities, and difference (Springgay & Freedman, 2007).

I am hyper-aware that this 'retrospective return' (Kristeva, 2002, p. 100) structures my perceptual experiences, organizes my memories, and provides purpose to my life events (Bruner, 2004). Jerome Bruner (2004) reminds us: 'In the end, we *become* the autobiographical narratives by which we "tell about" our lives' (p. 694). I see this retrospection, however, as a space to encourage, what Wanda Pillow (2003) refers to as, a 'reflexivity of discomfort' (p. 181): a reflexivity that is tentative, uncertain, and vague; a reflexivity that disrupts and renders issues malleable and in motion (Ellsworth, 2005); a reflexivity that challenges me/the reader, to make sense of who I/they might become (Miller, 2005).

I begin by discussing my theoretical framework, Kristeva's (2002) notions of intimate revolt. I then move on to analyse my memories. Understand that I do not intend to neatly resolve the issue of male circumcision or my process of revolt within the context of this chapter. Rather, I want to emphasize possibilities for deliberation and scrutiny and for multiple understandings of ideas and experiences (Lummis, 1996) with respect to mothering, pedagogy, and a bodied curriculum.

Revolt, She Said

I re-turn to my memories of the decision of whether or not to circumcise my son, through a Kristevian lens of revolt. Julia Kristeva (2002)
explains that the word *revolt* 'comes from a Sanskrit root that means
to discover, open, but also to turn, to return. This meaning also refers
to the revolution of the earth around the sun, for example. It has an
astronomical meaning, the eternal return' (p. 100). This returning, for
Kristeva, signifies an intimate revolt that allows for individual questioning of laws, norms, and values; it is a 'searching for truth through
a return to the past' (p. 100); it is an intimate revolt that is fragmented
with 'division, conflict, pleasure, and jouissance' (p.100).

Kelly Oliver (2005) explains, 'By revolt, Kristeva points to a challenge to authority and tradition, analogous to political revolt, that
takes place within an individual and is essential to psychic development' (p.77). This type of revolt is not mired in politics, but is situated
with/in the psyche – focused on change, mutation, questions, and
transformations (Bach, 2010; Oliver, 2005). Kristeva (2002) clarifies:
'it's precisely by putting things into question that "values" stop being
frozen dividends and acquire a sense of mobility, polyvalence and life'
(p. 12). This questioning, this intimate revolt, then, can be described
as 'an interrogation rather than a rejection' (Oliver, 2005, p. 80) – an
interrogation that allows for unlimited possibilities, support of self,
and connection with others (Oliver, 2005). As Oliver (2005) notes, this
type of revolt, while intimate and interior, still 'enables us to live as
individuals connected to others' (p. 77). She continues, 'We become
who we are through questioning and we remain open to meaning and
creativity only by continuing to question, continuing with this infinite psychic revolt. Indeed, psychic space is sustained by infinite revolt or questioning. These small revolts ensure both the individual's
autonomy and his or her assimilation or belonging within the social
symbolic order' (pp. 79–80).

Connection with others and awareness of the social symbolic order
is what makes revolt possible. As Hongyu Wang (2010) argues, 'There
is no revolt without a certain sense of the limit'(p. 380). She explains,
and 'interrogation of the limit does not mean overthrowing the limit
once and for all, but bringing more variety and flexibility to the limit'
(p. 380). That is, this type of revolt allows for a pedagogy that provides
for freedom within limits rather than constraint.

Oy Vey, Circumcision!

Twenty-four weeks into my pregnancy, the sonogram technician told us that the baby in my uterus was a boy. Koushik, my husband, wasted no time texting family and friends the news. And while Koushik was texting, and the sonogram technician babbled on about the position of the baby, I thought to myself, 'Oy Vey, circumcision! How are we going to manage circumcision?'

Judaism is matrilineal; Jewish law states that all children born to a Jewish mother are Jewish. Jewish boys are marked, however, by/through the act of circumcision. The Jewish ritual of *brit milah* – circumcision – is performed 8 days after the birth of a boy. *Brit* refers to the covenant/partnership between Abraham and God; *milah* means 'word' or 'to cut.' Although consideration is given if there are health concerns, the commandment in Genesis 17:10–14 orders the removal of the foreskin of the penis on the 8th day of the boy's life:

10 This *is* my covenant, which ye shall keep, between me and you and thy seed after thee; Every man child among you shall be circumcised.

11 And ye shall circumcise the flesh of your foreskin; and it shall be a token of the covenant betwixt me and you.

12 And he that is eight days old shall be circumcised among you, every man child in your generations, he that is born in the house, or bought with money of any stranger, which *is* not of thy seed.

13 He that is born in thy house, and he that is bought with thy money, must be circumcised: and my covenant shall be in your flesh for an everlasting covenant.

14 And the uncircumcised man child whose flesh of his foreskin is not circumcised, that soul shall be cut off from his people; he hath broken my covenant.

Jewish circumcision is celebrated. It is usually performed in public, by a *mohel* (the person who performs the cutting). And while the mohel performs the act of circumcision, it is the father's responsibility for bringing the boy to the mohel in order to fulfil the commandment. A big party follows the ceremony symbolizing the boy's entrance into the Jewish community.

My nephew's circumcision was a public celebration, a spectacle. Held at my sister's house, the whole family was there. I remember standing in the living room with a group of people. Not watching the circumcision, but watching the reactions of the men in the room. All seemed to be cupping their hands over their respective groin, pursing their lips to stifle yelps of pain, and suppressing in one moment, yet remembering and feeling in the next, the long forgotten body memories of their circumcision (Ahmed & Stacey, 2001; Butler-Sanders & Oliver, 2001; Irwin, 2000; Rhinehart, 1999; Springgay, 2003).

I must admit that I had never questioned the act of male circumcision, let alone my Jewish identity before. In fact, before I met Koushik, I took it for granted that *all* men were circumcised right after they were born, even those who were not Jewish. I understood the act of circumcision as a sign of belonging within the Jewish community, as a sign of Jewish identity, and as a surgery carried out because of health concerns (Pollack, 1995; Salecl, 2001). If I did not circumcise my son, the Jewish community certainly would reject him; if I did not circumcise my son, I would be sacrificing his Jewish identity (Pollack, 1995; Salecl, 2001).

Consumed by the commandment, caught up in dogmatism, slow to question, I thought circumcision was the norm. Kristeva wonders if revolt is even possible in today's current society:

> She claims that, within postindustrial and post-Communist democracies, we are confronted with a new political and social economy governed by the spectacle within which it becomes increasingly difficult to think of the possibility of revolt. The two main reasons are that, within media culture, the status of power and the status of the individual have changed. In contemporary culture, there is a power vacuum that results in the inability to locate the agent or agency of power and authority or to assign responsibility. We live in a no-fault society in which crime has become a media friendly spectacle and government and social institutions normalize rather than prohibit. (Oliver, 2005, p. 78)

I have vague memories of my initial, clumsy attempts to convince Koushik[1] that we needed to circumcise our not yet born son: 'I am Jewish, my son will be Jewish, it is a covenant with God, it is a commandment, so we have to circumcise.' Koushik, in his inimitable, 'quietest' way,[2] simply stated, 'I am okay if you want to circumcise; but you have to know why you are doing it. You cannot just say it is a commandment.'

Kristeva (2002) explains that, often, 'religions express a need for purity' (p. 105). She stresses, however, that the desire for purity should be situated within a context of revolt that does not get 'strangled by dogmatism' (p. 106), and she is aware of the 'spiritual anxiety driving religious dogma' (p. 106). Koushik's statement disrupted me, challenging me to re-turn to my understandings of Judaism. I suddenly found myself researching Torah stories of Sarah and Zipporah and re-turning to my mother's story of her role in my brother's circumcision.

Thinking Back through Our Mothers

Madeleine Grumet (1988) reminds us that the process of 'thinking back through our mothers' is 'an archaeology not of them but of our relation to them. It is the question of how to be separate and still recognize them in us, us in them, and us in each other' (p. 191). Grumet (1988) goes on to say that 'it invites us to recollect, to re-collect the process of our own formation . . . Because our separation from our mothers is rarely as defined as that of our brothers, we are more modest, a bit unsure. Beginnings and endings are not quite clear to us, where one leaves off and another begins' (p. 191).

Sarah and Zipporah

Traditionally, the role of the mother, within the ritual of circumcision, is not attended to or addressed. Haberman (2003) explains that 'circumcision is usually contained within the province of male ritual, performed by men upon the male organ' (p. 22). That is, God's commandment was given to Abraham only. It is Abraham, the father, who must perform the ritual cutting. Pollack (1995) notes that this absence of the matriarch begins with the Akedah, the story of the binding of Isaac. As the story goes, Abraham is called by God to sacrifice his son Isaac in an effort to show his faith in God. Abraham takes Isaac to be sacrificed without question. An Angel of God stops Abraham, saving Isaac at the last moment. Abraham instead sacrifices a ram.

God addresses Abraham, alone. Sarah – Isaac's mother, Abraham's wife, matriarch of Judaism – is not consulted. In fact, Sarah is not mentioned throughout the incident. At the beginning of the next chapter, there is a brief mention of Sarah's death. Pollack (1995) reads Sarah's exclusion, her ultimate demise, as a subversion of mother's authority, the death of the matriarch, and she writes:

I submit that this story, which lies at the nucleus of our religious and historical identity, is not only about faith. It is also, and most profoundly, about the shift of power and authority from women to men, about male domination which is always undergirded by the threat or implied threat of violence. The *akedah* is the definitive narrative of this paradigm shift . . . Circumcision arose to compete with matrilineal culture. It permitted the transfer of inheritance through patrilineal descent. Just as the *akedah* bound Isaac and Abraham to the male God, so circumcision bonds the male child to the men of his community throughout time and space and to the male God.

Haberman (2003), however, explains that '[viewing] Sarah as a passive, faint, misinformed mother contradicts the rabbinic view that counts Sarah among the righteous people for whom God causes the sun to rise and set' (p. 20). Instead, Haberman (2003) presents a more active reading of Sarah's death, understanding Sarah's death as the ultimate limit: 'Sarah drew her last breath, dispatching her soul as a messenger, racing to stay the blade. God, witnessing and apprehending the totality of her commitment, assented' (p. 20). Haberman's interpretation facilitates the continued existence of matriarchal power within Judaism, as he explains: 'Sarah argued that bestowing upon humanity the creative potency of childbearing is incompatible with the command for sacrificial life-taking. For Sarah, the sacrifice undermined nothing less than a foundation of Creation; humanity is empowered to participate in bringing forth and sustaining life, but not to control the taking of it by murder or sacrifice. The partnership with God that Sarah embodied as a life-giver, created in the divine image, was utterly undone by pitting love and loyalty to God against love and loyalty to child' (p. 20).

Sarah was aware of her duty to protect her child Isaac; her covenant was with her child, not God (Lummis, 1996). Haberman goes on in her re-reading of Sarah's actions during the binding of Isaac to note that, instead of sacrifice, the act of male circumcision would meet God's requirements of devotion.

Pollack (1995) and Haberman (2002) offer two completely different readings of Sarah. One reading condemns patriarchy and understands Sarah's absence as the ultimate death of the matriarch; the other finds strength and authority in the possibility of Sarah's actions. In either case, though, Sarah dies; the ritual of male circumcision is preserved as a body marking that confirms devotion and binds men, as a sign of belonging, within their community and to a male God.

There is only one mention of a woman performing circumcision, Zipporah, Moses' wife. As the story goes, on their way to Egypt, God confronts Moses, Zipporah, and their children. At that moment, Zipporah believes that God is going to kill either Moses or her uncircumcised son. In her effort to save Moses and/or the boy, Zipporah grabs a sharp stone and uses it to cut off the foreskin from her son's penis. Haberman (2003) explains that 'Zipporah's scene invites feminist access to the text and to an act from which women have mainly been excluded' (p. 22). Yet, Zipporah's reasoning is unclear to me. Is she showing devotion to a vengeful male God through the marking of the male body when she circumcises her son? Or, is she only circumcising in an effort to save her son's life and the life of her husband – which does not seem to be the intended reason for circumcision?

I did not feel connected to or included with/in these particular Torah stories nor did they help me to make sense of who I wanted to be as a Jewish mother. They made me question God and caused me to wonder what kind of a God would punish or kill a mother or a father for refusing to kill a son and/or for refusing to circumcise a son (Lummis, 1996)? For me these stories did not provoke devotion, rather, they caused ambivalence, hesitancy, and uncertainty. Moreover, they caused me to question my belief in a God who would punish me for refusing to carry out such a commandment, any commandment (Lummis, 1996).

My Mother

My identity, my understandings of who I am as a Jewish woman come from my mother. I grew up in a family with an eclectic mixture of Orthodox and Reform Jewish traditions. And while we belonged to a Reform temple, it was my mother's experiences growing up in an Orthodox Jewish home in the Fairfax Avenue area of Los Angeles that influenced my Jewish upbringing and identity. My mother was the keeper of religion in my family. She kept a kosher kitchen. She taught us to observe and celebrate Jewish holidays. She spoke using Yiddish words and phrases. She took us to Torah School every Sunday. She hoped all her children would marry someone who was Jewish.

It was difficult telling my mother that I was questioning whether or not to circumcise my unborn son. I was concerned she would take offence at my challenge of tradition and Jewish identity; but I was more anxious that she would feel I was confronting her decision to circumcise my brother. And while she retold the story of my brother's circumcision with ease, I could tell by the tone in her voice that my questioning made her a bit uncomfortable:

> Bubbe, grandma, daddy and I took Richard to Dr Persky's office. There was a rabbi who said some prayers. Even Dr Persky said some prayers. After it was over, Richard fell asleep in my arms on the drive home. I brought him in the house and he slept while family came over. To make everyone happy we had cold cuts for lunch. All the family in San Diego came. There was never any question, Richard would be circumcised; we were definitely going to do it, but I didn't want a public display. I didn't want the circumcision to happen in front of people. Bubbe wasn't happy about that.

Although there was a circumcision (note that my mother would *never* have questioned the act of circumcision), my mother did not acquiesce to Jewish convention by hosting a public ceremony. For her, *brit milah* was a private act, and she was going to play a role, a major role, in maintaining that privacy. In that moment, my mother was fully aware of who she was as a Jewish mother; she was engaged, present, conscious of her relationship with her son, with her husband, with her mother, with her in-laws, with her God, and with her Jewish identity. For me, my mother's authority in the story of my brother's circumcision, her renegotiation of the limits of Jewish culture, her revolt against the public nature of *brit milah*, caused me to wonder about ways I might be able to creatively re-negotiate the limits for my own son.

Provocation and a Call to Invention

I found myself seeking guidance from my family rabbi. I do not think I was looking for an answer; I was looking, however, for ways to negotiate, for ways to make sense of my own experience, and for possibilities for participating in a history that I was only beginning to make sense of. In that moment I was having difficulty with the either/or proposition of the commandment – *And the uncircumcised man child whose flesh of his foreskin is not circumcised, that soul shall be cut off from his people; he hath broken my covenant*. I thought the rabbi from my childhood might be able to offer some insight, some dialogue with/in a Jewish framework. I called him on the phone. Our conversation was brief:

RABBI: Hello Debbie. How are your parents?

DEB: They are fine.

RABBI: What can I do for you?

DEB: I am pregnant and we recently discovered that we are having a boy. I am conflicted about the issue of circumcision. My husband is not Jewish; he is not circumcised. And because I am Jewish the child is Jewish. I was just searching for some insight . . .

RABBI: Well, there is no question; you have to circumcise the baby. That is what you must decide.

DEB: Why?

RABBI: What is your address? I will send you some articles.

I hung up the phone feeling quite disconnected, suddenly constrained by an imposed limit (Wang, 2010). There was no deliberation, no debate. He was not interested in any questions I might have. For him, there was only one answer – 'you have to circumcise the baby.' For him, circumcision was not a commandment to be interrogated. Mark (2003) notes that many Jews, who often enter into spirited and even subversive debates concerning Judaism and Jewish culture, are hesitant to enter into discussions concerning the topic of male circumcision: 'Many [express] apprehension about drawing attention to circumcision, as if any kind of close look, no matter how historical or scholarly or textually based, just might undermine the vigorous YES that Jews have given this sign of the covenant over millennia' (p. xvi). Questioning male circumcision was a challenge to Jewish norms; it was an interrogation of Jewish universalisms and hierarchies. I seemed to be asking questions that shook the very foundations of Judaism. And yet, I had always understood Judaism as a religion that provided open spaces for questions, for debate, for multiple understandings, and varied interpretations. In this moment, it seems, I was to be compliant, docile, and obedient to my faith. I was not to question or complicate matters.

Dewey (1938/1997) reminds that 'mankind likes to think in terms of extreme opposites. It is given to formulating its beliefs in terms of *Either-Ors*, between which it recognizes no intermediate possibilities' (p. 17). The tensions and contradictions of my life, however, are much more complex than simple either-or propositions (Luke, 2010); I live in-between. Koushik and I have tried to blend our religious and cultural identities together in a postmodern meshing. *HindJew* was the phrase coined by my father-in-law at our wedding when he noticed how we were asking the Pundit and the Rabbi to intermingle our respective rituals. We continue to maintain and to re-present this merger in our dual-culture household – a Ganesha and a Mezuzah can be found on opposite sides of our front doorpost; our Ketubah and the image of the family Gods Sri Balah and Padmayati hang on opposite walls in our kitchen. On a daily basis, however, we manage and 'experience diverse and often ideologically conflicting sources of formal and informal pedagogies that often add both a special burden and a unique complexion to [our respective] identity formation' (Luke, 2010, p. 135). We each understand the world in different ways, our backgrounds so different – countries of origin, religions – yet sometimes so similar. Cultural clash and dissonance are a part of our daily lived reality (Luke, 2010).

I cannot help myself from thinking about the commandments from God in Exodus every time I look at the Hindu Gods in my house – *Do not have any other gods before me. You shall not make for yourself an idol, whether in the form of anything that is in heaven above, or that is on the earth beneath, or that is in the water under the earth.* But the wonderings I have are not about whose knowledges are of most worth or whose knowledges should be taught in our home, rather, the wonderings I have are of deeper pedagogical concerns, that is, how can I 'use what has already been thought as a provocation and a call to invention' (Ellsworth, 2005, p. 165)?

Revolt as Permanent Anxiety

Before my son was born, I was mired in literature, both for and against, male circumcision. The topic became our dinner conversation with friends. I knew who among our friends was circumcised; I knew who wasn't. I read and heard all sorts of arguments: Circumcision prevents disease; there is a higher rate of penile cancer in men who are not circumcised; I would never circumcise my son because it is just not natural; it is a tradition; I wanted my son circumcised because I'm circumcised; the American Pediatric Association does not recommend the routine practice of circumcision.

Most compelling for me was the issue of pain. Rhinehart (1999) explores the traumatic nature of circumcision in his psychotherapeutic practice with adult males, noting that 'various disturbing mental images and intense feelings often accompany the reemergence of this body memory, including the feel of sharp metallic instruments cutting into one's flesh (anesthesia is normally not used in circumcision), the sense of being overpowered by big people, being alone and helpless, feelings of terror, and a sense of paralysis and immobilization' (para. 6).

Mark (2003) also explains that many Jewish sources acknowledge the distress the infant experiences as a result of circumcision. For example, out of respect for the baby's situation, the Talmud stipulates the omission of the phrase 'happiness in his [God's] abode' from the blessings recited after the festive meal at a *brit milah*. As well, Mark (2003) explains that the medieval rabbi and pre-eminent torah scholar, Maimonides noted circumcision must be performed on babies because it minimized the pain of the surgery – 'the child does not suffer as much pain as a grown-up man because his membrane is still soft and his imagination is weak' (as cited in Mark, 2003, p. xvii) – and if the surgery was postponed to adulthood, the surgery would no doubt be avoided.

How could I believe in a God who commanded that a child's body be cut on the 8th day of his life with the intention of maintaining (or was it forcing) connection to a group and to a God (Salecl, 2001)? I was filled with such anxiety, not a stifling neurotic anxiety, but an anxiety that provoked me, challenged me. Kristeva (2002) understands 'revolt as permanent anxiety' (p. 104). She explains that this type of anxiety is not pathological, rather this type of anxiety causes one to explore identities, incessantly ask questions, and plunge into sensations. This type of anxiety is an intellectual work that lies midway between anxiety as a pathological state and anxiety as a manipulated consumer who accepts without question.

For me, this type of anxiety also connected with Dewey's understanding of inquiry as *trans-formation*. Dewey (as cited in Garrison, 1999) understood inquiry as an intimate relationship, a relationship in which experience (based on happenings and possibilities within our environment) and education become entangled in an effort to move the learner beyond what was previously understood. Dewey wrote, 'The resolution of a problematic situation may involve transforming the inquirer, the environment, and often both. The emphasis is on trans-formation' (p. 11). This trans-formation is a moving beyond formation, is a moving beyond taken for granted customs, traditions, institutions, and policies. Kristeva (2002) might also refer to this process as 'transformative creativity' (p. 101) – the ability to see another way, to move beyond compromise, to interrogate, to doubt.

None of this anxiety, none of this trans-formation, none of this transformative creativity, however, can be without the existence of the loving third. Oliver explains,

156   Debra Freedman

Intimate revolt is the process by which the subject-in-process displaces
the authority of the law, which it takes to be outside of itself onto its own
individual authority, which it takes to be inside itself. In this way, the individual belongs to the social in a way that supports its own sense of self
as well as its relations to others. This revolt is dependent upon a loving
imaginary third who beyond the punishing father of the law accepts the
individual/infant into the social through forgiveness . . . the individual's
revolt against the father of the law requires the prior guarantee, so to
speak, of the loving third's forgiveness and support. Intimate revolt requires a sense that love is the other side of the law and that the individual
can belong to the social. (p. 86)

For me, this loving third presented itself through Koushik's initial
provocation, my mother's ultimate acceptance of my inquiry, and my
belief that Judaism was a religion that allowed for questioning, debate, and deliberation (despite the obstacles I encountered). This loving third provoked my anxiety and caused me to question. This loving
third moved me to struggle with my identity as a Jewish mother in
relation to and with other Jewish mothers – to be comfortable with my
history (Gilbert, 2010), to be comfortable living with ambiguity, doubt,
and uncertainty. Pedagogically, this loving third calls us to re-consider
learning as a site of permanent anxiety. Wang (2010) speaks of playing
with limits; Lather (2007) writes about getting lost in the limits, of refusing a desire to know, to 'find what goes beyond what we know' (p. 13).
Getting lost, Lather argues, is a way of living with risk, anxiety, and
in tension. It is a process by which foundational, fixed, all-assuming
knowledge becomes unhinged:

if there are foundations – principles, rules, codes, laws of universal
validity – then all that is asked of us is to conform to them: to stick to the
rules, to learn the codes, to ingest knowledge, to implement the standards.
But if there are no foundations, then there is space for personal agency
and responsibility, for making meaning and taking decisions – while at the
same time recognizing the complexity and uncertainty that are an inevitable consequence of being human beings and not gods. (Dahlberg, Moss, &
Pence, 2007, p. 117)

On the 10th day of my son's life we named him, Samuel Amritya.[3]
The ceremony, like our wedding was a *HindJew* celebration. Surrounded
by family and friends, we welcomed Samuel into our community. We

whispered his name into his ear. We blessed him with the priestly benediction – May Adonai bless you and keep you; may Adonai's face shine upon you and be gracious unto you; may Adonai lift his face onto you and give you peace. We put silver bangles on his ankles. We said prayers in Sanskrit and Hebrew. And we told him, 'Be who you are, and may you be blessed in all that you are.' There was no mohel present.

Notes

1 Koushik was born in India and raised in a Hindu home. According to the Hindu belief system, Ahimsa (non-violence), circumcision is not a common practice. Historically, circumcision is a marker of difference between Muslims, Christians, and Hindus in India.
2 Owen Flanagan (2002) explains in *The Problem of the Soul* that [the quietist thinks that there is nothing worth saying, nothing sensible to be said, either about any conceivable positive characterization of God or about the denial of any characterization. Some people will see this quietist as tantamount to an atheist, and that may be a reasonable way to understand her. But she is not an atheist who disbelieves a certain conception of God. She sees no basis to coherently believe to be true or false any claim for any God' (pp. 207–208).
3 We chose the 10th day as it was a little over half-way between the 8th day circumcision ceremony in Judaism and the 11th day naming ceremony in Hinduism that South Indian traditions specify.

References

Ahmed, S., & Stacey, J. (Eds.). (2001). *Thinking through skin*. London: Routledge.

Bach, J. (2010, May). *'Just reading the book is not enough': Enacting revolt with middle and high school students*. Paper presented at Annual Meeting of American Educational Research Association, Denver, Colorado.

Bruner, J. (2004). Life as narrative. *Social Research, 71* (3), 691–710.

Butler-Sanders, L., & Oliver, K. (2001). The role of physical activity in the lives of researchers: A body-narrative. *Studies in Philosophy and Education, 20,* 507–520.

Dahlberg, G., Moss, P., & Pence, A. (2007). *Beyond quality in early childhood education and care*. New York: Routledge.

Dewey, J. (1938/1997). *Experience and education*. New York: Simon & Schuster.

Ellsworth, E. (2005). *Places of learning: Media, architecture, and pedagogy*. New York: Routledge.

Flanagan, O. (2002).*The problem of the soul: Two visions of mind and how to reconcile them.* New York: Basic Books.

Garrison, J. (1999). John Dewey. *Encyclopaedia of philosophy of education.* Retrieved 24 February 2010, from http://www.ffst.hr/ENCYCLOPAEDIA/doku.php?id=dewey_john.

Gilbert, J. (2010). Reading histories: Curriculum theory, psychoanalysis, and generational violence. In E. Malewski (Ed.), *Curriculum studies handbook: The next moment* (pp. 63–72). New York: Routledge.

Grumet, M.R. (1988). *Bitter milk: Women and teaching.* Amherst, MA: University of Massachusetts Press.

Haberman, B.D. (2003). Foreskin sacrifice: Zipporah's ritual and the bloody bridegroom. In E.W. Mark (Ed.), *The covenant of circumcision* (pp. 18–29). Hanover, NH: University Press of New England.

Irwin, R. (2000). Facing oneself: An embodied pedagogy. *Arts and Learning Research Journal, 16* (1), 82–86.

Kristeva, J. (2002). *Revolt, she said.* London: Semiotext(e).

Lather, P. (2007). *Getting lost: Feminist efforts toward a double(d) science.* Albany, NY: State University of New York Press.

Luke, C. (2010). Introduction: Feminisms and pedagogies of everyday life. In J.A. Sandlin, B.D. Schultz, & J. Burdick (Eds.), *Handbook of public pedagogy* (pp. 130–138). New York: Routledge.

Lummis, C.D. (1996). *Radical democracy.* Ithaca, NY: Cornell University Press.

Mark (2003). *The covenant of circumcision: New perspectives on an ancient Jewish rite.* Waltham, MA: Brandeis University Press.

Miller, J. (2005). *Sounds of silence breaking: Women, autobiography, curriculum.* New York: Peter Lang.

Oliver, K. (2005). Revolt and forgiveness. In T. Chanter & E. Plonowsk (Eds.), *Revolt, affect, collectivity* (pp. 77–82). Albany: State University of New York Press.

Pillow, W.S. (2003). Confession, catharsis, or cure? Rethinking the uses of reflexivity as methodological power in qualitative research. *International Journal of Qualitative Studies in Education, 16,* 175–196.

Pollack, M. (1995). Circumcision: A Jewish feminist perspective. In K. Weiner & A. Moon (Eds.), *Jewish women speak out: Expanding the boundaries of psychology.* Canopy Press. http://www.noharmm.org/pollack.htm.

Rhinehart, J. (1999). Neonatal circumcision reconsidered. *Transactional Analysis Journal, 29* (3), 215–221. Retrieved 24 March 2010, from ttp://www.cirp.org/library/psych/rhinehart1/.

Salecl, R. (2001). Cut in the body, from clitoridectomy to body art. In S. Ahmed & J. Stacey (Eds.), *Thinking through skin* (pp. 21–35). London: Routledge.

Springgay, S. (2003). Cloth as intercorporeality: Touch, fantasy, and performance and the construction of body knowledge. *International Journal of Education and the Arts, 4* (5). http://ijea.asu.edu/v4n5/.

Springgay, S., & Freedman, D. (2007). *Curriculum and the cultural body*. New York: Peter Lang.

Wang, H. (2010). Intimate revolt and third possibilities. In E. Malewski (Ed.), *Curriculum studies handbook: The next moment* (pp. 374–386). New York: Routledge.

9 Navigating M/other-Son Plots as a Migrant Act: Autobiography, *Currere*, and Gender

NICHOLAS NG-A-FOOK

> We must make peace with the women who teach our children and acknowledge our solidarity with the mothers of the other people's children if we are going to reclaim the classroom as a place where we nurture children.
>
> – Grumet, *Bitter Milk*

We start life swimming in suspense within our mothers' wombs. After crowning our entry into the world, labouring for that first breath, and severing our bodily entanglements with the placenta, how do men learn to re-member our first steps towards relational intimacies, and our infinite returns to those desired places of love and hate, life and death? And, as men, at what points in our journeys towards cultural conceptions of 'manhood' does the taste of 'feminine' love, turn towards *bitter milk?* Until recently, I knew little about my mother's life narratives that gave birth to the multiplicities of 'I' sitting here before you writing.[1] Elizabeth Gray has always existed to some extent, as the ideal mother I imagined she was, was not, or ought to be. Like the sands of time, my understanding of who she is, as mother, continually slips through my interpretive grasp and remains the silhouette of a diasporic narrative mirage:

> My name is Elizabeth Gray and in 1952 I was delivered at home into the hands of a midwife. During WWII, the Germans bombed the shipping yards on the Clyde River in Glasgow Scotland, across from my family's flat. Edward Gray, my father, served in the British army during the Second World War. When father visited us in Canada, he shared stories

with my children about the War, the Celtics' victorious soccer matches, or the most recent spy novel he was reading. Injured during a bombing raid at Windsor Palace, he was forced to leave the armed services. After the war my father worked from across our flat, as an invoice clerk, for Harland and Wolff, a company that built warships.

In this chapter, I migrate across the various shifting international landscapes of curriculum studies. I seek to understand how re/reading one's life narratives against/within/alongside this interdisciplinary landscape can provide a theoretical prism for navigating how mother-son relations are potentially conceived and delivered as men's life narratives. In turn, reading the works of various critical gender theorists as a politically pro-feminist conscious act provides a methodological filter, if you will, for how we might navigate our interpretations of such life narratives (Hesford, 1999; Pease, 2000). Feminist and masculinist theorists (such as but not limited to Digby, 1998; Gilmore, 1994, 2001; Munro, 1998a, 1998b), along with Pinar's (1994, 2000a, 2004; and in Pinar, Reynolds, Slattery, & Taubman, 1995) autobiographical method of *currere*,[2] have helped to shape how I de/re/construct the mother-son plots represented within this chapter. Between these intertextual margins, then, I draw on Pease's (2000) memory work with men to provide the reader an engagement with *currere* that works to stitch together mother-son narrative patterns of distancing, devaluing, blaming, and dependency. In turn, I illustrate how such narrative plots are often projected – acted out – on education's centre stage. Although women currently constitute the majority of all public school instructional personnel, like many mothers' life narratives, teachers' experiences, their respective narratives, still remain, as Miller (2004) reminds us, the sounds of silence breaking in the classroom.

Often mother-son relationships are delivered as autobiographical narratives of separation, separating, severance, severing, and the archaic condition of severalty, of being separate, rather than conceptions of interconnections and reunions.[3] Why is such severance necessary, and how is it deployed to support (symbolic) narratives of patriarchy? How is separation culturally, socially, psychologically, and economically re/produced through men's life narratives? In turn, how do such 'masculine' accountings provide the means to support such ideological re/productions? In such retellings, then, how do concepts of connection and attachment encompass our narrative navigations between the shores of mother-son plots and their bodily territories? How do narratives of connection and attachment provide a place, inside and outside of homes and schools, for severance to birth its existence into our lives? And, how do the constructions of such homes, the families within them, inform conceptions of distancing, devaluing, blaming, and dependency on education's centre stage? The vast limitless possibilities of complicating and engaging all of these questions go beyond the scope of this chapter.

> My grandmother was from a very wealthy family. She was Protestant and her family disowned her for marrying my grandfather, a devout Catholic. Her daughter, my mother, earned her living as a nurse and was born in Chapelizod, a subdivision in Dublin, Ireland. I remember after the war was over, waiting in line with our food stamps for butter, sugar, and oranges at the grocery stores. Mother gave birth to sister Caroline, stillborn between my eldest brother Eddy and Colin. She also had a miscarriage after me.

If in autobiographical writing, as a migrant act, mother and son life narratives are reproduced as a curriculum that pulls on the shifting tensions between separations and impossible reunions, how then, can one write autobiographically about relationships of love and hate without effacing a mother's life narrative, when writing itself entails effacement? And, to what educational purposes does such writing lend itself? Must it? How might I migrate autobiographically through my mother's life narratives and represent parts of her subjectivities without reducing her to a white, manic-depressive, alcoholic, first-generation immigrant to Canada, with her own traumas of premature deaths, while also expressing her agency, domestic authority, violence, and the feminine love she has for three sons, a husband, daughter-in-law, and three grandchildren? I wonder. And, how might we disrupt our capacities to wonder about our mothers' otherness? Indeed, who are migrant mothers before they land in new countries, give birth to sons, daughters, and/or marry (perhaps even trafficked to) husbands, that relegate (regulate) them to the corsets of domesticated spheres?

> My father was born in Glasgow, Scotland. His mother was from Dublin and his father was from the Isle of Barra. He injured his back while guarding German prisoners in Thurso. At some point during his duty at this prison, he slipped down some stairs and injured his back. In 1947,

he had to have a disc removed from his back and was demobilized from the British army. Then in 1959, he had to have two more discs removed. As a result of this injury, my mother took up employment as a nurse. I would later train at the same hospital. I am sure it was stressful for both of them because this was while the war was going on and my mother could see from the hospital windows the skies illuminating the docks as they bombed the shipyards.

In the first section of this chapter our mother-son's relational curriculum manoeuvres the rigorous and shifting terrains of collective memories, their mapped dis-comfort, in order to study and problematize the 'normative' injunctions of Pease's (2000) four mother-son narrative patterns. The second section works towards provoking the possible narrative limit-situations that emerge when mother-son narrative patterns are plotted on education's centre stage. Drawing on Grumet's (1988) and Pinar's (2004) theoretical works, in the last section I suggest that much like sons, politicians and bureaucrats need to rethink their imagined relationships with mothers and teachers, in order to understand how the gendered limit-situations of the idealized mother-son curricular plots are projected onto education's centre stage.

Narrative Injunctions between Mothers and Sons: Distancing, Devaluing, Dependency, and Blame

In his book *Recreating Men* (2000), Pease asks us to reconsider the four following 'normative' relationships of dis/ease between mothers and sons: distancing, devaluing, dependence, and blaming. Through interviews with men, Pease illustrates how the limit-situations of these discomforting narrative patterns work, in turn, to shape men's future relational conceptions of women's lives. 'Men's struggles with women in relationships,' Osherson (1992) maintains, 'are often based on unfinished attachment struggles with mother – their simultaneous desire to be close and separate' (quoted in Pease, 2000, p. 67). The American and Canadian public school curricula often teach boys to disavow (rationalize) a need for their mothers' feminine love, instead, reconstituting such curricular and pedagogical feminine love as *bitter milk*. However, 'whilst men and masculinity literature,' its canonical pen-man-ship, describes a boy's navigational separation from his mother as a wounding experience, 'one has to ask whether boys need to separate from their mothers' at all (Pease, 2000, p. 67). Instead, men must learn, Pease

suggests, to honour their mothers and develop relationships of interdependence with them, where narratives of separation and attachment
complement each other.

According to Pinar (2001), this wounding relation between mother-
child can be referred to as the matrifocality thesis which, in turn, places
'the mother as the key "object" in the process of social development,
and, more specifically, of gender identity formation' (p. 889). Boys are
expected, Pinar tells us, to reject their pre-Oedipal relation with their
mother during the positive Oedipal phase: 'Due to the rejection and
subsequent loss of the maternal identification boys lose (relatively
speaking) access to emotion, intuition, and relational potential' (p. 890).
The psychosocial construction of a boys' life narrative thus becomes
e/motionless and often shipwrecked at sea. Consequently, boys become more violent through 're-enacting the intrapsychic violence of
their identificatory separation from the mother' (p. 890). In the public
eyes of others, in the schoolyard, on the soccer field, in the hallways,
I never wanted to be socially recognized as a mummy's boy, nor remain in *Herland* (Gilman, 1979), to depend on mother for e/motional
support. Sliding along the backslash of such e/motional disavowal
introduces Pease's first narrative pattern – sons distancing mothers.
Before we travel towards mother-son plots, I would like to emphasize
to the reader that the following narrative navigations of distancing,
devaluing, dependency, and blaming, their pen-man-ships, are always
con(text)ually situated and, thus, forever on the way.

Escaping the Domestic Corsets of Herland

My memories of M-other-land and their narrative landscape begin with
a desire to be *Lost in the Barrens*, beyond the intertextual margins of
feminine love. Within the domestic landscape inside our home, I interpreted mother's authority as a barrier to the *Call of the Wild*, to its
patriarchal wilderness. At that time, I read her domestic authority as an
obstacle preventing my becoming a primordial manly beast. In turn, I
challenged her authority in order to escape to that imagined 'frontier'
of 'great' men – the public battleground that shapes 'perfect' men (Kasson, 2001). I assumed that escaping the hearth of our nuclear family
involved occupying, taming, and conquering the territories of a public
sphere. For me, this imagined public place, its patriarchal wilderness
was where the birth markings of manhood and its ritualized manly
metamorphisms awaited (Pagano, 1990). After losing such battles with

mother, I was relegated to my bedroom longing for the *Green Hills of Africa* (Hemmingway, 1935), to be Tarzan, or the Lone Ranger – masking myself with narratives of manliness. Like Terry O. Nicholson, my daydreams conjured up migrant narratives of escaping the perceived confines of *Herland* (Gilman, 1979).

> There were many ghosts present and absent lying on that couch, son. The childhood trauma of my parents' separation, the abuse and madness that took place in the asylum of our home, my depression at 17 as a nurse in the face of institutional patriarchy and the insanity of the psychiatric ward, my mother's suicide, with the migration and loss of family, alienation living in a new country, the loss of my uterus to cancer after giving birth to a third son. And, each time, each time, there was no time to mourn. Breakfast, lunch, dinners, playing the doctor's wife, the perfect hostess, the small town gossip, taking and picking you all up after school, to soccer practice, music lessons, volunteering at the music festival, with the badminton club, coaching soccer, teacher-parents' night, sitting and reading with you, teaching you how to add and write. And again each time, each time, there was no time for mourning what I had lost or sacrificed as a daughter, woman, a mother, and your first teacher.

In school, we (re)read his/stories, where immigrants migrated to North America to live a-merry-co-manly dream. Later, I learned on the schoolyard from other boys and men, and by watching my father interact with mother, that for a Chinese Guyanese man to accept his Irish 'white' mother's private authority, or feminine love in public, was to lose his self-respect (Pease, 2000). On this public stage, in the eyes of other boys, no man in his right (rational) mind wants to be called a 'mamma's boy.' Or, so some of us are taught. As a teenager, I did not understand why mother wanted me to stay suspended inside, while she was sleeping on the couch, or when she was passed out. Was she resting from the demands of domestic labour, or escaping its nuclear isolation? The living room sometimes had a familiar smell of alcohol. Mother often looked dead, lying there, ghostlike. An empty glass and favourite bottle rested at the edge of the couch, just out of reach of her extended lily-white arm, freckled with sadness. My immigrant father was absent, like many fathers are, at work, or off hunting and fishing in those evergreen woods of Canada.

I was always scared to wake mother. Possibly, it was not only mother's authority and love I was trying to escape, but also her illness of depression. Her alcoholism and/or manic-depressive illness were not acknowledged at the time. My escape was conflated with the asylum of a domestic sphere, mother's authority, an absent father, dis/ease and mental illness. Or, was it rather her dis/ease with immigrating to a new country and separating from her family? Or, was it the loss of her uterus after giving birth to her third son – prematurely losing a capacity to physically reconceptualize life in her curricular womb? I could not and did not understand her narratives of dis/ease and depression as a child. I was too preoccupied with my own dis/ease, like many boys are, of taking refuge within the asylum of a domestic sphere, while at the same time trying to escape its housed asylum of madness. At that time of reflection, of memory, of temporality, I was not aware of the traumatic severance (of suicide) between a daughter and her mother. Sometimes migrant sons justify leaving M-other-lands behind through narratives of devaluation, hoping to ease the bitter seasickness of such divided bodily and psychic territories. It is towards these devalued places that this narrative heads next.

> I had my first major depression at 16. I was always anxious. As a child every fall I felt sad. I recall going to the doctor who delivered me and he gave pills which just made me sleep. I was not able to function so I stopped taking them. I was working then at Ingram Brothers and needed my wits about me to work out the foreign currency exchange on their garments. Today, I know all about Seasonal Affective Disorder.

Motherhood Imagined as a Domestic Engineer

As young boys, my brothers and I sometimes watched my father yell and criticize my mother for her 'apparent' inadequacies, whether it was her drinking, her social skills at dinners with other doctors and their wives, her lack of 'formal' education, and/or simply her performances of domestication. Later, as I grew older and identified more with father's performance of patriarchy, I often ganged up with my brothers when taunting mother. We also learned a certain type of 'masculinity' taunting each other. I assumed that the place and practice of 'domestic engineering' was women's work, hence, believing in the normalcy of mother's, and in general women's, devalued labour. As young boys, we rarely offered to contribute to the domestic labour of the household. Perhaps my mother's hiring of a 'domestic engineer' helped in compounding how we coded, gendered, and devalued women's labour as simply taken-for-granted housekeeping.

> I left high school at 16 with my O-levels. I then worked for Ingram Brothers as an international bookkeeper. In high school I had been awarded a Royal Society of London certificate for excellence in accounting courses. After a year of working there I left because I was bored. During my time with the company I was offered three banking jobs but declined to take them because I did not envision myself working as a bank teller.
>
> In December of 1970, after turning 17, I applied to Nursing School. Although I missed the application deadline, I was able to work as an assistant nurse until I was able to officially enroll. I trained for 3 years. During my first year of training on the psychiatric ward I met your father who was in Glasgow University's medical school.

According to Pease (2000), 'a boy learns that if he wants to be accepted into a patriarchal society, he has to turn his back on his mother' (p. 71). One way to legitimize emigrating from M-other-land, and turn your back on its mothered landscape, is to devalue the social and cultural capital of *Herland* (Gilman, 1979). We fastened a corset around my mother's intelligence and suffocated the social, cultural, and economic capital placed on the labour she provided within this domestic sphere. Yet, I now realize that such domesticated labour, the subtleness of her feminine love, her performances of an Irish Glaswegian whiteness, its accentuated sociocultural capital, afforded her biracialized sons the 'democratic' freedom to participate in the daily world of Canada's public affairs.

Back then, I devalued and relegated the multiplicities of her subjectivities to the suffocating gendered constraints of a domesticated corset. At the same time, mother had agency and authority within the whiteness of this gendered corset. Behind closed doors, in the privacy of our house, although I challenged her authority, my access to the various social constructions of white masculinity, my navigations of the public space, and my educational survival depended on mother's nurturance of an Anglo-Canadian curriculum. Just as migrants depended on the stability and buoyancy of the different narrative ships that brought them across to North America, so do boys depend on their mothers. And, the conditions for surviving such racialized and gendered migrations depend on how our narrative relationships of dependence are conceived.

> One of my problems was a sense of being left behind. As a mother of three I was so busy with all of you. All I knew was domesticity. And after a while, I felt like an intellectual part of me was standing still. As a consequence, I would get depressed and drink to ease the pain.

Depending on a Mother's Feminine Love

The first and last time I drank alcohol with mother was at the age of 18 while we were in Glasgow Scotland for a cousin's wedding. The night before the wedding, mother and I stayed up late drinking, sharing her childhood stories of poverty, abuse, humour, life, and death. During that night of storytelling was the first time I learned about grandmother's suicide. Mother was only 20 at the time. Before then, the sober story was that she died of a heart attack. She remains the absent presence of drunken stories.

A few months after our return to Canada, I heard my father cussing at mother late one night. It was again about her drinking. The door slammed, as he left the house. The next day mother was in tears. She asked me to drive her to a friend's place, and to tell my father that she was leaving for Toronto to check into a rehabilitation centre. The first part of the program lasted for 3 months. Mother has not had a drink since. As the eldest son, it was my responsibility to take care of my youngest brother while she was away. We all came to realize that we depended on mother for her physical, emotional, and spiritual support. I remember being excited when she first returned. Yet, when I went to ask her to do the things she once did, she replied that part of the rehabilitation program was to take care of her/self first. The 'all-giving mother' that I fantasized about and depended on was no longer there. Was my idealization of mother, as Benjamin (1988) reminds us, a desire to dominate? I also resented acknowledging my dependence on her.

> My mother's grandfather, who fought with the original Irish Republican Army, was a Kenny and a 'wanted man' by the British army. My mother gave birth to three boys, Edward, Colin, Denis, and me. The first school that I remember attending was St Ninians, a co-educational public school. After I turned 7, my parents separated. I remember moving around a

lot with mother. Thirteen years later, at the age of 20, soon after my first child's birth, mother committed suicide.

Men are able to be supportive, Pease (2000) explains, but at the emotional expense of acknowledging their own needs and feelings. At times, putting one's needs aside becomes destructive and one's own neediness, Pease continues, can erupt in its relationships with other women. Rather than seeing such dependence as a sign of weakness, Pease suggests that men must learn how to develop interdependent relationships with their mothers and women. In turn, men might learn how to express their psychosocial needs in alter/native ways rather than demanding them. Yet, how do men (rationalize) blame the feminine love that supports a son's neediness?

Blaming Mothers

In April of 2004, my parents visited me in Baton Rouge. Near the end of our meal one night, mother shared stories of how her father used to beat my grandmother and uncles. The night before grandmother escaped her domestic corset, she took a steak knife to grandfather. In grandmother's absence before she committed suicide, grandfather made my mother and her brother Denis sit on the couch and watch him beat their brother Colin. As a result, Denis would constantly wet the bed at night, and my mother developed chronic bowl disorder.

My uncle Denis died of liver cirrhosis a few years ago. After the funeral, my grandfather and my uncle Colin approached mother and my youngest brother in the parking lot. They blamed mother for her lack of presence (feminine love) in Glasgow, bringing my mother once again to tears. My uncle Colin's unresolved issues with his mother, his loss of her to suicide, were often projected onto his sister in the form of a blaming narrative.

At the dinner table, father told mother that her life narratives always situate herself as the victim. He then referred to an incident that happened 3 years before this, while they were visiting me in Baton Rouge. He suggested that her constant victimization and our mother-son conspiracy led to the blowout and the eruption of my father wound 2 years ago.[4] That night I said everything that I had wanted to tell my father as a child and later an adolescent. I confronted, although with words, quite violently his patriarchal oppression. I threw my glass of wine against the wall after my father refused to apologize, and he then threw his along with the bottle. Like Laertes and Oedipus, we were two men at the crossroads of shattered egos, and this remains a deeply wounding experience for both of us. I then left the apartment slamming the door, unable to pick up the pieces of broken glass.

After his return to Canada, father later called to try and work through what had happened, which we did. Yet, at the restaurant that night in Baton Rouge, he blamed mother for that past incident. Perhaps, he was referring to the nights that mother and I stayed up crying together because of his patriarchal tantrums upon his return from work. Or, maybe it was due to his frustrations with the daily institutional racism he encountered, as a Chinese Guyanese doctor working at a remote rural hospital in northern Ontario. Or, maybe it was my mother's use of father's authority in his absence. 'Wait until your father comes home' was a common phrase. And, often it was not unwarranted. It was a way for my mother to implement what Grumet (1988) calls a pedagogy of patriarchy. Upon his return, father would have to discipline, often in colonial style caning my body and mind, on mother's request. Sometimes, it was on father's own accord. Other times, in her drunkenness, mother was the source of such violence. These incidences would provide mother with an opportunity to protect and console me after experiencing such violence. This is sometimes the madness children experience inside the asylum of the home.

I don't think that your father deliberately wanted to embody patriarchal performances of fathering you all. Looking back now, I would say that the performance of public authority is more of an expected cultural performance with Asian men among his family. However, in reality, women are in charge of the home and the children. And, it is a conscious choice that one of us had to stay home to take care of the children and the business. Your father's absence had to do with his work most of the time.

He was building a new medical practice. Also as a dedicated rural family physician he looked after a nursing home in Kapuskasing, worked long hours in the Emergency Room, and did obstetrics. He was on several committees. So, in essence, whatever time he had, which was little, he would go hunting and fishing which was always part of his culture. Yes, his absence was there, but for the majority of time it was for a good reason. Most importantly, he wanted to provide a better life for his family, which as an immigrant family takes hard work. And to this day, for the most part, our family has had a good life. ·

In such relationships mothers are sometimes blamed for conspiring with their sons and interfering with father-son relationships. Men who perceive such relationships as ones of over-mothering are led to calling others girly men. In fact, Pease suggests that pro-feminist men are sometimes referred to as 'mummy's boys.' A desire to become a feminist man is also seen as a desire to be dominated by the women he admires (Pease, 2000). His fascination with pro-feminism, Pease continues, is therefore regarded as a form of masochism. Perhaps mother-son relations migrate between sadism and masochism, domination and (gracious) submission (Benjamin, 1988; Pinar, 2004). The concept of blame sails on many different narrative ships – between the tumultuous e/motional seas of absence and over-mothering. Therefore, it is important to realize that the concepts of separation, distancing, devaluing, dependency, and blaming can also travel on many differing narrative ships that take different navigational headings from and towards their respective M-other-lands. Furthermore, such e/motional memories are constructed within the narrative layering of a theoretical womb, and hence, their social, cultural, and psychic constructions remain forever on the move. Let us now navigate our autobiographical headings towards other narrative headings.

Autobiographical Headings, Heading towards the Other

Although Pease (2000) constructs these four narrative patterns from memory work conducted with different men, I suggest that a man experiences one, or more of the aforementioned mother-son relationships at the same time or at different times in his life. Just as migrants arrive from different lands on specific narratives, ships that leave their Mother-lands and Father-lands behind, so do sons. Furthermore, Pease's analysis of men's memory work does not examine the psychosocial and political effects of race or heteronormativity on the relationships between mothers-sons (for examples, see the autobiographical works of Als, 1996; Gilmore, 2001; McBride, 1996; Sedaris, 2000). Nor does he cross-examine the historical, social, philosophical, and cultural constructions of an 'ideal mother' in his four narratives (see Kristeva, 1985). Narratives of biracialism, multiculturalism, dual citizenship, nationality, linguistic plurality, and place would further complicate the psychosocial constructions of our mother-son plot (see Ng-A-Fook, 2007, 2009). Do men's relationships with their mothers produce these four narrative patterns, or are these narratives used to reproduce such relationships? When writing their autobiographies, men must consider how certain life narratives of memories reduce mother-son relationships, their subjectivities, to a singular idiom. As a result of these concerns, I have strategically situated representations of mother's voice within intertextual excerpts in this chapter. For many men, it is important to emphasize that mothers have their own life narratives, desires, and conceptions of mother-son relationships. Yet, how might one plot, project, and act out the interpellations of such possible mother-son relationships on education's centre stage? As we migrate through the last part of this narrative landscape, let us re-member the aforementioned mother-son conceptions of distancing, devaluing, depending, blaming, and in turn, the 'ideological couplings' between the family and education.

> I need to challenge your autobiographical interpretations. You are holding a magnifying glass over the narrative trouble spots of your life. I feel you need to balance this mother-son plot with some positive narratives like your educational experiences with soccer, music, swimming, and playing badminton professionally. These are things I feel facilitated a strong source of positive self-esteem and in turn helped you to navigate your failures and successes in life.

Drawing on African-American autobiographical practices, Pinar (2004) asks us to re/consider autobiography as a revolutionary act that responds to the sustained bureaucratic and patriarchal epistemic violence of teaching and learning. 'Psychoanalytically,' Pinar (2004) maintains, 'that *currere* invites the interpretation of educational experience, scrutinizing manifest and latent meanings, conscious and unconscious content of language, as well as the political subtext of such reflection and interpretation' (p. 58). Engaging *currere* as an aesthetic writing praxis has afforded me a psychic and material place to scrutinize representational mappings of educational experiences, identities, ideologies, and subjectivities, as well as to study the relationships between such self-formations and the institutional foundations of schooling that shape them.

Here, Althusser's (1971/2001) theorization of the 'ideological State apparatus' might help us to understand how mother-son narratives are normalized within the institutional matrix of schooling. In *Ideology and the State* (1971/2001), Althusser explains,

> It [ideological State apparatus] takes children from every class at infant-school age, and then for years, the years, in which the child is most 'vulnerable,' squeezed between the family State apparatus and the educational State apparatus, it drums into them, whether it uses new or old methods, a certain amount of 'know-how' wrapped in the ruling ideology (French, arithmetic, natural history, the sciences, literature) or simply the ruling ideology in its pure state (ethics, civic instruction, philosophy). Somewhere around the age of sixteen, a huge mass of children is ejected 'into production': these are the workers or small peasants. (pp. 104–105)

The educational state apparatus is, then, an extension of a 'mode of production,' of re-production (in this case knowledge), which makes the (colonizing) tools of corporate exploitation and extortion possible.[5] Although teachers and students have already experienced educational systems of interpellation, autobiography provides the possibility to jive to a different educational dance, a democratic dance yet to come, within the current standardized beats of corporate North America. There is a historical relationship between the emergence of industrialization, corporatism, and capitalism on separating the spheres of (public) absent fathers and (private) domesticated mothers. Here is where this narrative can trace boys' separation from their mothers and the educational apparatus's alienation of certain bodies of knowledge.

There is an ideological state apparatus coupling (a patriarchal coupling, if you will) between family and education that continues to help North American corporate leaders to reproduce the necessary conditions for their (patriarchal) power to exist. In this coupling, relationship of bondage, fantasy of guarding the gates of epistemological migration, and construction of static ideals, teachers are placed under house arrest and submitted to the domesticated constraints of curricular corsets like an 'ideal mother' of an imagined 'bygone era.'[6] Let us turn this narrative towards such educational plots.

Plotting Mother-Son Navigations on Education's Centre Stage

I am a teacher, and I am a woman. I am a woman who teaches. I am a female teacher. I don't mean that I am a teacher because I am a woman. In my case I am a teacher despite my being a woman. This is important

to everything that follows. Until I actually began teaching, I disdained the
profession because of its association with women's work.
                                        – Pagano, Exiles and Communities

I attended André Carré, a French Roman Catholic school in northern
Ontario, from grades 5 to 8. In Grade 7 my identification with father and
my awareness of sexual desire intensified at home, on my migrations to
and from school, in the schoolyard, and during class. At the same time,
a longing to escape from M-other-land to an imagined patriarchal wilderness beckoned me. My first years in a faith-based elementary school
system, within its rural civilizing walls, were very difficult. Not only
was it hard because I had to learn French, a foreign colonial language, it
was also hard trying to speak this new language. Often other children
laughed at the way I enunciated its accented words. At times, although
I knew the answers to questions posed by the teacher, I remained silent
fearing that my peers would laugh at me. Consequently, I learned to
inhabit this civilizing place, in between its institutional walls of loneliness, with a sense of loss within my mother tongue, while fantasizing
about a patriarchal wilderness that still beckoned me.

  During the reprieves of recess, I often engaged in the violent 'manly'
dance of fisticuffs with other boys in the schoolyard because of their
unexplained laughter in class. Such laughter translated into a form of
questioning one's manliness. On many days, I had to stay after school
because of the violent physicality of such rural responses to this form
of gendered and racialized questioning. Some teachers, unbeknownst
to them, did not appease this pedagogical sense of institutional loneliness, of its soundless curricular dance. Instead, some made me stay
after school, to repetitively rewrite and erase myself on the blackboard,
if they heard the invisible accentuations of my mother tongue in class,
the hallways, or the schoolyard. In turn, I disrupted the beats of a teacher's daily pedagogical dance knowing that sitting in the hallway and
being a wallflower provided a temporary asylum from the laughter
and constant correction of the teacher. At the time, I could not foresee
the benefits of appropriating the curricular and pedagogical accentuations of a foreign tongue.

After my parents' separation I attended many schools across the
United Kingdom. Initially we moved to Nottingham, and lived with
my mother's sister. At the local school I was ahead of my grade level.

The administrators did not know where to place me. At first, they decided to put me into the 11+ class, which would enable me to go to high school the next year. They later reconsidered thinking that it would be too difficult for me to adjust socially to this older age group. For 6 months I learned utter nonsense at school. I remember a lot of painting. But, for the most part it was really boring. I worried of falling behind the other students back in Scotland.

And we did return to Glasgow after 6 months. I then went to St Peter Primary School. The teachers were made up mostly of nuns. The headmistress was Sister Mary Francis. And later it was sisters Mary Joseph and Theresa. All were great. And of course I was 6 months' behind the other students. So I had to work hard to catch up. Not too many kids wanted to associate with me. At first, I could not figure out why. Until one day, I was leaving with a girl, and her mother said, 'Don't play with her. Her mother is a bad woman. She is divorced.' After that incident, the other students ostracized me. I would stay after school, chat with the nuns, water the plants, and listen to some of their worldly wisdom. It was lonely, but I had been by myself for some time now and enjoyed the solitude. But, I was also no saint and spent time repenting for it in front of Our Lady of Fatima.

The name Ng-A-Fook was definitely not the norm among names such as *Trottier, Carriere,* or *Courshesne.* The Franco-Ontario students were aware of this and exploited it in the schoolyard. I was called names such as *Ng-A-Spook, Ning-A-Gook,* or *N_ _ _ _r-Fuck,* chink, and even slanted-eyes. As students developed their skills in oral storytelling, the racial jokes about Chinese people, and other outsiders, were often the focus of discussion in those small groups you see clustered around the schoolyard. The public space of the schoolyard is a theoretical womb where some of our first skills are developed to promote racism and misogyny. I never did come home and ask mother about the racial incidents that took place within the wilderness of the schoolyard. I was led to believe by my peers and some teachers that it was a 'normal' part of growing up. This informal form of schooling, its hidden curriculum, was an initiatory process of becoming part of a civilized society, of becoming a man. Yet, at the same time, confusion unsettled me, in the stories I shared about my narrative identities. At that time, I did not understand why other children made fun of me, for speaking a foreign language, of being racialized as different. Here is when I first learned to see my mother and father as racialized and gendered others, the differences between Chinese and white.

In these rural racialized, gendered, and linguistic territories of this religious schooling system, no one pulled me aside to explain the spirituality of being part this and/or part that. The teachers did not explain the partial knowledge we all did or did not have (Ellsworth, 1992). It seemed that my last name was the reductive signifier for constructing the multiple narratives for performing and representing an autobiographical 'I.' In high school, my accentuated performance of a foreign tongue did get better as did my performances of racialized and misogynistic comments. I became quite good in the schoolyard rhetoric of racial slurs. Some students would tell me, 'Chink get back on your boat!' Often, I would respond, 'At least my father can afford one!' Frequently, those who are oppressed become the gravest of oppressors. Paulo Freire (1970) explains that the oppressed 'are at one and the same time themselves and the oppressor whose consciousness they have internalized' (p. 32). As a doctor's son, I had quick responses for working-class students whose parents worked at the pulp and paper mill.

I turned away from my studies, and instead, attempted to empower a 'manly' self within the public sphere of sports like soccer. Much like being a 'momma's boy,' I was also made to feel ashamed of my father's Chinese Guyanese identity. As a socially constructed biracialized child, I thought I was privileged in the sense that I could abandon one identity construction for the other. Yet, in this abandonment, I left myself and became not an inhabitant within myself but 'un-homed,' within my mind, body, and soul. 'Being un-homed,' Tyson (1999) tells us, 'is not the same as being homeless' (p. 336). 'To be un-homed,' he continues, 'is to feel not at home even in your own home because you are not at home in yourself: your cultural identity crisis has made you a psychological refugee, so to speak' (p. 366). In Grade 8 the school administration placed me with a teacher who implemented a core curriculum and practised rote memorization as a pedagogical philosophy. They also separated me from a community of classroom friends. By mid-year, I was tired of completing worksheets. As a result, I was 'at risk' of failing that school year. I now remember experiencing the institutional alienation and isolation of assembly-line work with no sense of classroom friendships, or part of the community I had been part of the year before. One day, I broke down and told mother, 'I no longer want to be in school.' Narratives of separation and reunion were once again at work here.

I recall the summer of 1960. For the first time my father had agreed to come to Ireland with Mammy, Denis, and me. I was so happy. We went for a beautiful boat ride on the river Liffey near my Granny's house. One night Dad had gone out. Early the next morning, my grandmother was sitting on the top stairs, with a broom, waiting patiently. I sat down beside her. But, she told me to go back to bed. I was just about to, when I heard the gate open and my father walking toward the house. Granny pulled open the door, took the broom, and started to wallop him. 'You bring shame to this house and my name!' She told him. Afterwards, I never really gave it much thought. Inside, Granny told Mammy she had better do something, to think about her children. We returned home and things seemed normal. Later that summer we moved into a new house. And, I finally had my own room. Then November came and my eldest brother Eddie was home from his service at sea, which was odd.

One day, I returned from school and Mammy was preparing dinner as usual. I asked if I could play with the girl next door, a new friend. 'Yes,' she said. I was so happy and off I went. About an hour later Eddie came to get me. Of course, I always had to question why. But this time his tone indicated something wrong was happening.

After I entered the front door I could hear my parents shouting and screaming. Dad was sitting in his chair and mother was standing in her nurse's uniform. Mother was leaving dad. She was not taking any of us with her. I started to cry and begged her to take me. She told me to hurry up. On the pulley in the kitchen I had a favourite dress, which her sister made for me in the United States. I asked her, 'Please can I get my dress?'Mammy said, 'No you either come now, or I am leaving!' With one eye on her, and the other on the dress, we left. My fear of being abandoned was so great, in the end what was a dress? In the span of an hour my whole world had gone astray. No more house, no more fun with my brothers, only the clothes I stood in. That experience of loss was immense at that age. And, probably from that time on I suffered depression although no one ever talked about it. In fact, that hour changed our lives forever.

The isolation that many children and women experience in the nuclear home, at least since the industrialized era, is now found within the schools. Munro (1998a) stresses that the isolation of teachers and students resulted from the centralization of the curriculum, and its bureaucratization, in turn, functioned to disempower teachers (women) by removing the decision-making power over the curriculum from teachers and handing it to the supposed experts (men). I also remember progressive teachers who subverted the standardized and techno-corporate curriculum behind closed doors. At mother's request, the administration transferred me to the other classroom where the teacher, always behind closed doors, taught progressively. My grades improved by the end of that school year. I was happier at home. As a young boy, I continued to struggle, however, with my migrations between the domesticated spaces of the home and the public territories of a Catholic elementary school, where through female teachers the implementation of patriarchal pedagogies (of absent fathers) took place.

At present, in the United States, the No Child Left Behind Act and its current political plot featuring standardization and accountability work to reinscribe Pease's (2000) four mother-son narratives – distancing, devaluing, dependency, and blaming – onto education's centre stage. Politicians, most of whom are men, have distanced themselves, like absent fathers, through the implementation of standardized exams. Teachers in the public educational system, mainly women, are asked to implement, often oppressively, an absent father's national 'core curriculum' and its 'pedagogy of patriarchy' (see Grumet, 1988; Hirsh, 1999; Ravitch, 2000; Pinar, 2004). Not only does the continued pressure for a factory model of efficiency and standardization reduce teachers to automata, it also works to ensure that teachers (mothers) do not let our boys go soft (Pinar, 2004). As a result, teachers have lost, university educators are now losing their academic freedom to educational organizations, and in turn, their capacity to labour and conceive a curricular language, an institutional agency that provokes and questions the oppressive curriculum of an absent father. Teachers are, therefore, asked, coerced, to remain 'dutiful daughters' (Munro, 1998a), to perform their 'identification with fathers' (Grumet, 1988), and to comply with the politicians' insistence on our 'gracious submission' (Pinar, 2004). Like mothers of a 'bygone era,' teachers are thus ordered to sport teacher-proof curricular corsets.

In 1994, I decided to go back to school. At the time, two sons were away at university. Our youngest, in Grade 9, was still living with us. My experiences in the British educational system were completely different from what I encountered upon my return to schooling here in Canada. I remember our exams were all essays. There were no multiple choice, group projects, quizzes, or mid-terms. Instead, it was just one exam, which was pass or fail. We were taught to learn, memorize, and regurgitate. For two years I studied Social Work. We had a sister as our main teacher. It was stressful, but I enjoyed learning and being in school again. What amazed me was calling upon all my skills both as a mother and businesswoman. I was still running a home and the bookkeeping for my husband's family practice. I received my diploma in 1996. What I learned from those 2 years is that you are never too old to go back to school.

The current rhetoric of accountability suggests that we can depend on our teachers (our mothers) to save us economically and militarily. After the launch of Sputnik and during the Cold War anxieties, Kennedy became the first President of the United States to implement a policy for national curriculum reform. 'It expressed through innuendo,' Pinar (2004) maintains, 'that women – mothers and schoolteachers – were blameworthy in allowing American youth, specifically white male youth, to go soft' (p. 84). Is it the son's fear of dependency, the lack of permission to express male vulnerability, the desire to remain that heroic masked man that are once again at play on education's centre stage? Pinar (2004) continues, ' "accountability" would seem to be nothing more than a "projection" onto educators of what many businessmen and politicians themselves lack' (p. 164). Such reactions are possibly a man's misrecognition of himself, where in his repudiation of 'femininity,' imagined metamorphosis towards manhood, is projected as a lack of 'masculinity,' onto the schooling system. Our mothers, first teachers, daughters, and sisters have become political scapegoats, constructed by narratives of distancing, dependency, blaming, and devaluing. In their nightmares, in their narrative accountings, politicians imagine that teachers in the public schools are failing North America's children and neglecting their civic duties. This is, as Pinar (2004) stresses, the present nightmare of schooling.

If we depend on teachers, on M-other-land, to fulfil the future hopes and needs of our children, why is the labour of teaching continually devalued? Teaching remains, at least in the United States, one of the poorest paid professions. Consequently, its labour and capital returns remain corseted within the suffocating gendered straitjackets of motherhood and its respective affiliated domestic duties. Here bureaucrats assume, perhaps like sons, that an 'ideal teacher' should be the 'ideal all-giving mother.' There is a mother-son devaluation of domestic labour at play on education's centre stage. In reading Grumet (1988), Pinar (2004), and Munro (1998a), we can trace the genealogical feminization of education through Pease's mother-son plots of distancing, devaluing, dependency, and blaming. Men, politicians and educational bureaucrats, need to de/re/construct these curricular plots in order to develop and affirm policies that support interdependent relations that value and honour a teacher's ability to teach other parents' children. The No Child Left Behind Act may be a valuable diagnostic tool to measure the social inequities in certain American neighbourhoods. But the prognosis of such social inequities should not remove a teacher's agency to labour and conceive relationships between the school, curricula, and child.

Thinking Back through Our Mothers

> We, women who educate, are the ones who lead the children from first to second nature. *Educere*, 'to lead out,' to take the child by the hand to the bus stop, to the school, to the disciplines, to discipline. When we take them to school we take them to our father's house.
>
> – Grumet, *Bitter Milk*

It is late at night. I am at the office now as an absent father. There are no windows for me to look outside, while I try to work within. This father's academic house is cold and empty. As an assistant professor, I struggle with the institutional demands of Father-land. The silences of the hallways echo memories of a childhood 'left behind.' On this night, within the institutional walls of solitude, I am reminded that the synthetical, the last stage of *currere*, is the moment when one brings together past, present, and future limitations and possibilities in order to re-enter the present moment, hopefully, with greater self-knowledge. Nonetheless, I am having difficulty migrating across the various academic borderlands, through curriculum theory's customs, mired within an engendered and racialized history of national curricular policies. How, as teachers, might we reread and rewrite our narrative couplings between school and family? How, as men and sons, can we snuggle as writers with the discomforting memory work of distancing, devaluing, blaming, and depending? In turn, how might we continue to provoke how mother-son plots and their narrative constructions are acted out on education's centre stage?

Autobiographical writing, as *currere*, is a migratory praxis. Its narrative migrations, between regression, progression, analysis, and synthesis, have afforded me a place without an originary departure or final return, where I might critically examine past memories, present educational experiences, and future hopes within a Father-land's academic institution. 'When women think back through our mothers,' Grumet

(1988) explains, 'we look past the natural order expressed in physics, astronomy, biology, our second nature, to the first nature that male identity and male science have repressed' (p. 184). Therefore, must men think back through their mothers in order to reconnect with that first nature? If so, perhaps autobiographical writing, as *currere*, affords such an opportunity. Thinking back through our mothers can help sons, men, politicians, and educational bureaucrats to question the ways in which a national curriculum of disavowed 'femininity' projects onto – dominating through 'masculine' epistemologies and patriarchal ideologies – education's centre stage.

Autobiographical writing, as *currere*, supports a curriculum-lived-as-migrancy, one in continual transit, of departing, returning, thinking back, and writing forward. 'Migration offers us,' Rushdie (1991) writes, 'one of the richest metaphors of our age' (p. 278). 'The very word metaphor,' he continues, 'with its roots in the Greek words for *bearing across*, describes a sort of migration, the migration of ideas into images' (p. 278). Re-visiting life narratives through a praxis of autobiographical writing, as a migration between the shifting limits of M-other-land and Father-land, 'femininity' and 'masculinity,' provides a possible space for men to displace 'masculine' ideologies, its patriarchal baggage, and projected material images.

Looking back, I only wished I had gone for help sooner for my depression and drinking. Back then I was ashamed. I have many regrets about this. My family would not have suffered. And, my children would not have felt abandoned for 11 years. But, I cannot bring those years back. I have apologized to my sons and husband for what I put them through. I don't think for one moment it was easy for their father, let alone them.

Having said that, mothers need to know that their sons love them, too. Not just with a hug or a card, but by actually hearing them say these words. I can honestly say that I never heard my brothers say it once to our mother. This may have made a difference in her life. Once I was officially diagnosed with manic depression (bi-polar 2) and SAD, my life has been better.

I have been sober since 8 August 1991. I now pace myself and take my medication to keep my stress levels manageable. When my stress is high, I feel overwhelmed and begin to feel the ill affects of anxiety. Now when the fall comes I look forward to getting together with our quilting community to stitch & bitch. Beginning new projects with them helps me cope. I also plan for a trip somewhere sunny if possible during the winter with your father, and to visit our three grandsons.

In order for men, who are often politicians and educational bureaucrats, to reconnect with mothers and attune to our M-other-lands, to hear teachers talk back, perhaps such sons need to critically examine the general and specific ways in which they do or do not represent mothers within their life narratives. Men, sons, future fathers, can then, perhaps, reimagine and relearn how to love their mothers and ultimately themselves differently on either side of the border zones characterized by distancing, devaluing, blaming, and dependency. Engaging the aesthetic praxis of autobiographical writing, as an act of migration, as *currere*, then, provides men a place to reimagine, reconstruct, and reconceive the curricular and cultural corsets not only placed on mother-son relations, 'masculinity' and 'femininity,' but also on how such familial relations are acted on education's centre stage.

An understanding of mother-son plots and their couplings to education's centre stage, curriculum, and main actors is not fixed or final. On the contrary, like the relationships between mothers, fathers, sons, daughters, brothers, sisters, friends, students and teachers, school and family, self and other, such understanding continues to live inside a theoretical womb where the self is attached to others, where learning is suspended between life and death, reappropriating our curricular conversations and our representations, reuniting them or re-differing them, their bodily entanglements, their places; therefore, opening our capacities to conceive a perpetual birthing of otherness.

Notes

1 In the following pages, the life narratives situated in the displayed extracts represent my mother's voice. All of these life narratives are from various interviews conducted with my mother.
2 *Currere* is the Latin infinitive form for curriculum and means to run the course. Pinar's (2004) method of currere consists of the four following intertwining parts: regressive, progressive, analytical, and synthetical. In the regressive phase, one conducts free association with memories in order to collect autobiographical data. The purpose is to try and re-enter the past in order to enlarge and transform one's memories. The second phase, or the progressive, is where one looks towards what is not yet present. In the analytical stage, one examines how both the past and future inhabit the present. How might my future desires and/or interpretations of the past influence present understandings of our mother-son relationship, for example? At the analytical stage, how might I bracket such experiences in order to loosen emotional attachments and their respective limit-situations?

The synthetical is the last stage, where one brings together past, present, and future limitations and possibilities in order to re-enter the present moment, hopefully, with a sense of greater self-knowledge.

3 The *Concise Oxford Dictionary* defines *severance* as 'the action of ending a connection or relationship: the severance and disestablishment of the Irish Church; the state of being separated or cut off; dismissal or discharge from employment.'

4 The most damaging of wounds for sons, Pease (2000) maintains, is caused by the father's remoteness, lack of fatherly attention, and absence. But physical and emotional violence during the presence of the father also wounds.

5 Althusser (1971/2001) makes a distinction between what he called the repressive state apparatus (RSA) and ideological state apparatus (ISA). The former consists of the state and its various political branches and activities. The latter is comprised of the schools, family, religions, and religious institutions that are worked more by ideology than by power and politics. The role of ISA, according to Althusser, like that of education, is to impose particular 'subjectivities' through interpellation (where individuals internalize certain self-definitions). Such internalization provides the necessary conditions (of exploitation and extortion) for capitalism (corporatism) to take place.

6 Grumet (1988) explains that male educators invited women into schools in the 1900s expecting that they would reclaim their mothers. Women accepted, hoping they would identify with their fathers. This gendered interpellation 'encouraged a conservatism that accepted the epistemological and social configurations of schooling as given' (p. 56). Therefore, female teachers complied with the rationalization and bureaucratization of an industrialized cultural era. Within this educational system, women were asked to break the continuous and extended binding relationship between a mother and her maturing child. Furthermore, in such common school classrooms women were socially isolated from each other and asked to teach individualism while taking care of large numbers of others' children. The gender discrimination of that era deprived women not only of a classical education, and thus, the professional faculties to question the bestowed curriculum, but also of the opportunity to occupy administrative positions.

References

Als, H. (1996). *The women*. New York: Farrar, Straus, & Giroux.

Althusser, L. (1971/2001). Ideology and ideological state apparatuses: Notes toward and investigation. In L. Althusser (Ed.), *Lenin and philosophy and other essays*. New York: Monthly Review Press.

Benjamin, J. (1988). *The bonds of love*. New York: Pantheon.

Britzman, D. (1998). *Lost subjects, contested objects: Toward a psychoanalytic inquiry of learning*. New York: State University of New York Press.

Digby, T. (1998). *Men doing feminism*. New York: Routledge.

Ellsworth, E. (1992). Why doesn't this feel empowering? Working through the repressive myths of critical pedagogy. In C. Luke & J. Gore (Eds.), *Feminisms and critical pedagogy*. New York: Routledge.

Freire, P. (1970/1990). *Pedagogy of the oppressed*. New York: Continuum.

Gilman, C.P. (1979). *Herland*. New York: Pantheon.

Gilmore, L. (1994). *Autobiographics: A feminist theory of women's self-representation*. Ithaca, NY: Cornell University Press.

Gilmore, L. (2001). *The limits of autobiography: Trauma and testimony*. Ithaca, NY: Cornell University Press.

Grumet, M.R. (1988). *Bitter milk: Woman and teaching*. Amherst, MA: University of Massachusetts Press.

Hemmingway, E. (1935). *Green hills of Africa*. New York: Scribner's.

Hesford, W. (1999). *Framing identities: Autobiography and the politics of pedagogy*. Minneapolis, MN: University of Minnesota Press.

Hirsch, Jr, E.D. (1999). *The schools we need and why we don't have them*. New York: Anchor.

Huebner, D. (1959). A capacity to wonder. In V. Hillis (Ed.), *The lure of the transcendent*. New York: Lawrence Erlbaum.

Kasson, J.F. (2001). *Houdini, Tarzan, and the perfect man*. New York: Hill & Wang.

Kristeva, J. (1985). Stabat mater. In S.R. Suleiman (Ed.), *The female body in Western culture: Contemporary Perspectives*. Cambridge, MA: Harvard University Press.

Loomba, A. (1992). *Colonial/postcolonial*. New York: Routledge Falmer.

McBride, J. (1996). *The color of water*. New York: Riverhead.

Miller, J. (2004). *Sounds of silence breaking*. New York: Peter Lang.

Munro, P. (1998a). Engendering curriculum history. In W. Pinar (Ed.), *Toward new identities*. New York: Garland.

Munro, P. (1998b). *Subject to fiction*. Buckingham: Open University Press.

Ng-A-Fook, N. (2007). *An indigenous curriculum of place*. New York: Peter Lang.

Ng-A-Fook, N. (2009). Inhabiting the hyphenated spaces of alienation and appropriation: *Currere*, language, and postcolonial migrant subjectivities. In J. Nahachewsky & I. Johnson (Eds.), *Beyond presentism*. Rotterdam: Sense Publishing.

Pagano, J. (1990). *Exiles and communities: Teaching in the patriarchal wilderness*. New York: State University of New York Press.

Pease, B., (2000). *Recreating masculinity: Postmodern masculinity politics*. Seven Oaks, CA: Sage.

Pinar, W.F. (1994). *Autobiography, politics and sexuality: Essays in curriculum theory*. New York: Peter Lang.

Pinar, W.F. (1998) A farewell and a celebration. In W. Pinar (Ed.), *Contemporary curriculum discourses*. New York: Peter Lang.

Pinar, W.F. (2000a). Search for a method. In W. Pinar (Ed.), *Curriculum studies: The reconceptualization* (pp. 415–424). Troy, NY: Educator's International Press.

Pinar, W.F. (2000b). Strange fruit: Race, sex and an autobiographics of alterity. In P. Trifonas (Ed.), *Revolutionary pedagogies: Cultural politics, instituting education, and the discourse of theory*. New York: Routledge Falmer.

Pinar, W.F. (2001). *The gender of racial politics and violence in America*. New York: Peter Lang.

Pinar, W.F. (Ed.). (2003). *The internationalization handbook of curriculum research*. Mahwah, NJ: Lawrence Erlbaum.

Pinar, W.F. (2004). *What is curriculum theory?* Mahwah. NJ: Lawrence Erlbaum.

Pinar, W., Reynolds, W., Slattery, P., & Taubman, P. (1995). *Understanding curriculum*. New York: Peter Lang.

Ravitch, D. (2000). *Left back*. New York: Simon & Schuster.

Rushdie, D. (1991). *Imaginary homelands*. New York: Penguin.

Sedaris, D. (2000). *Me talk pretty one day*. New York: Back Bay.

Tyson, L. (1999). *Critical theory today: A user friendly guide*. New York: Garland.

10 Where Desire Endures: Intimacy and Mothering a Bodied Curriculum

UGENA WHITLOCK

For 16 years I was homesick for my mother. For all those years, while I was married to a man, I had a recurring dream that I was home. Each dream was made up of scenes with mother: riding in the car, shucking corn from the garden, looking for something together. They were very complex dreams, very real, and they always occurred right before I awakened. And in that split second that my eyes were opening – just for the time it took to blink once – I believed I was back home. And for that second, I was happy. When I blinked again, I knew, and was sick for home, for her. For mother.

I did not know at the time that it was my mother for whom I yearned. I always termed it 'home.' In the edited collection by Catherine Reid and Holly Iglesias, entitled *Every Woman I've Ever Loved: Lesbian Writers on Their Mothers* (1997), Reid writes,

> I have wanted to find my mother in every woman I've ever loved. I have ached to find traces of her smell, her touch, the way she would cradle the back of my head, her songs. I had to turn forty before I could admit this to myself or acknowledge how often a similar yearning shows up in the people around me. For everyone – women, men, heterosexuals, homosexuals – our relationships with our mothers are complicated. Rarely do we see them as complex, flawed beings. We revere them; we put them on pedestals. Or we do the reverse and cast them as the foes we must forever guard against . . . From our mothers come most of what we know about love and touch, about caring and connection. (p. ix)

Reid's last sentence interests me most. What if in our relating, in my case to my own daughter, or to my lovers, we feel insufficient in what we know of love and touch, caring and connection? *How* does what we know of these things come from 'our mothers,' and how do we shoulder the vast responsibility of imparting them to our daughters? And, to extend Reid's thoughts connecting mother-longing and sexual desire, how might conventional thinking on mother-daughter relating be destabilized when one is a lover of women? What, then, might be understood by giving account of mother-daughter relating, of the performing of mothering?

My mother has made two attempts to communicate with me – really communicate. The first was when I was 11 years old. A bibliophile and bookworm even then, I formed attachments to certain books and carried them around with me for days, starting with my first 'real' book from first grade, *Under the Apple Tree,* and continuing with *Harriet the Spy.* I still have these within my line of sight in my office. They are the meatloaf of books: comfort food for the mind and I love them. In 1974, mother had just ordered Rose Kennedy's *Times to Remember* for me from the Doubleday Book Club. The book is long, and I was on my second week of carrying it around – to the dinner table, trips to town, to bed – when I noticed my mother's handwriting on the card-stock page just inside the back cover. Mother had written a letter, the only one I had ever seen from her. More words than I had ever seen written by her in one place, other than on a recipe card. She wrote how proud she was of me. She knew, she wrote, that I was so smart, and that if it did not always seem like she and my daddy appreciated this, it was because she felt I was so much smarter and had so much more potential than could be accounted for in my raising – by them.

I wish I could say that I treasured the letter and have kept it in a special place where I read and reread it from time to time. That is not what happened, and all I can say is that I was a less-than-sensitive 11-year-old. That would be putting it mildly. Perhaps the overture at intimacy, a kind of hidden intimacy at that, startled and embarrassed me. Perhaps I was 11 years old and not accustomed to intimacy of this nature from either parent. Regardless, I had barely finished reading the letter before I ripped it out and threw it away. And while I have thought of it often over the years, neither of us ever mentioned its existence. For almost 30 years it was the only time my mother overtly expressed her feelings for me, her child. What does it say about me, and her, that she would write it, not on a piece of paper and give it to me or place it where I would find it, but in my favourite book? As though the letter by itself would not be sufficient for me to treasure;

that it would have to be attached to something I loved better than her. It was an acknowledgment that I loved something better than her.

When I was 37, mother tried again, this time with much more success. I had just gotten divorced after 16 years of marriage to a controlling man who, it turns out, had issues with his own sexuality. Throughout those years mother and I had both been in denial about the state of the marriage, me as a survival technique and to keep my parents from worrying, and her in her own survival mode to reassure herself that I was fine. Raised in a strict fundamentalist household that stressed adultery or fornication as the only scriptural basis for divorce, I had believed my parents would not support me divorcing my husband for any lesser cause, was afraid they would send me back, much like that first blink. When the conflict became sexual, I saw my out, and they were sympathetic. A few months later, mother and I were sitting together watching television – Fox news, my parents' news source, something we had done many times over the years. Mother looked over at me and said, 'I am so sorry. I should have known, should have known how bad it was. If I had known, I would have gotten you out of there. I know you have been miserable. I am sorry for being such a bad mother that I did not know, that you could not tell me.' I told her about my fear of rejection and non-support. She said, 'You are my child; I would have gotten you out.' Maybe, I should have kept the letter.

Reid (1997, in writing about the essays in the collection, states, 'Perhaps the strongest connection between these narratives resides in the reasons for writing them – to pay tribute, to hack away stigma, to bare the truths of a love that did or didn't protect or sustain us'(p. xvii). This essay attends to each of these reasons in some way, but it is primarily my writing through that desire I have for my mother to sustain me. Painful and arduous as it was for me to come to the realization that I could not sustain my own daughter, I have had no such realization concerning my mother. Does she, I continue to wonder – hope, believe she can; does she wish to; does she know of my desire? I hope that looking at both of these relationships in the same place – and in the same psychic space – will allow me to bear truths, even as I bear witness, about the self in relation to mother.

I am aware that I have written extensively over the last few years about my parents. They remain at the forefront of my memory as my thinking turns back upon itself in my autobiographical research on place. My parents make up what I think of when I think of Southern homeplace; when I consider my growing up – so essential to my theorizing identity and place – my parents are central characters. Specifically, I have written more about my father, a modern-day prophet and elder in his church who sees to his flock's edification with epic fervour. I have written about mother, too, but not as much. Mostly I have written of her life in terms of class and family structures in the rural South. What I have not done is write about her in terms of being my mother. This chapter in a collection on 'mothering a bodied curriculum' allows me space and reason to do so.

I am also aware that I have written very little about my children; when I think of home, it is the home where I was a child. When I think of family, it is the family of my birth. When I think of the most influential people in my life, they are my mother and daddy. And then I ask myself why these things are so. A quick, too-easy answer is that I write about past-in-place, about nostalgia, and these contexts generally require a backward-looking perspective. Yet, this answer ignores my need to look backward in an almost soothing attempt to return to home. It suppresses the more painful realities of the present and resists mindfulness. I have been guilty of that which I have challenged my South in my previous writing: preferencing and privileging the past because the present is simply not comfortable, thus ascribing through implication a false coherence to both place and time. In this chapter, I reconceptualize mothering as a bodied curriculum through my own performance of mothering, examining self and other by merging two mother-daughter relationships: my mother's and mine, and mine and my daughter's. It is my own intergenerational attempt to craft what Julia Kristeva called a new discourse of maternity.

This essay is queer, feminist autobiographical narrative inquiry in which I offer a conceptualization of mothering as the performance of refraction. To frame my narrative on mothering, I turn to Kristeva's seminal work on maternal discourse, 'Stabat Mater' (1977/1986), and to prominent psychoanalytical Kristeva scholar Kelly Oliver, whose *Reading Kristeva: Unraveling the Double-Bind* (1993), provides much-appreciated insight and analysis of Kristeva's theories for a Kristeva neophyte like me. Mothering becomes a performative act by the self, the bending of thought and consciousness across time and place in a backward/forward motion that de-centres self through the negotiations of relational processes. More specifically, I examine my experiences as my mother's daughter and my daughter's mother and contemplate the incongruencies and ruptures that lie within the intersections of both roles. Through anecdotes and reflections that are sometimes poignant, always unstable and destabilizing, I locate my self in-between: as being mothered and being mother in a queer move that disrupts conventional social and cultural constructions of maternity as mother *'or other'* and invites conversations of mother *'as* other.'

Throughout the essay I make reference to 'performance' and 'performativity.' There are, I am aware, vast differences between the two. And while I sometimes feel my grasp is tenuous, I use them with a sort of deliberate ambiguity, encouraging readers to consider exactly what kind of 'doing' we are doing. Everyday performances of mothering include the various acts by which 'motherhood' and acts of motherly love and care have been constructed and institutionalized as systematic truth from an essentialist paradigm. 'Mother-as-performative' is a spontaneous way of being (whose performance is not limited to female-bodied 'mothers'); 'performative' implies a sense of spontaneity (then, also repetition), which gives an interpellation of someone-as-mother. Eschewing a discussion of linguistics and Lacanian psychoanalysis with how 'mother' is then perceived in development, and what 'mother' then signifies, we can (simply) differentiate the everyday from the doings of mothering that are reiterations or citations, reproductions of norms that may either subvert or reinscribe conventional, hegemonic practice. These practices are, according to Judith Butler, the practices 'by which discourse produces the effects that it names' (1993, p. 2). For Butler, the body is a 'mode of becoming' (1998, p. 33), and thus may be a means of performing, *do*-ing, gender (2004), and by extension for our purposes, for performing or do-ing, mother. And, as Butler goes on to state, 'Although there are norms that govern what will and will not be real, and what will and will not be intelligible, they are called into question and reiterated at the moment in which performativity begins its citational practice. One surely cites norms that already exist, but these norms can be significantly deterritorialized through the citation' (2004, p. 218). Although Butler is referring to reproductions of gender, we can apply the destabilizing, subversive attributes of the performative to performing mother. In other words, the doing-into-being of mothering, the performative, occurs as day-to-day performances of mothering are enacted. The performative deterritorializes, I suggest, *queers*, mothering as an unfitting space, which is why I find Janet Miller's (2005) notions of autobiography as a queer curriculum practice most helpful to my theorizing mothering, self, body, and curriculum.

I consider mothering a bodied curriculum as *curriculum* work. By examining practices and performances of mothering and the maternal as contested, unfamiliar, unnatural sites by which identity is destabilized and reinscribed, I suggest an unnatural discourse of mothering might help us think about unnatural discourses of curriculum and teaching to disrupt standardized, universal, solidified, and normalized educational practices. I find Miller's (2005) theorizing of women, teachers, and curriculum through autobiographical methodologies invaluable to making these connections among unnatural identities. She describes a 'queered' use of autobiography as a curriculum practice that 'produce stories of self and other with which one cannot identify' (p. 224), one that might 'cast in new terms the ways in which we might investigate our multiple, intersecting, unpredictable, and unassimilatable identities' (p. 220). Queering the maternal and education claims the unnatural-ness of both and opens spaces of being and belonging and becoming that are unavailable when the entities are fixed.

The title of this piece, 'Where Desire Endures,' comes from Lauren Berlant's introduction to *Intimacy* (2000), which 'takes on as a problem how to articulate the ways the utopian, optimism-sustaining versions of intimacy meet the normative practices, fantasies, institutions, and ideologies that organize people's worlds' (p. 2). In other words, according to Berlant, having a life means having an *intimate* life and so, I would say, this personal desire naturally translates into our public lives, our public spaces, and our public 'processes of attachment' (p. 4). Finding Berlant's depictions of intimacy and our desire for intimacy particularly useful to my own discussion of mothering, I seek to consider the relationality of mothering, and of being mothered, as a desire for and negotiating for intimacy. Within Berlant's frame of personal/public intimacies, I contend that a bodied curriculum is at the same time highly personal and public, as are conventional discourses on the maternal. Both are contested sites where desire endures.

Mothering Intimacy

Whenever I go home, Mother and I go to the grocery store. Although she could go before I arrive, or I could stay at the house while she shops, it has become our 'mother-daughter time.' At this writing, I am 46 years old and I still walk behind her as she pushes the cart, as I have done for as long as I can remember. Sometimes, someone wants to come along, and while I do not object, I secretly hope they will not. It is a simple thing, walking through every aisle, simultaneously checking the grocery list against the sales flyer, but it is the image

I will call forth from now on. It is time-in-place I share with my mother. The crowded, maddeningly bustling food carnival is often the most intimate experience we share. I do not know what she feels being there with me, but when we are together there, I am blessedly present in that moment. I am with my mother.

She has a saying about familial affection: 'We never did hug or say "I love you," but we always *knew* we *did*.' I do not know if she says this to reassure herself or me. Whichever the case, I did not grow up in a home where intimacy was displayed or expressed. And yet, my parents often declare that we are a close family. In this look at maternal intimacy, I search for the obscured intimacies of my childhood home by re-memorying my relation with my mother, making this essentially a mother-daughter piece. Berlant (2000) notes the 'eloquent' and 'inward' qualities of intimacy, that it is a 'narrative about something shared . . . within zones of familiarity and comfort' (p. 1), and how it is yet a 'public mode of identification and self-development' (p. 3). I approach the topic as a lesbian who is not out to my parents; therefore, I do not have the luxury of examining an 'honest' relationship, with its careful manoeuvrings to redefine and reconfigure the mother-daughter dynamic; given that, there is only so much sharing I can do. Instead, the careful manoeuvrings that *are* considered are the moves to love without being intimate and exposing the self – loving without intimacy. And yet, perhaps a reconfiguring of the notion of *intimacy* – private and public – remains from this study of mothering, an untangling of the fantasy of maternal intimacy that impacts understandings of the self and self in relation to other. Berlant (2000) suggests what rethinking intimacy might mean: 'Rethinking intimacy calls out not only for redescription but for transformative analyses of the rhetorical and material conditions that enable hegemonic fantasies to thrive in the minds and on the bodies of subjects while, at the same time, attachments are developing that might redirect the different routes taken by history and biography. To rethink intimacy is to appraise how we have been and how we live and how we might imagine lives that make more sense than the ones so many are living' (p. 6).

If my interrelatedness with my mother has raised questions about my own capacity for intimacy and my being in a state of it with other(s), then my relationality with my daughter might point to ruptures in intimacy – and mothering – fantasies I have heretofore held. I might, then, complicate and 'imagine lives that make more sense' in light of performances of mothering. Perhaps I will find intimacy is like the Wizard's gifts in Oz – here all along.

I think about how I always considered my mother a 'natural' at mothering, and I am reminded of Berlant's (2000) question as to 'why, when there are so many people, only one plot counts as "life" (first comes love, then...)?' (p. 6). For me, my mother's 'plot' was the one that for me 'counts' as mothering. She loved babies, would have had more, she told me once. She is so gentle and giving, patient and tireless. And I have come to realize she is one of the most complicated people I have ever known. More complicated than my mythologies of her as mother would indicate. Somewhere in my mid-30s I began seeing my mother not as maternal caregiving other, but as (an)other. It was, for me, a de-centring of my own little universe, and opens up other plots, other discourses, that count. My oldest friend once told me, 'Everybody thinks that your mother is the warm, caring one and that your daddy is stern and strict. They're wrong; it's your mother who is the cold one.' It dawned on me that in some deep place I had known this all along. It is a testament to her performativity of the maternal, and what my friend termed 'cold' was perhaps a space mother kept for herself. And much as she likes to remind me, particularly when I am an aggravation to her, 'You are just like your daddy,' I have come to know that as mother and lover, I too, possess a similar space of cold.

This cold space that represents, I think, what Berlant (2000) terms the 'amnesia around which desire's optimism and its ruthlessness converge' (p. 2). I do not know what lies within my mother's space, but within my own lies the longing for shared emotions and caring. It is a reflexive longing that plays out with nuances of difference; I long for it with my mother, and grieve its absence with my daughter. I need more than want it with one, it seems, and want more than need it with the other. Of course, want suggests need, just as need usually leads to want; still, I am troubled by my own situating of the two. By placing value on need versus want, I have placed a value on the self being mothered and the self as mother and thus value on the lack found in both; however, this articulation, this laying-out maternal intimacies, prompts and frees me to differentiate between intimacy and love. It allows me space to say that I do not love one above the other, as love – like mothering – has different, but not necessarily hierarchical – configurations. The discussion here, then, explores intersections among performing 'mother,' desiring intimacies, and those differing configurations.

Berlant (2000 writes, 'It becomes clear that virtually no one knows how to do intimacy; that everyone feels expert about it; and that mass fascination with the aggression, incoherence, vulnerability, and ambivalence at the scene of desire somehow escalates the demand for the traditional promise of intimate happiness to be fulfilled in everyone's everyday life' (p. 2). If we substitute the words 'mothering' and 'maternal' for 'intimacy' and 'intimate' in Berlant's quote, we may be struck with similar conclusions. 'Doing' motherhood is elusive precisely because everyone feels 'expert,' due to conventional, fixed maternal discourses. And yet, we demand its coherence as we tentatively acknowledge the incoherence and ambivalence of its being and becoming. There is a promise in the maternal that proliferates in our everyday lives, private and public. But how do we 'do' it?

If I hold certain mythologies and assumptions towards my mother as she both constitutes and is constituted by my conceptions of mothering as a natural, identifiable state of being and doing – I hold equally debilitating ones for myself, as not fitting into motherhood-as-natural. The first is the ongoing narrative claim that 'I should never have had children.' It has been my statement of last resort when the mothering got tough, and during one such time I told this to my daughter – a most reprehensible and regrettable disclosure. Kristeva contends that we must abject, lose, our mothers to become mothers ourselves, and in her proposed new discourse on maternity – beyond those commonly available to Western cultures from religion and science – we might also find ourselves as women. Oliver (1993) contends, 'The main threat to the fledgling subject is his or her dependence upon the maternal body. Therefore, abjection is fundamentally related to the maternal function' (p. 56). What happens, though, when we abject our children, when we abject not the object (mother) that created us, but rather the object (child) we have created? The verbal erasure of my daughter by my disclosure to her marked the point at which I knew that my consideration of family and relationality would no longer be confined to the family of my own birth, but must also include those to whom I gave birth. I knew I would have to write about Jessica. And I knew I would never again utter the words, 'I should never have had children.'

Stood the Mother

Kristeva's essay on the 'cult of the Virgin Mary and its implications for the Catholic understanding of motherhood and femininity'

(1977/1986, p. 160) is a reflection of her own experience of maternity, and can, according to Oliver (1993), 'be read as Kristeva's own identification with the Virgin' (p. 53). It is the only *consecrated* image of maternity, and an enduringly problematic one: it fails to articulate motherhood/mothering for mothers – the connections and intimacies of mother and child. In the first part of the essay, Kristeva discusses the historical development of the cult of the Virgin; her premise is that with the decline of religion – Catholicism – a site wherein exists a discourse on woman and mother, there remain insufficient and incomplete discourses to emerge in its place. Kristeva structured the piece using an unconventional 'split' text to represent the ebbing discourse of the Virgin juxtaposed with birth and woman as mother. The split itself represents the mother's sex, the birth canal to which is tied so closely the woman mother's identity, and in what Oliver calls this 'journey into the maternal function . . . traced as a journey into the maternal body' (p. 5), Kristeva calls for new understandings of motherhood and the mother's body, specifically seeking to bestir feminist interest in investigating new and possible discourses. 'The scar,' continues Oliver, 'can also be read as the loss of the child. Through the split columns of the mother's sex comes the child. It is necessary for the mother to lose her child in childbirth in order to have her child. Also, as Kristeva describes, it is necessary for the new mother to lose her child in order to rediscover her own mother' (p. 54). Thus, out of loss comes the mother, the mothering subject more than the child who was lost to Other and the woman who has lost Other. This mother, who has gained child and mother and self, is no unitary, essentialized, transcendent Mother; rather, she is shaped by the social, cultural, historical, sexual, and political contexts that have constructed the scar itself. New discourses on the maternal must assume it to be as partial, provisional, and contingent as the woman subject who performs it.

The title of the piece intrigues me most: *Stabat Mater*, an abbreviated version of a very old hymn about the agony of the Virgin Mary as her son's crucifixion begins, *Stabat mater dolorosa*, or, *stood the Mother, full of grief*. Stood the mother, full of grief. I have stated on more than one occasion that my daughter 'like to have killed me!' which, I suppose, is a country Southern phrase for causing me grief. I am sure the Renaissance masters had a more profound conception of grief in mind when they composed the hymn *Stabat Mater*, but parents of teenage daughters everywhere will know what I mean. Giving birth to my daughter was easy; raising her was hard. I know what it feels like to feel aggrieved, to stand alone, isolated and helpless, knowing that my child is in trouble, in danger, or worse, lost to me. With a nod to Kristeva, losing one's child does not necessarily happen in childbirth or in psychic, primordial spaces. If, as she suggests, I must lose my child to find her, and subsequently, (my)self, I have, in standing alone in my grief, believed myself to have lost us both.

One note: I do not attempt here to craft a fixed autobiographical narrative of motherhood that consists mainly of difficult lived experiences involving my child. This is no transcendent story of overcoming adversity and arriving at illumination. This is a hard story of birth. And, like Kristeva's split text, it is not singular. This is me, mothering. These are hard stories to remember and tell, and this chapter is turning out to be the most wrenching piece I have ever written. They are hard, in part, because of the insufficiency of maternal discourses available to me, and to others, by which I might conceptualize and make meaning from loving and mothering my girl child. So, I attempt to theorize these experiences and psychic grapplings through Kristeva's notions of abjection and Other in order to grow understanding of the fluidity of the mothering self and Others. Throughout the narrative, I attempt to give symbolic meaning to an experience that lacks cultural representation. I do this as a curriculum theorist by trade, an autobiographical feminist researcher who does this work to also make meaning of 'mothering a bodied curriculum.'

Based upon my preconceptions and assumptions about conventional maternal thoughts and acts, rethinking mothering is a disruption to existing scripts. I therefore turn to Miller's feminist curriculum theory work on 'autobiography-in-the-making' (2005, p. 232), as well as her 'autobiography as a queer curriculum practice' (1998, title), to bridge these seemingly divergent and unrelated lines of thought, as mothering, for me, is always also 'in-the-making' and 'queered.' Miller's autobiography-in-the-making includes 'multiple tellings, multiple questionings of those tellings, and multiple angles on representations of "self" that give strategic leverage' (2005, p. 232) to questions we raise about the self and identities. Like Miller, rather than use autobiography to 'delineate completed, wholly conscious and linear representations' (p. 233), in my case, as mother, writer, scholar, teacher, I employ it to call into question conventional, and often debilitating discourses on mothering. I suggest that mothering identities, like those of women, teachers, academics, etc., are, as Miller notes, 'provisional and contingent'

(p. 137). If mothering is also in-the-making, then there is also transformative meaning to be explored in a mother standing, full of grief – beyond an identity fixed by historical, social, and religious constructions of Motherhood. It is, perhaps, a kind of motherhood where I might fit. I hope so.

She was conceived as the result of a fit. A newlywed of only 2 months, I did not want a child. I was sick for home, isolated, alone all day waiting for my husband to come home. I had thought we – he and I – might come to know one another better, might cultivate the kind of relationship like the only one I knew: that of my own parents, fictional as I later came to know it was. I had thought he would let me go to school, but my confinement became more and more clear. A baby would tie me to him, but in my skewed survivalist thinking, might rather tether than tie, giving me enough rope to go to school. He talked about a baby, about how wonderful it would be to have a baby, about how we would have fun, about how he had wanted a family. He took us to the bookstore and bought a standard baby book, *What to Expect When You're Expecting*. He bought two little glass clowns for the baby's room. I felt sick. I felt college and intellectual life slipping away like a vapour as he spoke. I did not speak.

One night, I ventured into delicate territory. As gingerly as I could, I told my husband that if I could only start to school in the fall, we could plan for a baby then. He became enraged, literally ripping the book I was reading in half and hurling it across the living room. I do not remember what he said then, but I remember him taking the clowns and knocking them from the shelf onto the floor; I remember looking at their chipped and cracked figures and realizing the life I was locked into. I became pregnant 3 months later, and he bought a new book.

Jessica was born on the first day of March, the day they said she would come. I had no profound Kristevan reflections upon her birth, did not fall in love with her when I looked upon her and held her. I loved her. The only secret desire I had when she was born was that my mother would come and live with me for a while, not to 'help out' with the baby, but to allow me to feel home again. She came with my husband's mother and planned only a day trip. I was heartsick and felt her leaving as soon as she walked in the door, resentful of the woman who would take her away. Resentful that the other woman would have stayed for a month if I had asked *her*. It was Jessica who caused Mother to stay with me. I had tried to feed her from my breast since her birth. I could not, but did not know it. She cried violently and tried to nurse;

I did not know there was no milk. Mother watched me feed her and declared, 'She's starving. She will starve to death.' She went to the kitchen, sterilized a bottle, filled it with canned evaporated milk and water, and fed my child. The other woman, the unwanted one, was sent away, and my mother stayed with me for the week. It was she who fell in love with the baby.

Even now, even when I desire and attempt to write about my daughter, I do so in terms of my mother. Where is the language to speak of the child? Kristeva found it, in often graphic, adoring, raw words. She spoke of a new language of the mother woman, one of music and beauty. A new discourse of maternity. Finding only the language of (my)self as child, my mother's music calls to me, and not my own. What Kristeva suggests in 'Stabat Mater,' according to Oliver (1993, p. 52) is that 'what we need is an ear for listening to motherhood' (p. 263). Oliver elaborates, connecting religious and spiritual ecstasy with childbirth: 'Kristeva's left column is the flesh become word. The fleshed mother with her jouissance, her "sexual-intellectual-physical passion of death," replaces the Mother-God. We no longer need goddesses, says Kristeva, when we have the mothers' love and music. Her left column is some of this mother's music' (p. 53). Performances of mothering, othering, is, in the Kristevan sense, the Word-made-flesh-made-word in that identifications with the Virgin, mother of the Christ child and Other to the child Christ, the Mother is deprived of death through her Son and he is human only through his mother (Kristeva, 1971/1986, pp. 162, 164). Subjective being, then, for both is reciprocal and co-constitutive. Given the social, psychoanalytical, and historical implications of the maternal that Kristeva assumes, becoming conscious of and listening to the mother's love and music is facilitated by autobiographical moves that consider subjects as irreducibly multiple. The autobiographical work of questioning fixed universal constructions of mothering and the self in relation to them disrupts notions of unified, rational, coherent, autonomous 'whole' (Miller, 2005, p. 47) mother-woman identities and is suggestive of new meaning making and reconceived subjectivities.

How do I talk about mothering my child, about being with her as other? What is mothering as a bodied curriculum in relational encounters with my child? I feel insufficient to even discuss it. The 'truth' is, for all the time I was 'mothering' Jessica, I was tenaciously attempting to maintain my identity and subjectivity, and not as 'woman' or 'mother,' as I understood them at that time. Because I did not adapt to conventional notions of mothering as I understood them at that time, I felt then, as now, that I failed at it, failed the child who was other.

I would like, at this point, to consider Kristeva's accounting of 'abjection' in relation to the maternal body in an autobiographical move to challenge 'essentialist constructions' (Miller, 2005, p. 49) of mothering and the maternal, and to consider multiple and incoherent ways of being. I turn to Oliver's analysis of abjection in the Kristevan sense to frame my discussion. According to Oliver (1993), the abject is 'something repulsive that both attracts and repels. It holds you there in spite of your disgust. It fascinates' (p. 55). Some bodily functions, to put it delicately (as it were), are abject, as is sin – to some of us – or passing a car wreck. The abject 'threatens' identity and 'destroys identity, system, order' (p. 56) and 'calls into question the boundaries upon which [the unity/identity of both society and the subject] are constructed' and 'points to the fragility of those borders' (p. 56). Yet, the corollary of abjection is love, and if abjection marks separation, love marks connection and intimacy (S. Keltner, personal communication, October 2009). Abjection, then, may be considered from an autobiographical standpoint, as autobiography in the postmodern, post-structuralist sense works in similar ways upon the social constructedness of identity.

Her father and I divorced the summer of her ninth grade year. I watched her proceed to transform herself, and stood, watching, as she began choosing the kind of life she wanted to live. Why stand and watch? Why not *parent*, might be the obvious questions. Oh, I imposed curfews (which she broke), set consequences (which she subverted), and issued ultimatums (which she called me on). When she was barely 16, I found a note in her pocket in which she was explaining to a friend how devastated she was about a rumour of how she had given a classmate a blow job in the parking lot during a football game. I remembered the game; I had allowed her to go, checked out the older girl she was riding with, an honours student of mine with whom I would trust my child. I also knew the alleged blow job recipient and wondered how in the world I would be able to pass him in the hall again. This explained the whispers and glances I had witnessed in class and had chalked up to teenage drama. I wondered, why couldn't my kid be one of the 'good kids' – the kind I taught? They were teachers' children, middle class, grade-conscious, pleasant – and they liked me, all in stark contrast to my perception of my own child.

Not long after, one of them asked her out. Jessica had had a crush on the boy – football player, member of the drama club, all-around-nice-guy – for a year. She was happy – I noted, for she seldom displayed much I could identify as happiness – as she made preparations for their date. He picked her up, and I saw them off, hopeful, as I still was prone to be concerning her then. He dropped her in the driveway barely an hour later. I knew what had happened before she told me. He had heard the rumours about her, she said. He drove them to the Monte Sano Mountain overlook and parked the car, before even taking her to dinner. He told her if she was giving out blow jobs, she might as well give him one, too. She refused. I was distraught and furious, but not indignant. This night was a consequence. My daughter was paying for her behaviour; I was paying for my sins.

Towards the middle of her junior year, Jessica was driving, which meant she skipped school at every opportunity. I always knew by the end of second period, as soon as morning attendance slips had been recorded in the office. The vice-principal in charge of attendance and discipline was my friend Charlie. Charlie and I were from the same hometown and were distantly related, but we got to know each other from our interactions concerning Jessica's behaviour. During one visit to the office, she called him a 'fucking idiot,' and the vein was still bulging in his neck as he told me that because it was me, he would put her into in-school suspension for her latest offence, rather than recommend expulsion.

On this particular day, Charlie called to tell me she had been reported absent from her first period class. I hoped she was just late and went to try and find her. I was sick as I drove home. I entered the house to find her dishevelled and crying. She had almost been raped, she told me. She had been changing clothes, getting ready for school, when a classmate saw her car in the driveway and dropped in. She let him in and he had tried to rape her, she explained. 'So you said no,' I asked. 'Yes,' she replied, 'I said no.' This time I was indignant; throughout the years, I had counselled many students that 'no means no.' Demanding to know the boy's name, I called his parents and asked them if they knew what their son had attempted. Then his mother stopped me. 'Yes, we know, but you should also know this. Your daughter was barely dressed and enticed him. She seduced him and continued dressing in front of him. Before you continue with your accusing, you need to talk to your kid.' I hung up the phone in silence and dejection. I told her to get dressed and took her to school.

For years I thought my daughter a sweet child who took an adolescent turn. But she remembers herself as having a rebellious, risky side that she kept to herself. She felt an apartness from me that went beyond 'we were never close.' Rather, it was more like an ongoing but hidden opposition, to paraphrase her words. To illustrate, she related a visit to a friend's house for dinner. They had sat down to a meal the mother had cooked, then proceeded to talk around the dinner table. It made her realize, she said, that I had not been that kind of mother. Furthermore, I had been the kind of mother who had deprived her of opening presents on Christmas morning at our home by insisting we be at my parents' for Christmas every year. To me, this presented a kind of daily life and yearly assessment of mothering, salient to my discussion here of abjection.

What I heard that day was blame, yet what Jessica described, in her own way and without articulating it as such, was the processing of being the abject subject, repulsed at both separating from and identifying the maternal, yet drawn by the desire for both. Her own reflective thought examined physical and psychological connections to me as maternal in terms of my performed functions of mothering. She was at the same time expressing desire and revulsion, love and anger, longing and disgust, as I became abject other 'in order to facilitate' the separation (Oliver, 1993, p. 56). Oliver writes, 'The child becomes the abject in order to avoid both separation from, and identification with, the maternal body – both equally painful, both equally impossible ... The "subject" discovers itself as the impossible separation/identity of the maternal body. It hates that body but only because it can't be free of it. That body, the body without borders, is the body out of which this abject subject came, is impossible. It is a horrifying, devouring body. It is a body that evokes rage and fear' (p. 60). In her new abject relation to me, she was, as she was coming to understand, 'not yet separated but no longer identical' (p. 57) with me. She raged; I grieved, standing.

There are risks involved in negotiating spaces of mothering and exploring mother/child relationality, rather than acquiescing to the complacency of conventional 'truths.' In fact, there are risks involved to the child and mother as individuals, as well as to the ways they relate to one (an)other. For, according to Oliver (1993), 'A woman risks losing herself when she loses her mother . . . This reunion (of childbirth) is bittersweet because it reminds the new mother of what she has lost . . . it is reunion through lack' (p. 54). While there exists the possibility for exploring identity, subjectivity, and agency, there is also the possibility for unrealized loss. In telling my hard stories, I not only note the distance between my self and my child, but I also feel abjection towards my mother; she seems nowhere to be found in these stories, and that loss is also pronounced. What is left is enduring desire of the self, abject, left to make meaning of subjectivity in relation to the lost others. Troubling the enduring desire for personal-public intimacy and incongruencies/threatened breakdowns in meanings between self and other lies at the heart of considering mothering a bodied curriculum. If a bodied curriculum involves in part ' "being-with" other bodies differ-ently and to the different knowledges such bodily encounters produce' (Springgay & Freedman, 2007), then considering the maternal body as a performative, socialized, inscribed political site is a fitting location for discussing curriculum as the interpretation of lived experiences – by bodied subjects.

Mothering a Bodied Curriculum

When she was 24 years old, my daughter admitted she was an alco-holic. My young, beautiful girl struggled with a demon I had foolishly relegated to someone *else*. Her boyfriend had delivered her to rehab after finding nine empty vodka bottles in her car. Confronting her ad-diction shattered what remained of my identity as a mother; in other words, I took this upon myself. If I were a better mother, if I had worked harder to raise her, if I had been more attentive – more engaged – if I had been more, I would have had a 'normal, productive child.' How-ever, this road, the arduous journey of learning to engage relationally with (an)(alcoholic)other who happens to be my daughter, opens a space for undermining scripts of the maternal that would fix women's ways of being, of being with each-other, such as roles, feelings, behav-iours, and ways of relating. The truth, my secret truth, is that for the almost decade of her active addiction, I had not *wanted* to relate with her. My guilt and sense of lacking as mother was joined by fear – of having to help, to *do* something, to confront so much. I held my breath and felt relief at the silence and absence. When she was living in her car, she was not asking something of me; when she bounced from one dilapidated apartment to another, at least I did not have to house her; when there were no phone calls, I did not have to think about my child, and therefore, about my self. Gender-, sexuality-, religious-, race-, and class-based discourses on mothering allow no spaces for incoherencies such as addiction. Static, universal conceptualizations limit us to being long-suffering, mothers, who, like Mary, hold our secrets in our hearts in some noble, loving altruistic transcendent state called Motherhood.

These discourses have nothing to offer mothers who hide. There are, of course, obvious parallels and similarities in the gendered work of curriculum and teaching.

Reflecting upon my unrealistic and unquestioned assumptions about mothering, I am reminded of Janet Miller's (1990) work with classroom teachers, in which they struggle with naming the questions that will guide their work. While they may in their various positions as educators and researchers identify initial questions for the sake of beginning their investigations of sexed, gendered, classed, teacher-selves in the classroom, the questions almost always change dramatically as they come to realize that curriculum research must begin within themselves. They began to pose very private, very intimate questions that reflected both the 'uncertainties' and 'dissonance' (pp. 77, 85) of being teachers and researchers. Miller and her fellow teacher researchers grappled with the oppressive 'layers of internalized assumptions and expectations' (p. 153) that had imposed both questions and answers upon them. Post-structuralist feminist discourses of knowing include a bodied curriculum that not only shatters imposed, conventional, fixed assumptions, but allows us to challenge as bodied subjects, social, political, institutionalized structures that construct such assumptions. An unfitting discourse, one of music from the scar, of rethinking the maternal container, is born, literally and figuratively, of love – the source of Kristeva's music. Oliver (1993) writes, 'The child must separate from its mother in order to be an autonomous being. It cannot remain dependent on her. It is the mother's love and her love for her own mother . . . It is this love that fills language with meaning . . . Perhaps primary identification is not with the mother's body but with the mother's love' (p. 68).

I write about love in, from, and for a variety of contexts and forms. Love, like grief, can be powerful and generative, and can work in mutuality to allow for the emergence of the autonomous subject. Love, like grief, is a continual working of emotional, psychic, and embodied being. Love, like grief, involves informed acts. I do not idealize or romanticize love, no more than I do the notion of Motherhood; love to me is most often fierce, similar to that of the God of the Hebrew people, one who, incidentally, sent his Son to die, in the Christian account, for love. It is a love that is present at our childbirth and in our classrooms. It is a love that demands something of us, as women, mothers, teachers, researchers. It demands our discomfort, our dissonance, our questioning. Love is the labour.

This is no progression narrative, no success story of overcoming. One trap of loving an alcoholic is the strong urge to start hoping that the storm has passed. Instead, I have had to begin to think of my daughter's life – and my part in it – in terms of climate rather than weather. There will be fronts and flows and movements daily, yet I am the mother of an alcoholic for the long run. Any mothering discourse available to me, then, must allow me to work the tensions of a hard relationship that must be worked and reworked as identities shift and contrive – even if I have to shape the discourse as I go along. There is no more unstable or uncertain, un-fixed context through which to consider maternal identity. She looks haggard to me, older than her 26 years. 'Hard livin',' as my folks would say, has taken its toll. She does her self-work; after several false starts, she is finally working on her major, marine biology, as she works full-time. We talk now; she contacts me almost every day, and I am glad to hear from her. She tenaciously trudges through her 12 steps and allows me to see something of her process. I am now often in awe of her and wonder when and how she became so insightful. She also raises her own daughter, Layla, who exudes joy and love. She is a good mother, who, like my own mother, impresses me with the care and tenderness with which she interacts with her child. I think, maybe, that in Layla Jessica hears her music.

Two Thanksgivings ago, Jessica had decided to leave her boyfriend and the stifling small town life that entrapped her. We had gathered, as we always have, at my parents' house. This time, when she hugged me goodbye, she whispered, 'I don't want to go, Mom.' 'I know,' I whispered back, 'but make a plan and get out.' She buckled Layla into her carseat and got in the car. As they drove away, my family – as we do – stood to wave goodbye until the car was out of site. I stood there by mother, grief visible, external, tangible. It was then she taught me her secret, and I realized the maternal in her is neither myth nor magic – nor natural. Seeing me heartbroken over my lost girl, my mother spoke as sternly and directly as she had ever spoken to me. 'Smile,' she said. 'Don't you let her see you upset. Don't you let that be the last thing she sees.' And that is what I did. I stood there, with my mother, smiling and waving and not knowing. I remember that now, writing this essay, and I note something now I did not realize then: I stood, but not alone. Two mothers stood that day, watching the third leave us, and the three grieved, each in her own way, for her own reasons – in her own abjection and to her own music.

Epilogue

Before this piece went to press, I decided to show it to my daughter and make sure I had her permission to make public these episodes of her life. I am glad I did. The following are points she would like to make sure readers know about her:

- She got a C in advanced placement calculus in high school while she was skipping class and graduated with a 3.7 grade point average.
- She is not only working on a major in marine biology, but she also gets A's in courses such as organic chemistry and histiology (the study of tissues).
- Not only does she not dwell on these experiences of the past, she draws from them as learning experiences.
- She concedes that while 'happy endings' may not be realistic or accurate, she is happy and life is good.
- She is working her program.
- She and her husband Jason continue to improve their marriage, and she is blessed to be married to a man who loves her child.
- She thinks this piece is the most depressing writing she has ever read and wonders how I can do this for a living.
- She asked whether all curriculum theorists are as egotistical as I come across in the essay (I told her we all are).
- She does not look haggard.

And, come to think of it, she doesn't. She is my beautiful, beautiful child.

Acknowledgment

I would like to thank my friend and colleague, Stacy Keltner, for her feedback on my interpretation of Kristeva, and Kennesaw State University student Matthew Stewart, for explaining Judith Butler to me. I would like to think my daughter, Jessica Elizabeth Hyde Nash, for helping me with perspective.

References

Berlant, L. (Ed.). (2000). *Intimacy*. Chicago, IL: University of Chicago Press.
Butler, J. (1993). *Bodies that matter: On the discursive limits of sex*. New York: Routledge.

Butler, J. (1998). Sex and gender in Simone de Beauvoir's *Second Sex*. In
   E. Fallaize (Ed.), *Simone de Beauvoir: A critical reader* (pp. 29–42). New York:
   Routledge.
Butler, J. (2004). *Undoing gender*. New York: Routledge.
Kristeva, J. (1977/1986). Stabat mater. In T. Moi (Ed.), *The Kristeva reader*
   (pp. 160–186). New York: Columbia University Press.
Miller, J.L. (1990). *Creating spaces and finding voices: Teachers collaborating for
   empowerment*. Albany, NY: State University of New York Press.
Miller, J.L. (1998). Autobiography as a queer curriculum practice. In W.F. Pinar
   (Ed.), *Queer theory in education* (pp. 365–373). Mahwah, NJ: Lawrence
   Erlbaum.
Miller, J.L. (2005). *Sounds of silence breaking: Women, autobiography, curriculum*.
   New York: Peter Lang.
Oliver, K. (1993). *Reading Kristeva: Unraveling the double-bind*. Bloomington,
   IN: Indiana University Press.
Reid, C., & Iglesias, H. (Eds.). (1997). *Every woman I've ever loved: Lesbian
   writers on their mothers* (pp. ix–xviii). San Francisco, CA: Cleis Press.
Springgay & Freedman. (2007). *Curriculum and the cultural body*. New York:
   Peter Lang.

11 (Lesbian) M/otherhood as Contradiction: Love, Sexuality, and Other (Imagined) Wonders

KATHLEEN GALLAGHER WITH CAROLINE FUSCO

Conception

Lesbian motherhood was more or less invisible prior to the 1970s (Shore, 1996; Arnup, 1995). In its relatively short history, academics in this area have focused considerable attention on the resistance/assimilation challenge of this walking, breathing, breeding, loving contradiction. Hequembourg (2007) asks: 'Do lesbian mothers challenge the very foundations of patriarchal ideologies that centralize biological ties and heterosexual unions as the basis for "family"? Or, are lesbian families just like other families?' (p. 11). However provocative a question, albeit relying on the overdetermined binary of resistance and assimilation, I will not set out to answer it here. More interesting to me is the idea that, by and large, I am living in a time when my desire, for lover and child, is no longer seen to be in conflict; a time when, in other words, the contradiction of lesbian motherhood is no longer an anomaly. There are, of course, science and technologies that explain the greater frequency and visibility of lesbian mothers, but I am more fascinated by the re-alignments of social discourse and relations that make this contradiction conceivable in the first instance. It would be a mistake to see this simply as a sign of progress, an inevitable outcome of queer rights and progressive social policy. It is all of these things, of course, but it is also a victory of the *imagination*.

The *fact* of lesbian motherhood has major implications for social, political, and economic policy. In the arena of education policy, the place where this sea change will be most acutely felt is in the small world of the classroom, in the space of curriculum, the site of the most significant relational exchanges and knowledge construction in schools: the place where imagination is either fed or starved.

Lesbian motherhood produces a certain kind of contradiction, to be sure, but to be a *mother*, full stop, is to embody contradiction. Motherhood itself, as institution and experience, is laden with paradoxical axioms. Strong and tender. Sexual and chaste. Loving and controlling. Motherhood and its Double. Motherhood *is* Otherhood, even though it is the only single shared experience of all human and non-human life. Adrienne Rich (1976), in the foreword to her famous exploration *Of Woman Born* said, 'All human life on the planet is born of woman' (p. 11). Of course, a truism we take for granted. But coupled with her next observation, the politics of the field begin to take shape, 'We know more about the air we breathe, the seas we travel, than about the nature and meaning of motherhood' (p. 11).

For me, it has been an induction into the most ordinary of jobs, but one that demands of me the greatest creativity, the most fluid and flexible curriculum, and the deepest engagement with another human I have ever experienced. I am not an expert in this field; in fact, I have no expertise at all. But in this chapter I hope to use the scholarship available to me and this new corporeal ground of intelligence opened up to me through my experience, a fleeting two years in, of motherhood.

What Labour Does (Lesbian) Motherhood Perform?

Lesbian motherhood challenges both social structures and biology. In legal, academic, and popular discourses, writers have carefully examined the 'work' accomplished and the institutions challenged, by the fact of lesbian motherhood. But, Wald (1997 cited in Heqeumbourg 2007, p. 182) outlines an even more radical view: 'Lesbian motherhood exposes the social creation of gender.' Although motherhood is always inflected with race, ethnicity, culture, age, able-bodiedness, socioeconomic status, marital status, etc., *sexuality*, lived openly, requires that we look again at the givens of gender. Sexuality does not simply interplay, as other social categories might, with gender, it exposes the ground upon which gender is constructed and its essential/izing role in the construction of 'family life.'

A mother (and grandmother), a curriculum theorist, and a profoundly influential scholar, Madeleine Grumet, in her seminal work, *Bitter Milk: Women and Teaching* (1988), could be seen to be making the antecedent argument to any new look at the role and function of gender in the home and in the classroom. In this work, Grumet argues that women were recruited (and actively recruited in the nineteenth century) to do the job of preparing children for the productive world. But Grumet thinks the classroom can be influenced by the wisdom and knowledge of the reproductive world, the way we learn through relationship, movement, eros, play, and touch in the pre-Oedipal phase. Further, Grumet makes a very explicit connection between aesthetics and the reproductive world in the classroom. For her, aesthetics appears to be a way of knowing through our bodies and knowing by way of relationships and nurturing. It is here that I insert my idea of the place of the imagination in the curriculum, brought from home to the classroom.

To escape the simple trap of identity politics demands an imaginative leap. I am not suggesting that real, material, hegemonic, and naturalized discourses do not shape the experiences of women who are both lesbians and mothers. But when, and through what experiences, they 'came out' sexually and when they 'came into' the experience of motherhood distinctively shape such women's relationship to the deceptively coherent title of 'lesbian mother.'

A Curriculum of Becoming or Productively Losing 'Identity' as a Defining Category

I scarcely know how to speak of curriculum without thinking about drama pedagogy, its embodied quality, and its flights of fancy. It continues to inspire me here. 'Mothering a bodied curriculum,' for me, means using and losing identity to take flight in the classroom. The curriculum of the school must be the ultimate practice run for a life curriculum in which the imagination is central.

In his lecture at the Sorbonne in the spring of 1960, Jean-Paul Sartre claimed that sculpture represents the *form* of the body and theatre, the *act* of the body. The problem with the bourgeois theatre of his time, he asserted, was that it neither intellectually challenged nor aesthetically engaged its public. What was inadequate in the theatre of Sartre's day is also inadequate in today's classrooms. Sartre argues for a theatre of situations, not of characters. It is, therefore, our actions in a given situation that create our character(s) and thus our life. What does this mean for a classroom? As student I might ponder: Under what conditions would I make my idea public? In which dialogues will I participate? How could I extend the input of another? What positions of compromise allow me to collaborate? How do this situation and these people shape my performance? In other words, Sartre's imagined *theatre of situation* helps to better elucidate the private and public, the reproductive and productive choices that both students and teacher make in the pedagogical contract.

In Sartre's analysis, psychology provided too thin an explanation for the richness that life is. And on stage, psychology and its stories of characters and motivations was often embarrassing to witness. If, as Sartre believed, 'man' could choose his freedom or not, given a situation, then theatre ought to show 'man' choosing what he will be, in a given situation. When we delve, instead, into the psychological conundrums of characters on stage (or in classrooms), we lose the act of the body. In much the same way, therefore, psychology is inadequate in the classroom; it does not allow the full range of choice, the full engagement of imagination that might be possible in a given set of circumstances. At times, what is needed in a classroom is a brief moment of imagination to break the predictability. And if pedagogy can create an intentionally interrogative space, it might extend the body's knowing beyond its own situatedness. How do I come to know within *and* beyond the categories of 'lesbian' and 'mother'? Imagination.

One of the lesser-known contributions of Sartre, but very important in the context of my interests here, is his 1962 examination of the imagination, called *Imagination: A Psychological Critique*. Because early thinkers on imagination, like Hussrel and other phenomenologists, had settled upon the images we create in our minds and their relationship to thinking as central to any understanding of the imagination, Sartre usefully challenged what he perceived as an error. An image, he said, is *an act*, not some thing in our heads. Images are not things. To believe this, he said, is to ignore the important role played by imagination in thinking. It is this idea, I think, that has most pedagogical weight, an area to which I now turn.

Imagination: What's Love Got to Do with It?

It [imagination] is *the* meaning and purpose of each individual's existence. Nothing matters as much.

– Armstrong, *Conditions of Love*

Being a mother has made me want to close the divide between reasoned judgment and emotional expression. In other words, awakening critical thinking now has something more to do with love, as a disruptive force. Of course, Dewey long ago was inviting reason to turn to imagination, too, but what I could not find in that earlier work was the attention to imaginative action and change that I desired, that my gendered subjectivity demanded. Didier Maleuvre's (2005) more recent conception of aesthetic education illustrates how teaching and learning have the power not only to train critical thinking, but also to awaken the more tender faculties of the mind, kindling generosity, kindness, and love. These ideas are not new, although my interest in Romanticism and pedagogy is. Pedagogy, as a critical and political act, has not easily shared intellectual space with ideas of beauty and love, more common in Romantic texts on education. But might there be a way to accommodate such old ideas of Romanticism in new ways? As it turns out, many others have asked this very question. Daniel Cho (2005) claims that love not only has a place in pedagogy, but is necessary for it. For others, Dewey is taken up anew: 'teaching depends upon [teachers'] wisdom about the ways of love,' according to Garrison (1997, p. 1).

Maxine Green, of course, made the way easier for many with such interests. She has, for a very long time, been talking about learning and teaching with passion, perhaps even love, and with imagination, or 'wide-awakeness' (see Greene 1995). In her view, classrooms can be nurturing, thoughtful, and just simultaneously. She even urges us to 'look into each other's eyes and urge each other on to new beginnings' (p. 46). I think this is a pedagogy of love. At the risk of essentializing, I think this is motherhood, not the institution but the impulse, in teaching.

In chasing down these newer conceptions, in an effort to better accommodate this boundless love of new motherhood I felt with an idea of education as essentially a critical, imaginative, but also loving act, I discovered the work of David Halpin (2007). His basic orientation to the imagination and to love in teaching follows: 'While the imagination is commonly thought of as an aspect of the private "inner" mental world of an individual, it is in fact indivisible from the public "outer" one within which people exist and which, through their actions, they routinely socially reproduce' (p.103). So the imagination is also embodied, an idea with little currency in historical accounts of it. Halpin's study helpfully positions the imagination in time and space, illustrating how the imagination has always been harnessed to the needs of particular groups and, certainly, that the imagination, therefore, is not something that is always good by definition. In other words, it isn't necessarily a 'lack of imagination' that may make teachers and other children misunderstand and/or fear my son's non-normative home, it may indeed be an act of imagination and, furthermore, that act of imagination has embodied features. Halpin traces early conceptions of the imagination through German idealist thought and strongly to Kant's psychological theory of cognition.[1] The pedagogical piece of importance here is a theory of the mind that enables people to create another nature out of the material that actual nature has given them in the first place, *through experience*. In other words, the imagination is not just a psychological theory but also a method, a way of being. The pedagogical question, therefore, is what kind of 'method' enables the ideals of justice to drive imaginative thought? When imaginative acts might go off in any number of directions, what would orient children (and teachers) towards an imagination of inclusive thought and action? Of course, 'inclusive' is a slippery if not inadequate word, but it is at least a place to begin.

Even as I write it, I hesitate to use the word imagination. It has been overused in contemporary educational discourse, has lost its meaning. In 1961, E.J. Furlong published a little text on the many uses and meanings of imagination in early Romantic thought. One might easily produce the same review now from educational discourse. Sometimes imagination appears as the proxy for 'feeling,' but this is too vague to be helpful; other times, it seems to stand in for the sense of invention. Furlong pulls out two very important ideas about the imagination, tracing them back to Hume, which I think should animate any further work on the imagination in pedagogy and education today. They are, simply, that any theory of thinking will necessarily be a theory of imagination and that some of our most important beliefs are the result not of a sense of reason but of imagination (see pp. 99–113).

Given this, the road to school is an important one, and the imagined curriculum is the centre of it. Tolstoy was a critic of school and a radical educator in his time, I have learned. His view of traditional schools was clear. In 1860, in an essay on 'Popular Education,' he wrote: 'Every curriculum ought to be a response to answers posed by life, whereas school does not only not come up with questions, but does not even answer those posed by life. School eternally answers the same questions posed by humankind several centuries ago rather than those questions springing from the intellect of the child – the educator is not interested by these' (in Blaisdell & Edgar, 2000, p. 175). A believer in the pedagogical imagination, Tolstoy saw teaching as an 'art.' He also considered that the main function of a school is to allow for experimentation.

Off to School

> Education is the tendency of one man to make another just like himself.
> — Leo Tolstoy, in Blaisdell & Edgar, *Tolstoy as Teacher*

> Now this process of selection, this determination that something matters, is the very heart of curriculum. The choosing and naming of what matters and the presentation of those values for the perception and engaged participation of others are the deliberations that constitute curriculum development. And we learn how to do it – or how not to do it – at home.
> — Grumet, 'Curriculum and the Art of Daily Life'

As compelled as I am by Grumet's analysis of reproductive knowledge and her plea for its place within institutional learning, as a lesbian mother, I anticipate the harm done by the projection of a certain kind of home that permeates the discourses, explicit and implicit, of most classroom relationships. Although Grumet might reassure me that no one actually has that ideal home that is invoked in our collective mind, I am suggesting that the interplay of gender and sexuality make a different difference when it comes to configurations of home. At the heart of my discomfort is a simple question, one asked by many Other mothers everywhere: what imposition of 'home' will limit my son's capacity to imagine otherwise? Already, my son has gone from being described as a 'very affectionate baby,' the 'kissing bandit,' the 'Walmart greeter' in his infant daycare room, to an 'unusually affectionate' toddler, in his toddler room, 'very affectionate ... *for a boy.*' How is home being read here?

When home is suspect, so must be the knowledge that comes from it. Deficit thinking about all kinds of non-mainstream homes has been the focus of much academic writing. Far, indeed, is this from Grumet's 'sensuous possibility of home' (1991, p. 88) brought into our classrooms. The home of lesbian mothers is too luxurious. It is missing the hardness that makes children normal. It is leaking affect everywhere. But it is not, simply, issues of representation or even homophobia that scare me most, it is the worry that school is never the space where new ways of being or relating can be imagined, let alone rehearsed. Again, Grumet (1991) distils the problem I believe to be at the centre of a crisis of imagination in schools: 'we fail to distinguish the world we received as children from the one we are responsible to create as adults' (p. 80). Here, she is being critical of our 'ahistorical narcissism,' when it comes to presuming that our generation faces greater challenges than any other before it. But what I hear of value in this observation is that teachers, as the makers of curriculum, can only naturalize what it is we already know from home and for those who have a poor repertoire to draw upon, we select from the palette of normativity on offer, in dominant culture. The myth of home is ubiquitous; the particular of home is lost. What might a curriculum look like that could release a child from the inevitable processes of internalization, from the confines of a home they do not know? If so many children we teach come from families and homes that do not reflect the hyper-idealized and normative one implicit in most teaching discourses and curriculum materials, how can we even begin a discussion about 'inclusion' or imaginative pedagogies? And from my small corner of the world, I wonder what a curriculum would look like that makes gender *and* sexuality a part of the aesthetic nomenclature that is home?

Mothers and Other-Mothers

Surely, it is not just a slip of the gender that our son has two mothers, but not a mother and a father. Two loving adults, but not two different sexes. A soft-shoe move. A gender slide. Two mothers, partner-mothers, not just any two mothers. *Mothers who are lovers.* Mothers who love each other and him.

Maidin (a Gaelic word pronounced Ma-Jeen, meaning 'morning') is her parental name, like Mommy is mine. In the last few weeks of our son's life, he has begun to say '*My* Maidin.' As in 'Where is my Maidin?' when I pick him up from daycare. The possessive denotes something extremely important. It's no longer just her name; it's also her function. When I noticed this shift, I imagined the whole world changing. But how does the other-mother experience the multiple contradictions of her role? I asked her, and she replied as follows. Caroline Fusco (aka Maidin):

What do two mothers do to *re*imagine the social spaces of the family differently? What are the daily contradictions and counterpoints and the little 'tactics of habitat' (Foucault, 1980), that we engage in order to undo the weight of the matrix of heterosexual intelligibility (Butler, 1990) that defines and confirms 'the family'? How do mommy and Maidin reconfigure the heteronormative familial practices of the everyday in order to make our lived space/s other than mommy-daddy?

we were two lovers of one gender, we were two women of one generation. (Rich, 1993, p. 31)

At one time I thought that being a (lesbian) mother was not possible for me: it was outside the realm of my imagination when I was living at home in Ireland. Being a lesbian mother was a contradiction. Growing up under Irish Catholicism rendered lesbian motherhood wholly and an unholy Other. Here, now, I cannot imagine being otherwise. I am the other mother, the other lesbian mother, the other lesbian Catholic mother in our household. This identity provided one of the first contradictions of my motherhood. Identifying as a 'lesbian Catholic mother' is important because the resulting tension in these mother identities required a suspension of disbelief, literally and figuratively, on our behalf and on the Church's behalf early in our son's life. 'Bundled' into an individualized baptism class in the basement of a church, away from the gaze of the 'faithful,' we, along with our non-practising Catholic godparents, declared that the son of lesbian mothers was ready to be baptized. Scheduled at a time when no one else would witness the baptism or hear the mothers' names over and over again in the ceremony, we, a subversive priest, and our friends and family, including the other Irish Catholic mother ('in-law'), created a profound (20-minute) counter-narrative to the Church's foundational heterosexual procreation narrative. As Father E called on us, the loving (lesbian) parents, to 'give' our son to the Church, I wondered (and still do) what right/ rites this Church has to my son? The history of this Church is marred by patriarchy and inquisitions and persecutions, and women, particularly, have not faired at all well in this institution. As a woman, and now as a mother, who grew up attached to its ritual but loathing its vilification of difference, what could this Church offer our son? Whatever we imagined it to be, it seemed to be worth signing him on. It should be his right to reject the Church if he chooses. His other mother signed her full name, but for the record, for all perpetuity, and for all (not) to see, his second mother signed only her first initial and surname in the *official* baptism register. Father E was worried about any future inquisitions; this was the compromise we struck. But, as the second mother, I remain the absent-presence on the register, my incomplete signature a testament (no pun intended) to the misunderstanding of the fullness I feel as a mother. Then again, this is not the only place where incompleteness and fullness are in tension in my 'other-mother life.'

this is how we tried to love, and these are the forces they had ranged against us,
and these are the forces we had ranged within us, within us against us, against us,
within us. (Rich, 1993, p. 31)

Usually it is only within my own imaginary that I have thoughts of
incompleteness and contradiction because the people, parents, and daycare workers I interact with are, from what I can tell, very accepting of
our son's Maidin, his other mother. We have been two mothers at the
daycare mothers' day celebration – two gifts made for us by our son for
his two mothers. We have had our godfather attend the fathers' day celebration with us. They have to accept us; we take our place in this family
space. We often wonder if our son's daycare pals ask their parents why
they do not have a Maidin? Despite this, even when I am called mother
or Maidin (by others) I often wonder, what do they really think about
this name and about the bearer of such a name? Who do they think this
person is in this little boy's life? Do they think about whether our son
knows that his Maidin is not a daddy? Do they wonder whether his
Maidin will teach him daddy things? Do they see Maidin as ≠ mother
and ≠ father, and two mothers as = 1 not = 2 (as in mommy + daddy)?
Our son is surrounded by these other mommies and daddies. I am the
only 'Maidin' he knows, I am the only other parent he has known in his
life. When he calls, 'Maidin,' I do not ever stop to wonder what he is
thinking, I just respond. In the morning ('ar maidin' in Gaelige), at night,
and at all other times I take my Maidin role very seriously. But even
these moments can be undone and feelings of incompleteness pervade
my psyche when our son asks 'where is my mommy' or sobs 'I want
my mommy.' It is heart wrenching when I say, 'mommy Maidin is here
sweetheart,' and he cries, 'I want my other mommy.' Instantaneously,
I wonder what we have done in the naming of ourselves as mommy
and Maidin and not mommy and mommy? Does he see me as ≠ mother
because of this naming and because he sees otherwise in his life outside
our family? I have to think that it is not a rejection of Maidin as mother
but of anyone (even 'a daddy') other than the mother who he so desper-
ately needs at that moment. And in those moments, I have to remember
that our son now says, 'Where is my Maidin?' To him I am ≠ his mother
and ≠ daddy. I = Maidin, the only one he will ever have. For him, there
is no contradiction. Yet.

In public, some people have not known what to make of me; I am
not a daddy, neither do I look like my son. Not knowing how to make
sense of me, I have been mistaken for my partner's mother, our son's

grandmother. Some synonyms for 'grand' are: impressive, distinguished, fantastic, large, and all-inclusive. I'd like to believe that I am all of these things in my son's life, so perhaps when I hear this again I can bring myself to answer, 'well, actually, I am his Maidin, which is a "grand" mother of sorts.' Adrienne Rich (1993) wrote: 'Two women together is a work nothing in civilization has made simple' (p. 35). Two women, who are lovers and mothers, is also a work, 'heroic in its ordinariness … where the fiercest attention becomes routine – look at the faces of those who have chosen it' (p. 35). Always in progress, constantly taking a 'line of flight' (Deleuze & Guattari, 1987), away from the Oedipal family and towards a becoming-family, becoming-different, becoming (im)perceptible to him, to us, to everyone.

> *the air through which child and mother*
> *are running the boy singing*
> *the woman eyes sharpened in the light*
> *heart stumbling making for the open*
> (Rich, 1993, p. 59)

Home Time: Now and Then

Contemplation about the circular notion of parenting, being parented and now parenting, captivates me. Coming back home to one's experience of childhood, through one's experience of parenthood, is something of a fascination. What is the same? What is different? How do we escape this 'parented' feeling, embrace it, accommodate it, deny it, reproduce it, consider it? Where does the parenting home fit with the home of childhood? Intensely loving a parent as a young child is different in quality and kind from loving one's own child. Surely. Or is it just the same? In another key perhaps? Transposed but recognizable? What is the quality of that move to the other side of unconditional love, if you have, as I have, been so lucky to have experienced it that way. Unconditional love. It even sounds impossible. Hard to say. Too much movement in the mouth. But it is just that. Fraught though it might be at times, I have arrived on the other side, able to say, finally… ahhh. I know. I understand. Thank you mom and dad. The project is now clearer. Your deaths interrupted an important continuity, but now the thread's been taken up again. Dropped a stitch, but here we are again. Thank you.

My own mother wasn't a typical mother of her generation, the 1950s. She didn't much like domestic chores even though she was 'at home' with her five children until I, her youngest, hit about age 12. It's hard to say whether she would have liked domestic life more if she hadn't had such illness. With so much pain, my father picked up several of the domestic tasks. Typical gender roles were a little wonky in my house. Not by today's standard's perhaps, but certainly in their time and working-class space. And my father loved parenting. I knew it because I felt it; he loved being a father. But that is a different chapter. I would like to close with a very small reflection about my mother.

In the last many weeks of her life, she was bedridden. She was in her home, my father had just died, and she was being cared for not by her nurse of 40 years, my father, but by each of her five children, who shared the care among them, each one having her/his special night/day/time with her. We all did different activities when we were with her. We had our own separate relationships with her, and so we did the different things we each liked to do when she was on our watch. I often brushed her hair, or rubbed cream on her leg, the amputated one. Others read to her or simply talked or, one of my mother's special gifts, sat silently together with her. When my mother died, and we were left to sort out the house, we, each of us, wanted to keep the music CD that was my mother's very favourite, the one we always listened to with her over the last months. These turned out to be five different CDs. (Mine, by the way, was *Unforgettable* with Nat and Natalie King Cole). She had, or so we had imagined, told each of us that a different CD was, in fact, her very favourite one. She'd allowed us to believe, as she had in our childhoods, that what we loved was also what she loved. For me, this tiny discovery retold the story of my mother's life as a mother. Not self-sacrifice, but a way of ensuring that each of us felt special, individual, and that we could count upon her fascination with anything we deemed important. When I now make my son's bed, in his room when he's gone, or when I am sitting very still breastfeeding, staring into his eyes, I remember this feeling of the affirmation of the universe. All is well. Love, embodied, unadulterated. And a deeply imaginative act.

So here is our starting place. Two mothers on a course. We will draw from many places, intellectually, emotionally, imaginatively. And we will make a work of our mother-partnership. A kind of promise. To him. To each other. To ourselves.

Note

1 For a comprehensive framing of Kant's theory and German idealist thought more generally, see his *Critique of Judgment* (1790).

References

Armstrong, L. (2003). *Conditions of love: The philosophy of intimacy.* London: Penguin.

Arnup, K. (1995). *Lesbian parenting: Living with pride and prejudice.* Charlottetown, PEI: Gynergy.

Blaisdell, B., & Edgar, C. (2000). *Tolstoy as teacher: Leo Tolstoy's writings on education.* New York: Teachers and Writers Collaborative.

Butler, J. (1990). *Gender trouble: Feminism and the subversion of identity.* New York: Routledge.

Cho, D. (2005). Lessons of love: Psychoanalysis and teacher-student love. *Educational Theory, 55* (1), 79–92.

Deleuze, G., & Guattari, F. (1987). *A thousand plateaus: Capitalism and schizophrenia.* Minneapolis, MN: University of Minnesota Press.

Foucault, M. (1980). *Power/knowledge: Selected interviews and other writings, 1972–1977.* Trans. C. Gordon. New York: Pantheon.

Furlong, E.J. (1961). *Imagination.* London: George Allen & Unwin.

Garrison, J. (1997). *Dewey and Eros: Wisdom and desire in the art of teaching.* New York: Teachers College Press.

Greene, M. (1995). *Releasing the imagination: Essays on education, the arts, and social change.* San Francisco, CA: Jossey-Bass.

Grumet, M. (1988). *Bitter milk: Women and teaching.* Amherst, MA: University of Massachusetts Press.

Grumet, M. (1991). Curriculum and the art of daily life. In G. Willis & W. Shubert (Eds.), *Reflections from the heart of educational inquiry: Understanding curriculum and teaching through the arts* (pp. 74–89). Albany, NY: State University of New York Press.

Halpin, D. (2007). *Romanticism and education: Love, heroism and imagination in pedagogy.* London: Continuum.

Heqeumbourg, A. (2007). *Lesbian motherhood: Stories of becoming.* New York: Harrington Park.

Maleuvre, D. (2005). Art and the teaching of love. *Journal of Aesthetics Education, 39* (1), 229–253.

Rich, A. (1976). *Of woman born.* New York: Norton.

Rich, A. (1993). *The dream of a common language*. New York: Norton.

Sartre, J.-P. (1960/2000). Trans. Reck. Beyond bourgeois theatre. In C. Martin & H. Bial (Eds.), *Brecht sourcebook* (pp. 50–57). London: Routledge.

Sartre, J.-P. (1962). *Imagination: A psychological critique*. Ann Arbor, MI: University of Michigan Press.

Shore, A.E. (1996). What kind of a lesbian is a mother? *Journal of Feminist Family Therapy, 8* (3), 45–62.

12 M/othering Multiculturalism: Adoption, Diversity, and Nomadic Subjects

JENNIFER EISENHAUER

In the evenings before bedtime, my 3-year-old daughter Xinyan and I sit in the rocking chair in her room reading books. Her selection of books has followed various interests including the weeks we spent reading books with pictures of moons. However, more recently she selected a book we had not read before, *I Love You Like Crazy Cakes*, by Rose Lewis. The story begins with an image of a room with a row of cribs each holding two babies attended by Chinese women wearing what looks somewhat like white lab coats. It reads: 'Once upon a time in China there was a baby girl who lived in a big room with lots of other babies. The girls shared cribs with one another and became great friends. The girls had nannies to take care of them, but each was missing something – a mother' (Lewis, 2000, not paginated).

On the next page the illustration is of a Caucasian woman with brown hair sitting pensively at a table with white paper, a pen, a small lamp, and a cup of tea. The story continues: 'Far away across the ocean was a woman who also had many friends, but she was missing something, too – a baby. That woman was me. So I wrote a letter to officials in China and asked if I could adopt one of the babies who lived in the big room. Months later, I received a letter with a picture of a beautiful baby girl . . . that was you. The people in China said I could adopt you if I promised to take good care of you. I promised I would' (Lewis, 2000, n.p.).

In the remainder of the book, the story follows this mother's journey to China to meet her child including images of airplanes, a tearful union, playing in the hotel room, taking pictures, and returning home to a crowd of excited relatives bringing presents and affection to their newly arrived relative. The story ends with the mother embracing her sleeping baby and concludes: 'I held you tightly, kissed you softly, and cried. The tears were for your Chinese mother, who could not keep you. I wanted her to know that we would always remember her. And I hoped somehow she knew you were safe and happy in the world' (Lewis, 2000, n.p.).

In these three pages, this storybook establishes a number of ideas common within the popular discourse of adoption of mostly girls from China that began in the early 1990s in part as a response to the One-Child Policy established by the Chinese government. *I Love You Like Crazy Cakes* navigates the challenging narratives of abandonment, cross-cultural exchange, gender, and class that are inherent to the adoption of young girls from China into Western families. In particular, this story exemplifies the way in which these complex relationships are constructed through maternal bodies. There is no adoptive father or birthfather in *I Love You Like Crazy Cakes*. Both this book by Rose Lewis and the companion book, *Every Year on Your Birthday* (2007), are based on her own adoption as a single mother of a baby from China. However, this first person narrative becomes the reader's narrative, as was clear when after one reading, my daughter, who I and my husband adopted from China, pointed to the Chinese baby in the story and told me that the baby in the book was her.

The exclusion and marginalization of fathers is common within Chinese-American adoption narratives. This marginalization reflects a larger discourse that emphasizes the maternal in constructing understandings of the complex process and experience of transnational adoption. Even when adoptive fathers are included in the narrative, it is consistently the adoptive mother who is depicted as reaching for and holding the babies during the literal and symbolic exchange most often represented as an orphanage nanny handing the child to his or her adoptive parents for the first time.

Transnational adoption from China emerges as a form of cultural exchange, mediated immigration, and multiracial/multicultural familial construction that involves maternal bodies (both birth mother and adoptive mother) as the locations of abandonment and conservation, lack and plentitude, and communism and capitalism. Dorow (2006) explores the maternal in discourses of Chinese adoption: 'Indeed, much of adoption discourse in both China and the United States is about the specularized absence or presence of a mother's love and the contradictions of journeying between two mothers juxtaposed by class, nation, and race. This is why scholars have increasingly recognized that adoption remakes the agency and meaning of motherhood in divergent ways' (pp. 164–165).

Amid these constructs of motherhood, both birth mothers and adoptive mothers are depicted as loving their children. Abandonment is carefully located not as the breaking of a bonding love between birth mother and child, but as a natural maternal relationship disrupted by material consequences, that is, poverty and China's One-Child Policy, that leave no other options. As the narrative concludes in *I Love You Like Crazy Cakes*, 'The tears were for your Chinese mother, who could not keep you' (Lewis, 2000, n.p.). It is not the birth father that cannot keep the child. Although probably more accurate in many experiences, the narrative does not conclude, *we don't know for sure why your birth parents couldn't keep you*.

Volkman (2003) suggests that the anxiety that arises surrounding the loss of the birth mother's body, comes to be relocated in a search not for the birth mother, but her surrogate form, that is, birth culture: 'Beyond the efforts to instill a kind of protective cultural pride, it is this sadness and desire, I suggest, that may incite tremendous interest in the child's "culture." In the absence of the mother's body, the longing for origins may be displaced onto the body of the nation and its imagined culture . . . The world of adoption has come up with a term that seems to express this, a paradoxical formulation: *birth culture*' (p. 42).

It is the relationship between maternal bodies, subjectivity, and culture that I will explore in this chapter as a way to inform not only understandings of adoption discourse, but also to provide a path through which to examine a parallel and, at times, intersecting discourse of multiculturalism. In particular, I will be exploring how an understanding of the adoptive mother's body as a 'meeting place' of nomadic subjects and a critical engagement with the social and cultural realities of global families provides additional vantages through which to critically engage multiculturalism and multiculturalism within education.

Does She Have a Nickname? Adopted Children and Nomadic Subjectivity

The circumstances and ideas surrounding our daughter's naming are indicative of the complex interrelationships of culture, race, gender, and socioeconomic status characteristic of her nomadic subjectivity. Our daughter, Xinyan, was not given a name that we know of by her birth parents. Rather, when she arrived at the orphanage as a newborn

she was given the name Cao Xin Yan. All of the children in the orphanage born in that year, were given the same surname, Cao. Like any expecting parents, my husband and I debated the possibility of multiple
names that 'we would give her.' We didn't question the practice of re-
naming adopted children. Eventually, we opted to create a combination
of Eastern and Western names with Xinyan, spelled as one word, for
her middle name.

When we met our daughter for the first time, however, she was 16
months old, and the only thing that we said that she could understand
was her name. We did not speak Mandarin and she did not speak English. To call her anything else in this moment where she struggled to understand what was happening to her felt alienating for her and selfish
on our part. This decision to continue calling her by her Chinese name
resulted in a reconsideration of why we had given her a Western first
name in the first place and two years later she continues to be called,
Xinyan. Ultimately, her name will be her choice.

Her naming has resulted in a number of experiences that reveal
the Eurocentric, racist, and sexist challenges facing a family created
through such hybrid cultural and racial identities. Not surprisingly, it
is common to be asked to repeat her name, and people not familiar with
Mandarin pronunciation struggle with a name that doesn't correspond
to English phonetics. Comments and 'suggestions' regarding her name
often extend beyond simple pronunciation issues.

Once, after hearing me say her name, a gymnastics teacher asked if
she had a nickname. I realized that her request for an alternative name
did not stem from a desire to create intimacy, as is often the case with
nicknames that come from one's interactions with others or as indica-
tors of affection. Rather, this was, in part, an issue of convenience and
perhaps American arrogance. Our daughter's name required too much
of her attention and our daughter's failure to assimilate with her Caucasian middle-class classmates, none of whom were asked if they had
nicknames, made the instructor uncomfortable.

We also have entertained suggestions from others ranging from
changing the spelling of her name to make it more 'pronounceable'
to outright 'phasing out' her Chinese name. What remains veiled for
many are the ways in which these 'suggestions' can emerge from an assimilationist mindset grounded in Eurocentrism and racism that views
our decision to understand our daughter's cultural identity as *a coming
together of* rather than *a becoming changed into* as a parenting problem.
As our daughter now begins to understand that there is a relationship

between herself and other things and people that are labelled 'Chinese,' other naming issues have emerged. This year when decorating for the Lunar New Year our daughter pointed to herself when we described one of the decorations in our home as Chinese. Later, friends witnessing our daughter's emerging understanding of cultural naming reminded her (and us) that she was 'Chinese American.' It was quite clear that the transgression was in the failure to include the word American and that it would be unlikely that the omission of the word Chinese (i.e., calling her 'American') would elicit such commentary. In many ways, the challenges that emerge regarding our daughter's naming are reflective of larger issues about how to best understand the complex identity of the transnationally adopted child beyond assimilationist discourses and practices that have dominated earlier moments in the history of transnational adoption. As Yngvesson asks, is the child an 'open cultural space' or is he or she inextricably 'rooted in national soil' (in Volkman, 2003, 35)?

Mary Watkins (2006) proposes an understanding of the transnationally adopted child as a nomadic subject through a consideration of Rosi Braidotti's (1994) discussions of nomadism, gender, and feminism. Watkins is interested in 're-conceiving' the identity of transnationally adopted children as characterized by complexity and multiplicity rather than as fixed and singular. In particular, Watkins is interested in how the identities of transnationally adopted children can be understood as nomadic subjects. Watkins (2006) applies Braidotti's understanding of the nomadic subject as characterized by ' "the simultaneity of complex and multi-layered identities" where the axes like class, race, ethnicity, gender, age and others interact with each other' (p. 265). Watkins continues, submitting that 'a nomadic self continues to be a "self-in-process," a continuous becoming that moves against the fixity of identity' (p. 266).

Braidotti (1994) articulates nomadic subjectivity not as resulting from literal travel, but from transgression and subversion: 'Though the image of "nomadic subjects" is inspired by the experience of people or cultures that are literally nomadic, the nomadism in question here refers to the kind of critical consciousness that resists settling into socially coded modes of thought and behavior. Not all nomads are world travelers; some of the greatest trips one can take without physically moving from one's habitat. It is the subversion of set conventions that defines the nomadic state, not the literal act of traveling' (p., 5).

Watkins (2006) also applies Braidotti's distinction between the migrant, exile, and nomad to thinking about the transnationally adopted child's subjectivity. The adopted child is not a migrant brought from one culture to another: 'She moves between multiple cultural locations in the present, not just two' (p, 265). Likewise, Watkins suggests that the adopted child is not an exile because she can or has returned to her birth place. However, this is a somewhat literal interpretation of Braidotti's distinction between the migrant, exile, and nomad.

Braidotti (1994) describes the 'exile style' like·this: 'The mode and tense of exile style are based on an acute sense of foreignness, coupled with the often-hostile perception of the host country. Exile literature, for instance, is marked by a sense of loss or separation from the home country, which, often for political reasons, is a lost horizon; there is a diasporic side to it. Memory, recollection, and the rumination of acoustic traces of the mother tongue are central to this literary genre' (p. 24).' In contrast, Braidotti describes the nomadic style as being about 'transitions and passages without predetermined destinations or lost homelands' (p. 25). The nomad is not homeless or the result of compulsive displacement. Rather, the nomad is a 'figuration for the kind of subject who has relinquished all idea, desire, or nostalgia for fixity. This figuration expresses the desire for an identity made of transitions, successive shifts, and coordinated changes, without or against an essential unity' (p. 22).

Rather than situating the adopted child as one in search of or dislocated from her 'roots,' or her 'essential identity' (Braidotti, 1994, p. 22), an understanding of the adopted child as *nomadic subject* positions her not as 'lacking roots,' but rather that her 'roots are rhizomatic in nature, allowing her to emerge into situations marked by different ethnic sensibilities, supported by her own experience that links them' (Watkins, 2006, p. 12). By referencing Deleuze and Guattari's (1987) discussion of the rhizome, Watkins challenges arborescent conceptualizations of personal and familial histories as not being represented by a family tree, but by a non-hierarchical matrix of connections. As Deleuze and Guattari (1987) write, 'Principles of connection and heterogeneity: any point of a rhizome can be connected to anything other, and must be. This is very different from the tree or root, which plots a point, fixes an order' (p. 7). However, how does this understanding of the child's nomadic subjectivity as rhizomatic impact understandings of the maternal and the relationship between child and mother within transnational adoption discourses? Are adoptive mothers also nomadic subjects?

Wandering Wombs: Adoptive Mothers as Embodied Nomadic Subjects

The bond between mother and child is often situated within biological discourses that attribute notions of connectedness with the physical act of carrying a child in the uterus. Labelling women who do not give birth to biological offspring as barren positions their bodies and identity as lacking, uninhabitable, and unproductive. When these understandings of the maternal body intersect with discourses of adoption, people will sometimes remark that adoptive parents were not able to have a child *of their own* or refer to adopted children as not being the couple's *real* child. Ultimately, adoption is positioned as a second choice to biological reproduction with most people not even considering the possibility that adoption might not be the result of 'failing' to get pregnant, but rather as it was for my own family, chosen instead of biological reproduction.

The privileging of maternal bodies that give birth has positioned the adoptive maternal body not only as lacking, but also as pathological (i.e., a wandering womb). Among other symptoms and conditions linked to the womb, one cause of the historical diagnosis of hysteria was those things that related to the reproductive system. Briggs (2000) explains, 'In fact, a great many divergent kinds and causes of "civilized" women's infertility were simultaneously proclaimed to have a relationship to nervous illness, from failure to conceive to miscarriage to abortion' (p. 246). An early example is Plato's positioning of the 'unfruitful' womb as pathological. Plato writes about 'the so-called womb or matrix of women' (as cited in Merskey & Merskey, 1993, p. 401), and describes, 'the animal within them is desirous of procreating children, and when remaining unfruitful long beyond its proper time, gets discontented and angry and wandering in every direction through the body, closes up the passages of the breath, and, by obstructing respiration, drives them to extremity, causing all varieties of disease' (p. 401).

An early phrase used to describe what later became more commonly called 'hysteria' was 'the suffocation of the mother' (Briggs, 2000; Merskey & Merskey, 1993). The suffocation of the mother refers to the belief that the womb could travel through the body and impinge on other organs and bodily functions. This wandering womb can be thought of as not simply leading to the suffocation the literal 'mother,' but also of the role of the maternal, understood as the primary role of the biological female. The linguistic and conceptual construction of this condition as suffocating the 'mother' rather than the 'female' or 'woman' is quite revealing of the strong connection between the female reproductive system and role as a predisposition to 'madness.'

Rather than positioning the adoptive mother's body as a lack and absence, I am interested in how a reconsideration of the adoptive mother's embodiment and subjectivity might challenge assumptions inherent to privileging biologically based mother-child relationships. In particular, I am interested in repositioning the wandering womb of the adoptive mother as one characterized by multiplicity and change with the potential to disrupt gendered, cultural, biological, socioeconomic, and racial (among other) boundaries. What if the woman with a 'wandering womb' is understood not as lacking, pathological, and desperate, but as a nomadic maternal subject? What if the relationship between mothers and children united through adoption is not understood simply as one that aims to replicate the ties assumed to be inherent to biological relationships, but that rather opens opportunities for considering divergent ways of understanding the maternal? As Volkman (2003) inquires, 'Is adoption inescapably bound to the effort to replicate, echo, or mirror the family formed by biological ties? Or is a more radical transformation possible, as Yngvesson (1997) suggests in her analysis of open adoption? The practices of contemporary Chinese (and other forms of transnational) adoption reveal both the pull of the genealogical model and the impulse to transcend it and create new forms of kinship beyond blood' (p. 48).

In returning to Braidotti's discussion of nomadic subjectivity, rather than understanding the adoptive mother as 'mov[ing] *toward* nomadicism,' as Watkins (2006, emphasis added) proposes, I am suggesting that the adoptive mother be recognized also as a nomadic subject. I am not suggesting that the adoptive mother experiences the same mix of social, political, cultural, class, and gendered experiential layers lived by her transnationally adopted child. Rather, the adoptive mother's subjectivity is no more fixed, singular, and predetermined and is no less an embodied experience, even when the physicality of birth is absent from her lived experience. In particular, a recognition of both mother and child as having independent, but connected subjectivities is important to more broadly defined understandings of mothers and children. Drucilla Cornell (2004), who is the mother of a daughter adopted from Paraguay, writes, 'Parenting involves the acceptance that a child never belongs to the parent' (p. 140).

Within the contexts of transnational adoption from China, the adopted child also does not belong to the birth parents or the birth nation. However, it remains important that the birth parents are not understood as an absence and a lack. In one sense, the birth parents are always present in the physical body of the child constructed through a connected genetic relationship, the bellybutton a reminder of a maternal physical connection and separation. However, the birth parents and the circumstances surrounding their loss of a child and the adoptive parents being united with this child remain an important presence in the familial construct and the understanding of adoptive maternal subjects.

These subjectivities, experiences, practices, and circumstances also position 'the post-colonial condition' as a part of the familial narrative and of the wandering womb (Cornell, 2004, p. 119). Cornell writes about the complexity of transnational adoption including the ways in which transnational adoption embodies what Gayatri Spivak describes as an 'enabling violation' (as cited in Cornell, p. 119):

> Due to the horrifying economic inequalities that separate countries in the global North and the global South, many children are left in serious poverty. These inequalities are created and sustained by the very countries that allow some of us the resources to adopt in the first place. Thus, what can be enabling for certain children – parents who adopt them and, in many cases, enable them to stay alive – is inseparable from the violation perpetuated through systematic inequalities . . . Being part of the scene of adoption forces us to acknowledge the great extent to which the post-colonial predicament is about the continuing legitimation of inequalities between northern and southern countries.

Therefore, the wandering womb of the adoptive maternal subject does not reference an idealistic, romantic, and salvation-oriented nomadism. Rather, this nomadism is at times trespassing, and the maternal body is not simply a nurturing haven, but also a locus of abandonment, colonization, and inequity. This wandering womb is a location of beginnings and a 'mourning of injustice' (Cornell, 2004, p. 142).

Considering this framing, how can the adoptive mother be understood as an embodied subject in a way that realizes the complexities that surround transnational adoption? Rather than seeing the nomad as without place, I am interested in how the wandering womb of the maternal nomadic body and subject can be understood as what Massey (1994) describes as a 'meeting place.' This is not a maternal embodied subject defined through a fixed notion of rootedness, but a meeting place, a moment of intersection (p.154): 'What gives a place its specificity is not some long internalized history but the fact that it is constructed out of a particular constellation of social relations, meeting and weaving together at a particular locus . . . Instead then, of thinking of places as areas without boundaries around, they can be imagined as articulated moments in networks of social relations and understandings, but where a large proportion of those relations, experiences, and understandings are constructed on a far larger scale than what we happen to define for the moment as the place itself' (p. 154).

This meeting place can be understood as reflecting 'nomadic shifts' that 'designate . . . a creative sort of becoming; a performative metaphor that allows for otherwise unlikely encounters and unsuspected sources of interaction of experience and of knowledge' (Braidotti, 1994, p. 6). The wandering womb of the adoptive maternal subject is not a location of reproduction, but one of connections, intersections, and multiplicities.

An understanding of nomadism requires a willingness to have one's understandings of social and cultural constructs disrupted. Within the contexts of transnational adoption, oversimplifying, non-reflexive, and non-critical ways of envisioning the social and cultural aspects of multiracial and multicultural families formed through adoption can be of significant consequence. In what follows, I will explore issues raised regarding social and cultural understandings in the context of transnational adoption and explore these issues as they pertain to understandings of multiculturalism and multicultural education.

Mothering, Multiculturalism, and Multicultural Education

Volkman (2003) describes how the 'social pendulum has swung from the virtual denial of adoption and the biological beginnings of the adopted child to an insistent ideology that *without* embrace of those beginnings there will forever be a gaping hole, a primal wound, an incomplete self' (p. 43). This is quite different from earlier assimilationist discourses within transnational adoption that asserted that the child's cultural experience should mirror that of the adoptive parents with little to no attention given to the multiple racial and/or cultural locations experienced by the adopted child. This is a challenging reality, as 'adoptive parents struggle with the contradictions as they seek to imbue a child with a love of China *and* an understanding of the harsh realities that probably inform her personal history' (p. 43, emphasis added). Multicultural education reflects a similar struggle.

Adoptive parents often incorporate things like holidays and cultural celebrations into the familial tapestry in an attempt to maintain the adopted child's connection to her 'birth culture.' However, as Anagnost (2000) cautions, 'The danger lies in constructing a culture that is purely celebratory and devoid of history' (p. 390). Cornell (2004) describes how the adoptive parents can inadvertently maintain assimilation within overt attempts of encouraging the adopted child to embrace her 'birth culture': 'Because whiteness is the color that erases itself, the parents saw themselves as without a color, as without an ethnicity other than American. Thus, in the very attempt to recognize their children's uniqueness, the parents thwarted their need to identify as Americans "like them"' (p. 139).

Similarly, Eng (2003) raises the issue that while attitudes towards adoption have changed considerably, 'given the ways in which difference is often appropriated and reinscribed by a politics of weak multiculturalism, the current acknowledgement of the adoptee's past may not have shifted this management of affect in any significant manner' (p. 16).

These critical questions raised about a multiculturalism situated in a predominantly celebratory discourse point to the ways in which multiculturalism 'sets up the paradox of absorbing "difference" into the intimate space of the familial while also reinscribing it' (Anagnost, 2000, p. 390). As Eng (2003) asks, 'How are discourses of multiculturalism being invoked to manage, to aestheticize, to reinscribe, and finally to deracinate culture of all meaningful difference' (p. 12)? The challenges surrounding constructions of multiculturalism within the global family formed through transnational adoption raise important questions not only for issues of identity within the family, but they also point to how similar issues arise within constructions of multiculturalism in education. What can this critical engagement with the negotiations of social and cultural realities within the family formed through transnational adoption offer to challenging the problematic outcomes of a celebratory multiculturalism equally devoid of a consideration of the historical and contemporary complexities of cultural and racial diversities?

In his discussion of anti-oppressive education, Kevin Kumashiro (2002) provides a critique of different approaches to multiculturalism within education. Two of the approaches he examines are what he calls 'education for the Other' and 'education about the Other.' Common manifestations of multiculturalism within both adoptive familial and educational discourses are similar to Kumashiro's descriptions of education for the Other, and education about the Other.

Education for the Other begins with the idea that children experience harmful places in relation to their diversity and that providing students with 'helpful' places can address the issues they experience surrounding their diversities. Within schools, an example of this approach would be to create a group for LGBTQ (lesbian, gay, bisexual, transgender, and questioning) students. Kumashiro critiques this approach in its failure to address the ways in which oppression is not simply the result of marginalizing the Other, but also of privileging what is considered to be normal. Such an approach inadvertently positions the Other as the problem to be contended with. Likewise, this approach does not address or challenge people and students who are not part of marginalized groups (i.e., white, American, and middle class). Within adoptive families, multiculturalism as education for the Other can result in providing adopted children with opportunities to learn cultural 'traditions' related to such things as dance, language, and art while seeing these experiences as being primarily for the sake of the child. A consideration of how issues surrounding racial and cultural diversity are relevant to everyone in the family and not just the child who is perceived as Other is often lacking.

Education about the Other includes both those in marginalized and non-marginalized groups in a celebration of the cultural traditions of Others, but it equally fails to challenge the racial, cultural, social, gender, and class issues that lead to the marginalization of some groups and the privileging of others. Within education this is a common form of multiculturalism that focuses school-based lessons in diversity as exploring, much like tourists, the cultural traditions of diverse groups. These explorations focus on that which is perceived as 'traditional' and 'authentic,' rarely entertaining contemporary realities and more often completely avoiding questions related to social and cultural injustice. Likewise, the adoptive parents may actively participate in cultural events with their child, but equally overlook the more complex issues surrounding the lived experience of racial, cultural, and class-based differences. Anagnost (2003) comments on a similar issue regarding adoption and celebratory multicultural discourses: 'certain modes of institutionalized multiculturalism carry the potential to aestheticize racial and cultural difference. At their worst, they can box people into stereotypical images as insistently as the representational regimes associated with colonial histories. The politics of inclusion can so easily be subverted (as it often is in public schooling) to the controlled insertion of culturally inflected signs devoid of history (such as Chinese New Year, the dragon, the Chinese writing system, or ethnic cuisine)' (p. 412).

In Braidotti's (1994) discussion of Trinh T. Minh-ha's perception of multiculturalism, she explains that multiculturalism should be understood not only as a difference *between* other cultures, but also as a difference *within* the same culture, within every self. Such a shift necessitates an understanding of the relationship between 'histories of colonialism, military intervention, capitalist exploitation, racism, and gender discrimination . . . and histories of imperialism, immigration, racialized exploitation, and gendered commodification' (Eng, 2003, p. 9); the ways in which *both* parents and children are racialized; and how 'dehistoricization also maintains the separations that constitute racialized boundaries in U.S. society historically' (Anagnost, 2000, p. 391).

Understanding nomadic subjectivity as a 'nomadic consciousness [that] is a form of political resistance to hegemonic and exclusionary views of subjectivity' opens opportunities for reconsidering some forms of multiculturalism (Braidotti, 1994, p. 23). Such a nomadic consciousness speaks to a deconstruction of the adoptive maternal subject through 'narratives of salvation – from poverty, disease, and the barbarism of the Third World' (Eng, 2003, p. 9). This conceptualization of transnational adoption can provide an 'exemplary – perhaps radical – opportunity for white, middle-class subjects to confront and to negotiate difference ethically within the social configurations of the new global family' (p. 33).

Discourses surrounding transnational adoption often emphasize the maternal in attempting to navigate the complex body of issues and realities surrounding one mother's loss and another mother's union with the same child. In the absence of the birth mother's body, a search for the child's 'birth culture' often becomes the substitute (Volkman, 2003). However, forms of multiculturalism dominated by a celebratory orientation often overlook the social and cultural injustices that can surround why transnational adoptees are separated from their birth parents and can remove historical realities and contexts from discussions of culture.

Likewise, understandings of multiculturalism lacking critical engagement with social and cultural realities and history cannot adequately
represent and provide locations for the complex, multiply defined, and
continually changing subjectivities. This questioning and reconsideration of discourses of multiculturalism shared by both education and
transnational adoption communities can complicate and address diversity not simply as a celebration of difference, but also as a location of
inequality and injustice.

From Family Tree to Rhizome

My daughter never knew my womb as a fetal hand reaching into
the warm darkness. Her bellybutton didn't connect to me through a
twisted cord. I wove paperwork into ropes that led me to her, and I
flew in the belly of a 747 to meet her for the first time. When I am asked
why I chose to adopt or why I didn't have a child of 'my own,' I am
being asked about my body. I am being asked if my body is 'broken,' if
it nearly denied me motherhood, and it is never assumed that adoption
might be the path my body chose.

Adoption makes our family one of three wombs: my own and those
of my daughter and her birth mother. We are a family of wandering
wombs. Not ones identical to those of the history of hysteria, but wandering as nomads: complex, multiple, in process, and subversive. Our
DNA is not that of fallen ladders, but of rhizomes. So, teachers, please
don't ask my daughter to draw her family tree when she is a rhizome.
Don't assume to know what a nomad might bring when asked to
bring a food from her culture. The nomad born from the wandering
womb questions the very meaning of culture. She provides us with an
opportunity to realize that celebrations do not exist in isolation from
challenges and pain. Self, do not mourn the loss of your daughter's
birth culture, but recognize the value of multiplicity. Tell her story
honestly, but gently, just as a mother would.

References

Anagnost, A. (2000). Scenes of misrecognition: Maternal citizenship in the
age of transnational adoption. *Positions: East Asia Cultures Critique, 8* (2),
389–421.
Braidotti, R. (1994). *Nomadic subjects.* New York: Columbia University Press.

Briggs, L. (2000). The race of hysteria: 'Overcivilization' and the 'savage' woman in later nineteenth-century obstetrics and gynecology. *American Quarterly, 52* (2), 246–273.

Cornell, D. (2004). Defending ideals: War, democracy, and political struggle. New York: Routledge.

Deleuze, G., & Guattari, F. (1987). *A thousand plateaus: Capitalism and schizophrenia.* Minneapolis, MN: University of Minnesota Press.

Dorow, S. (2006). Transnational adoption: A cultural economy of race, gender, and *kinship.* New York: New York University Press.

Eng, D. (2003). Transnational adoption and queer diasporas. *Social Text, 76* (21), 1–37.

Kumashiro, K. (2002) Troubling education: Queer activism and anti-oppressive *pedagogy.* New York: Routledge.

Lewis, R. (2000) *I love you like crazy cakes.* Bel Air, CA: Little, Brown.

Lewis, R. (2007). *Every year on your birthday.* Bel Air, CA: Little, Brown.

Massey, D. (1994) *Space, place, and gender.* Minneapolis, MN: University of Minneapolis Press.

Merskey, H., & Merskey, S. (1993). Hysteria, or 'suffocation of the mother.' *Canadian Medical Association Journal, 148* (3), 399–415.

Volkman, T. (2003). Embodying Chinese culture: Transnational adoption in North America. *Social Text, 74* (21), 29–55.

Watkins, M. (2006). Adoption and identity: Nomadic possibilities for reconceiving the self. In K. Wegar (Ed.), *Adoptive Families in a Diverse Society* (pp. 259–274). New Brunswick, NJ: Rutgers University Press.

13 Writing in the Shadows Cast by Moonlight

HEATHER PINEDO-BURNS

The rise of the sunlight spoke to us; it was late afternoon, we were not yet beyond the clearing and much was left to be done. We found ourselves deep in woods at the northeast corner of our family farm. The sunlight, golden and shimmering as if it were on a lake, not air, filtered through the needles of the pines and onto our faces. We had arrived in the hemlock forest, my father's beloved area of respite. My mom stopped working for a moment, gazing at the stories of the forest before her, 'This is my favorite part of the woods. I think you all were kids when I last came here.' I breathe in the cool air, noticing the texture of the bark on the scattered rows of trees, taking in these words of my mother.

–Pinedo-Burns, narrative, October 2008

Prior to setting out for this autumnal walk with my mother, I did not know my mother had a favourite part of the wood. I doubt I even contemplated this thought. With this glimmer of unsettled knowledge of not knowing, I began to consider my mother, positioned as mother. I thought of our shared history, the dynamics of our mother-daughter relationship, and her recent stories. My mother has begun to share stories I did not know, and stories I recall differently. Thus, I began this written endeavour, this book chapter, as a way to search out a method (Cixous, 1991) that 'leaves space for *the other*' (p. 62, original emphasis) as a way to explore these stories, and the differences in memory between my mother and me. As our stories are the accounts of memories of our shared experiences, I turn to Hélène Cixous, a feminist literary scholar and fiction writer who asks, 'How do we see what we no longer see?' (in Cixous & Calle-Gruber, 1994/1997, p. 4). I posit, what happens when a mother and daughter seek to address this question, working together?

Moonlight as Metaphor

To sense or see by the moonlight is to know only partially; it is to see an essence, never distinct, sure, or definite. To see by the light of the moon is to welcome the obscure, to knowingly not fully view the landscape of the other before you. The moonlight, although luminous, casts shadows about, diminishing and obscuring the focus of other possibilities of other meanings. I begin with the metaphor 'Writing in the Shadows Cast by Moonlight' as a way to explore our relational positions as mother and daughter in an effort to explore mothering, positioning the mother as other. This metaphor of the moon is inspired by French feminist Hélène Cixous's (in Cixous & Calle-Gruber, 1994/1997) concept of '"de lune à l'autre" from moon to the other' (p. 10). Cixous submits that 'the earth seen from the point of view of the moon is revived; it is unknown; to be rediscovered' (p. 10). To see the landscape of the other is to see differently. Cixous explains, 'Being geocentric, because we are geocentric, we say: from the earth to [sic]. And the moon is the other' (p. 10). This geocentric static approach limits understanding by beginning with the self, instead of seeking to work reciprocally with the other, or from the other, or of how the other sees and expresses her notion of the world. It is a metaphor for how we begin to understand others, by beginning with ourselves. Moonlight creates a narrow focus on what we can and choose to see, knowing our sight is imperfect, reflective of our experiences, histories, memories, biases, and beliefs.

'De lune à l'autre' is decentring work with the other. To work from the earth to the moon, a linear, one-way method forms, beginning with the self towards the other. By reframing the paradigm of geocentricism, to begin with the other and to move recursively within the same shadowy orbit, de lune à l'autre works to reorient the oft-accepted conceptualizations and hierarchies of working with the other. Cixous (in Cixous & Calle-Gruber, 1994/1997) explains, 'to whom I always say – silently looking at her – excuse me for acting as if you were the other, whereas you are the *lune*. Let us change points of view' (p. 10). This turn of perspectives is infinite, as Cixous describes, and so in this mother-daughter narrative inquiry my mother and I began by asking one another, 'Let us change points of view' (p. 10).

Method: Writing Together and Separate in the Moonlight Shadows

Cixous encourages writing as a way to express and explore the shadows of knowledge. Conceptualizing writing as feminine, Cixous (in Cixous & Clément 1975/2001) urges, 'Woman must write her body, must make up the unimpeded tongue that bursts partitions, classes, and rhetorics, orders and codes, must inundate, run through, go beyond the discourse with its last reserves' (p. 94). In the text, *Shared at Dawn*, Cixous (1998) positions herself as mother in relation to her daughter and her own mother, narrating, 'The house is full of remnants, it imprisons us in its memory of sorrows' (p. 175). As I walked with my mother through the halls of her home, gazing upon the shared artefacts, common objects in our lives, we created narratives of remembrance as they inspired, shadowed, illuminated, or silenced us. In this mother-daughter narrative inquiry, selected artefacts from our once-shared home serve as relics, as one means to view the other. Thus, we situated our stories within the mundane, selecting items we either see or once saw every day. For us, it was important to select a variety of items, many quotidian, as Cixous notes, 'in situations that are less acute one can also find material to work on and to rediscover what one has never had' (1998, p. 12). The stories we shared about these chosen artefacts work to obscure mother and daughter, allowing us to see the other in the shadows. Our purpose was to revisit together, to work towards understanding the other, knowing it is an impossibility, filled with shadows of what we choose to see, do not see, or choose not to see or say. Shadows are temporal, as are our stories, and our accounts of our memories within the stories we share.

My mother and I began with our telephone discussions: my vague descriptions of this mother-daughter narrative inquiry, her questions, and then my initial conceptual writings. To begin our initial written conversations I first sent her my vignette of our autumn day spent walking the woods together. The subsequent written vignettes, shared mostly through e-mail, were punctuated by our daily telephone conversations. I recall thinking my mother was unsure of the expectations, desiring more guidance than I was willing to give. I was worried about directing my mother's writing or pushing her beyond certain unspoken limits. I believed I wanted her to shape this project in her own way. I wanted her to share in the working of her own stories through the selection of the topics. We selected the artefacts to inspire our writing in the hopes of exploring the perspectives of the other, recognizing there would be stories left remaining deep in the shadows, silenced within. There were family tragedies, such as the death of my father, and a childhood accident involving my brother that remained silenced even within these writings. I chose not to select artefacts that would directly recall these painful shared memories, in an attempt to provide a comfortable place within which my mother and I could write and work.

Recognizing the recursive nature of narrative inquiry, we were not simply 'telling stories' (Miller, 2005), but also seeking to explore and express our individual thoughts, emotions, processes, interpretations, and silences at a moment in time (Chase, 2005; Miller, 2005). Through our writing my mother and I were not only searching for meaning, but we were also creating meaning (Richardson, 2000). We began writing together, separately, knowing there would be deep levels of comfort and discomfort accented with numerous emotions of in-betweeness. I say that, not really knowing if my mother considered that there may be deep levels of discomfort. Throughout this process I was unsure how my mother would read my writing. I am still unsure of her reading, knowing that I can never fully know or understand her thoughts and responses to this project (Ellis & Bochner, 2000; Pillow, 1997). As with many research endeavours, my original conception of this chapter and its eventual development are distinguishable. Thus, our engagement in our writing by which we worked in de lune à l'autre became our common focus. Like many mothers and their grown daughters, my mother and I live apart; she in the country and I in the city. Too far for a day trip or impromptu visit, geographical distance shaped our physical and metaphorical 'entredeux' (Cixous & Calle-Gruber, 1994/1997), or passage between one another. Writing together and separately, we worked towards creating 'writing that chooses the interval space, the between, the in-between, the entredeux, and that works in the place of otherness' (p. 8).

Initially, I expected we would send the selected writing pieces back and forth, via e-mail, having given up on the romantic notion of sending the writing as letters through the postal service. But that did not happen. We wrote separately, as I had imagined and intended, but then the sharing piece, the piece I was most concerned about changed. We agreed not to read each other's writings until we had written our own accounts. I had thought my mother would travel to my apartment, having printed and read my writing side by side with her own. Instead, she arrived in New York ready to read the pieces *with* me. Anxiety filled me. I would witness my mother's less-censored responses to my writing.

In many ways, this move of my mother, the action of not reading our shared writings till she sat with me in person, helped shape and direct our project in unintended ways. While my role as initiator certainly shaped our joint writing endeavour, our mother-daughter narrative inquiry, my mother asserted her power by not reading our writing till we were together, fashioning our entredeux. Her actions pushed us to move from the detachment of the written word, to recognize the corporeal presence of the other within the telling of our stories (Pillow, 1997). Thus, on a Saturday and Sunday, together we sat in the old wooden chairs I had inherited from my father's family, in my living room, reading each other's writing. Marking my notations, my questions, and my revisions in a purple pen, my mother then scribed her thoughts, her side-stories, and her reminiscences in a pen of pink ink. These documents became our shared focus. As we read each other's writings and notations, we chatted, and laughed over a weekend's visit. Sharing our writing together created new impressions of the written memories, as 'telling the stories changes the memory of the stream of events' (Michielsens, 2004, p. 184). We remarked how we recalled stories differently; or how the story sparked a thought of another memory; or how another story was woven within our memories, but remained untold in our writing. As we worked that weekend, I sensed a mutual hesitancy to tread too deeply into the shadows of our memories. While my mother noted her thoughts on our writings, I wrote:

The things I did not realize
    (will it be we?)
The things I have no memory of but I believe
The things I have different memories of…
The things I remember differently

The stories beneath, woven within
The shared stories – the family lore
To begin – the reminiscing –

our distancing from certain stories
The stories untold.
The stories we both chose to not tell
The stories I did not know
The metaphors – the realizations

The stories I still don't know

The stories I will not know.

(Pinedo-Burns, narrative notes, January 2009)

The Entredeux, Our Passage to the Other

My mother lives alone in the country on a large 40-acre non-working farm surrounded by dense woods. Living in the country, large land-owners are required to 'post' their property This entails a physical walking of the property line, hanging notices or signs on trees warning trespassers or hunters that they are on private property and to stay off the land. This work is a full day, or weekend job, often considered the work of men, a chore completed each fall by the father and/or sons of the family. This narrative below is based on one such fall day spent with my mother posting her property. This vignette follows the earlier narrative at the start of this chapter, occurring later that evening. I sent this writing to my mother to introduce this narrative inquiry:

> Later, walking through the thick brambles of the overgrown forest, my mother and I exit the woods having performed never before considered roles within our family. These are the fall-time duties of a large-land holder in the country, a farmer, a worker, not that of a nurse or a teacher, a mother or a daughter. The staple gun dangles from my hand, while my mother cradles the roll of posted signs, the no-trespassing signs, those orange, yellow or white signs, stapled to trees, now boldly outlining the borders of the family's farm. The responsibility of the yearly posting of the property, the hanging of the no-trespassing signs, the tracing of the borders of the land once fell to my father and my brothers. With my father dead, and my brothers working overseas, my mother and I dressed in my father's yellow hunting jacket and vest, mud-boots on our feet, staple guns in our hands, having set out to chores with the goal of finishing before dusk. Tired at the end of our day, I pause and look up at the approaching darkness of the evening sky, towards the crescent moon. (Pinedo-Burns, narrative, October 2008)

This posting of the property is a tedious all-day process. Each fall my mother insists on joining me; she is 75 years old now, and is slow. Yet, it is this recollection of a fall day in the country that provoked me to reconsider the notion of boundaries and trespassing within narrative inquiry, to rethink possibilities of my own trespassing words in relation to my mother as mother. The possible boundary between the stories that can and cannot be shared is uncertain, and formed by our relationship as mother and daughter. Cixous shapes the concept of 'entredeux' as a means of addressing the in-betweens of otherness. As Cixous (in Cixous & Calle-Gruber, 1994/1997) explains, entredeux is neither fixed nor stagnant, but always in 'passage from the one to the other' (p. 10). Thus, I consider mothering, the act of forcing the identity of mother as other as creating a problematic dualistic identity and denying the multiple dimensions of self. Through immersion in the 'entredeux,' as conceived by Cixous, we explored the working memory parley (Michielsens, 2004; Lacey, 2000), as my mother and I searched for a means to explore the self, the other, and the in-betweens. It was this experience of posting the property with my mother that made me reflect upon our roles as mother and daughter in our family. Using the no-trespassing posted sign, as our first subject, these are my mother's words:

When I first moved out here in the country, I didn't even know what a posted sign was, what it looked like, or why people would put one up and where they would use it. My husband, Milt, knew a lot about rural life even though he had been raised in the city of Albany, like myself. He did have the experience, however, of spending every summer for at least a month up in Ogdensburg, NY, at his aunt and paternal uncle's house where he shared dairy farm chores with them and their daughters, his cousins.

The posting season usually started in October in preparation for the hunting weeks. By this tenth month, it was easier (perhaps) to walk the land as some of the vegetation had died off and bees and bugs were at a minimal. Unless it was an unusually wet fall, the land was fairly dry making the walk-about more pleasant, especially on a beautiful crisp fall day.

Another year Heather came up for the weekend with the primary purpose of posting the land. I know she felt she had 'inherited' the responsibility as both brothers were working out of the country. She knew I couldn't do it myself. I did take up the role of making sure the supplies were on hand beforehand. It was a cold and wet miserable day and we were thankful when the job was completed. Heather did all the work and I would hand her the equipment and keep her company. (Burns, narrative, December 2008)

Within my mother's writings, I note my perceived conceptions of mother, daughter, and family responsibility. In her work, Cixous explores the roles and concepts of mothers and motherhood in her writing (Hanrahan, 2004). Her work on mothers and difference has been described as an 'endeavor to open up the space between them necessary for her mother to have, in writing, a place of her own' (p. 19). To create such spaces for the entredeux, this passage between my mother and me, I felt that my mother was still deferential to me as her daughter and to my late-father, by placing a value of my father, others, and me above her own. I worry that in her writing she dismisses her own importance, noting, 'Heather did all the work.'. Perhaps this was my mother's work of 'de lune à l'autre,' complicated by the entredeux of my mother's insistence on maintaining familial positions and relations (Cixous & Calle-Gruber, 1994/1997, p. 10). In exploring bodily writing, writing of the body, Cixous (1976) asserts, 'Woman is never far from the "mother" (I do not mean her role functions: the "mother" as noname and as source of goods). There is always within her at least a little of that good milk. She writes in white ink' (p. 882). I cannot but imagine the way white ink fades into the page of white paper, just as my mother dismisses her role in maintaining her home and property.

In addressing Cixous's writings and the role of her father, Mairéad Hanrahan (2004) explores the permanency that the role of the dead father has: 'The mother does not just evolve within space: she *is herself* the space through which she passes ...Whereas death fixed the father, the mother is constantly changing' (p. 11). Throughout our writings, there are similar sightings of my father, and my mother's father. Like Cixous's, my father died while I was young, and my mother's father died when she was even younger (Cixous & Calle-Gruber, 1994/1997). This role of the dead father lingers throughout our writings. Although the stories of the memories we share of my father are never-changing, my mother, her life and stories, and therefore our shared memories are still ever-changing. Although this mutability of our memories complicates our work, it also offers opportunities; as Cixous (in Cixous & Calle-Gruber, 1994/1997) notes, 'To write we must be faithful to this unfaithfulness' (p. 8). All of our writing is reflective of this moment in time, discursively situated, and never fully consciously known.

'Faithful to This Unfaithfulness': Risks of Betrayal and Stories Untold

Writing about Hélène Cixous's writing of her mother, Hanrahan (2004) notes, 'The question is thus not how not to betray her mother but how to mitigate or minimize the betrayal, how to betray her the least' (p. 7). New questions surfaced within the shadows of our written work. What happens when the participant in your research is your mother? How do familial relationships shape the method and process of research? Would my words betray my mother? Much of my writing and my responses to my mother's writing were shaped by a worry of betrayal. I must ponder if my mother was attentive to the possibility of betrayal as she concluded her writing on the no-trespassing posted sign by saying:

> Now as I drive along any highway and see a posted sign, I respect what that owner had to go through and what they expect. Clearly the bright yellow signs all say the same thing: 'Posted Private Property. Hunting, Fishing, Trapping, or Trespassing for any purpose is strictly forbidden. Violators will be prosecuted.' (Burns, narrative, December 2008)

Heeding my mother's admonition, would we risk trespassing within our writing? What would be the consequences of our violations? What were the possibilities? Through embarking on this project together, we shared vulnerability with one another. In intimately writing and reading together, 'there's the vulnerability of revealing yourself, not being able to take back what you've written or having any control over how readers interpret it' (Ellis & Bochner, 2000, p. 738). This vulnerability is ceaseless, and it is full of risk and possible betrayal. Amid these risks, there is potential within the shadows for a working of the entredeux, which is possible and wanted.

When writing about family, Laurel Richardson (2000) notes feelings of restriction and hesitation, negotiating the value of the narrative and the intimacies of family. While writing my narratives, I searched within the shadowy haze of boundaries, the stories I could and could not tell. As my mother and I wrote together, we evoked memories, participating in 'a conscious and purposeful performance of memory' (Kuhn, 1995, p. 157). These fragmented writings became our working 'material for interpretation' (p. 157). Selecting certain narratives and leaving other stories within our memories influences the ways in which stories are told and the importance we place on each event (Pinar, Reynolds, Slattery, & Taubman, 1994/2004). There was an unspoken pact of sorts, between my mother and me, pieces of our memories that we will not make public. And yet, I question, how are these untold stories determined?

What are the intended and unintended consequences of these silenced stories? Did we write for each other or for ourselves?

Thus, within this next set of vignettes, we addressed issues of vulnerability and choice of story within narrative, as 'the stories are, like the memories and secrets out of which they are born, only *traces* of the *whole* story' (Poulos, 2008, p. 64, original emphasis). In my mother's home sits a jewelry box with a delicate necklace known as a lavaliere that shaped our next set of vignettes. Within her writing my mother shared the history of this family heirloom:

> My mom, Heather's grandmother, had very little 'good' jewelry. From the time I was quite young until the day she died, there were only four pieces that stood out in my mind that were her favorites:
>
> Pearl button clip-on earrings (costume jewelry)
> Gold locket with a small diamond in the center (she bought that after my Dad died so she could place his picture in it)
> White gold wedding band and a diamond engagement ring also of white gold
> A lavaliere
>
> I was always fascinated by the delicate, intricate nature of the lavaliere – so lacy, feminine and beautiful. It was not your average piece of jewelry that you would wear with everything, although some owners do just this. Even though I don't remember my Mom wearing it that often, I do know that she liked it. Because of its delicate nature and appearance, perhaps this is why she didn't wear it very often for fear that something would happen to it.
>
> My mother never talked much about how or why she got the lavaliere. I remember her telling me that her stepmother, Adelaide, had given it to her. I don't know if it was purchased new for her or if it had been Adelaide's or belonged in her family. That was never discussed. Since Adelaide died about 1930, the necklace dates back to at least 75 or more years. (Burns, narrative, December 2008)

My mother's words, 'that was never discussed,' suggests the multifaceted nature of each of the narratives we created. Within our writing there are other stories, stories that have been revised, abridged, simplified, or simply left out. Our narrations 'are necessarily incomplete, and therefore, perhaps, inaccurate' (Poulos, 2008, p. 53). Accuracy, a comparison or contrast, was not our goal; rather, it was an exploration of narratives, a working of the entredeux. Rather, our focus remained, what happens when we engage in working the entredeux, through writing exploring the indistinct limitations and explorations of our stories? Within the narrations my mother often eludes to family stories, now family lore, and family secrets, stories my mother and I know well but chose not to discuss, not to commit to paper. Carolyn Ellis and Arthur Bochner (2000) question and respond to the impossibilities of narrative inquiry noting, 'Doesn't this mean that the stories we tell always run the risk of distorting the past? Of course it does. After all, stories rearrange, redescribe, invent, omit, and revise. They can be wrong in numerous ways – tone, detail, substance, etc.' (p. 745). And yet, these are the stories we chose to tell, to share, and to discuss. These stories, as are all narratives, are fragmented, written memories as recalled by particular people at specific times and places.

If I were to tell this story, how my grandmother came to own the lavaliere, there are numerous possible threads for me to weave, consciously and unconsciously deciding which story it is that I choose to tell. As Sidonie Smith and Julia Watson (2001) note, memories are constructions of the fragments of recollections of experiences, always subject to change and to revision. Thus, these are our narrations, the stories we wish to share (Poulos, 2008). My mother's narration of the lavaliere continues:

> My mother, Heather's grandmother, never offered to let us borrow her lavaliere but for one exception. She said I could borrow it for my wedding day. I was thrilled since I loved that piece of jewelry, and I was honored. It would go perfect with my wedding gown as the lines of the bodice top were simple. The gown had three-quarter length sleeves and a scoop neckline. Yes, it would go well and would look very pretty and feminine.
>
> After the wedding, I returned the lavaliere to my mother and she continued to wear it occasionally.
>
> After Mom died, my two sisters and I were dividing up some of her personal jewelry. When it came time to discuss the lavaliere, I immediately spoke up and said I would like to be considered its new owner and why – because it was part of my wedding outfit. My two sisters were very understanding about it and without hesitation said I should have it.
>
> I have not worn it very often, perhaps for the same reason I think my mother didn't wear it very much either: it looks very delicate and for fear of something happening to it. I had it in my jewelry box and hadn't looked at it in a while. However, in my mind from the time I was little, it has

always been the same image in my mind and I have never forgotten how it looked. It is has a very lacey appearance. In the center is a small but beautiful diamond. At the bottom of the ornament is a dangling gemstone. My Mom referred to it as a seed pearl.

My visual perception of the lavaliere never changed – through all these years, I remember every detail and even after long periods of not looking at it, I remember it in the same way. Nothing has changed my perception of it. Perhaps this is one of the reasons why families often choose it to be an heirloom – it represents the balance between delicate structure yet the stability of precious metals and jewels, a fine blend of qualities. (Burns, narrative, December 2008)

As I first read my mother's words about the lavaliere I questioned the narratives that she chose to forefront. I believed my mother took a differenced approach to this writing about the lavaliere. My mother highlighted her history of the lavaliere, eliminating the unnecessary, messy, controversial details. Yet, who am I to question the stories we choose to say aloud, to risk a commitment to paper, and those that we choose to keep in our hearts and minds? Or, perhaps I questioned my mother's memory because these are not memories I expected or desired to hear. 'We are not simply the stories we tell as much as we are the modes of relation to others our stories imply, modes of relation implied by what we delete as much as what we include' (Pinar, 1988, p. 28). I now realize the expectations I carried with me, turning to note my mother's perspective, I try to view this story from my mother's perspective, a way of working the entredeux. I note this, as I finally share the thoughts on the lavaliere that have lingered in far reaches of my memories, my concern for over six years. I wrote:

On August 17, 2002, my wedding day, I too was to wear the lavaliere. A few weeks before the day, my mother carefully packed it up and ceremoniously hand delivered the necklace to my home.

August 17th was a hot and humid day; the skies carried that vibrant hue of deep blue that signals an impending storm. As my mother and I opened the doors to my tiny compact car, I realized my brothers packed the car leaving no space on the passenger side for my mother's feet. Nonplussed, my mother said, 'Don't worry, I've been doing yoga,' and swiftly seated herself with her legs elegantly raised and crossed. Thus, my Mom and I set off to deliver boxes of candles, programs, and paper fans my brother Scott brought from Japan to St Joseph's Park where my husband and I would marry. While driving, a gentle five-minute thunderstorm fell, the only rain of the day, and we laughed at my insistence on an outdoor wedding. When my mother and I returned from the church, having completed our errands, there, waiting for me on the kitchen table was a velvet blue box and a note from my soon to be husband. Inside rested pearl earrings and a necklace shaped like branches of woven pussy-willows.

The lavaliere remained in its careful packaging that day, unnoticed beside the unread books, loose change, and bottles of perfume on my dresser.

To wear both would have been tacky, not stylish. I wore the new gift from my husband, and by so doing, neglected and rejected the tradition of the lavaliere.

I recall making this decision, knowing there would be consequences. And yet, I would say, without hesitation that I chose the gift of my husband, and not the offering of my mother.

On my wedding day I made the decision to choose my husband. On that day, I left behind my mother.

It was a brief moment. As we dressed, laughed, and took photographs, my smiling mother assisted me in my preparations, carefully closing the clasp on the pussy-willow necklace I wore on my wedding day. (Pinedo-Burns, narrative, December 2008)

'Cixous exhorts her readers to write with one hand and experience pain with the other: "With one hand, suffering, living, putting your finger on pain, loss. But there is the other hand: the one that writes"' (Lie, 1999, p. 17). Thus, I included some pieces of the painful fragmented stories we chose to tell in our writing. As more exists within our working writing, more exists within our memories – it is impossible to tell it all. Most difficult for me, was sharing my writing on the lavaliere. I had never spoken of this with my mother, and therefore I was concerned, was this working the entredeux simply working up trouble? I am humbled to read my mother's response to my work, a handwritten notation at the end of her narration, *Some traditions have to be put aside! And that is O.K. They should never become a hardship or produce regret'* (Burns, narrative note, January 2009). When we talked, my mother spoke of learning that lesson over the holidays, as new traditions begin, some must end. I did not realize the struggles she experienced negotiating this when my brothers and I were young – she made it seem effortless. I wonder now, did my mother mean that, or was she just fulfilling her role as 'the good mother'? It was, as the writer Amy Tan (2003) says when she shares her experiences with story and her mother, 'How wonderful to hear her say what was never true, yet now would be forever so' (p. 214). Thus, these acts of remembering, writing, and sharing weave together to create alternative memories that may or may not resemble the memories of our past. 'Cixous accentuates that love is reaching towards the other, and towards writing and life in general' (Lie, 1999, p.18). I ponder, in an effort of love, as Cixous describes, if my writing forced my mother further into the position of mother as other? Was she playing the role of the 'good mother' and pushing aside her feelings, or am I still unable to view the moonlit landscape of my mother without the shadowy haze of my conceptions and understandings? I am reminded of Cixous's question, 'But are we not *always* prey to otherness?' (p. 9, original emphasis), as I reflect upon my actions of mothering, seeking to glimpse the perspective of my mother's memories, but failing to do so.

As Cixous (in Cixous & Calle-Gruber, 1994/1997) states, 'All biographies like all autobiographies like all narratives tell one story in place of another story' (p. 178). Joan Didion (2005) speaks of choice often recognizing how she secretly chooses to act one way, but thinks privately in another form. Thus, Didion's autobiographical text, *The Year of Magical Thinking* reads like memory. Near the end of her book, she recalls a long-departed former home once shared with her family. She walks the halls and gazes at the rooms in her mind: 'Later in the day I realized that I had forgotten one' (p. 226). There are numerous forgotten rooms within our memories; there are rooms that are created yet never were. Choice in memory is powerful. Consciously and unconsciously, we revise and edit our memories to meet our temporal needs. Yet, a weaving of stories and paths chosen was not the priority of this written exploration into the entredeux: 'I see that almost everything that we went through has been carried away by time. What came to pass has gone away, I've forgotten it all' (Cixous, 1998, p. 180). In our entredeux, there was often a working messiness, parallel stories, and stories that sadly remained disconnected. There were also things we did not risk to say to one another. Thoughts I knew would hurt, challenge, and upset. I do not speak directly of the family affairs, I do not mention my mother's ever-increasing frailty, my worries about her isolation, widowed, living alone on a desolate farm, and more I still will not verbalize today. There were things I knew I could not say. I cannot say. I can only imagine my mother experienced similar thoughts, though I cannot imagine what those thoughts might be for my mother. Laurel Richardson (2000) notes, 'Each writing-story offers its writer an opportunity to make a situated and pragmatic ethical decision about whether and where to publish the story' (p. 932). Within each vignette shared with one another there were stories shared and selectively forgotten for the moment. There were some objects chosen that my mother refused to write about, penning a few distant lines, almost fulfilling her duties of the task, but quietly stating, *I don't want to talk about this.*

At times I found these disconnects surprising, as I was caught off guard by my own presumptions. While we met to read and respond to one another's narratives, I turned to my mother and described an old black and white photograph that exists in the back of mind, one that served as an inspiration for one of my vignettes. My mother turned her head slightly cocked to the side, questioning, unclear, uncertain what photograph I may have been referring to, her countenance incredulous. I was surprised, I thought she would immediately respond to my description, but this is a memory we do not share:

> An old black and white photograph immediately comes to mind when I think of the old 'climbing' tree in our front yard. My mother is standing, smiling into the camera that I presume my father was holding. In her arms is her first cat, Timmie, wearing a collar and leash. My mother is dressed in a white shirt, with pants suited for an expedition; an explorer's air floated about her. This photo, taken before my parents had any children, presumably shows my mother to be gloriously happy, relishing in her new home in the country filled with her chosen pets, a few bits of antique furniture, and the excitement and anticipation of life yet to come. (Pinedo-Burns, narrative, December 2008)

I am saddened that my mother does not recall this photograph of herself, as I describe. There she is seemingly young, unencumbered by the (im)possibilities of mother. Within this same written narrative, juxtaposed with this vision of my mother's youth and possibility, I am struck by my own writing, and its reference to my mother's age:

> In the winter, we often hang large white Christmas lights about the front door entrance facing the tree, silhouetted by its the wide hanging branches. Though, now I can recall, it has been some years since that has

happened. My mother no longer risks standing on chairs on old cement stoops for items and ideas as frivolous as decorations. (Pinedo-Burns, narrative, December 2008)

Here I hint at a piece I realize now I silenced, my mother's age, and my concept of her ever-increasing physical fragility. After our writings and our readings, I must question what else did we leave remaining in the shadows, silenced? Cixous (in Cixous & Calle-Gruber, 1994/1997) says, 'At the end of the path of attention, of reception, which is not interrupted but which continues into what little by little becomes the opposite of comprehension. Loving not knowing. Loving: not knowing' (p. 17). As Didion (2005) reminds me, what rooms have we forgotten? This is yet to be known, if ever known. It is these shadows of the knowns and unknowns, our 'de lune à l'autre' which shaped our entredeux as mother and daughter in writing and in our lives as the other.

References

Burns, J.W. (2008, December). Unpublished raw data, narrative. In author's possession.

Burns, J.W. (2009, January). Unpublished raw data, narrative notes. In author's possession.

Chase, S.E. (2005). Narrative inquiry: Multiple lenses, approaches, voices. In N.K. Denzin & Y.S. Lincoln (Eds.), *Handbook of qualitative research* (3rd ed.; pp. 651–679). Thousand Oaks, CA: Sage.

Cixous, H. (1976). The laugh of the Medusa. Trans. K. Cohen & P. Cohen. *Signs. 1* (4), 875–893.

Cixous, H. (1991). Clarice Lispector: The approach. Trans. D. Jenson. In D. Jenson (Ed.), *Coming to writing: And other essays* (pp. 59–77). Cambridge, MA: Harvard University Press.

Cixous, H. (1998). Shared at dawn. Trans. K. Cohen. In *Stigmata: Escaping texts* (pp. 145–148). New York: Routledge.

Cixous, H., & Calle-Gruber, M. (1997). *Hélène Cixous rootprints: Memory and life writing.* Trans. E. Prenowitz. New York: Routledge. (Originally published 1994).

Cixous, H., & Clément, C. (2001). *The newly born woman.* Trans. B. Wing. Minneapolis: University of Minnesota Press. (Originally published in 1975).

Didion, J. (2005). *The year of magical thinking.* New York: Knopf.

Ellis, C., & Bochner, A.P. (2000). Autoethnography, personal narrative, reflexivity. In N.K. Denzin & Y.S. Lincoln (Eds.), *Handbook of qualitative research* (2nd ed.; pp. 733–768). Thousand Oaks, CA: Sage.

Hanrahan, M. (2004). The place of the mother: Hélène Cixous's Osnabrück. *Paragraph, 27* (1), 6–20.

Kuhn, A. (1995). *Family secrets: Acts of memory and imagination.* London: Verso.

Lacey, J. (2000). *Subject to representation: Essays on the politics of representation.* Ottawa: Gallery 101.

Lie, S. (1999). Life makes text from my body: A reading of Hélène Cixous' la venue à l'écriture. In L.E. Jacobus & R. Barreca (Eds.), *Helene Cixous: Critical impressions* (pp. 1–22). Florence, KY: Gordon & Breach.

Michielsens, M. (200). Memory frames: The role of concepts and cognition in telling life-stories. In T. Cosslett, C. Lury, & P. Summerfield (Eds.), *Feminism and autobiography: Texts, theories, methods* (pp. 183–200). New York: Routledge.

Miller, J.L. (2005). *Sounds of silence breaking.* New York: Peter Lang.

Pillow, W.S. (1997). Exposed methodology: The body as a deconstructive practice. *Qualitative Studies in Education, 10* (3), 349–363.

Pinar, W. (1988). Autobiography and the architecture of the self. *Journal of Curriculum Theorizing, 8* (1), 7–36.

Pinar, W.F., Reynolds, W.M., Slattery, P., & Taubman, P.M. (1995/2004). *Understanding curriculum.* New York: Peter Lang.

Pinedo-Burns, H.J. (2008, October). Unpublished raw data, narrative. In author's possession.

Pinedo-Burns, H.J. (2008, December). Unpublished raw data, narrative. In author's possession.

Pinedo-Burns, H.J. (2009, January). Unpublished raw data, narrative notes. In author's possession.

Poulos, C.N. (2008). Narrative conscience and the autoethnographic adventure: Probing memories, secrets, shadows, and possibilities. *Qualitative Inquiry, 14* (1), 46–66.

Richardson, L. (2000). Writing: A method of inquiry. In N.K. Denzin & Y.S. Lincoln (Eds.), *Handbook of qualitative research* (2nd ed., pp. 923–948). Thousand Oaks, CA: Sage.

Smith, S., & Watson, J. (2001). *Reading autobiography: A guide for interpreting life narratives.* Minneapolis, MN: University of Minnesota Press.

Tan, A. (2003). *The opposite of fate: Memoirs of a writing life.* New York: Penguin.

PART 3

Affect

- difficult for me to
connect b/c I'm not sure
motherhood is understood in that
people want to understand it

⟶ hard, involved, 24/7 (obligations)

⟶ mom waking b/c worried about her
31 y old & their family of 6
& being a mother never ends

Mothers guilt...

14 Tasting the M/other as Sensational Pedagogy

STEPHANIE SPRINGGAY

Despite decades of feminist maternal theories, policies, and practices, motherhood remains in opposition to the ideologies of work, the one being intimate, emotional, nurturing, and private, the other detached, objective, logical, and public. This is even more divisive in the academy, where the intellect and the body are constantly severed (Evans & Grant, 2008) and reinforced by the dichotomy between reproduction and production.

Examining the ways that women's experiences of reproduction and nurturance are silenced, appropriated, and regulated in the discourses and practices of schooling, Madeleine Grumet (1988) wrote in her book, *Bitter Milk*, that if we 'interpret our reproductive experience (procreation and nurturance) and our productive practice (curriculum and teaching) each through the other's terms, not obliterating the differences between them but naming their contradictions and reconceiving our commitment to the care and education of children' (1988, p. 29), we might expose more generative connections between motherhood and education.

In this essay, I argue that the very ideologies and practices that delimit reproduction and production need to be re-visioned through a more *sensational accounting of difference*. Examining feminist maternal art, I propose a sensational pedagogy that would enable educators to re-conceptualize teaching and learning as embodied, affective, and as a co-ontological experience.

Many feminist visual artists wrestle with maternal ideologies present in Western representations of the 'good mother.' The ideal mother – white, middle-class, devoted, selfless, and heteronormative – has become the yardstick by which women are judged (Addison,

Goodwin-Kelly, Roth, 2009). Any deviation from this pattern is jus-
tification for suspicion, denigration, and surveillance. For example,
the large-format photographs created by Canadian Korean artist Jin-
me Yoon are attentive to the discourses that devalue the figure of the
mother while sanctifying the institution of motherhood. Produced in
the years following the birth of her children, the photographs converge
and wrestle with the gendered domains of work and caring for an
infant. The series of photographs titled 'Intersections' document the
artist, dressed in sombre black suits, her hair cut short, severe black
glasses, set against backdrops of intense colour. In all but one of the
images, the figure of the artist is desexualized through attention to
clothing, accessories, and pose. In all of the photographs, milk is used –
either dribbling out of the mother-artist's mouth, collecting in puddles,
or referenced through breast pumps and parts – inserting an element of
volatility into the scenes.

In the diptych 'Intersection 5' the artist is portrayed as a multi-limbed
octopus housing squirming children beneath her little black dress.
Lying on her back, milk seeps out of the neck of her dress, oozing past
her bourgeois pearl necklace to puddle on the floor. In the accompany-
ing image, two topless children seen from the back spurt forth a foun-
tain of milk. The diptych is imbued with both humour and horror – that
the children have literally sucked the life out of the mother and are now
wasting it by spitting it up into the air. A final sign of the sacrificial and
consumed mother is the strand of pearls, which lie discarded in a pool
of milk surrounding the children. Yoon's parasitic images suggest that
'the ethical imperative is to be found in an acute awareness of disgust'
(Probyn, 2000, p. 137). The tentacled mother wriggling in a puddle of
milk, the threat of hostile invasion immanent, ruptures the metaphor of
the sacrificial virgin by accounting for disgust in the maternal relationship. Although I have yet to literally writhe prostrate on the threshold
of my children's school amid the scattered remains of 'krispie pops,
milk, and banana peels,' as my 'flesh and blood' poke their chubby
child fingers into my eyes, thighs, and buttocks before scampering off
to their classrooms, 'the dilemma becomes how to speak of the difficulties and incomparable beauties of making space for another unknown
person without having those variously inflected and complex experiences turned into clichés of what enduring motherhood is supposed to
be' (Liss, 2009, n.p).

Resisting the growing tendency to theorize maternal subjectivity
through narratives of maternal experience, which rest on an idealized

perception of mothering as universal, essential, and sentimental, this essay will examine two works by contemporary artists, Jess Dobkin's 'The Lactation Station Breast Milk Bar' and Lyla Rye's 'Byte,' through an attention to affect and, in particular, *disgust*. I incorporate feminist cultural theorist Elspeth Probyn's thoughts on eating, Barbara Kennedy and Sarah Pink's work on sensation, and Felix Guttari's concern with the ethicoaesthetic in order to re-vision curriculum in terms of a visceral, embodied, and affective ethos. I recognize that both artists have an extensive body of artistic work, and that singling out one performance and one video might involuntarily place their work in a category of maternal art; however, I selected these two pieces for their attention to the *mouth*. It is the mouth in both pieces that causes an extreme embodied and sensational reaction to the work, particularly one of disgust. Disgust is engendered by the proximity of the body often through touch, taste, or smell. Thus, the mouth in terms of eating and otherness 'commands careful considerations of bodies and affective configurations' (Probyn, 2000, p. 133).

Throughout this chapter I entertain the questions: What if disgust were a proposal for rethinking the arrangements and assemblages of bodies? How might disgust cause us to reflect more generatively on difference, not as an affirmation of, but as an ethical embodiment of difference? And how might sensational aesthetics contribute to scholarship in the field denoted as curriculum studies? The artistic encounters I engage with in this chapter permit multiple and conflicting responses, creating a maternal subject that is intercorporeal and enfleshed in her own personhood, professionalism, and self-knowledge.

The Mouth: Disgust and Difference

Jess Dobkin's work 'The Lactation Station Breast Milk Bar,' which was presented at the Ontario College of Art and Design Presentation Gallery in 2006, offered audience participants the chance to taste samples of pasteurized human breast milk by six new mothers. A short video documentary of the work can be viewed at http://www.jessdobkin. com/videos/9. In the spirit of wine tasting, participants could saddle up to the bar and drink shot glass – sized samples of breast milk. The artist, from her position as bar tender, talks casually about the 'bouquet' of each donor's milk: 'When I interviewed this donor she talked about how much chocolate she ate during her pregnancy.' Over 300 people attended the event and more than 100 sampled the milk:

'Sweet, it's sweet,' says one participant. Another claims that her sample 'is a lot creamier than the first one,' and two men discuss the coconut flavour of their milk-shot. Cheerios are served in silver bowls to cleanse the pallet.

In an interview posted on her Website, Dobkin speaks about the impetus behind the work; her own inability to breastfeed her daughter, and the public discourses of being a single, queer mother. Wrestling with the social and political implications of what it means to be a good mother, Dobkin's performance explores the ambivalent and controversial relationship women in the West have with breastfeeding. At the time of the performance the *Globe and Mail* published an article stating that fewer than 15 per cent of new mothers in Canada meet the minimum standard of breastfeeding for 6 months (Picard, 2006). In North America, the medical community pushes the advantages of breast milk and assumes that mothers who do not breastfeed do so because they are unaware of the health benefits of breast milk. However, it is the public vilification of breastfeeding and the discomfort many women have (either physically or socially) that often prevents women from breastfeeding (Hausman, 2003; Kukla, 2006). 'This paradox – women who don't breast-feed often know they should – springs from a collision between the encoding of the breast as a maternal organ and of breast milk as an infant nutrient, on the one hand, and the competing interpretations of the breast as sexual fetish and of breast milk as abject bodily fluid' (Reeve, 2009, p. 65).

Respective of the discourses and implications surrounding the maternal body and breastfeeding, I want to proceed by focusing on the aversions to the adult consumption of breast milk that Dobkin's performance evokes; namely, *disgust*. Disgust is a bodily knowledge that, as Amanda Sinclair (1999), notes is immediate: 'A great deal happens before a person opens their mouth. Emotions are aroused, judgments are made. Comfort or discomfort levels are established well in advance of verbal communication. We unconsciously or consciously register and make judgments about stature and voice. Bodies elicit feelings of excitement and admiration, attraction and desire, envy and distaste' (p. 3).

In her book *Carnal Appetites: Food Sex Identities*, Probyn (2000) makes the case that a politics of representation – who and what are represented and the discourses surrounding their inclusions/exclusions – argues for 'more images of the right sort' (p. 126). Examples include the Dove and Benetton advertisements, which suggest that all bodies regardless of size, shape, age, or colour should be celebrated and embraced, emphasizing the affirmation of difference and uniqueness. Similarly, images of a naked and pregnant Demi Moore flaunt the swollen maternal body as a post-feminist sign of women's empowerment – we've arrived 'Ladies' and we can let it all hang out! Reading Dobkin's work as a celebration of the public side to lactation and mothering, simply reifies without critical examination, that which we find disgusting to begin with – tasting human milk.

The breast, Iris Young (2005) reminds us, is sexual and thus, 'the feeding function of the breasts must be suppressed, and when the breasts are nursing they are desexualized' (p. 88). Probyn's (2000, 2006) thinking about disgust and shame provides us with a more complex and untidy understanding of tasting breast milk – or quite frankly, of 'eating the other' (hooks, 1992). Probyn (2000) writes, 'In shame, in disgust, the body displays knowledges that may yet surprise us, that point to new corporeal connections' (p. 128).

Analysing the 'The Lactation Station Breast Milk Bar' through affective responses, I argue, disrupts a culture of blame and demands that we examine why and what we feel is disgusting. Probyn (2000, 2006) argues that, in many instances, the response to feelings of disgust is to work through them and reclaim them with pride. For example, the disgust one might have for the extremely obese female body is replaced with an image of 'love your curves.' Or in lactation culture, take the position that breastfeeding is a moral choice to provide the best healthy food for your child (Kukla, 2006), despite the fact that both the public imaginary and lactating mothers experience disgust in relation to breastfeeding. Not to denigrate such models of affirmation, Probyn (2000) contends that in such moves disgust is repressed, disavowed, and erased. This stifles any potential reflection on the production of disgust and 'the power of our bodies to react' (p. 129). In the case of 'The Lactation Station,' disgust is registered as the mouth takes in the human milk, evoking a visceral response, which then expels it and spits it out. And despite the fact that the milk was ingested via clean and sanitized wine goblets, one can't help but imagine the taking in of the breast in order to consume the milk. Disgust becomes scandalous because breasts 'shatter the border between motherhood and sexuality (Young, 2005, p. 88).

Before proceeding further with my analysis I want to introduce Lyla Rye's video work 'Byte' in which the mouth also figures prominently. On the multichannel video installation of stacked monitors (see http://www.lylarye.com/Byte1.html), we witness a mother (the artist) and her child engage in a sensual game of singing into each other's mouths; a game abruptly terminated when the child bites her mother's lower lip. On the screen, however, their actions are ambiguous, and we wonder if they are kissing, fighting, or resuscitating each other. The image, which is clear at first, becomes blurred and pixilated, further alarming the viewer – just what are we not supposed to be watching here? Is it the touching of mouths that provokes a sense of disgust and perversion in the viewer?

It is in proximity that disgust is generated. Engendered through the fear of contact – the coming together of bodies – disgust operates on a visceral level forcing us to turn away. According to Sarah Ahmed (2004), the association of what is bad is 'bound up with questions of familiarity and strangeness' (p. 83). Food – or breast milk – is significant 'because disgust is a matter of taste as well as touch – as senses that require proximity to that which is sensed – but also because food is "taken into" the body' (p. 83). Ahmed notes the contradiction inherent in food. It is the stuff of survival, but in taking it in we open up our body to that which is not us; to the other. Breast milk is food and a nutrient for infants, but outside of that dyad it is the abject, the excess that is repelled, repressed, and disposed of. Thus, breast milk is not inherently unpleasant, but when it is brought into contact with our body through the mouth, then this proximity is felt as offensive. Ahmed suggests, however, that disgust, although felt in and on the surface of the body, is not just a gut feeling or reaction. Rather, it is 'mediated by ideas that are already implicated in the very impressions we make of others and the ways those impressions surface as bodies' (Ahmed, 2004, p. 83). So while many audience participants could critically articulate the social and political ideologies behind finding public tasting of breast milk so disgusting, they found themselves still squeamish about tasting the milk themselves. Their distaste for or refusal to drink the milk emphasizes the fear of contamination and the boundaries between subjects coming undone. Coco Fusco (1995) suggests that the flipside of repulsion is the fetishistic fascination with the exotic in which the performance of identity of an Other for a 'white' audience is consumed by a rhetoric of multiculturalism. She writes, 'The threatening reminder of difference is that the original body, or the physical and visual presence of the cultural Other, must be fetishized, silenced, subjugated, or otherwise controlled to be "appreciated"' (p. 45). The attempt at neutralizing the public fear of breast milk by pasteurizing it and serving it in a bourgeois bar-type setting amplified the violent erasure of the Other and the colonization of 'indigenous foodstuff,' by turning it into something exotic and consuming it in a bar-type setting, which implied 'good taste' and a refined social class. The sensory politics of tasting art call into question the maintenance of economic and racial stratification, where 'food' marks a body as distinctively other.

In offering an affective reading of 'The Lactation Station,' I want to argue that Dobkin's work, intended as a satirical commentary on the West's self-consciousness of the (lactating) breast, politicized the exoticness of eating something foreign. In much the same way that Torontonians can eat and appreciate food from all over the world, tasting breast milk gestures, as Probyn (2000) states, 'to the pleasure of control, the desire revealed in constraint' (p. 18) that threaten to colonize the body. To the right of the milk bar was a large video projection of Dobkin's interviews with the six mothers who had donated the milk. Although this video enabled a more phenomenological and intimate narrative of the breastfeeding mothers' diverse experiences, the audience-participants' actions – ingesting the milk, noting its various flavours, and the repulsion and/or fascination with tasting – forced the spectacle of Otherness out into the open. Whereas the pervasiveness of food in art and culture can create spaces of 'affiliation by merging difference under the rubric of congeniality, food can also underscore and exacerbate difference by framing otherness in culinary terms' (Drobnick, 1999, pp. 77–78). Writing about her own performance, 'The Couple in the Cage,' Fusco (1995) notes that 'even those who saw our performance as art rather than artifact appeared to take great pleasure in engaging in the fiction, by paying money to see us enact completely nonsensical or humiliating tasks ... audiences invariably revealed their familiarity with the scenario to which we alluded' (p. 50). Commodified by an art institution, audiences were all too happy to sit comfortably at the bar as a gesture that breast milk wasn't all that threatening and thereby consume difference palatably. This reminds me of Moira Gatens and Genevieve Lloyd's (1999) comments on the symbiotic relationship of the body: 'Each body exists in relations of interdependence with other bodies and these relations form a "world" in which individuals of all kinds exchange their constitutive parts – leading to the enrichment of some and the demise of others (e.g., eating involves the destruction of one body at the same time as it involves the enhancement of the other)' (p. 101).

In concert with the 'live' performance, there was another layer of disgust that permeated the work. The media seemed to fixate on the moral indignation that Dobkin's work was funded through the Canada Council for the Arts, yet this was merely a veil behind which hid the threat of the queer maternal body.[1] If, as Deleuze and Guattari (1988) contend, eating reveals 'a precise state of intermingling of bodies in a society, including all the attractions and repulsions, sympathies and antipathies, alterations, amalgamations, penetrations and expansions that affect bodies of all kinds in their relations with one another' (p. 90), then the real threat was the opening up – the penetration – of the heteronormative body to other bodies. As such, 'The Lactation Station Breast Milk Bar' exposes socio-ultural assumptions about what is edible and what is in 'good taste.'

In *Powers of Horror,* Julia Kristeva (1982) suggests that the relationship between disgust and abjection is the border (like the skin that forms on milk). It is not that the abject has gotten inside of us but that it existed there all along turning inside out and outside in.

In the case of 'Byte,' it is the dissolution of boundaries between mother and child that repulses the viewer. Just as touch produces disgust, disgust turns us away: 'it pulls away with an intense movement that registers in the pit of the stomach' (Ahmed, 2004, p. 84). It is the movement, the vacillation between touching and repulsion that is disgust: 'To feel disgust is to be fully, indeed physically, conscious of being within the realm of uneasy categories: merely saying that something disgusts me is to have placed myself beyond it; yet my embarrassment at being caught within this categorical play may entail some level of self-disgust. Simply put, one of the effects of experiencing shame and disgust is a sense that categories of right and wrong, agreeable and distasteful, desirous and abominable, are rendered pressing and tangible' (Probyn, 2000, p. 132). There is too much of this mother and child interaction. Both heads and mouths loom large in the video frame, then fragmented and pixilated in a series of unending biting mouths. We register disgust socially, assuming some inappropriate mothering behaviour has transpired, and we respond with disgust as the image synasethetically spills over the edges of the video frame – touching us.

Touch dissolves the boundaries between subject and object, in both a sense of being in contact with another body and by way of being moved; an affect of being in proximity (Springgay, 2008). The hegemony of touch is at play in 'Byte' in how we ought to touch or not touch. If disgust is generated from coming too close, then the sensory morphology of mouths produces enlivened zones of intensity and force, connecting the mouth to the anus. Symbolically what goes in must come out. Although, 'Byte' does not reference food explicitly, the attention to the mouth and the biting action, articulates the complex ways that the mouth produces identity: 'we eat into culture, continually oscillating between primary, natural and necessary acts, as simultaneously, we consume and ingest our identities' (Probyn, 2006, p. 17).

The same principles are at work when we examine the corporeality of eating and biting, 'the point of which is the opening up of the body to reveal a multitude of surfaces that seek out contact with other surfaces near or far' (Probyn, 2000, p. 61). As the infant's mouth latches onto the mother's the viewer feels a sense of moving at different speeds, which Deleuze and Guattari (1987) contend is the phenomena of 'lines of flight, movements of deterritorialization and destratification' (p. 4). The point is that lines of force that regulate and produce us are always already in motion, which in turn, create new assemblages and other ways of 'living social patterns' (p. 61). Bound to values of power, the act of eating or biting, Probyn (2000) compels us 'to think about an ethics of living – other ways of being': 'If "ethics" cannot be reified as an object, but always consists of practices that foreground how we relate to ourselves and to others, then the task of thinking ethics will necessarily be a doubled one' (p. 64). This doubling requires that we seek out an ethical practice that 'disturbs, opens up and rearranges different parts of ourselves' (p. 70). The ethical dimensions of eating would mean that the body no longer passively accepts what goes into it; rather the body opens itself up to deterritorializations, a multitude of surfaces, or what Felix Guattari calls an 'ethicoaesthetics'; 'a call to creativity, a call to become actively involved in various strategies and practices that will allow us to produce/transform, and perhaps even go beyond, our habitual selves' (Sullivan, 2007). In the next section, I will examine the politics of taste that compels us to think about an ethics of living, of other ways of being.

The implications of ethicoaesthetics for rethinking a sensational pedagogy consists not of objects, but of sensational practices that foreground how we relate to ourselves and to others.

Tasting' Ethicoaesthetic Encounters and a Sensational Curriculum

Taste is a sense that signifies discrimination, whether in the Kantian sense of aesthetics, moral value, or social decorum, or in relationship to the sensory experiences of the mouth. According to Kant (1790/1951) the 'faculty of taste' was the means by which one aesthetically judged beauty, which differed from 'the culture of taste' or the sensory qualities of the mouth. Eating was assumed to be an individual act and expressed as either pleasant or unpleasant, whereas the faculty of taste was a transcendent point of view, equated with vision and reason. As Jennifer Fisher (1999) notes, 'taste evolved as a term to describe the formal judgments of aesthetic value as well as the unspoken, but enacted, codes for conduct or "good taste"' (p. 31). In contrast to the contiguous experience of tasting something with our tongue, taste as a form of judgment was embedded in the notion of rational thought, and thus associated with distance and separation of the mind and body (Vasseleu, 1998). Michael Peters (2004) contends that in education this separation of mind and body 'stands for a host of optional metaphors that serve to dualize or bifurcate reason and emotion, metaphors in their application and formalisation, have become the substance of educational practice' (p. 14). Moreover, education has traditionally emphasized linguistic, aural, and visual learning, whereas emotions, physical responses, and the senses are bodily responses that must be tamed or controlled to achieve cognitive performance. What little attention has been paid to the senses is often wrapped up in theories of somatic or tacit knowing. For instance, somatic knowledge is an awareness of what is going on 'within' a person, thus integrating the mind and body in processes of learning. As I have argued elsewhere (see Springgay, 2008), this continues to reify a universal and autonomous approach to experiential knowledge, and does not attend to affect, difference, and the relational – the intercorporeality – of knowledge production. Rarely do we encounter educational research that examines the senses as epistemological or ontological.

The ideologies and practices of this scopic regime are evidenced not only in art and education but in the very ways we understand the maternal body. For example, breastfeeding practices are affected by the values, attitudes, histories, and knowledges we have of food and the breast. Here, 'good taste' refers to moral symbolism and discretion. For instance, Alison Bartlett (2005) concludes that examples of scandalous public breastfeeding always have to do with white middle-class urban women. Public lactation by a white middle-class heteronormative and married mother represents a threat to particular social values, which are assumed to be 'average' or 'normative.' She argues that women's use of public space to breastfeed challenges dominant understandings of public citizenry, which are implied in white middle-class values. It is significant that indigenous, ethnic, and lower socioeconomic groups of women are less likely to be publically shunned from breastfeeding outside of the home, as the moral symbolism of 'taste' would imply that such groups would always participate in public forms of breast-feeding and thus embody 'poor taste.' If whiteness becomes a marker for ideal motherhood and breastfeeding has often been linked to the project of nation forming, then it follows that mothers who deviate from such inscriptions would be deemed unfit and lacking 'taste' (Bartlett, 2005).

In this sense, then, 'The Lactation Station Breast Milk Bar' converges the discriminatory practices of taste with the sensational experiences of tasting. For instance, Jennifer Fisher (1999) writes that 'eating in the white cube of the gallery space disturbs the modernist paradigm of a purely visualist taste' (p. 29), and thus, tasting art contradicts our ob-session with scopic consumption. Likewise, taste, even defined as bad or digusting, 'shows us how the boundaries that allow the distinction between subjects and objects are undone in the moment of their mak-ing' (Ahmed, 2004, p. 83). Things we taste merge with our bodies, and thus, we become aware of our own body in space. I want to turn now to examine contemporary art in relation to pedagogy and its implications for education. In particular, I want to offer a divergent understanding of participation in contemporary art, given that proximity engenders a consideration of the politics of sense and sensation.

Over the past decade, there has been an emphasis on contemporary artists who engage in relational art practices as ways to counter our overreliance on visual and alienating modes of living. According to Claire Bishop (2006), these art practices, whether we call them 'so-cially engaged art, community-based art, experimental communities, dialogic art, littoral art, participatory, interventionist, research-based, or collaborative art,' are 'less interested in a relational aesthetic than in the creative rewards of collaborative activity – whether in the form of working with preexisting communities or establishing one's own interdisciplinary network' (n.p.). This 'pedagogical or social turn' in art is linked 'by a belief in the empowering creativity of collective action and shared ideas' and the imperative that 'the creative energy of participatory practices rehumanizes – or at least de-alienates – a society rendered numb and fragmented by the repressive instrumen-tality of capitalism' (n.p.). In her essay, 'The Social Turn: Collabo-ration and Its Discontents,' Bishop argues that many advocates of service-based artwork have denounced aesthetics in favour of 'an ethics of authorial renunciation' (n.p.), where one work is deemed better than another because it exemplifies a superior model of collaborative practice. Co-participation and co-authorship, as opposed to artistic mastery, therefore, become the tenets of benevolent socially engaged art. Although I might be inclined to agree with her point that determining the value of a work of art based on 'ethical judgments on working procedure and intentionality' (n.p.) has its flaws, and that we can't assume that participation automatically engenders a greater degree of agency and empowerment, I want to argue that perhaps the knowledge that comes from collectivity, which she so easily dismisses, might in fact, be located in an ethicoaesthetics, a way of questioning what it is to be.

For example, sliding up to the breast milk bar, imbibing a few shots of breast milk, while talking to the bar tender/artist and fellow imbibers, might constitute what Maria Lind (2004) defines as art that creates and recreates new relations between people. Similarly, the processes of participation simultaneously further bifurcate and fetishize the Other through a politics of the senses – we are, after all, consuming the mother – taking her in and incorporating her into our own body. However, if we turn our attention to the proximal encounter, to affect and disgust, then how would such an ethicoaesthetics work? How can we think through disgust in a way that works with the complicated relations between bodies? Disgust is dependent on proximity. The object that we find disgusting must be close to us to register in intensity. It is through sensation that the object is 'felt to be so "offensive" that it sickens and over takes the body' (Ahmed, 2004, p. 85).

Brian Massumi (2002) describes sensation as pertaining 'to the dimension of passage, or the continuity of immediate experience' (p. 258). Likewise, sensation, according to Elizabeth Grosz (2008), 'is the zone of indeterminacy between subject and object, the bloc that erupts from the encounter of the one with the other. Sensation impacts the body, not through the brain, not through representations, signs, images, or fantasies, but directly on the body's own internal forces, on cells, organs, the nervous system' (p. 73). According to Deleuze, affect is the effect another body has upon my own body, experienced in time and as duration. It is of the body, and as such, produces bodily knowledge. Affects are passages of intensity, a reaction in or on the body at the level of matter. Affects are the becomings of my own body as they encounter another body as difference, constituting a capacity to act in the world.

Affects are not the signification of meaning, but felt experience, the molecular, a happening, an event through which relational becomings are continuously reconfigured (Braidotti, 2006; Kennedy, 2004). This, then, is a pedagogy premised on movement, and process, on machinic connections as assemblage. Being in the presence of tastes has the potential to connect us with other bodies, be it pleasantly or not, through memories and sensory associations. When we encounter the affective through taste 'the thickness of communication includes what is *not* communicated, what may not even be identified as more than a potentiality. Affect is incommunicable per se; and that is its virtue' (Marks, 2008, p. 135, original emphasis). As you sip your wine goblet of breast milk, you may have common reactions to others around you, 'but that response will be enriched and complexified by a core of absolutely individual and relatively incommunicable experience' (p. 135) emplacing you, affecting you. Relational art does not readily confer a participatory experience that is pleasurable or even positive. In fact, it is more likely that the hundreds of milk-tasting participants were complicit in their colonizing gestures of power. It's the new craze, after all, to be part of an artist's work, to feel responsive to something through different means. A sensational pedagogy strategically negotiates between engrained codes of taste and embraces the complexities of lived, affective experience. The dilemma becomes how to speak of those difficulties and incommensurable experiences of being in proximity without having those intensities and complex occurrences turned into easily packaged and fetishized objects of pleasure. In thinking the maternal, we need to work against the essentialized and romanticized understandings that silence, misrepresent, and bifurcate reproduction and production. In thinking sensationally, how might we think outside of the perfect ethical relation – the mother responding to her child over her own needs – and, instead, think about how that coupling relationship, the coming too close engenders other ways of thinking and being in difference.

Note

1 See http://www.jessdobkin.com/index.html/8-press/pages/5-articles.

References

Addison, H., Goodwin-Kelly, M.K., & Roth, E. (Eds.). (2009). *Motherhood misconceived: Representing the maternal in film*. New York: State University of New York Press.

Ahmed, S. (2004). *The cultural politics of emotion*. New York: Routledge.

Bartlett, A. (2005). *Breastwork: Rethinking breastfeeding*. Sydney, Australia: University of New South Wales.

Bishop, C. (2006). *Participation*. Cambridge, MA: MIT Press.

Braidotti, R. (2006). *Transpositions*. Cambridge, MA: Polity.

Deleuze, G., & Guattari, F. (1987). *A thousand plateaus: Capitalism and schizophrenia*. Minneapolis, MN: University of Minnesota Press.

Drobnick, J. (1999). Recipes for the cube: Aromatic and edible practices in contemporary art. In B. Fischer (Ed.), *Foodculture: Tasting identities and geographies in art* (pp. 69–80). Toronto: YYZ.

Evans, E., & Grant, C. (2008). *Mama PhD: Women write about motherhood and academic life*. New York: Rutgers University Press.

Fisher, J. (1999). Performing taste. In B. Fischer (Ed.). *Foodculture: Tasting identities and geographies in art* (pp. 29–48). Toronto: YYZ.

Fusco, C. (1995). *English is broken here*. New York: New Press.

Gatens, M. & Lloyd, G. (1999). *Collective imaginings: Spinoza past and present*. New York: Routledge.

Grosz, E. (2008). *Chaos, territory, art: Deleuze and the framing of the earth*. New York: Columbia University Press.

Grumet, M. (1988). *Biter milk: Women and teaching*. Amherst, MA: University of Massachusetts Press.

Hausman, B. (2003). *Mother's milk: Breastfeeding controversies in American Culture*. New York: Routledge.

hooks, b. (1992). *Black looks: Race and representation*. London: South End Press.

Kant, E. (1790/1951). *Critique of judgment*. New York: Macmillan.

Kennedy, B. (2004). *Deleuze and cinema: The aesthetics of sensation*. Edinburgh: Edinburgh University Press.

Kristeva, J. (1982). *Powers of horror: An essay on abjection*. New York: Columbia University Press.

Kukla, R. (2006). Ethics and ideology in breastfeeding advocacy campaigns. *Hypatia, 21* (1), 165–180.

Lind, M. (2004). Oda Projesi. In C. Doherty (Ed.). *From studio to situations: Contemporary art and the question of context*. New York: Black Dog.

Liss, A. (2009). *Feminist art and the maternal*. Minneapolis, MN: University of Minnesota Press.

Marks, L. (2008). Thinking multisensory culture. *Paragraph, 31* (2), 123–137.

Massumi, B. (2002). *Parables for the virtual: Movement, affect, sensation.* Durham, NC: Duke University Press.

Peters, M. (2004). Education and the philosophy of the body: Bodies of knowledge and knowledges of the body. In L. Bresler (Ed.), *Knowing bodies, moving minds: Towards embodied teaching and learning* (pp. 13–28). New York: Springer.

Picard, A. (2006). Second opinion: Most mothers quit breast-feeding far too soon. *Globe and Mail,* 15 June.

Probyn, E. (2000). *Carnal appetites: Food sex identities.* New York: Routledge.

Probyn, E. (2006). *Blush: Faces of shame.* Minneapolis, MN: University of Minnesota Press.

Reeve, C. (2009). The kindness of human milk: Jess Dobkin's Lactation Station Breast Milk Bar. *Gastronomica: Journal of Food and Culture, 9* (1), 66–73.

Springgay, S. (2008). *Body knowledge and curriculum: Pedagogies of touch in youth and visual culture.* New York: Peter Lang.

Sullivan, S. (2007). *Academy: The production of subjectivity.* Retrieved February 2010, from http://summit.kein.org/node/240.

Vasseleu, C. (1998). *Textures of light: Vision and touch in Irigaray, Levinas, and Merleau-Ponty.* New York: Routledge.

Young, I. (2005). *On female body experience: 'Throwing like a girl' and other essays.* New York: Oxford University Press.

15 Breastfeeding Mothers and Lovers: An Ebbing and Flowing Curriculum of the Fluid Embrace

REBECCA LLOYD

My 4-year-old son Otis is often a source of comic inspiration in my full yet depleted life as a mother/academic. One day, while I was breast-feeding his little brother Ian, he said, 'Mommy, did you know that one side is vanilla and the other is chocolate?' Vanilla and chocolate, hmm, who knew? Perhaps that is why my right breast was his favourite when he first suckled. His words have me drift back in time to the first week of his life when I recall the uneven swelling and painful moments of my newly lactating breasts. The right one responded to his angelic little mouth ready to suck the life juices out of me. My left resisted with inverted resolve. With careful massage, I convinced my nipple that it could withstand the vacuum-like seal as I breathed through tears that clouded my fixed gaze on the mantelpiece clock. Two minutes. I just had to make it through the timed interval of sadomasochistic-like fore-play before I would experience the inevitable bliss of 'let down.' My labour lasted *only* 48 hours, and I was as prepared as I could be for that glorious day when I first became a mother. I attended courses at the hospital, read books, and even devised a 'birthing plan.' No one prepared me for what I was about to experience in the minutes, hours, weeks, and months to come.

The lived curriculum of breastfeeding is very much hidden in West-ern communities until, of course, one is able to produce a child. From lactation consultations to singsong circles and mom-and-baby fitness classes, breasts, breastfeeding techniques, and breastfeeding as a way of mothering (e.g., La Leche League International, 2004) emerge ev-erywhere. There is comfort in surrounding oneself with other sleep-deprived mothers who know what it is like to vacillate between tears of profound joy and rock-bottom frustration and fatigue, as we compare hours of sleep and explosions of poop amid the spraying of milk. But what about the mother who ventures out of her cocoon of like-minded mothers and feeds her baby while writing an academic chapter, or does so during a meeting in an academic setting? Although much may be said about the political nature of such an act (e.g., Davidson & Langan, 2006) as 'breastfeeding [has become] a way to demonstrate women's power and importance' (Kendrowski & Lipscomb, 2008, p. 8), this inquiry acknowledges yet also delves deeply into the existential nature of the breastfeeding experience. Specifically, this inquiry questions what it is like to be in the symbiotic relation of mother and child in blissful moments of fluid embrace. It also explores what is it like to experience moments of mother-child disconnection, a complicating longing to be doing something else while breastfeeding, and what that says about the phenomenon of living life fully and freely as a mother and academic who experiences ebbing, surging, cresting, waning, and weaning experiences of flow.

In describing my experience of breastfeeding phenomenologically (van Manen, 1997) with motion-sensitivity (Lloyd & Smith, 2006a, 2006b), I aim to contribute to Miller's (1982) breaking of silence to which Pinar, Reynolds, Slattery, and Taubman (2000) refer, 'the silence of women's experience, the splitting of women's lived worlds from the public discourse of education' (p. 381) and describe intimacies inherent in the various viscosities of self-other-world fluidity. For breastfeeding is more than a means to provide babies with vital sustenance. A relational reciprocity may surface, one that may shape the ways in which mother and child move in response and be with each other. It also provides a metaphorical model for exploring the multiplicities of relational consciousness, the surging and waning of motile expression, what Stern (1993, 2004) and Sheets-Johnstone (1999) describe as 'vitality affects' that are not only present within the mother-child dynamic, but any relation, such as marriage, friendship, and for those who choose academia, life in the classroom and beyond.

The 'logic' of my inquiry will be very much related to the various stages I experienced within my journey of breastfeeding, my painful beginnings to my eventual experience of 'flow.' It will also be framed around various registers of interrelational movement consciousness, which have emerged from recent phenomenological inquiries within interdisciplinary, movement education contexts (Lloyd & Smith, 2006a, 2006b, 2009, 2010, in press; Smith & Lloyd, 2006, 2007. I will thus reacquaint myself with the joys and tensions of breastfeeding with the intention of becoming more viscerally in touch with others and the world. From superficial explanations of objective kinetic function to deep, moving experiences of primordial bliss, this inquiry will draw attention to the surges, swells, waning, and weaning experiences of living life as a breastfeeding mother, professor, lover, and friend within and beyond the fluid embrace.

A Kinetic Embrace: Mobilizing Objects of Desire

Moments after I bear down and give my last guttural push, Otis is received by Rose, the fourth doctor on call during my two-day labour, the only doctor with small enough hands to reach up and adjust his posterior position. He is placed on my chest, ear turned towards my heart. My eyes glisten, not from residual pain but fathomless joy. I am a mother. I have a son. He is no longer within me, stretching my torso with alien-like pokes from his elbows, fists, and feet. His delicate flesh rests on my bare chest, and for the first time, I offer him my breast. He takes me in and we christen our new relation, our way of being close, so much so that I don't want to let go, not ever. Not knowing that I should have brought an extra pillow to prop under my elbows, my arms bear Otis's 8.6 pounds of loveliness. The first few hours of holding my child were blessed. I was filled with overwhelming emotion but, later, my gestural love for my child becomes strained. Burning biceps, levator scapulae, scalene, and upper trapezius muscles remind me that I need to seek guidance from a lactation consultant not only from the exhaustion I experience in supporting my child but the agony I am also experiencing with bleeding, misshapen, swelling, and on occasion inverting nipples – an act of preservation perhaps.

Objects of Desire within the Kinetic Embrace

Now that Otis's lips regularly form a seal around my nipple, my bodily way of being in the world is forever changed. A walk down the street remains just that, a walk. No longer able to run, jump, and soar my way through life, my shift from a perky size 'A' is weighed down to a monstrous 'E,' the largest size made available in Motherhood Maternity™ stores. Although my friend from the gym jokingly comments that I have 'porn star' boobs, not for any other reason than personal comfort and perhaps instinct, I have purposefully removed them from the relational dance within my marital embrace as they are filled with newfound purpose. My desire to remove my breasts from sexual fore-play fits with the way most cultures experience the breast as only '13 out of 190 cultures report male manipulation of female breasts as a pre-cursor or accompaniment of sexual intercourse' (Kendrowski & Lip-scomb, 2008, p. 23). But however removed the experience of offering the protrusion of my nipple into the moistened mouth of my newborn infant is from my personal experience of sexual bliss,[1] the breast, more specifically the enlarged, lactating breast exemplifies an object of desire in Western culture (Bartlett, 2005). Freud latches on to such tendencies, as he proclaims that the state of being 'filled up with mother's milk [becomes] a blissful satisfaction that will be a standard for all requited love to come' (translator's preface to Freud, 2003, p. x). Accordingly, the breast forms the hub of psychoanalytical object-relations theory, and the drive for both Eros and life, since Freud contends that 'hunger and love make the world go round' (1958, p. 68), thereby problematizing the act of breastfeeding for many women who reportedly choose not to breastfeed because of 'self-conscious' and 'prudish' feelings (Sloan, Sneddon, Stewart, & Iwaniec, 2006, p. 289).

As an alternative to discounting the breast as an object of hunger and desire or succumbing to feelings of prudish restraint, Bartlett (2005) in-vites us to reconsider 'what we understand as sexual' (p. 68). She delves beneath object-subject discourse and reinscribes breastfeeding 'as an embodied experience which involves intense physical exchanges: skin touching, hands stroking, holding and playing, bodies sharing, hor-mones pulsing, as well as an emotional relation of intimacy, care often passionate engagements' (p. 68). Bartlett also explains that 'breast-feeding is understood and experienced – made meaningful – through a number of intersecting discourses which are filtered through each woman's embodiment as it is lived and subjectivity as it forms her on-going sense of self' (p. 69).

And so, I return to my lived experience as a newly lactating mother to make sense of my new feelings of embodiment associated with a trickling drip of colostrum that opens my relational existence in the world beyond the surface of my flesh. But is what I am feeling truly embodied? Perhaps the visceral awareness now coursing within and through me bursts the 'embodiment' bubble, a term that carries the no-tion of being 'packaged,' as it 'fails to do justice to animate form; it fails to recognize the primacy of movement and its dynamic tactile-kinesthetic-kinetic correlates' (Sheets-Johnstone, 1999, pp. 359–360). The fluid embrace, however painful as I acquaint myself with a new way of being visceral in the world, thus reminds me that I, my breast, is so much more than an object for my child and something to be objectified by the gaze of others since my viscerality flows from and through me and connects a false divide between what may be considered internal and external (Shusterman, 2008a).

Mobilizing the Kinetic Embrace with Medical and Mechanical Milk

I have been breastfeeding for 2 weeks now, and I take my lactation consultant's advice to walk around topless to help my nipples recover (*thank God for blinds*). Feelings of comfort begin to emerge. The group of breastfeeding mothers I met one week prior to giving birth, mothers associated with a Toronto chapter of La Leche League, were right. *It does get better.* Had I not heard that unanimous verdict that was the only commonality among the various tips and suggestions each of the 14 women had to offer, I think I would have given up. They provided me with enough hope to persevere. My eyes no longer look towards the mantelpiece clock as I blink away 2 minutes of tears; they attend to Otis, my sweet Otis, as he coos, squirms, and on occasion, cries. He never leaves my side, we are attached, and my breasts fill and empty in response to his desire to suckle. I feel that I have finally gotten a handle on mothering, so to speak, and a fragile confidence is beginning to surface until. . . . my parents visit.

'When I breastfed you and your brothers, I gave you 5 minutes per side once every 4 hours,' my mother says with concern. My Dad, a medical doctor who 'delivered' babies for more than 25 years during his ongoing practice, chimes in,

> 'Babies haven't changed since you were born. You should listen to your mother. You turned out okay. We worry about how tired you are. I used to give mom a break and give you all a bottle of formula at least once per day. You look so tired. . . Once every 4 hours is enough.' My mother adds, 'Yes Rebecca, once every 4 hours is enough to form a bond.'

I am thankful that my mother breastfed me and shared her story of not only forming a bond through the act of breastfeeding but also learning how she found a way to manage her depleting energy. I can imagine how difficult it must have been for my parents to see their daughter, a former fitness champion and professional dancer with endless motile exuberance, struggle for the first time in her life to stay awake. Meg Daley Olmert (2009) explains that the demands on new mothers are extraordinary: 'Their bodies manage to produce thousands of extra calories per day to keep themselves and their babies alive' (p. 26). She continues by saying, 'Above all, despite their overwhelming new responsibility they must relax both body and mind so that their love and milk will flow' (p. 27). Biologically speaking, the more one breastfeeds, the more one will experience the flow of oxytocin, a hormone found within breast milk that quiets 'the sympathetic nerves and inhibit[s] the production of stress hormones, [hence nature's] antistress strategy that minimizes wear and tear on a mother's body' (p. 27). And as far as forming a bond is concerned, it 'is from oxytocin-rich mothers that we have learned so much about the chemistry that makes us the kind of mammal that can form deep and long-lasting emotional attachments to our babies, our friends, our mates, our pets, even our planet' (p. 26).

And so I question my parents' advice to schedule my newly forming fluid relation with my child 'once every 4 hours,' not only in relation to stress management but also in relation to the primordial nature of forming and experiencing a bond. To give context to what timing an act of fluid and loving interconnectivity might be like, Bartlett (2005) invites us to consider what scheduling the sexual act in relation to a fixed number of minutes would do to 'coital frigidity.' Just imagine the absurdity: *'Honey, it's time,'* as clothes drop to the floor. No time 'fore' play. Penetration, intense gyration with one purpose in mind – male satisfaction, ejaculation as the primary goal. – soft gentle caresses and licks dismissed, not prioritized for waves of female pleasure ebb and flow within the nuances of a lived moment, not intervals that are timed by a ticking clock. Similarly, the time it takes for an infant to satiate his hunger varies considerably. I return for a third visit to the lactation department of Women's College Hospital in an effort to stabilize my wavering confidence and learn that it is normal to have a baby suckle for an indeterminate amount of time. My jovial consultant with an Australian accent explains,

> Some babies guzzle as if they are eating fast food and finish in 5 minutes or less, while others like to savour a gourmet delight.

My way of mothering, feeding 'on cue,' or what my mother describes as 'on demand,' stands in contrast to my British heritage, just as 'English society women started scheduling their feeding regime in order to combine motherhood and social responsibilities [as early as] 1750 AD' (Jansen, Weerth, & Riksen-Walraven, 2008, p. 514). Breast-feeding, thus, shifted from a way of being fluidly connected with one's child to an objective act of providing nutrition, so much so that this Victorian time period was marked by the emergence of infant formula. Schwab (1996) explains, 'Infant formula was first created in Victorian Europe, yet the state of mind from which it emerged was the mechanistic philosophy of the 17th century, with its belief that the body, like all of nature, is a machine, fixed in specific patterns of behavior – a clock or a factory, rationally designed and managed by the Great Engineer in the sky' (p. 480).

Although much can be said about the life-saving potential that formula provides for mothers who, for a number of reasons, cannot or choose not to breastfeed (DiGirolamo, Thompson, Martorell, Fein, & Grummer-Strawn, 2005; Sloan et al., 2006), we may question the practice of scheduling bottle and breastfeeding by the objective measure of time. In fact, we may question living life at large by the hands of a mechanical clock, the icon of the scientific age and the tendency of 'coloniz[ing] the natural rhythms of the day, the month, the year' (Schwab, 1996, p. 480). When one thinks back to some of the most memorable moments one experiences in life, what some may describe as 'peak' experiences, there is a tendency to completely lose oneself in the moment, and time takes on an existential, living quality. Time shifts from sequential clock, or 'chronos' time, to 'kairos' time (Stern, 2004; van Manen, 1997), where moments of significance seem to either speed up, slow down, or feel suspended (Stern, 2004; Csikszentmihalyi, 2000). Feeding and caring for an infant through experiential time, thus, shifts the emphasis from an objective measure to a motile responsiveness, one that, at times, regulates into a predictable pattern, but at others, shifts towards moments that may be described as 'cluster' feeding patterns where the child stimulates more milk production through prolonged sucking at a mother's breast. Through such interactions, breast milk becomes 'something more vital, a living, constantly changing and responsive substance, homeostatically regulated' (Schwab, 1996, p. 488), and thus, a fluid relation emerges.

An Aesthetic Embrace: Forming a Flowing Relation

As I continue to breastfeed, my comfort in experiencing life beyond the hands of a ticking clock not only begins to grow, my tactile way of being with my child takes on a new quality. I am beginning to perfect the 'cross-cradle hold,' a position where my baby's full spine, from head to bottom is supported by my forearm that is resting upon my new wrap-around breastfeeding pillow. I take my lactation consultant's advice and cease to pump and support my lactating breast with my free hand, a technique I learned from reading my *Dr Jack Newman's Guide to Breastfeeding* book. In response to watching Otis's pattern of sucking and swallowing, my consultant assures me that I have enough milk and do not need to coax it out. Instead, she suggests that I learn to relax my hand, my arm, and the whole carriage of my upper body as she gently massages my bare shoulders and encourages Martin, my husband, to do the same. Instead of pumping the breast, she explains that I simply need to draw the baby's bottom towards my torso, as the relative positioning of a baby acts like a rudder for intensity. I watch in amazement as the closer I draw Otis in, his pace and depth of suckling increase. For the first time, an act that felt utterly painful and awkward is taking on an aesthetic quality.

Aesthetics, a school of thought traditionally associated with appreciating beauty in art and nature (Menke, 2008; Carlson & Berleant, 2004), may also apply to the art of everyday living (Shusterman, 2008b). I open my La Leche League International (2004) text entitled, *The Womanly Art of Breastfeeding,* and read about the various ways in which I may hold and position both my baby and myself. From the nuances of cultivating an effective and comfortable latch, a gesture initiated by gentle stroking of my nipple on his nose and upper lip to encourage an open-mouth like yawn, wide enough to 'take a large portion of [my] areola into his mouth along with the nipple' (p. 48), to the multiple positions I am in the process of refining, this new, fluid embrace has an emerging aesthetic quality. If something is not quite right I writhe in pain and shove my finger between my nipple and his lip to break the seal or Otis cries out in frustration. In some way he is my biggest but also my most honest critic. Babies do not feign comfort. Hearing him joyfully suck and swallow my milk, especially after so many weeks of trepidation, is a small miracle in and of itself. And so I return to Shusterman's (2000) notion of aesthetic experience, one that he defines as being 'essentially valuable and enjoyable; [. . .] vividly felt and subjectively savored, affectively absorbing [to the extent where we] focus [. . .] our attention on its immediate presence and [it] thus stand[s] out from ordinary flow of routine experience' (p. 17). I am assured that yes, breastfeeding as an act in and of itself and also as an act of responsiveness to coos, reaches, and murmurs (as a full-throttle cry is somewhat of a nightmare to soothe), may fall within the realm of the aesthetic. Perhaps it is this quality that is now emanating from my mother-infant interactions is helping my parents accept my seemingly unorthodox way of feeding my child and the frequent glasses of water I consume. The stress I initially absorbed in relation to their concern for scientific frequency and function of milk production now rolls off my back as I embrace a 'science of sensuous knowledge' (Menke, 2008, p. 60). Aesthetics, as introduced by Baumgarten's *Aesthetica* from 1750 (Menke, 2008), thus takes a new hold on my consciousness. I continue to experiment with new holds and positions, the 'football,' the 'side-lying,' and to my amazement, the 'side-lying switch.' Much like the change of position may bring a new sense of excitement within a marital embrace, an experimental phenomenon that led to the cracking of my IKEA bed frame that we were unfortunately not able to replace, but I digress, the refinement of a new breastfeeding position may be regarded as beautiful, a new art form. In accordance with Shusterman's (2008b) contention that 'sexual experience can be aesthetic,' that we can experience sexual union beyond 'unimaginative, thoughtlessly mechanical and insensitive copulation' (p. 93), we can become imaginative in breastfeeding, beyond the confines of my home.

At first I try to copy other mothers in my mom-and-baby fitness class and begin to feed Otis within a tentlike cocoon of a flannel baby blanket draped from my shoulder. I quickly learn that the blanket-shield will have no part of our fluid embrace. He wants to be close. More than mouth on nipple, his hands and feet kick the blanket until he can fully take me in. I don't force the act of covering up and find a way for him to latch with utmost discretion. Perhaps it was the challenge of mastering the unclipping of a sports bra and offering him my breast in an effective manner during fitness classes that softened future possible anxieties of lifting loose-fitting tops and lowering bras designed for easy access. I soon became a 'pro' and fed Otis anywhere and everywhere, his doctor's office, restaurants so that my husband and I could continue to enjoy fancy meals together, the park which enabled me to organize a walking group with my new mom-and-baby-fitness friends, parties, the hair salon, the spa, church, and on planes, as I often travelled to present fitness education workshops in places such as New York, Miami, Chicago, and Florida. *If only my marital embrace was as adventurous . . . Hmmm . . . perhaps that is a good thing.*

As Shusterman (2008b) approaches the aesthetics of sex by 'valuing it for its own sake rather than its role in producing children' (p. 92), I too, experience the full appreciation of relaxing and being close with Otis and the sensations such proximity holds.

A Kinaesthetic Embrace: Vital Mergings of Flowing Flesh

> Breastfeeding is in some sense a testimony to vitalism, and to women's power.
>
> – Schwab, 'Mechanical Milk'

There is something so intimate in the gesture of a mother reaching towards her baby, gathering him close, nose to nipple. The scent of her flesh lets him know it is time to open, time to form a seal and 'educere' or draw out his vital sustenance, a milky dream of protein, water, and oxytocin. Figuratively and fluidly speaking, he sucks his way into existence and in so doing transforms a mother's existence and way of being in the world. Beyond an appreciation for the aesthetic nature of such a transformation, where breastfeeding may thus be understood beyond the scientific principles of 'mechanism,' measured quantities, and the nutritional value of breast milk, as such, we may also consider attuning towards the kinaesthetic sensations of experiencing life in fluid relation. Vitalism, the counter-movement of mechanism (Schwab, 1996), embraces the presence of life, an ontology that is perfectly represented in experiencing an ebbing, flowing relation not only between mother and child but with what Abram (1996) so eloquently describes as the more-than-human world.

Breasts, my breasts, have thus shifted from soft, perky protuberances my husband once described as perfect handfuls, to enlarged, engorged, spraying, depleting, and refilling modalities that move in response to the nutritional and nurturing needs of my little one. No longer identified by and through my bodily surface, I have become a perpetual moving tide of 'interpenetrating waves [. . .] movements of an unspeakable love. A love that makes it possible for flesh to drop away' (Conrad, 2007, p. 322).

The flesh of my breast, my child, my world dissolves in the bliss of a fluid embrace. Such intertwining delves beneath Merleau-Ponty's (1968) object-subject, perceiver-perceived, two-sided leaves of living 'flesh,' a chiasm predominantly understood in relation to what is 'visible' and what is not with respect to bodily surface. More than an aesthetic experience of form in the various ways I now am able to hold my child and the appreciation such a vision holds, I delve beneath the surface of our intertwining flesh. The presence of vitality surges and swells within me and is freely expressed as my love flows forth.

The fluid embrace of breastfeeding thus affords a modality of exploring the 'symbiotic relation of mother and child [beneath the] gaze of misunderstanding' (Grumet, 1988, p. 97), a look that acknowledges the infant's 'all-inclusive identification that does not recognize her' (p. 97). As an alternative to seeking the 'discontinuity between herself and others' (p. 98), and the establishment of a sense of self through the lens of psychoanalysis, what if we turn towards the motions, gestures, and fluid ways in which we may enhance our sensibilities of interconnection? While Merleau-Ponty and Grumet were primarily drawn to explore perception through vision, what could be considered the most distancing of senses however 'palpable' as 'synaesthetic perception' affords (Merleau-Ponty, 1962), what might we learn from attending not only to the aesthetic qualities of the maternal embrace but also the kinaesthetic flow of gestural motions within such envelopment? Leder (1990) invites us to consider the felt sense of our 'viscerality, not visibility' (p. 206), a 'visceral invisibility that is never fully written within Merleau-Ponty's text' (p. 207). And in so doing, we may consider 'the hidden vitality that courses within' (p. 204) and the 'deeper magic [that] takes hold' (p. 203) beyond the sensorimotor expressive nature of Merleau-Ponty's 'I can,' the conscious apprehension of 'the surface body' (p. 203), and acknowledge our 'viscero-aesthesiological being' (p. 204).

I heard a baby cry in the hallway during my lecture at the university today, and a strange thing happened. More than 6 months have passed since I weaned my second baby, yet a throb of bodily remembrance surged deep within my flesh. When I teach, I am usually always in the moment, and my attention is purposefully directed to facilitating a flowing conversation within our four walls. Today, beyond where my eyes were looking, my breasts viscerally attended elsewhere in surging and ebbing waves of awareness that very much moved in accordance with the intensity and phraselike quality of the baby's cries of distress. For this reason, my cousin Vikki, a physician who returned to part-time work when her infants were 4 months old, felt the need to wean. The involuntary surging, swelling, and expression of milk from her breasts in a hospital setting was too much of a distraction from the concentration she needed to do her job. Luckily, the university seldom echoes reverberating baby cries, and I was able to maintain my fluid relation until both Ian and Otis were 14 months old. What baffles me now, however, is that the feeling of fluid responsiveness still surges within. Although no milk was expressed, my fluid way of relating to babies emerged in a gestalt of remembered responsiveness. As much as I wanted to embrace my class and hear Stacy's story from her recent practicum,[2] a longing to pick up, rock, and sway the baby in our hallway took hold of my throbbing and engorging visceral consciousness.

The concept of Leder's (1990) 'viscero-aesthesiological being' in relation to the kinaesthetic sensations a breastfeeding mother experiences, thus, adds, even disrupts, the chiasm of conscious and unconscious awareness put forth. On the one hand, there is a conscious separation from our deepest motility that Leder describes within the realm of 'it can' in relation to acts such as digestion, where it is simply 'accomplished within me, without my intervention, guidance, or skill' (p. 203). Similarly, the production of milk and the fluid, *expressive* responsiveness to a baby's cry, any baby's cry, also falls beneath the Merleau-Pontian sensorimotor realm of the ' "I can" of the surface body' (p. 203). What is unique to the surging tide within a woman's breast is that such fluid responsiveness, however primordially mediated, enters into the realm of conscious apprehension. While digestion may happen deep beneath one's surface, the seeping out of milk or even the remembrance of milk preparing to spray forth becomes imminently conscious. And paired with the kinaesthetic awareness associated with the actual release of milk into the mouth of an infant is an emotional affordance of complete bliss:

One quiet evening as I nursed my daughter to sleep, I reflected on the term 'let down' and I began to wonder how this term came to be used in regard to breastfeeding. It usually means disappointment and hurt. The total opposite is what occurs when I nurse my infant daughter. The breastfeeding let-down was by then a very familiar feeling to me, yet it can't really be described. My daughter sucked and wriggled and sucked more to coax the milk out. After a few brief moments, I felt the fullness – almost an ache – my breasts seemed hard and ready to overflow. And then the change in her breathing as she began drinking in with long, slow gulps, eyes closed, in utter abandonment. I looked down at this small being who was cradled against my body. As I stroked her soft, sweet skin, I felt the overwhelming

release of love which to me, is what the let down truly is. (La Leche League
International, 2004, p. 54)

More than a 'look' of love between infant and child, a gaze of reciprocity that matures by 6 weeks, the kinaesthetic sensations of let down
draw us deeply towards waves of motile responsiveness. The release
of love, a letting out of tension, therefore, somewhat coincides with
Freud's theory of affect, a kernel concept where 'affect [may be con-
ceived] as the build-up and fall-off of stimulation and tension' (Stern,
2002, p. 84). In contrast to Freud's extreme position, however, where
'the build-up side [of tension] was solely unpleasurable and the fall-off
side purely pleasurable' (p. 84), Stern (1993) suggests that *all* categorical affects such as happiness, anger, and sadness have in-built surging
and fading qualities. Affect may be thus understood as a temporal dynamic, a musical phrase of building and fading emotion, what Stern
refers to as a 'vitality affect,' which represents the presence of dynamic
life within the micro-experience of an emotion. While 'psychology has
[largely] ignored temporal dynamics' (p. 13), the fading, accelerating,
cresting, and swelling qualities of tension, phenomenologists such as
Sheets-Johnstone (1999) have concluded that a vitality affect is always
present in some shape and form. The gestures we associate with expression such as a smile, therefore, not only have a discernible temporal
quality in and of themselves, they reverberate in a full-bodied way. An
infant's smile, the gradual opening and upward turning of a baby's
mouth releasing his latch from a nipple, for example, is also accompa-
nied by a series of vitality affects communicated in the way his limbs
reach out, his hands open and shut, as well as the tonal rise and fall of
his soft, happy gurgles.

Through Stern's theory of temporal affect, one that draws upon the
felt sense of bodily tension, we may approach the experience of 'let
down' through a visceral motile consciousness. More than a static feeling of bliss, a state that may be interchanged with Csikszentmihalyi's
(1997, 2000) theory of flow that athletes, artists, and yes, even teachers
or professors use to describe the phenomenon of a 'peak experience'
or 'being in the zone,' a state where time takes on an existential quality
and action merges with awareness, we may seep out of the Cartesian
coordinates used to psychologically profile the phenomenon. Beyond
the $X = Y$, upwardly expanding relationship of matching one's skill
level with a corresponding challenge (Csikszentmihalyi, 1997, 2000),
the act of breastfeeding, once mastered and refined through aesthetic

sensitivity, does not continue to climb in skilful, measures that can be graphed. The experience of flow or motile 'bliss' within a breastfeeding embrace comes and goes like an ebbing and flowing tide. It is not confined to a practised performance, the feeling of love not only climbs as a mother becomes more proficient at holding and feeding her child, the feeling of being close, of feeling a sense of fluid love is infinite, off the Cartesian chart, so to speak. The experience of flow within the fluid mother-child embrace thus draws one beneath the elemental intertwining of Merleau-Ponty's (1968) chiasm of flesh, beyond Leder's (1990) visceral addition he terms 'blood,' as in the 'flesh and blood' of the world, and into the temporal dynamics of expression (Stern, 2002) that connect Abram's (1996) 'rhythms of the more-than-human cosmos' (p. 187) to Conrad's (2007) description of 'consciously entering into the fluid system of [her] own bodily tissues' and entertain the possibility of a 'different order of existence [that so] emerges' (p. 4).

A Somaesthetic Embrace: A Reflective Ebb of Intertwining

A visceral, seamless connection to the world experienced within what Csikszentmihalyi (2000) profiles as flow is, therefore, possible. But, the phenomenon of feeling a blissful connection to a lived moment, what Stern (2004) describes as a musical phrase or arc that carries the expansiveness of the 'small momentary events that make up our worlds of experience' (p. xi), is not always present. As much as we are predisposed to experience sensations of ultimate connection to others and the world in flow, we humans also have the ability to disconnect from our actions of daily life and reflect. Shusterman's (2008b) concept of somaesthetics carries just that, a reflective consciousness that supersedes Merleau-Ponty's (1962) notion of a preconscious 'direct and primitive contact with the world' (p. v). Within the realm of somaesthetics, Shusterman (2008b) invites us to acknowledge the following senses, namely, the 'exteroceptive (relating to stimuli outside the body and felt on the skin), proprioceptive (initiated within the body and concerned with the orientation of body parts relative to one another and the orientation of the body in space), and visceral or interoceptive (deriving from internal organs and usually associated with pain)' (p. 2).

When one analyses one's relation to others and to the world through these modalities, there is a sense of separation from the bliss of 'going with the flow' of 'let down' and the overwhelming sense of joy and love such an experience holds. I, for one, have disconnected from the immediacy of my direct experience and have been caught in moments of reflection, moments where I purposefully shifted my relational perception within and beyond the fluid embrace. With the help of a breastfeeding pillow and soothed state of my sleepy, suckling infant, for example, I have purposefully attended to reading journal articles, writing academic texts, watching television, or during moments of excruciating pain at the onset of breastfeeding, the hands of a ticking clock. The surges, swells, gushes, waning, and weaning experiences of milk within my breast, therefore, not only remind me of my ability to aesthetically (in reference to appreciating outer form) and kinaesthetically (in relation to proprioceptively feeling inner sensation) experience my viscerality but become aware of the ebbs and flows of consciousness in any relational existence between self, other, and our mostly fluid world.

Today, as I continue to breastfeed, the aesthetic and kinaesthetic qualities of the experience slowly begin to wane, and the experience of lactation no longer seems to stand out or apart from the ordinary. I no longer 'fully' soak in my child, his delicate little fingers, his tiny toes while I caress his soft fine hair in rhythmical strokes in time with the beat of his latest baby CD, a Jamaican remix of *London Bridges Falling Down*. My eyes drift beyond the pane of my two-bedroom apartment kitchen window and softly cloud over, as a perplexing feeling of discontent emerges. Much of my existence as of late may be described by the idiomatic expression of 'being a boob.' Etymology Online (2009) reveals that a 'boob,' a term that originated in 1909, is used to describe a stupid person and yes, the descriptor fits. I want my short-term memory back. I want to be able to start a sentence and have enough 'with-it-ness' to end it. A longing to be more than a lactating mother surges within. Memories of my former life as a doctoral student and part-time professor surface, as do my buried hopes and dreams of securing a tenure-track academic position.

A mix of guilt and anguish churn. How dare I think about a life beyond mothering? How dare I feel jealous of my husband's frequent correspondence on his handheld Blackberry™? Should I not be content with the fact that my baby is happy and healthy? Why are tears rolling down my face? Why do I feel that mothering is not enough? It was the epitome of my mother's existence. She was the mother of all mothers and continues to define herself through her love of babies, her fascination with sleeping and feeding routines, the ideal diaper size and sleeper length, ways to tuck in a blanket, and story upon story of what she did for my brothers and me. I do not care about such things, but feel that I am supposed to. I feel caught in the cycle of what Grumet (1988) describes as 'maintenance, [an existence] repeated in daily chores required merely to sustain life, not to change it' (p. 24), and I know deep down, I need more. I am not my mother. I do not take pleasure in folding onesies into little squares, organized by size and colour. I have a large shelving unit with 'areas' for sleepers, pants, and socks. It works most of the time, until I seem to be forcing his chubby feet into the legs of a sleeper that just doesn't have enough stretch. My mother is flabbergasted: 'Rebecca, that suit is for a 3-month old! You need to put all of the smaller ones away and get organized!' I silently respond, 'Kill me now, seriously.'

Nancy Chodorow (1978), in *The Reproduction of Mothering* (1978), explains through a psychoanalysis of biology and culture why, for so many reasons, it is me who mothers, just as my mother mothered me. It is not my husband, who spends his days at Chiropractic College and anticipated future in a clinic. More than a biological need for my child to be at my breast, Chodorow (1978) invites us to 'understand the mechanisms which produce [the sexual division of labor] in the first place' (p. 215) and consider the possibility of 'men and women parent[ing] equally' (p. 217). She suggests 'that infants require the whole parenting of warmth, contact, and reliable care, and not the specific feeding relationship itself' (p. 217). I pause to consider such a possibility and question how much longer will I continue to live life as a 'boob'? How much longer will my intelligence, alertness, and desire to do something with my Ph.D. get sucked away? Although my stroller walks on cold winter days are always filled with rays of sparkling sunshine, my dreams of an academic life are very much suspended at present through my breast, a sentiment echoed by Grumet (1988). She elaborates, 'The sucking infant drains her mother's swollen breasts of milk, reasserting the dominance of the child's time over the mother's as lactation and sleep as well respond to the duration and strength of the child's hunger and vigor' (p. 10).

I have been exclusively breastfeeding for 5 months now, and while I wouldn't describe my child's relation to me as one of dominance, I know that I am destined for so much more. A year and a half have passed since I graduated from my doctoral program and I worry that if I don't apply soon, I may miss my window of opportunity to secure an academic position. Perhaps it is luck or coincidence but within 2 weeks of following leads I am contacted by McGill University for an interview by their Kinesiology and Physical Education Department. My husband Martin, in full support, joins both Otis and me as we head to Montreal. For the first time in a long time, I contemplate a life of becoming a professor.

In order to assume the look of a professor, as clothing often 'reveal[s] a great deal about [one's] pedagogical beliefs' (Weber & Mitchell, 1995, p. 580), I squeeze my breasts into a button-down shirt and step into my Holt Renfrew grey tweed suit, the suit I purchased for my graduation. I am amazed that I can do up the waist, as I am at least 15 pounds heavier, and laugh as I attempt to close my jacket button. 'Oh well, I guess I will have to leave it open,' I giggle to myself.

There is something to be said for 'looking the part,' as my identity as a mother was suspended on that crisp January day. I left my hotel room and walked to the McGill campus with a quiet confidence, a certainty that I can carry a conversation that does not revolve around diapers, baby poop, and a lack of sleep. I am greeted by approximately 12 professors and I take a significant liking to Joe Kincheloe, the invited external member of the hiring committee. We have a very enjoyable debate on the difference between 'essence' and 'essencing,' as well as 'lived' and 'living,' particularities that I introduce within my motion-sensitive phenomenological approach; so much so that by the end of my presentation, he invites me to write a chapter in his education research methods text (now published, see Lloyd & Smith, 2006a). I also meet Enrique Garcia Bengoechea, a person with whom I have stayed in touch, and one who has recently asked me to contribute to a book chapter in an international physical education text (Lloyd, Garcia Bengoechea, & Smith, 2010). And so, I met two 'kindreds,' two very special souls in what could have been a very stressful situation and was filled with renewed hope.

'I did it... I really did it, I think I got the job,' I tell my husband, who is pushing our sleeping Otis in the stroller. The details of the day cascade off my tongue as I float down the sidewalk and Martin smiles. For the first time in a long time, I am bursting at the seams in a different way. My husband sees how a turquoise fish hanging from a simple silver chain in a store window catches my eye and urges me to forget about our student budget and purchase it as a way to remember this special day. We continue to walk in and out of shops, and although the January air is cold and brisk, the sunshine seeps into my every pore as we head back to our hotel. My life seems to be turning in a new direction until . . . I experience a bursting swell of a different kind. Otis begins to stir and my button-down shirt no longer fits as it did earlier that day. My usual way of discretely merging with Otis is blocked by the tightness of the pressed and stretched cotton. Within the privacy of our hotel room I have to completely remove my shirt to unclip my bra. I offer Otis my breast and hold him close. Mommy had a big day today, goodler,[3] I softly say as he nuzzles and guzzles. Our glorious night continues. We change before heading out to a celebratory dinner.

But wait . . . What have I done? I sit up in our hotel bed in the middle of the night and begin to cry with remorse. What if I do get the job? Who will take care of Otis? How could I possibly think of leaving him? Martin's hug calms the momentum I am generating in my back-and-forth pacing, and I pause to catch my breath between sobs. My thoughts drift to a future of dedicating my best energy and time to an institution, to others, and not my son, my baby Otis. I love Otis so very much that the thought of separating and living a life where there will be more absence than presence of his laughter, his curious nature, his moments of fear or fascination with the cat or the toilet will be lost to someone who doesn't care as much as I do is more than I can bear. I am not ready to leave him, not yet.

An Energetic Embrace: Renewing and Refining
My Visceral Connection to the World

More than 3 years have passed since my interview at McGill. I am a mother of two boys, now weaned and aged 20 months and 4 years. I am also a tenure-rack professor bursting at the seams. I teach five classes, apply for two or more grants per annum, supervise students, promote equity on a formalized committee, look forward to chairing a national physical and health education conference as well as to organizing a symposium on health-related fitness pedagogy. I also trail run, do yoga, walk my dog, grocery shop, cook feasts for my family, make love to my husband, go out dancing with friends at least twice a year, and for the first time since I have had children, plan to take up snowboarding again this winter.

No longer sitting at home with the comfort of my breastfeeding pillow supporting the recline of Otis where I am able to soak in his miraculous features, his little fingers, his perfectly formed eyebrows, his little, and might I add, beautiful clusters of earwax that I delicately clear out as he reciprocally soaks in me, I attune to a 'let down' of a different kind. Salty tears stream down my face when I pause to consider what it is like to disconnect from the 'sensation of "eternity," [. . .] something limitless, unbounded, something "oceanic"' (Freud, 1958, p. 2), an existence and phenomenon, however primordial, questioned by Freud through his object-relations theory of 'discontent.' Living the life of an academic requires that, at times, I leave my children in the arms of someone else. While ebbs and flows of interconnectivity do exist in my relational connections to others, my students, my writing, and my colleagues, there are many moments where life seems to be passing me by, almost leaving me, as my bath of primordial bliss on occasion becomes an ocean where I struggle to stay afloat.

As much as I enjoy the many things I do, accepting the invitation to write this chapter has also evoked feelings of sadness, concern, and longing to form deeper, visceral connections, not only with my children but in everything I do. Recalling past moments of bliss within my prior life as a breastfeeding mother sends a reverberating memory of my former existence beneath the now-hardened surface of my flesh. My breasts no longer engorge as visceral, intersubjective reminders that it is time to reconnect with my loved ones. I am guilty of reverting back to Western time where 'speed gets noticed [where] speed is the ultimate defence, the antidote to stopping and really [feeling] what we [are] doing' (Whyte, 2002, pp. 117–118). Ironically, the push I needed to write this chapter over the past month has prompted me to close my door for the first time while working in my office. No longer greeted by fluid waves of inquiring students and smiling colleagues, I have purposefully closed myself off in an effort to bear down and make just one more *dead*line. I am left questioning my *life*line,[4] the importance of feeling joyfully connected to others and experiencing not only the peaks of Csikszentmihalyi's (2000) flow when I return to snowboarding this winter, but a longing to renew an energetic, renewing, and revitalizing fluid embrace of the world:

> A realm of gestural identifications is herby opened up – one that has deep ecological value – by this turn to the primary motions of what would normally be considered the affectivities of human relationality. A fully fleshed-out analysis of the embrace is needed. What is its Oedipal significance as indicated above? What human relations are engendered by an embrace that seemingly carries women's affectivities for the ocean, the tides, water and its circulations? What is the emotional expressivity in the motions of the elemental flesh? For the moment, however, it will have to

suffice to indicate a promising direction of such an analysis. In this regard we need glance no further than the landscape and to those deep ecological renditions of landscape connection that highlight the primary motions of connection and identification, not just as metaphors, but as tangible, palpable ways of being in touch with the flesh [and blood] of the world. (Smith, 2006, p. 7)

I may conclude that the viscerality of my life as a breastfeeding mother is not all together weaned. Although milk no longer seeps and expresses out and bursts my imposed bubble of productivity, I know that the fluid ebbing and flowing tide of cosmic interconnectivity continues to surge within. Conrad (2007) reminds us that our 'bodies are mostly water, and yet [we] move about the Earth in this apparently solid way' (p. 8). From fluid steps that spontaneously tread on fresh-fallen snow in my evening dog walk to all encompassing gestures of love that care for my little one who wakes up in the middle of the night with a stomach ache, and a resolve to return to work with my door wide open, I know that I may become more attuned to experience the multiplicities of flow. This reflection on my experience as a breastfeeding mother has thus inspired me to reclaim what Irigaray (1992) describes as the 'full extent of my flow. Of my fluidity' (p. 45), a liquidity which Conrad (2007) asserts may be experienced as the 'movement of water on land' (p. 7), as I reawaken my sensitivities to existing within what Mazis (2002) describes as a flowing reciprocity within the world and return to the bliss of a fluid embrace. And so I leave you with the poetic text of Irigaray, who articulates the invisible, visceral sensations of an embrace, one that may be experienced within a mother's and lover's interconnection within a human and more-than-human world, one that I believe is also within our grasp:

Deeper, deeper than the greatest depth your daylight could imagine, once again I caress you. Luminous night, touched with a quickening whose denseness never appears in the light. Neither permanently fixed, nor shifting and fickle. Nothing solid survives, yet that thickness responding to its own rhythms is not nothing. Quickening in movements both expected and unexpected. Your space, your time are unable to grasp their regularity or contain their foldings and unfoldings. The force unleashed has an intensity which cannot anywhere be measured, nor contained. Can never be obliterated unless it is poured out in mortal ecstasy. (Irigaray, 1992, p. 13)

Notes

1 Julia Kristeva (2001) describes the metaphorical connection between the breast and penis, explaining that 'the penis is thus assimilated into the mother's breast, and the vagina assumes the passive role of a sucking mouth' (p. 122).
2 Note that a pseudonym was used to protect the identity of my student.
3 Otis's first utterances sounded like, 'goodle, goodle, goodle,' hence, the affectionate nickname 'Goodler' emerged, one that carried over to our second-born son even though he never 'goodled' in the same way.
4 A term inspired by the poetics of Celeste Snowber (2011). She writes: Some of you just don't give me enough attention; you think your deadlines are more important. Well your deadlines are not lifelines. I am your lifeline, your lifeblood and I wait for you to come home and find release in just the sheer joy of being alive (p. 193).

References

Abram, D. (1996). *The spell of the sensuous*. New York: Vintage.

Bartlett, A. (2005). Maternal sexuality and breastfeeding. *Sex Education: Sexuality, Society and Learning, 5* (1), 67–77.

Carlson, A., & Berleant, A. (2004). *The aesthetics of natural environments*. Peterborough, ON: Broadview.

Chodorow, N.J. (1978). *The reproduction of mothering*. Berkeley, CA: University of California Press.

Conrad, E. (2007). *Life on land: The story of continuum*. Berkeley, CA: North Atlantic Books.

Csikszentmihalyi, M. (1997). *Finding flow: The psychology of engagement with everyday life*. New York: Basic Books.

Csikszentmihalyi, M. (2000). *Beyond boredom and anxiety: Experiencing flow in work and play*. San Francisco, CA: Jossey-Bass.

Davidson, D., & Langan, D. (2006). The breastfeeding incident: Teaching and learning through transgression. *Studies in Higher Education, 31* (4), 439–452.

DiGirolamo, A., Thompson, N., Martorell, R., Fein, S., & Grummer-Strawn, L. (2005). Intention or experience? Predictors of continued breastfeeding. *Health Education & Behavior, 32* (2), 208–226.

Etymology Online. (2009). Boobs. Accessed 10 November 2009, from http://www.etymonline.com/index.php?term=boobs.

Freud, S. (1958). *Civilization and its discontents*. Trans. J. Riviere. New York: Doubleday Anchor Books.

Freud, S. (2003). *Beyond the pleasure principle and other writings*. Trans. J. Reddick. London: Penguin.

Grumet, M. (1988). *Bitter milk*. Amherst, MA: University of Massachusetts Press.

Irigaray, L. (1992) *Elemental passions*. Trans. J. Collie & J. Still. London: Athlone.

Jansen, J., Weerth, C., & Riksen-Walraven, M. (2008). Breastfeeding and the mother-infant relationship – A review. *Developmental Review, 28*, 503–521.

Kendrowski, K.M., & Lipscomb, M.E. (2008). *Breastfeeding rights in the United States*. Westport, CT: Praeger.

Kristeva, J. (2001). *Melanie Klein*. Trans. R. Guberman. New York: Columbia University Press.

La Leche League International. (2004). *The womanly art of breastfeeding* (7th rev. ed.). Schaumburg: La Leche League International.

Leder, D. (1990). Flesh and blood: A proposed supplement to Merleau-Ponty. *Human Studies, 13*, 209–19. In D. Welton (Ed.), *The Body* (pp. 200–210). Malden, MA: Blackwell.

Lloyd, R.J., & Smith, S.J. (2006a). Motion-sensitive phenomenology. In K. Tobin & J. Kincheloe (Eds.), *Doing educational research: A handbook* (pp. 289–309). Boston, MA: Sense Publishing.

Lloyd, R.J., & Smith, S.J. (2006b). Interactive flow in exercise pedagogy. *Quest, 58*, 222–241.

Lloyd, R.J., & Smith, S.J. (2009). Enlivening the curriculum of health-related fitness. *Educational Insights, 13* (4). Available at http://www.ccfi.educ.ubc.ca/publication/insights/v13n04/articles/lloyd_smith/index.html.

Lloyd, R.J., & Smith, S.J. (2010). Feeling 'flow motion' in games and sports. In J. Butler & L. Griffin (Eds.), *Teaching games for understanding* (pp. 89–103). Champaign: Human Kinetics.

Lloyd, R. J., & Smith, S. J. (in press). Health-related fitness: Enlivening the physical education experience. In E. Singleton & A. Varpalotai (Eds.), *Pedagogy for the moving body: Establishing a community of inquiry for studies in human movement* (pp. 1–33). London, ON: Althouse Press.

Lloyd, R.J., Garcia Bengoechea, E., & Smith, S.J. (2010). Theories of learning. In R. Bailey (Ed.), *Physical education for learning: A guide for secondary schools* (pp. 187–196). London: Continuum.

Mazis, G.A. (2002) *Earthbodies: Rediscovering our planetary senses*. Albany, NY: State University of New York Press.

Menke, C. (2008). The dialectic of aesthetics: The new strife between philosophy and art. In R. Shusterman & A. Tomlin (Eds.) *Aesthetic experience* (pp. 59–76). New York: Routledge.

Merleau-Ponty, M. (1962). *Phenomenology of perception*. Trans. C. Smith. London: Routledge & Kegan Paul.

Merleau-Ponty, M. (1968). *The visible and the invisible*. Trans. A. Lingis. Evanston, IL: Northwestern University Press.

Miller, J. (1982). The sound of silence breaking: Feminist pedagogy and curriculum theory. *Journal of Curriculum Theory, 4* (1), 5–11.

Newman, J., & Pitman, T. (2003). *Dr Jack Newman's guide to breastfeeding*. Toronto: Collins Canada.

Olmert, M.D. (2009). *Made for each other: The biology of the human-animal bond*. Cambridge, MA: Da Capro Press.

Pinar, W.F., Reynolds, W.M., Slattery, P., & Taubman, P.M. (2000) *Understanding curriculum*. New York: Peter Lang.

Schwab, M.G. (1996). Mechanical milk: An essay on the social history of infant formula. *Childhood: A Global Journal of Child Research, 3* (4), 479–497.

Sheets-Johnstone, M. (1999). *The primacy of movement*. Philadelphia, PA: John Benjamins.

Shusterman, R. (2000). *Performing live*. London: Cornell University Press.

Shusterman, R. (2008a). *Body consciousness: A philosophy of mindfulness and somaesthetics*. New York: Cambridge University Press.

Shusterman, R. (2008b). Aesthetic experience: From analysis to Eros. In R. Shusterman & A. Tomlin (Eds.), *Aesthetic experience* (pp.79–97). New York: Routledge.

Sloan, S., Sneddon, H., Stewart, M., & Iwaniec, D. (2006). Breast is best? Reasons why mothers decide to breastfeed or bottlefeed their babies and factors influencing the duration of breastfeeding. *Child Care in Practice, 12* (3), 283–297.

Smith, S.J. (2006). Gesture, landscape and embrace: A phenomenological analysis of elemental motions. *Indo-Pacific Journal of Phenomenology, 6* (1), 1–10.

Smith, S.J., & Lloyd, R.J. (2006). Promoting vitality in health and physical education. *Qualitative Health Research, 16* (2), 245–267.

Smith, S.J., & Lloyd, R.J. (2007). The assessment of vitality: An alternative to quantifying the health-related fitness experience. *AVANTE, 11* (3), 66–76.

Snowber, C. (2011). Let the body out: A love letter to the academy from the body. In E. Malewski & N. Jaramillo (Eds.), *Epistemologies of ignorance in education* (pp. 187–198). Charlotte, NC: Information Age.

Stern, D.N. (1993). The role of feelings for an interpersonal self. In U. Neisser (Ed.), *The perceived self: Ecological and interpersonal sources of self knowledge* (pp. 205–215). Cambridge: Cambridge University Press.

Stern, D.N. (2002). *The first relationship: Infant and mother*. Cambridge, MA: Harvard University Press.

Stern, D.N. (2004). *The present moment in psychotherapy and everyday life*. New York: Norton.

Van Manen, M. (1997). *Researching lived experience: Human science for an action sensitive pedagogy*. London, ON: Althouse Press.

Weber, S., & Mitchell, C. (1995). *That's funny, you don't look like a teacher! Interrogating images and identity in popular culture*. Washington, DC: Falmer.

Whyte, D. (2002). *Crossing the Unknown Sea: Work as a Pilgrimage of Identity*. New York: Riverhead Books.

16 The Breastfeeding Curriculum: Stories of Queer, Female, Unruly Learning

KARLEEN PENDLETON JIMÉNEZ

It is this ability of bodies to always extend the frameworks which attempt to contain them, to remain permeable and uncertain …
— Springgay & Freedman, *Curriculum and the Cultural Body*

A Disciplined Body

1 September 2009

Breast one, breast two, lactation aid one, lactation aid two, no finger feeding. You have to do it on the sly. The nurses at the clinic prefer the small cup that the baby laps up like a cat. I try not to laugh when she does it. What is most crucial is the breast. What is most crucial is the latch. Lips facing out from all sides. Must open her mouth wide enough. The neck raised and tilted by the curve of my wrist. A ballet position. Is she down far enough? Is she up far enough? I am to learn how to lead, and she to follow. My body responds to her demands. Can I maintain her position if I release and begin compressions? Or will her head move wildly and drop me?

It is stressful unless I continually remind myself that whether or not I get it right or wrong this time, I will have another try in just 4 more hours, and 4 hours after that, and another 4 after that.

'Why doesn't anyone tell you how hard it is?' the woman asked at a group of new mothers. I have asked the same question numerous times since my daughter was born 6 months ago. If breastfeeding does not come quickly, or easily, or painlessly, then the mother enters into a complex and contested terrain of information and learning. In my case, I could not produce enough milk, and my baby could not open her mouth wide enough for a proper latch. Between these two complications, my baby was starving. As the mother, watching my baby's weight drop sharply in her first few days, I turned frantically to the resources available for my education.

At the centre of my learning is a relationship between two bodies. At no other time in my memory have I been utterly dependent on my body and the body of another. Trained in a Western tradition where bodies are undervalued and excluded from learning (hooks, 1994), I am not accustomed to attending to the knowledge of the body. No matter that I read bell hooks years ago, and should know better, and should want more. It is not so easy to release one's body from the constraints of cultural practices and discourse. However, the dependency on my body and hers that I have experienced through breastfeeding has momentarily snapped me out of the Cartesian split between mind and body (Grosz, 1994, p. 7). I can leave neither my mind nor body behind, as both are needed to survive. It is a torturous experience, a loving relationship and an opportunity for learning, as bodies make available a wealth of knowledge. As Elizabeth Grosz articulates, 'If bodies are objects or things, they are like no others, for they are the centers of perspective, insight, reflection, desire, agency' (p. xi).

I write about the curriculum of bodies in the performance of breastfeeding. I draw upon William Pinar's notion that curriculum emerges from the infinitive *currere*, or a running of the course (2004, p. 35). Pinar asks us to build the course through an autobiographical method of inquiry where the writing of past experience and future fantasy deepen our experience of present living conditions (p. 4). I invoke the strategy in order 'to study the relations between academic knowledge and life-history in the interest of self-understanding and social reconstruction' (p. 35). Cindy Cruz (2006) urges the recovery of knowledge garnered through bodily experience for pedagogical theory. I choose to write about breastfeeding while immersed in the sensations of the act, while they are still tangible for me.

Breastfeeding is not only a mental exercise, but fixed in physical exertion. I am running a course. In my cycle of sleep deprivation and acrobatic manoeuvres, I imagine an athletic feat. There is a bright red track around a green football field. I feel the hot sun on my skin as I run. I run in long, broad circles. I cannot stop. It is a marathon. I begin to memorize the features of the landscape at each point along the circle, knowing I have seen them before, and that I will see them again on the next loop. Their increasingly familiar presence is reassuring. My muscles are sore and strained to exhaustion, but I keep going. There is no choice.

There actually are choices (multiple methods for breastfeeding, or the use of bottles and formula), but it doesn't feel like it. Instead, it feels like there are many ways to potentially feed my baby incorrectly. I have sought out and received contradictory knowledge, presented passionately and authoritatively. And while I am a teacher educator, specializing in critical literacy, particularly in relation to issues of equity and human development, I have fumbled for direction. I forgot Elizabeth Ellsworth's (1992) notion, that all knowledge is 'partial, interested, and potentially oppressive to others.' I have wanted the truth, the answer, the remedy that would make possible the simple desire to feed my baby. In my weary state, I have easily relinquished my body, its instincts, to the next available authority discourse.

Grosz (1994) investigates the subordinate position of the body to the mind and, in particular, the suppression of the female body, which accounts, to a certain degree, for the struggle I describe. Breastfeeding, with the body at the centre, is subjected to a proliferation of theories of control. Further, Aparna Mishra Tarc asserts that a discourse of parenting is directed at our bodies to ensure that we perform a proper role of mother (personal communication, 10 September 2010). The mother's body, and the way in which the mother's body comes into contact with the baby's body, are at issue. There is so little room between my body and my baby's. It is a cramped space; we are squished together, and yet the discourse is there between us.

There are various reasons for the professional knowledge developed around breastfeeding. There is a fundamental desire to offer our babies the healthiest possible lives. Sometimes we hope to create strong relationships between mother and baby. A few acknowledge a sense of woman's empowerment through the ability to feed her own baby. There is also an opportunity for profit; how can money be made from these tiniest of consumers? Or, how can the least amount of money be lost by a nation's health care system through healthy feeding techniques?

For roughly 150 years these desires collided or culminated, depending on the point of view, in the creation of baby formula. Baby formula has provided an alternative to breastfeeding or the use of wet nurses. Mothers have no longer had to use their bodies as a food source nor expose their breasts in public. Mothers could forget how to breastfeed. Baby formula also offered businessmen an opportunity to make a profit on an exchange between mother and child that would have otherwise excluded them. The well-researched fact that baby formula has never been as healthy for babies as breast milk (Harms, 2004; Kitzinger, 2003; Murkoff, 2003; Sears & Sears, 2003) has not prevented companies from marketing the product to the entire world. Baby formula has even been marketed to communities where there is a lack of clean drinking water, causing the formula to be dangerous for babies. There has been a massive boycott against Nestlé for selling baby formula to mothers in Africa since the 1970s (Miller, 1983).

As an adult, I have known about the Nestlé boycott. I learned through friends, books, and news sources that breast milk is better for infants than formula, that our mothers had been duped by formula companies. The evidence is overwhelming that breast milk is best for babies; it contains many nutrients not available in formula, it is 'custom-made' for your baby's precise needs, it is designed for a human baby's digestive system, 'it's safe,' 'it keeps allergies on hold,' 'it keeps diaper rash away,' 'it's an infection preventer,' 'it's a brain booster,' 'it builds stronger mouths,' 'it costs less,' it helps with postpartum recovery (Murkoff, 2003, pp. 3–5). I was taught not to use formula; I was taught to resist those who attempted to push formula between me and my baby. Formula is a capitalist scam that in 2009 I could resist as an educated, politicized woman. Finally, I live in the rich, progressive city of Toronto and have had access to breastfeeding support from family, friends, community groups, texts, the medical establishment, midwives, nurses, and one rogue doctor.

Therefore, there was no question that I would breastfeed. If I did not breastfeed, a number of friends would be disappointed. Not to mention that it's bad politics. If Western knowledge colonized women's uncredentialled knowledge, if they wiped away our ability to feed our own babies, so that we may consume products at the store, if I know better now, if I live in downtown Toronto and have the people and resources to support me to feed my own baby, well then, it would be an act of betrayal not to do so. I would be knowingly and consciously colonized, a victim, I wouldn't have tried hard enough, I would've given into the Man. I would be leaving my baby in a statistically poorer lifelong health situation. I would be a wimp.

And yet, I am the product of baby formula marketing. I was not breastfed, nor were my siblings, and I rarely saw women in my childhood breastfeeding their babies. Sheila Kitzinger (2008) writes, 'When women fail to breast-feed, it sometimes has less to do with failing to get the techniques right and more to do with the fact that breast-feeding can be a lonely struggle in a culture that disapproves of its being visible' (p. 404). Given the support available for breastfeeding in Toronto at this time in history, I do not feel lonely, nor suppressed by the culture around me. However, as I struggled unsuccessfully to feed my baby in the first months, I wondered how the invisibility of breastfeeding in many North American communities has thwarted those of us with the best of intentions. When problems arose, I had no experience with other mothers' problems or solutions. Although I recently made friends with other women who have also chosen to breastfeed, we have little history to fall back on. I had no idea how to solve my problem, nor whether the problem was common or obscure. I lacked tangible experience around real mothers' and babies' bodies feeding. I turned to books, to a community group, to a lactation clinic, to lactation nurse specialists, and to doctors for direction. It is a harsh irony; I have depended on professional knowledge for help, even though it was professional knowledge that taught us to buy formula and lose our ability to use our own breasts.

Doctors now, in principle, support breastfeeding because the research tells them to do so. However, this does not mean that they know what to say or do in order to make the practice successful. It also does not mean that they are considering the health of the mother or the learning for both mother and baby that occurs through the practice of breastfeeding. There is no mention of the relationship that is formed, or the hunger that drives the two together. Breastfeeding, as a medical practice, is abstract knowledge that does not account for the emotional body.

The directions for proper breastfeeding positions are more difficult to follow than IKEA instructions. They are reminiscent of Michel Foucault's (1995) discussion of 'docile bodies,' where beginning in the late eighteenth century it was believed that bodies could be trained. If instructed correctly, bodies could be put to optimal use if every position, gesture, and movement was precise. Breastfeeding positions, although offered with the best of intentions, are part of the paradigm of controlling and training bodies to perform at maximum potential.

In the following excerpts, I have juxtaposed an example Foucault (1995, p. 152) offers of the proper position for writing (including a long excerpt from La Salle, *Conduite* ..., 63–64) with instructions from Sears and Sears (2003, p.128) on the proper positioning in breastfeeding:

We cannot overemphasize the importance of proper position and latch-on. Most of the breastfeeding problems we see in our practice and breastfeeding center (sore nipples, insufficient milk, mothers not enjoying breastfeeding) are due to not using these basic right-start techniques.

Good handwriting, for example, presupposes a gymnastics – a whole routine whose rigorous code invests the body in its entirety, from the points of the feet to the tip of the index finger.

Position Yourself Correctly. Get comfortable before beginning to breastfeed. Milk flows better from a relaxed mother. Sitting up in bed or in a rocking chair or an armchair is the easiest position for breastfeeding. Pillows are essential for your comfort and the baby's positioning.

The pupils must always hold their bodies erect, somewhat turned and free on the left side, slightly inclined, so that, with the elbow placed on the table, the chin can be rested upon the hand, unless this were to interfere with the view; the left leg must be somewhat more forward under the table than the right.

Place one behind your back, one on your lap, and another under the arm that will support your baby ... To best prepare your mind and body, think baby, and think mothering. Position Baby Correctly ... 1. Nestle baby in your arm so that her neck rests in the bend of your elbow, her back along your forearm, and her buttocks in your hand.

A distance of two fingers must be left between the body and the table; for not only does one write with more alertness, but nothing is more harmful to the health than to acquire the habit of pressing one's stomach against the table; the part of the left arm from the elbow to the hand must be placed on the table.

2. Turn baby's entire body on its side so she is facing tummy to tummy. Her head and neck should be straight, not arched backward or turned sideways, in relation to the rest of her body. Baby should not have to turn her head or strain her neck to reach your nipple ... 3. Raise baby to the level of your breasts by putting her on a pillow on your lap and by using a footstool. Let the pillow on your lap support your arm and baby's weight ... bring baby up and in toward you rather than your leaning forward toward her.

The right arm must be at a distance from the body of about three fingers and be about five fingers from the table, on which it must rest lightly. The teacher will place the pupils in the posture that they should maintain when writing, and will correct it either by sign or otherwise, when they change this position.'

4. Get baby's interfering arms and hands out of the way. As you turn baby on her side tummy to tummy, tuck her lower arm into the soft pocket between her body and your midriff. If her upper arm keeps interfering, you can hold it down with the thumb of your hand that is holding her. 5. As you are positioning baby's arms, wrap her around you, tummy to tummy. This basic position is called the *cradle hold*.

A disciplined body is the prerequisite of an efficient gesture.

First, it is important to note that neither of these instructions is particularly easy to follow in the third dimension. Fingers and limbs are to be counted and measured. Props are needed to support body positions: pillows, foot-stools, desks, chairs. 'Interfering arms' must be restrained, 'pressing stomachs' are a problem. The health of everyone involved is at stake. Notice, also, how correct body positioning should result in the correct frame of mind, 'alertness' for the pupil, and 'comfort' or 'enjoyment' for the mother. Excellence will follow from form. And if the mother is disciplined and becomes a successful breastfeeder to her baby, Sears and Sears (2003) note one more final benefit for the future of your baby: 'In studying the long-term effects of breastfeeding on babies in my practice one feature stands out – these children are well disciplined' (p. 124).

I have often used the description of proper writing positioning to show teacher candidates an extreme example of control in the classroom. It generally evokes laughter, perhaps recognition of past experience with former teachers, and a questioning of how and why children are asked for any reason to have disciplined bodies in the classroom. Yet, when given my instructions for breastfeeding, I tried as hard as I could to get every piece of my body into order. With my baby's body at stake, I finally found something in my life important enough to submit to such formal procedure. At this point, I do not know whether such strict guidelines are right or wrong, but I do wish to know what learning based on the explicit disciplining of bodies feels like and offers us.

It was like learning to play the piano. It seems simple enough, the keys are all laid out before you. Your hands are ready; they're eager and agile. But when you bring your fingers to the keyboard, they fail you.

They are clumsy and slow. They touch the wrong notes and interrupt the melody you were certain you would find. There is no quick method to making the song. It will take many dedicated days, months, years of practice to reach a skill level that brings satisfaction. It is rote learning. It is physical exertion and exhaustion.

The nurses and doctors told me that if I kept trying, dedicated and disciplined, I would see results. The milk would probably come. The baby would probably learn to drink. There were no guarantees. There had been significant observation of mothers and justifiable predictions. Who has the patience and the faith to continue working at it for so long? As I struggled week after week, the nurses kept commenting how amazed they were that I kept trying. I know they meant to be supportive, yet their disbelief made me question whether my perseverance would really pay off.

A Graceful Body

> Disciplining and disappearing the body in schools are intrinsic to traditions of Western education and epistemology, and so it is no surprise that when we begin to readmit body consciousness to educational discourse, in the very presence of toes or navels, gonads or drool, we stood mute and awed.
> – Grumet, Foreword, in Springgay & Freedman, *Curriculum and the Cultural Body*

My body, though constrained by discipline, direction, sleep deprivation, and stress, performed magnificent feats. The first miraculous manoeuvre involved the brazen transformation of my breasts.

Before there were milk supply and baby latch issues, there was a concern over my gender. As a butch dyke, as transgender, I have had an ambivalent relationship with my breasts since they emerged at age 11. When they first grew, pink and swollen, painful, I thought I was going to die. If something that painful was part of my body, located right above my heart, I was certain that it was serious and deadly. I was terrified my mom would find out and be broken-hearted that I was dying. Later, she asked me if they were sore, and that was enough information to know that this pain was supposed to happen, but not enough information to know what to do about them. I wore baggier and baggier t-shirts, mortified that anyone would see them and see

302   Karleen Pendleton Jiménez

me as feminine or female. For the most part, nothing has changed since then.

At 27, I performed on stage as a drag king. I bound up my breasts with a bandage and duct tape. I admired my chest in the mirror, flat and firm under my suit. I performed my fantasy of myself for a few minutes on stage for a Saturday night crowd.

There are moments when I like my breasts. When I can see and feel them as beautiful. These moments are sporadic and few. Nevertheless, these moments do exist and make it worthwhile for me to keep my breasts; many of my butch/transgender friends do not experience this pleasure; many have had them surgically removed.

Although I wanted the best health for my baby, I wondered whether I would be able to breastfeed, whether the sensation would hurt me, whether the visibility would humiliate me. Knowing the hurt and shame that have dominated my relationship with my breasts, I doubted I could breastfeed. I read encouraging books such as *The Womanly Art of Breastfeeding* (La Leche League International, 2004), but felt lost in the message: 'For many mothers, breastfeeding is a fulfillment of what it means to be a woman' (p. 3). If feeling like a woman makes me uncomfortable, the promise of fulfilment as a woman was certainly something to avoid. Others around me questioned my intention to breastfeed. If breastfeeding is a relatively covert practice, breastfeeding performed by a butch woman is unheard of. I have never seen a butch woman breastfeed. Can our bodies learn physical feats when there is a complete lack of representation? If I could successfully breastfeed, in addition to the many benefits to mother and baby listed earlier, I would also be providing a queer intervention, disrupting the 'normal' course of events, hopefully causing people to question conforming gender expectation and bias (Jagose, 1996, p. 3). My butch breastfeeding could constitute an act of public education: 'A cornerstone of teaching queerly is to deconstruct these sexual and gender binaries ... that are the lynchpins of heteronormativity' (Sears, 1999, p. 6). However, I was aware that my political and pedagogical desires would have little influence upon my bodily capabilities.

What transpired was miraculous. From the moment my daughter was born and she instinctively climbed and clawed her way up my chest, my breasts transformed. They were suddenly responsive, capable, invincible. They were neither feminine nor masculine; in my mind they shed gender specificity. As Springgay and Freedman (2007) propose, 'a bodied curriculum not only resists the very notion of standards, hegemonic power positions, and categories of sameness, it dislodges and destabilizes "the center" from which the binaries and dualistic logic are produced and maintained' (p. xxvi). The sensation of my daughter's drinking has not harmed me; I am drawn to her and to the power of my body to sustain another. Stranger still, I experienced an immediate comfort with the new visibility of my breasts. While I fumble awkwardly with maternity bras, shirts, and shawls each time I need to feed her, I have not experienced the slightest concern over whether my body is visible to others. The radical metamorphosis seems impossible. One's body serves as the foundation for perspective, interaction, and relation. After 38 years I have come to assume certain proficiencies and limitations from my body. Living, now, with this significant change under my skin has instructed me that worldly structures, no matter how solid nor how certain I am of their composition and qualities, could fool me and surprise me. It is a revelation that broadens the imagination.

The second lesson I encountered is that miraculous changes may never happen, or occur slowly, practically undetectable over time. This is a lesson in patience and humility. No matter how badly I wanted to feed my daughter, my body had other plans. No matter how well I listened and followed orders, I could not convince my body to follow my will. No directions could fix the problems. No truths could save me.

Nevertheless, a collection of words, practices, and performances could ultimately guide my daughter and me. The midwife offered her expertise on body weight loss, formula feeding, and phone numbers for lactation specialists; a La Leche League facilitator made a home visit with tips and the name of a doctor who specializes in milk supply problems; a nurse came right away to show us how to provide supplement without undue pressure; a clinic spent hours observing and finessing my positions and gestures; a doctor prescribed the golden medication; books reassured me in the quiet moments at home; the community group offers ongoing dialogue and peer support; my girlfriend calms me, reassures me, and cleans bottles and equipment.

As individual components, none were sufficient to secure the offering of milk between mother and daughter. Often the items of advice contradicted each other: pumping or no pumping, medication or no medication, force feeding, suckling, weighing, fenugreek, blessed thistle, Guiness, Malta, skin-to-skin, push the chin down/leave it alone, every 2 hours, 3 hours, 5 hours? I had to choose. Some of the information offered felt like support, some felt like threat. The compilation of people and dis-course across a span of 100 days (at least 600 feedings), resulted finally in a round and strong baby. My body developed the capacity to sustain her. It is ecological learning, where interdependence between community, professionals, books, family, and bodies makes the connection possible:

14 December 2009
Elena is an expert at breastfeeding now. Her back is arched. She grasps my breast and pulls it toward her. Her mouth is wide open, lips rolled back. A perfect latch, even in her sleep. The drama of a couple months ago seems impossible, like an entirely different life.

Conclusion

Led by my body, I submitted to uncertainty. I had no control, no an-swers. I have tried to convince my students to approach human devel-opment theory with such ambiguity. I have lectured righteously that there is no Truth for them, just many ideas, all the while thrusting my own beloved theorists upon them as the ones who probably had the right answers. I learned the lesson thoroughly underneath my skin that there are no truths, no ready answers, but that a collection of knowl-edge would save me and my daughter. Each piece worked or failed on any given day, but brought together and implemented over time, my wish to feed her with my body was achieved. I have finally learned this lesson, but I could only do it through the imperfections and struggles of my body. I'll be more generous with my students now, knowing more intimately the desperation for truth.

I did not learn from my body how to cope with failure. No mat-ter how much I tried to convince myself intellectually that I was a worthy mother with or without breast milk to offer my baby, I was at the mercy of how well the feeding went each time I tried. If the baby could get little milk from me, opting instead to fall into sleep (because the effort required to retrieve my milk was too great), I could feel the shame fill my body. If the baby managed to drink, if I could identify her swallowing, the ever so slight movement of her throat, the small-est clicking sound, (easily missed), then I was overjoyed. I would feel a profound sense of pride. All the while I knew that I was on a crazy emotional rollercoaster, that she would thrive with or without my breast milk, that there was no need for such a dramatic response.

I did not know this in my body, though, it was far removed from my body.

In the months since my daughter's birth, dozens of women have approached me to meet the baby, ask her sex, her age, compliment her smile. Sometimes they ask about the birth experience, sometimes they want to know about breastfeeding. More often than not, they share their own struggle with breastfeeding, their war stories with doctors, hospitals, or relatives not supporting them. They know the same Toronto community and medical network for breastfeeding; they've tried the same medications; the outcomes vary. These informal women's communication systems defy a century of the formula consumer model of feeding one's baby and help to restore knowledge of the body.

In her essay on the medicalization of childbirth, Natalie Jolly (2007) argues that 'a curriculum of female embodiment that supports women's body confidence' (p. 187) is essential in convincing women that technological intervention is not the only answer to the challenges our bodies face. Just minutes after childbirth, 'experts' turn their attention to the difficulties of feeding the child. For the past century, baby formula has been offered as the scientific intervention to relieve women of the burden of breastfeeding. It is presented as an easier choice, and at times it has even been touted as a healthier alternative. It has since been proven that 'breast is best' for a child's health, not to mention that a mother may experience the pleasure of sustaining another life through her body. Breastfeeding could constitute precisely the type of embodied curriculum that Jolly calls for. However, the fact that breastfeeding offers substantive benefits for both mother and child does not make it any easier to perform. Because many women do not possess an innate ability to breastfeed, intervention is necessary. Because many women are shocked to discover that they lack an innate ability to breastfeed (and have no back-up plan), intervention needs to be readily accessible. What should be reconsidered, however, is the kind and the quality of that intervention. This is where current cultural norms of mothering have failed women, opting for a quick (profitable) commodity, instead of an investment in the power of the body. Rather than a solution that substitutes and rejects the body's gifts, I argue for an intervention based on collective teaching.

Informal women's social networks (new mothers beginning conversations with one another across the streets of Toronto) as well as the group of mothers in La Leche League, and progressive medical clinics

such as the Newman Breastfeeding Clinic and Institute, offer pedagogical alternatives to the science of baby formula. What I have found
most useful are the recurrent words of reassurance and faith that our
bodies can sustain our children. I have appreciated group conversations based on a model of critical pedagogy, where 'expert' knowledge
is questioned, and doubts and ideas are shared. I have learned as well
from physical lessons: having my own body pushed into position, and
watching other women breastfeed around me. The pedagogy of breastfeeding thrives through collective practice. It is both a skill and relationship that is difficult to achieve through the use of baby formula
(expert scientific knowledge), or through individual practice (women
who try to breastfeed without social support often fail).

An investment in collective practice has the potential to provide
broader types of learning. In *Communities of Practice*, Wenger (1998) argues that 'engagement in social practice is the fundamental process by
which we learn and so become who we are' (front cover). When we
learn to breastfeed within community contexts, we not only develop
a competence in a specific skill, we may also change how we see ourselves as women. We may learn to value our bodies and those of the
women around us. We may become active participants in women's
communities, less dependent on patriarchal social structures. We also
begin to develop our identities as mothers in relation to our children.

Breastfeeding is a primary practice in the learning and relearning of
the body. It is 'how [mother and child] learn about each other in those
first hours and days following birth' (La Leche League International,
2004, p. 4). It is the foundation for making meaning of one's world,
'from the threads of this deeply woven intersubjective communication
between mother and infant emerges a fabric upon which all subsequent
capacities for meaning making evolve' (Mishra Tarc, 2007, p. 37) It is
precisely because the body is at the centre of the art of breastfeeding,
unruly, non-compliant, and magical, that its study is significant to theories of learning. In this essay, I continue the custom I have encountered
of sharing my struggles with breastfeeding. I offer stories of my body as
curriculum. My mother body. My queer body. My insufficient body. It is
a curriculum of shame and pride. A curriculum of humility.

References

Cruz, C. (2006). Toward an epistemology of a brown body. In D. Delgado
   Bernal & C.A. Elenes (Eds.), *Chicana/Latina education in everyday life:*

Feminista perspectives on pedagogy and epistemology (pp. 59–75). Albany, NY: State University of New York Press.

Ellsworth, E. (1992). Why doesn't this feel empowering? Working through the repressive myths of critical pedagogy. In C. Luke & J. Gore (Eds.), *Feminisms and critical pedagogy* (pp. 90–119). New York: Routledge.

Harms, R.W. (Ed.). (2004). *Mayo Clinic guide to a healthy pregnancy*. New York: HarperCollins.

hooks, b. (1994). *Teaching to transgress: Education as the practice of freedom.* New York: Routledge.

Foucault, M. (1995). *Discipline and punish: The birth of the prison.* New York: Vintage.

Grosz, E. (1994). *Volatile bodies: Toward a corporeal feminism.* Bloomington, IN: Indiana University Press.

Grumet, M. (2007). Foreword. In S. Springgay & D. Freedman (Eds.), *Curriculum and the cultural body* (pp. xv–xvi). New York: Peter Lang.

Jagose, A. (1996). *Queer theory: An introduction.* New York: University Press.

Jolly, N. (2007). Cesarean, celebrity, and childbirth: Students encounter modern birth and the question of female embodiment. In S. Springgay & D. Freedman (Eds.), *Curriculum and the cultural body* (pp. 175–187). New York: Peter Lang.

Kitzinger, S. (2003). *The complete book of pregnancy and childbirth.* London: Dorling Kindersley.

La Leche League International. (2004). *The womanly art of breastfeeding.* New York: Plume.

Miller, F.D. (1983). *Out of the mouths of babes: The infant formula controversy.* Bowling Green, OH: Bowling Green State University.

Mishra Tarc, A. (2007). *Literacy of the other: Making relation to language.* Unpublished doctoral dissertation, York University, Toronto.

Murkoff, H. (2003). *What to expect: The first year.* New York: Workman.

Pinar, W. (2004). *What is curriculum theory?* Mahwah, NJ: Lawrence Erlbaum.

Sears, J.T. (1999). Teaching queerly: Some elementary propositions. In W.J. Letts & J.T. Sears (Eds.), *Queering elementary education: Advancing the dialogue about sexualities and schooling* (pp. 3–14). Lanham, MD: Rowman & Littlefield.

Sears, W., & Sears, M. (2003). *The baby book: Everything you need to know about your baby from birth to age two.* New York: Little, Brown.

Springgay, S., & D. Freedman, D. (2007) Introduction: On touching and a bodied curriculum. In S. Springgay & D. Freedman (Eds.), *Curriculum and the cultural body* (pp. xvii–xxvii). New York: Peter Lang.

Wenger, E. (1998). *Communities of practice: Learning, meaning, and identity.* New York: Cambridge University Press.

17 Multiple Stories: Alternate Constructions of M/othering in the Context of Family Violence

SASKIA STILLE

Change and transformation accompany the process of becoming mother, whether one is pregnant or not. My story of this process is a story of and in multiples: carrying, birthing, nursing, and mothering twins, and re/constructing the stories of family violence from my own childhood. Drawing upon narrative reflections of my past and present experience (Aoki, 2003; Pinar, 1994), in this chapter I take up a critical analysis of normative conceptions of intimacy and nurturance between mother and child. Exceeding the two, the intimate mother-child dyad, I engage with the idea of multiple stories to explore what happens when mothering is not just a relationship between two, when the intimacy between mother and child is ruptured, dislocated, and divided by violence and control perpetrated in the home. Multiple stories invite alternate, nuanced tellings of what is happening between mothers and their children and children and their mothers. Multiple stories also expand the sphere of influence upon children's lives, making space for other caring adults to mother a child. I turn to these multiple stories to speak to the relational implications of mothering in the context of family violence, and to a more ethical reading and production of mothered encounters with children experiencing this form of crisis.

Domestic or family violence can be described as one partner's attempt to take control over the other, which serves as a context for physical and/or sexual violence. This coercive control extends to emotional and economic abuse, isolation, blame, and intimidation. Where children are involved, they too, are drawn into this web of abuse as a means of control, with the perpetrating partner threatening to hurt them or take them away (Johnson, 2007). According to Johnson (2007), a gender theory of domestic violence foregrounds the intersection of gender and violence, which in heterosexual relationships is perpetrated almost entirely by men. In same-sex relationships some aspects of gender may also play a role in partner violence; gender alone inadequately accounts for domestic violence, as aspects of race, class, and culture can also shed light on theoretical understandings of domestic violence.

Throughout much of my childhood I witnessed my father's physical and emotional violence towards my mother. My mother was able to separate from my father when I was 6 years old, but like many women involved in violent relationships, several years passed before she truly escaped (Campbell, Rose, Kub, & Nedd, 1998). Visiting shelters, staying with family, and moving into short-term rental homes, my mother slowly gathered information and resources that finally helped her to leave. We moved to a remote Aboriginal community in northern Manitoba, 3,000 kilometres away, where my mother took a teaching job. My father found us there, and picked my brother and me up for the weekend, never to return. We didn't see my mother again for 4 months. It would be another 3 years before the battles between my mother and father subsided enough for me to have some semblance of normalcy in my life.

I went to five primary schools in 6 years. Maybe that is how it is when your mother is running. When you are like another bag hurriedly packed. I tell my children now 'safety first,' but of course, I am teaching them how to cross the road. But consider the following:

The rain came down. I watched the wipers carve sweeping arcs across the windshield. I sat in the passenger seat, too low to see anything but the dark sky. My brother curled up against me, asleep. My dad intent on the road. The same tapes playing over and over, superimposing a soundtrack on the experience. It was a really long drive, made longer by the uncertainty, the partial explanation of where we were coming from and where we were going to. I guess at some point it started to seem longer than a typical weekend visit.

How did my 8-year-old self take all of this in? I don't remember saying goodbye to my mother. So excited that my dad showed up (finally!). Maybe I didn't even see her before I left. What did my dad say to us to explain the drive across northern Manitoba back 'home' which I now know must have taken 2 days.

My friends must have seen an unusual car drive up – the big tall white man asking around for us. Did they watch us go? Were they standing right there? Or maybe they didn't, just maybe peeked through the cracks in the plastic covering their windows. I wonder what they told my mother when she asked.

How sick she must have been.

That is how we left Nelson House. I don't know the name of the school, but we walked 2 x 4s over boot-sucking mud to get there and back every day. We looked like jumbo jets queuing up on a runway, spreading our arms in the air as we flew over the narrow planks, yielding and converging as we met up with friends coming down the other branches and leading to the school doors. It was spring thaw, and mostly girls (and little brothers) went there because all the boys were trapping.

I don't know the name of one other school I went to. Selective memory helps forgetting. But I vividly recall the cream cheese and jelly sandwich that I didn't give to my brother one Wednesday. He crossed the gym floor sticky and hot to find me. My heart thumping in my ears so loud that I only watched his mouth and eyes plead. I would be in big trouble if I did: my brother wasn't to eat another thing until he finished Monday's dinner which was still in the fridge at home. (He didn't like corned beef and cabbage.) I tossed the soggy sandwich in the garbage. I remember how my brother threw up when he was allowed to eat again before we left for school on Thursday.

Ruptured: Mother-Daughter Relations in the Context of Family Violence

What it means to mother is something that has been woven into a well-worn cloth: a set of agreed-upon, normative actions and affects that are performed in public and private spaces. Stories of mothers and children whose experience differs from these dominant norms are essentially inaudible. Specifically, for families affected by violence in the home, this silence is made even more profound by their participation in hiding signs of violence. Covering up with clothing, makeup, or well-crafted excuses, mothers present a unified front that everything is all right. The home itself can be thought of as a symbolic container for domestic violence, walls blocking from outside a view of what happens within.

Nearly one in four women in the United States reports experiencing violence by a current or former spouse or boyfriend at some point in her life, and 15.5 million children live in families in which partner violence occurred at least once in the past year (Family Violence Prevention Fund, 2010). Considering these data, each of us must know women and children affected by family violence, yet how many of us hear it spoken about? As a child, I wished someone could come in, come help me make sense of my symbolic home, or else open a door for me to leave through. Instead, my deep processing of the circumstances of my upbringing happened years later, unfolding in increments as I became a mother. Meeting my children, watching them grow, the reality of what my father had done to our family hit me again and again.

Children experience a sense of dislocation arising from violence in the home. bell hooks describes this well: 'the world one has most intimately known, in which one felt relatively safe and secure, has collapsed' (p. 270). Safety and trust are most obviously broken, and so too, is the intimacy and nurturance between mother and child. These circumstances also rupture outsider assumptions about mother-child love: what kind of mother would allow her children to live with ongoing, enduring psychological and/or physical pain? From a normalized perspective, we assume love is good, but the contingent of this assumption implies that love can be suspect, too.

Understanding love and mothering in the context of family violence necessarily extends to messy, contradictory, and irrational aspects of love: my mother can love me and allow me to suffer. Problematizing mother-child love, I turn to Lily Bartolomé's (2008) elaboration of authentic love, or cariño, which she defines as a politically and ideologically informed kind of love. Bartolomé writes that love is not a neutral entity: 'loving . . . is insufficient unless the love and care are informed by authentic respect and a desire to equalize unequal [conditions]' (p. 2). In the context of family violence, love can be limiting and oppressive; children need more than love and care, they need respect, solidarity, and physically and psychologically healthy homes. Alternate stories of mothering highlight the different ways in which mothers cultivate authentic love and, at the same time, the inadequacies of this relationship to make up for all of the compromises that family violence imposes upon children.

Dislocated: Identity Construction in the Context of Family Violence

The kind of family violence that I describe is between partners/spouses. However, where children are involved, they are the unintended victims of control and assault. Victimization multiplies as children's' lived experience becomes undifferentiated as both witness/self/subject and mother/object (Grumet, 1988). This intersubjectivity patterns onto children's' identity constructions, overshadowing their own agentive subjectivity. Attempting to recover my location and subjectivity, as I grew older, I withdrew from my mother and my family for a while, hoping to free myself from the constricting bonds of mutually constitutive mother-child relations. For me, school eventually provided an ideal way of extricating myself from my childhood, offering the stability, consistency, and security that I needed. In school, I was unbound by historicity, and could relate to the world on my own terms. However, this severing was a radical negation of my past, removing myself from the good as well as the bad. To resolve this interruption, I worked towards surfacing the subjectivities of my experience (Pinar, 1998, p. 243). I found my way back across the most defining moments of my life to the smaller (less violent) influences that are equally constitutive of my embodied experience. I am not all broken.

Divided: Preserving the Integrity of Self in the Context of Family Violence

Without outside support, I made sense of the inner world of my family alone. Not knowing families to be anything different, I only realized in my teen years that my father was an angry man. As I grew older, I came to accept and integrate the circumstances of my family with my own identity, that although my family experience could be characterized as extreme, I was still a 'normal' woman, and I could be a good mother.

Mother and mothering are constructions that have been neatly packaged into categories that can dangerously fool us into believing that we know all the kinds of mother-child relationships that there are. We think we know the differences among families and their lived experience of these differences. Elizabeth Ellsworth (1989) calls these kinds of assumptions a 'violence of rationalism' (p. 304). Dismantling these 'mythical norms' (p. 310) requires problematizing the idea of how we come to know the Other. Reflecting on this critique, I wrote of my lived experience:

> I am physically repulsed by these thoughts that dis-voice me, that assume your story about me is the way things are. It helps to make life so knowable but you don't know me. You silence my story and I play along,

complicit in the hegemony of this epistemology. I am so good at deliver-
ing what you want to hear. Complicit. Waterboard me. Ram the water
down my throat, I still swallow.

I could claw the air for breath. I can hardly breathe through the stifling
cellophane of protection that guards me from the outside and holds what
is inside still in. I can't swallow any more. I have to push back against
these neat little categories. Struggling, struggling to free myself.

Women and children who are affected by family violence hold tenu-
ously to agentive subjectivity by sharing only safe tellings of the stories
of their lives. bell hooks (2007, p. 273) writes that women who have
been victimized by violence have to pay a price for breaking the silence and naming the problem, opening themselves to judgment and
critique. Having the choice of when to speak and what to say about my
experience is an agentive choice that I make after assessing my vulnerability. If asked about my childhood, my family, I might give a different
answer every time. Constructed in the moment, I make subconscious
decisions about which parts of myself to expose, and what is better left
unsaid.

Questions of representation arise when seeking to know and explain what is happening between mothers and children and children
and their mothers in the context of crisis. The private, domestic, intimate nature of mothering allows no space for distance and objectivity among children and mothers defining and interpreting their
relationship.

My writing, my analysis of mothering is necessarily shaped by an
embodied understanding and approach in which I am fully involved.
Helping me to understand what these kinds of investments mean for
research, Kathleen Gallagher (2008) writes that feminist approaches to
research have 'abandoned the pretense of objectivity' (p. 68), to connect knowledge with lived and felt experience. Gallagher's research approaches pedagogical spaces as research sites, where researchers shift
from observers to doers in order to be with and come to know students
differently. I draw upon this idea of 'being with' as a way to connect
with, understand, and support children who may be experiencing violence in the home.

The hidden experiences of pain at the hands of well- (or ill-)
intending adults 'come already validated in a radically different
arena of proof and carry no option or luxury of choice' (Bartolomé,
2008, p. 302). The telling of these experiences can have the effect

of re/inscribing abject feelings and identity constructions, particularly when others, through 'normative listening,' assign these experiences to conventional social categories and stereotypes. For some women and children who share their stories, the repeated experience of confrontation with powerful forms of normativity has the effect of making some experiences untellable (Zingaro, 2009, pp. 112–113). Silence and fictionalized 'counter-stories' are alternatives to sharing painful truths in situations of vulnerability. Silence and counter-stories should be seen as active, agentive choices that children might make in talking about themselves. Safely constructed counter-stories are as real to a child as experiences of pain and suffering; as though the telling of safe stories of happy, loving families might make them come true. When the pain of what children experience is locked away, protected by safer stories of their lives, researchers and teachers might never hear the 'truth' or 'real' stories about a child. In these circumstances, I wonder whether it matters if children share fact or fiction. Believing children's stories, or pretending to, might be a way to extend a hand to the child experiencing crisis, to help the child hold on to her or his precarious investment in and movement towards a reality that might be other/wise. Working with these ideas, I fondly remember a teacher who made a difference for me:

> Grade 6 was Ms. Kitamura's class. Blue scratchy carpet on the floor that I looked at up close at circle times. If you look hard enough at something you can kind of vanish and it's like you're not even there at all. The raucous cacophony of so many different faces, names, skin was beyond my knowing. Did I really look as lost as I felt. How did she know? She was just like the others (most). Lucky me. Oh lucky, lucky, lucky me. They saved my life, I think.

Extending a lifeline such as this required my teachers to look past what they could see and hear. To read the story of my life, teachers needed not only to watch me, but to be with me, listening with their hearts as well as their heads. Ms. Kitamura sometimes asked me why I didn't seem my usual 'bubbly' self. She brought me books about interesting young girls, and appointed me to the important task of answering the school phone during the secretary's morning breaks. Over and above the prescribed routines of school, Ms. Kitamura noticed me, talked with me. Although I never told her anything about my life, it seems I didn't need to. She heard me anyway.

I am pulled towards the dialogic possibilities of positive relationships that can be fostered between caring adults, such as teachers,
and children in crisis. I look to the ways in which we experience our
being through others (Fanon, 1967) to inform a pedagogy of being with
children in order to know and teach them differently. The pedagogical moves that my teachers made to 'know' me extended to me a different, and transformative way of knowing myself. Bringing authentic
cariño to the classroom, my Ms. Kitamura provided for me an opening
to engage with school. This idea is similar to Beauboeuf-Lafontant's
(2002) notion of 'politicized mothering' which describes teachers' advocacy for and struggle with children. Although we attempt to create
a safe and welcoming space for children to learn, we should also take
a critical stance towards this idea which does not conflate safety with
openness. Students' entrance to so-called safe spaces of classrooms is
partial, as only some differences are marked as legitimate and allowed
or brought into classrooms. Other differences are not spoken about;
more uncertain and complex. Simmering under the surface of classroom discourse, these differences are like the elephant in the room, and
filter every educational experience of children like me. Ellsworth (1989)
asks: 'what diversity do we silence in the name of "liberatory" pedagogy?' (p. 299). Classrooms, whether critical, progressive, or otherwise
labelled present little more than the illusion of wholeness, of safety. We
are always silencing someone.

Multiple Stories: Alternative Forms of Relation,
Perception, and Expression in Motherhood

Seeking to interrupt the rupture, dislocation, and divide that family
violence patterned upon my self and my life as a mother, I turn to
Helene Cixous' (1991) work with the feminine subject, in Coming to
Writing, to inform a different position and location for my self. I seek
an alternative form of relation that does not change what is different
about me, that accepts the experiences that have made me who I am.
Why should I have to give up something of myself to better fit the
idea that I had a good mother, that I am a good mother? Critiquing
idealized notions of mothering can help to 'rid our psyches of the
sense that we have failed in some way by not having such relationships' (hooks, 2007, p. 274). The subject of mothering in this book asks
that we think differently about mothering and how it has been positioned in our culture. Cixous' work exceeds the binary logic of good/
bad mothering and opens to multiple, hetergeneous possibilities that

are promoted by thinking of alternative forms of relation, perception, and expression.

Violence in our society is abject, an extreme state that we are conditioned to distance ourselves from. For children living in contexts of family violence, this distancing cuts them off not only from fitting in as normal, but also from themselves and their relationships with their mothers. Bridging this divide requires filling mother-child relations with new meaning. Becoming a mother, birthing my twin babies, helped me to this place. Cixous' (1991) writing connects the experiences of women in their bodies to relating with and knowing the other. She writes that giving birth is something our bodies do, without mastering by reason. An experience of the uncontrollable, birth itself is a bodied experience that produces a real new living being that is not what is already existing, not a reproduction of the past. With my children as they played on the beach, rode their bikes, and made up songs, I re/entered the world and found one joy after another, following my children to places and feelings I had forgotten.

> Flesh of my flesh, you remind me that I used to run on the beach, ride my bike, and make up songs, too.

Preoccupied with separating from my mother, I had forgotten that she taught me to read, that I rolled cookie dough at her side, that we went for long drives looking at beautiful houses together. She loved me. I loved her. My children have brought me back in touch with parts of me that my relationship with my mother represents. If maternal loves maps onto later love relationships, I struggle to hold tight to what I loved about loving my mother while letting go of the parts which exceed(ed) my rationality. I can rethink the rupture of my mother's love, transgressing the divide it created in me. Yes, my mother can love me and cause me to suffer at the same time. Flesh makes strangeness come through (Cixous, 1991).

Multiple births are complex, often the result of 'high-risk' pregnancies. Multiples (twins, triplets, and other higher-order births) exceed the norm, and I take up this excess to represent the multiple and often unknown possibilities that birth, that encounters with children stimulate for mothers. Forever altered, these exchanges tint us (Cixous, 1994). (My) children redirect my current hopes and aspirations towards a future that I cannot control but which I shape. Elizabeth Grosz (2005) explores the concept of time not as a rational marker but as continuity between past, present, and future. My own children embody a continuity that literally and metaphorically splits my present trajectories: one pregnancy, two children; sleeping, eating, crying, laughing differently, and at the same time. Who do I hold first, feed first, pay attention to? What happens when they both need me at the same time? Relating this experience to my understanding of myself, I see that, as a mother, I am at once mother and child, but also 'other,' something different from who I was before. As Grosz (2005) describes, my conception of time is divided into parts, 'one virtual, one actual, one open to anticipation and unknowable future, the other onto reminiscence and the past, functioning simultaneously as present and as the past of that present' (p. 4). A multiple orientation towards temporal moments and movement directs me simultaneously to the past and to the future, generating a multiplied present and directionality (p. 4). Watching my children grow, learn, speak, understand, they enable my life to continue to become in all the directions that time is moving. Both alone and together, we are, always, in the process of becoming something other than what we were and will be.

Conclusion

Family violence makes it difficult to accept that there is any integrity in mother-child relationships. Attempting to reclaim the integrity of the love and care that exists both in spite and because of violence is an empowering process that should be supported to assist women and children affected by violence in the home to gain a renewed sense of worth and value. Being with children as mother produces knowledge that is relational, subjective, and believing. Accepting the multiplicity and irrationality of different orientations to mothering, love, and family, even in the extreme, requires opening to the possibility of these differences and suspending disbelief. Doing so not only supports children in their moves towards agentive subjectivity, but also contests social and cultural contexts and processes that perpetuate the privileges of power, dominance, and normativity.

The ruptured stories of women and children affected by family violence are absent from educational discourse. Family violence is tolerated in the ways in which it is overlooked, so that the silence of women and children affected by violence in the home is reinforced by the silence on the topic in education and society at large. This silence-violence is a concern not just for individual families; it extends from individual relationships to the arrangement of power and authority in schools and society. Family violence has a context, and needs to be understood as within and relating to social experience. Bringing stories like mine into the discourse, I invite the merging and blurring of the public and the domestic, the fact and the fiction, and the ethical responsibilities of mothering and teaching other peoples' children.

References

Aoki, T.T. (2003). Locating living pedagogy in teacher 'research': Five metonymic moments. In E. Hasebe-Ludt & W. Hurren (Eds.), Curriculum intertext: Place/language/pedagogy (pp. 1–10). New York: Peter Lang.

Bartolomé, L. (2008). Authentic carino and respect in minority education: The political and ideological dimensions of love. *International Journal of Critical Pedagogy*, 1 (1), 1–17.

Beauboeuf-Lafontant, T. (2002). A womanist experience of caring: Understanding the pedagogy of exemplary black women teachers. *Urban Review*, 34 (1), 71–86.

Campbell, J.C., Rose, L., Kub, J., & Nedd, D. (1998) Voices of strength and resistance: A contextual and longitudinal analysis of women's responses to battering. *Journal of Interpersonal Violence*, 13 (6), 743–762.

Cixous, H. (1991). *'Coming to writing' and other essays*. Trans. S. Cornell. Cambridge, MA: Harvard University Press.

Cixous, H. (1994). Preface. In S. Sellers (Ed.), *Helene Cixous reader*. New York: Routledge.

Ellsworth, E. (1989). 'Why doesn't this feel empowering?' Working through the repressive myths of critical pedagogy. *Harvard Educational Review*, 59 (3), 297–322.

Gallagher, K. (2008). The art of methodology: A collaborative science. In K. Gallagher (Ed.), *The methodological dilemma: Creative, critical, and collaborative approaches to qualitative research* (pp. 67–82). New York: Routledge.

Grosz, E. (2005). *Time travels: Feminism, nature, power*. Durham, NC: Duke University Press.

Grumet, M. (1988). Conception, contradiction, and curriculum. In *Bitter milk: Women and teaching* (pp. 3–30). Amherst, MA: University of Massachusetts Press.

hooks, b. (2007). Violence in intimate relationships: A feminist perspective. In L.L. O'Toole, J.R. Schiffman, & M.L.K. Edwards (Eds.), *Gender violence: Interdisciplinary perspectives* (2nd ed., pp. 279–284). New York: New York University Press.

Family Violence Prevention Fund. (2010). Get the facts: The facts on domestic, dating, and sexual violence. Retrieved 17 February 2010, from www.endabuse.org/content/action_center/detail/754.

Fanon, F. (1967). The fact of blackness. In Black skin, white masks (pp. 109–140). New York: Grove Press.

Johnson, M.P. (2007). Domestic violence: The intersection of gender and control. In L.L. O'Toole, J.R. Schiffman, & M.L.K. Edwards (Eds.), *Gender violence: Interdisciplinary perspectives* (2nd ed.; pp. 257–268). New York: New York University Press.

Pinar, W.F. (1994). *Autobiography, politics, and sexuality.* New York: Peter Lang.

Pinar, W F. (1998). Understanding curriculum as gender text: Notes on reproduction, resistance, and male-male relations. In W.F. Pinar, *Queer theory in education* (pp. 221–244). Mahwah, NJ: Lawrence Erlbaum.

Zingaro, L. (2009). *Speaking out: Storytelling for social change.* Walnut Creek, CA: Left Coast Press.

18 First Reading: Troubling Maternity

APARNA MISHRA TARC

Troubling Maternity

> My children cause me the most exquisite suffering of which I have any experience. It is the suffering of ambivalence: the murderous alternation between bitter resentment and raw-edged nerves, and blissful gratification and tenderness. Sometimes I seem to myself, in *my feelings* towards these tiny guiltless beings, a monster of selfishness and intolerance.
> – Adrienne Rich, *Of Woman Born* (emphasis added)

In feminist motherhood's seminal text, *Of Woman Born,* Adrienne Rich powerfully demonstrates how motherhood works to secure women's bodies, and consequently those of their children, to ontological systems and institutions of human existence privileging man (Derrida, 1995). Rich (1981) de-stables romantic myths of motherhood by analysing representations of mother in Western literature and cultural texts. However, telling in Rich's critique of motherhood is the problem of what to do with the child. As she discloses, in the epigraph opening this chapter, the primary source that provokes Rich's feminist self to take on mother is her affective, troubling response to the fact of her children's existence. In these sparse, unforgettable lines Rich depicts the feeling power of the maternal relation as exquisite, deeply ambivalent, bodily suffering. Out of intense affect projected towards the child, Rich makes a 'monster' out of mother.

Rather than focus feminist critique on the affective substance of the grievance comprising her feelings, Rich produces a manifesto for woman to defend against motherhood made 'monstrous' by the agent of maternity's creator, patriarchy. In defence of woman and her body, Rich rewrites her journal-recorded feelings into an attack on colonizing, patriarchal motherhood. Although Rich does manage to put into question the Western patriarchal process by which woman becomes 'terribly' mother, something curious occurs in the body of her scholarly text. In her attempt to rewrite women as master of herself, Rich (1981) repeats the patriarchal logic she seeks to break down:'We need to imagine a world in which every woman is the presiding genius of her own body. In such a world women will truly create new life, bringing forth not only children (if and as we choose) but the visions, and the thinking, necessary to sustain, console, and alter human existence – a new relationship to the universe' (pp. 285–286).

Not only does Rich rely on an ontology of the agentic self on which to found a feminist project, but she also adopts a central patriarchal teleological end for man as the end of feminism: 'a world in which every woman is the presiding genius of own body' (p. 285). I theorize this normative end, of sovereignty for the self through mastery over the body, as untenable for human existence constituted both by its utter dependence on others (Lévinas, 1969) and its inability to articulate coherently the desires of the body in symbolic form without the loving support of a(n) (m)other (Freud, 1999/2008).[1] In this chapter, I recover the aspect of Rich's (1981) text that I find most enigmatic, insightful, and troubling for new feminist projects writing the maternal body – Rich's depiction of motherhood as an exquisite suffering that cannot be named but felt deeply within. Rich's stumbling upon the affective dimensions of maternity heightened by her attempts to relate to what she claims are 'tiny, guiltless beings' forms the basis for my unsettling maternity.

The earlier feminist critiques separating the mother from the child or equating the mother and child bond with woman's body is a questionable assumption underlying the separatist view of mother and woman. At the same time, powerful activist works, as is *Of Woman Born*, began to create a theoretical language for how subsequent generations might forge scholarly, social, political, artistic, and individual revisions of maternity. My own work would not be possible without the courageous intervention and heated discussions of feminist scholars and mothers Adrienne Rich (1981), Mary Daly (1978), and Audre Lorde (1984). Still, as Jacques Derrida (1995) points out, in some ways the early American, Australian, and European feminist project to reclaim maternity from man is doomed, if, in the first place, the woman's body feminists seek

to reclaim is the body 'inferred, constructed and interpreted as paternity' (p. 48).

In this chapter, I trouble dominant, Western, heteronormative assumptions of maternity using object relations theorist Melanie Klein's
(1935/1987) affective depiction of the maternal relation. I situate the
child's symbolic meaning-making practice in Klein's lifelong attempts
to learn to manage the affective workings of the body first experienced
in a pre-Oedipal, colonial, and conflict-ridden scene of infant-mother
relation. I term the scene of the infant's struggling to know her body
through the body of the mother's language, 'first reading,' forgotten
but marked as a 'felt,' affective trace somewhere within the deep re-
cesses of (pre)memory (Derrida, 1976/1995). Rather than see the body
and its theory of embodiment as providing relief from male-centred,
rational or normative accounts of motherhood, I return to Rich's depiction of unbearable motherhood to discuss the body's felt struggle
for meaning. Rethinking maternity, I draw on Klein's theory of affect
encompassing the body relations of mother/parent and child. The
enduring conflict of intolerable, felt suffering that encountering the
other's body animates in our own exemplifies the maternal relation.
Following Derrida (1978a), I suggest that there is no body feeling free
from the already socially determining and naming words used to represent those feelings. The maternal relation is many-times wounded
and made resilient by the discourses writing the bodies of woman and
child. When we speak of our bodies, we animate multiple and layered
competing desires that make the body an overdetermined and reinscribed text of great violence, suffering, and creativity. Our bodies are
terribly and beautifully entombed in language and social constraint.
To do justice to the inarticulateness, precariousness, and decay char-
acterizing the body's material condition requires a maternal, social
environment that learns to lovingly hold the body in its highly intelligent and unintelligible infancy. Although counterintuitive, Klein
found that the infantile body, not yet fully formed, in dire need of others for sustenance, mobility, and articulation contains within it an incredible, felt intelligence that cannot be replicated in any other time of
our development (1928/1987). And the reason for Klein's bold claim
is this: against all odds babies compel others to respond to their incho-
ate needs. Observing how infants, babies, and young children make
sense of their bodies in relation to objects and others, Klein provides
startling insights into the complex of body feeling comprising the maternal relation.

Klein (1935/1987) theorizes maternity as a psychical relation on which the baby depends for her very survival. To the merciful hands of mother, which I conceive both as a (m)other-person and a psychosocial environment, human being is born. Social-patriarchal cultural, in the form of the third or the father, overwrites the maternal relationship, while the child and (m)other make relations to each other (Kristeva, 2001). Through the infant's coming to sense, grieve, and come to terms with the proximal difference between her existence, which at infancy consists mostly of all-consuming, sensate feeling, and that of the symbolizing (m)other's composing the psychical and social realities of the infant, the child becomes particularly a human self.

Theorizing maternity as an external environment in which the child is thrust and received I suggest, following Deborah Britzman (2009), that natality poses certain questions of responsibility to those social beings and collectives entrusted with the infant's care. The infant's caregivers consist of the bodies making up the psychosocial maternal environment as well as the social institutions that materialize mother as a highly politicized entity securing the family, law, and education. So women alone are not solely responsible for the child's entry into an already formed social world, even if the mother labours, births, and nurses the child and, in doing so, is often charged with the primary care of the child. In my reading of mother, the mother's caregiver's body is an agent of competing affective desires and social-political forces, articulated by, what Karleen Pendleton Jiménez (personal communication, 15 May 2010) describes as 'bossy discourses.' The oppressive social relations and regimes that make mother into an overdetermined, psychosocial entity, agent, and myth also bear an ethical responsibility for supporting children, born of no fault of their own, into inhospitable social space with 'visions, and the thinking, necessary to sustain, console and alter human existence – a new relationship to the universe' (Rich, 1981, pp. 267–268). As Hannah Arendt (1993) rightly points out in her thoughts on education, the burden of changing the world is often futurist-oriented, thus placing the demand for change on the newly arrived rather on those collectively charged with the child's care and social development, those responsible to support the infant's reconciliation with the ruined worlds to which she is born.

Most previous theorizing on the subject of motherhood in the Western women's movement is of sides, of mother and of man. Derrida (1989/1995) writes that a theorizing of sides betrays in feminism a concealed, learned longing to inhabit the masterful logic of man: of reason, of autonomy, of individualization, of agency, and of freedom. I want to suggest that what is erased in the conflict of sides is that on the other of (m)other is not man but the child. And, as Rich (1981) agonizingly finds, the child as the other side seems to defy subordination, as is in any binary movement in the usual sense of opposing couplets (man/ woman, black/white). The infant, in her dependence as an unseeing, immobile, sensory creature, is a part of and beholden to (m)other in the most dramatic sense. The infant haunts the dream of woman's body unbound to the child because the infant's attachment to mother is infinite. If the mother is forced, by the social and cultural mandate of the third, to physically sever from her body the baby, if the cord must be cut, the psychical/physical injury caused to the child in necessarily forcing separation returns in unforeseen ways to haunt the mother and the social. The child, even as an adult, never quite leaves the psychical and social bond between herself and the deeply affective familial and cultural relations embodying mother.

Thinking through the institution of motherhood, we cannot avoid thinking the demands posed to mother by the fact of the child's existence, posed to self by the fact of the other's existence. African-American feminist Audre Lorde (1984) poses these demands of response made to mother this way:

The difference between poetry and rhetoric
is being
ready to kill yourself
instead of your children (p. 106).

In this passionate call to embrace the vulnerability of the child before the body of paternity instituting mother, of reinventing a poetics of infancy before the rhetoric instituting patriarchy, Lorde troubles Western conceptions of maternity. Her call is a stark warning to feminists to engage in a generative and reflexive psychosocial practice of painstakingly reworking dehumanizing forms and logics of language in the rearticulation of the maternal relation. Rewriting maternity as radically other, rather than in accordance to the self-aggrandizing terms of an already colonizing Western patriarchy, provides, in Lorde's political vision, the basis for maternal thought and action. Do not repeat the rhetoric-driven, self-justifying logics of patriarchy that would have you inhabit the same killing space of male-female relations with your own children, Lorde insists. Her caution is one that French and American post-structural feminists heed in the evolution of *l'écriture féminine*, seeking invention of new terms and conceptions for what woman and mother might mean (Cixous, 1976). However, as Gayatri Spivak (1981) shows through her critique of cultural strains in French feminist thinking, seductive is the pull of Western ontological, normative valuing and determination of bare human life. Maternal environments in other places and civilizations place Western conceptions of motherhood under great strain and might provide other means and practices by which to raise our children to become differently human. Analysing the child's psychosocial development as it materializes in motherhood practices at home and elsewhere can support new thinking on how to collectively raise our children to inhabit less violent and colonizing modes of existence.

First Readings: Bodies in Anguish

Bodily theories are used in both feminist and educational research as a means by which maternal knowledge might be studied and analysed for its ontological and epistemological significance. If the body cannot exist without the world, as Maurice Merleau-Ponty (1962) has argued, no world exists without the body. The body, in other words, is a somatic world residing within other worlds. We are never certain which world is more colonizing in the individual life of the child, the affective internal body world or the discursive external worlds of the body, and perhaps this enduring, ontological war of worlds waged within grounds the human's very crisis of existence from the onset of life.

Although curricular embodiment theorists (Springgay & Freedman, 2007) have powerfully analysed the effects of dominant Cartesian theories on dominant developmental, cognitive, and curricular theories in education, less attention is paid to Western ontological theories that violently split apart the bodies of infant, mother, and man, granting each self the illusion of agency where there is none. If our bodies are not split from our minds, they are also not split from the bodies of our others. Our bodies are not our own but bound to the body of others. We both desire and need the other's body to bring relief and meaning to our own. We are born and remain suspended throughout our lifetimes in deeply dependent, and binding kinship, libidinal, and social relations. If we learn to split ourselves from (m)others through language and socialization, part of our meaning making is always tending to the wounds that independence both necessarily and violently commits. Our bodies carry a primal severing from other, body feeling and inner life. (M)others hauntingly accompany our every attempt to rid ourselves of the losses to self that separation evokes. The struggle to be self and to be with other is traced in our discourses yearning for emancipation that learning to be an agentic subject demands.

With Madeleine Grumet (1988), I want to suggest that motherhood is bound to the experience of infancy and begins in the nonknowing time of conception and birth. Following Grumet, my own project (Mishra Tarc, 2007) of theorizing the process by which the child becomes particularly human through infantile language learning is bound 'to the experience of birth and nurturance of children' (Grumet, 1988, p. 9). As with Grumet, I draw from psychoanalysis and post-structural phenomenology to image and imagine the maternal relation. However, a reimagining of the maternal relation in my writing is of both infancy and (m)othering. Following Klein (1928/1987), I stake my claims for learning in the pre-Oedipal maternal relation, taking the child's nonsensical affective sense-making process as the basis for thinking and knowledge (Mishra Tarc, 2007). Male-dominated educational theories of mind and existence mark the Oedipal, or the fall into language, as the moment in which the human being's capacity for knowledge production begins. Privileging logical, symbolic human states reflects the patriarchal project, through language learning, to 'claim the child, to teach him or her to master the language, the rules, the games, and the names of the fathers' (Grumet, 1988, p. 21).

Preceding the child's fall into language is a set of intricate, complicated intelligent processes that lay the grounds and possibilities for meaning making. Although these psychical infantile processes cannot be empirically measured or verified, Klein (1928/1987) found, in her observation of the somatic outbursts of infants and children, that feeling plays a leading role in the development of the interpretive capacity of the child. Psychical processes are primitive and yet present in the infant's guttural sounds, cries, gestures, movements, etc. If managing body affects are terrifying for the mother, as Rich (1988) attests, they are unbearably so for the infant, as she has no recourse to articulating those body feelings in choate forms of speech and writing. The infant has no self-made means for knowing what it is she feels, yet she feels everything regardless of her initial incapacity for logos-driven articulation.

Educationalists have defined curriculum as the pedagogical and embodied texts by which knowledge comes to be focusing mostly on the symbolic forms of this process (Pinar, 1998). Drawing on this critical reconceptualization, I theorize the curricular as the transferential process by which the infant's affectively co-constructed desire to know or to have the content of the (m)other's body coincides with the symbolizing process of the infant's coming to make terrible and glorious sense of her own body. The yet-to-be worded, affective infantile existence is our first curriculum text. I suggest that man-made ontologies of wanting and abjecting the other give rise to the man-made epistemologies created expressly to stake claim over the child. And if mother is subordinate to this project, she is also implicated in and reproduces it through her 'first readings' of the child. By this I mean that the infantile body is a textual site upon which the mysteries of human existence unthinkably materialize. If the body is overdetermined by mother and/or the social, infantile flesh conceals its revolt and within revolt's concealment is waged the productive struggle between the baby's need to live and the mother's socialized, libidinal desire for the child to be. This struggle between the self's need and the other's desire is curricular; the infant's basic need collides with the mother's desire for baby: through the unconscious transferential communion of warring psychical material, competing and communing meanings of self and other are mysteriously made, ruined, and remade (Coleman, 2009).

Melanie Klein (1928/1987) characterizes this first reading of others or object relations as violent, conflict-ridden, and necessarily defensive. We experience affect in infancy by being born physically and mentally dependent on others. Without speech and left to the (m)other's mercy, the infant feels her way through affects of pleasure and pain and of love and hate to make sense of the world and others. The magical process of corresponding somatic sensations to objects/other is the child's primary mechanism for making sense and then symbol, for reading the world. As the infant wages war with threatening objects and others, defences are summoned; defending is also the process by which order (good and bad) is made and by which we begin to identify with the good and destroy the bad. As order and identification are made, anxiety lessens, and the child's mental processes begin to enter into a state of relative harmony. Still, Klein noticed that when children played with toys and things, they were often overtaken by affect manifesting in their fits of rage, anger, sorrow, and silence. As adults, conditioned by social norms and language, we learn to tune out affect. But infantile affect remains within our bodies, reminding us of our terror-filled dependence on other to mysteriously find its way into outbursts of a different kind. At an epistemological level, Derrida (1976) speculates that we can gain access into the affect structuring (Western) thought by deconstructing its trace left behind in writing.

Within the maternal relation, Britzman (2009) images the mother's body as subject to a site of affective, internal struggle that resembles that of the physically dependent, helpless, vulnerable, frail infant:

> While for the infant the mother is the first love object, her capacity to tolerate the infant's needs and to find pleasure in early care renders both parties vulnerable to times when care impinges upon both the infant's growing capacity to tolerate frustration and the mother's desire for freedom as a separate person. In psychoanalytic views, both parties are subject to this primal helplessness, feelings of violation, and hostility. Yet a significant dilemma for both social thought and the individual's desire for recognition is that it is difficult to symbolize this emotional life without falling into idealization or disparagement of the vicissitudes of maternal care, self-hood, and autonomy. After all, the infant is helpless and cannot meet her own needs. But this fact is often used to cover over the ways in which the infant's needs, by the very nature of the mother's care, turn into love, sexuality, and desire. The capacity to become a self, then, depends upon maternal care. (p. 778)

As Britzman powerfully depicts, and Rich (1981) so beautifully enacts in her suffering thoughts, the maternal relation is over-infused with sensate feelings that defy representation. The maternal relation is filled with the hatred of dependence experienced simultaneously yet uniquely by infant and mother. The feeling body attachment between both the infant and the mother is reckoned with in a silent warring between two entities that both love and cannot abide by the needs and desires of the other. If the relating entities are bound together through a primal, libidinal, physical, and socially constructed mythical bond of love, mother and infant are also constantly at odds with one another, invisibly combative, as one's needs compete unintelligibly with the desires of others. This abject conflict of need and desire is our first felt impression of love (Britzman, 2009).

Occupying different stages of development, as they do, sets up the potential for conflict between mother and child. The baby's limited ability to articulate the demands of her body to the (m)other, and vice versa, is another. And from here the confusion ensues, as child and mother are forced to make sense of each other through the unreliable work of first reading the affective pull of felt bodies. But even if the suffering is mutually felt, as Britzman (2009, p. 778) critically points out, the adult has the power and recourse to symbolize the baby's needs in relation to her own desire for the baby and is responsible for holding the baby's distress. The capacity to become a self, to become someone precariously hangs in the balance of the (m)other's care, care that can easily fall into the idealization and disparagement of the infant's need, care that, more often than not, falls into overdetermined, frustrated misreadings of the infant's corporeal pleasure and distress (Britzman, 2009).

The first few days of an infant's life are spent with infant and primary caretaker reading each other in the instinctual way that all other sentient beings learn to feel out their environments, in the sensory way all beings read the external world (Kamuf, 2000). The baby's coming into the world of others is grounded in her overwhelming need of others, while the mother's relation to the child is already determined through desires both individual and mandated by socialized and social forces within and beyond the self. According to Klein (1928/1987), for her very survival, the infant is forced to make her need of milk and comfort known through the functions of the body, mostly through crying, feeding, and sleeping. The mother, on the other hand, is afforded with the symbolic resources with which to make interpretations of the infant's behaviour. She can coherently read the baby according to the somatic signals the infant emits which are then subject to a well-developed interpretive apparatus. However, despite having what educational and philosophical theorists state is the higher-order capacity to reason or rationalize, mother is forced to make wild first readings on the non-speaking being for which she is entrusted to care. The newly arrived creature has no way of allowing mother the luxury of factually, cross-checking her wild intuitive, interpretations. So the mother must turn to a third, the father, the father's law, to verify uncertain readings. These third readings of culture and society override the mother's less verifiable affective readings of infant behaviour to powerfully rewrite and govern the mother's first data, the mother's felt and uncertain interpretations. The interpretations of her self by others are steadily taken in and projected out by baby, as she comes to terms with the affective fact of her self through the learning of language.

The baby's need of mother steadily develops into desire for other through the response she garners and receives from the mother. The mother's response consists of her speculation and/or calculations on the unknowable feelings and behaviours of the child by using learned or predetermined, competing, and intricate analytical yet strangely defensive strategies. Defences against an (im)possibly intuitive sense of what the child wants are handed down to mothers by mothers, by the social constraints of culture. The defensive first reading of mother support the new mother to make decisions out of the mother's unrelenting uncertainty of the baby's need, to make urgent sense out of aporetic gaps to mother that the baby's unknowable need continually and pressingly presents. However, our decisiveness is an illusion only temporarily relieving the tension that we feel in not knowing what the child wants. 'She's hungry,' we say when the child wants to be held. This paradoxical misreading constitutes the child's existence while she gains entry into the world of authority figures that comprise the social. As we gain the capacity to become a self, we are also bitter-sweetly subject to continuous misreadings, for better and worse, of our uniqueness by our maternal environment, by others, by language, and by the ornate social wrapping embalming our bodies in a perpetually tangled knot of misunderstanding and confusion. Our first readings are profound, if forgotten; first readings lay the grounds for how we relate to others, to external realities lived outside of the maternal relation. These readings also ground our interpretive capacity such that our primary relations invisibly guide the subsequent possible meanings we can make of the world and others.

Maternity as First Readings: Bodies in Anguish

When Adrienne Rich (1981) experiences the 'exquisite, murderous suffering' that coming to terms with her child's existence animates within, she also temporarily experiences the terror of infantile first reading. The baby's presence leaves her with little recourse but to regress into a state of not knowing what the other wants. Britzman (2009) suggests that, as with the infant, the mother is plunged back into a state of helpless dependence and fights angrily to rid herself of the hatred that dependence animates. And this confused inner-self state overwhelmed by the feelings of infantile affect is unbearable, unwieldy, and erratic, and it leads to the production of knowledge that both represents and defends against the body's feelings. To rid her self of the body's insufferable feelings, Rich produces a manifesto of woman's emancipation that has moved generations of women to thinking and acting for the first time in defence of the right to their bodies and their children. We often think that embodied writing is closer to the truth of our existence, when it might signify a defence of existence repeating the original desire of the father to misrepresent the life of woman and the child in defence of a man's self. And while the power of Rich's thought is undeniable and far reaching, it is also powerful for what it doesn't admit – that the maternal body is infinitely bound to the child. The infant's desires are so tied up in the mother's that mother cannot distinguish where her body begins and the infant's ends. Within dependent bodies, severed by sociality, the struggle to be heard, known, articulate, and survivable acts out an overwhelming passion on the pleasure and agony of dependence, in endless repetitive productions of language-instituting culture. Language and culture hold with or without mercy the body's exquisite suffering, as well as producing the source of the body's joy.

If we take the life-producing and barely known feelings of dependence as constituting the maternal relation, the suffering of bodies that are foreign to one another, we radically alter dominant social constructions of motherhood and the body. As those who have suffered with the facts of their body's revolt testify, embodiment is the body's attempt to express the body's internal struggle to reconcile itself to the fact of others, the others' language, the others' authority, the others' social constraints. If Sarah Kofman (in Derrida, 2007) wrote the body's suffering out in a philosophy of the mind that surpasses that of her male counterpoints, her autobiographical text gives us insight into how that philosophy never really addresses her woman's bodily suffering in a way that does justice to the felt life of the body (see Kofman, 1996). Language mediates unreliably our embodiments, misreads our existence, and produces something beautiful but perhaps always lacking in representation. Although art and drama might bring us closer to the truth of the body's exquisite suffering, these affective modes of symbolization are too limited by the discursive and logos-bound institutions of culture. Antonin Artaud (in Derrida, 1978b) expressed his despair with logos in the creation of the 'Theatre of Cruelty,' a movement to express the body's psychosocial revolt with social constraint. As Derrida (1978b) observes through the case of Artaud's lifelong dispute with language, the fact of the body is both necessarily and agonizingly excess to representation. We lose the ability to read excess when we become subjects of language – this originary, felt intelligence reminds us that we cannot be without a loving authority, a loving reader that both liberates and constrains our every utterance, gesture, and movement. Reading, in its primal sense-making function, bridges the inarticulable conflict of ambivalent affect. Our sense of the other allows us to receive comfort where words fail. And upon this intuitive sensing reinforced by our (m)other, prone to misreading and without distinct method, human existence depends.

Rather than focus on the body in its already formed states, as implied by the proper names baby, mother, father, etc., I want to suggest that curriculum is grounded in the body's attempt to manage, through 'first readings,' the war of epistemologies waged within and on the body's indelible surface, the skin of the flesh. Not knowing but needing to know the other's conditions of existence basic to the survival of both infant and mother is our 'first reading' of each other. Our first readings both mark and are marking our bodies with interpretations that are yet to be of reasonable use. Derrida (2007) refers to these markings as the secrets of the body that are defended against by the very words we use to make the body intelligible to ourselves and others (Butler, 2001). The secret contains the human being's very will, the body's resources, and recourse to survive. The body's epistemological defences and capacities are locked into this sensed but unknowable source of creative and destructive libidinal, affective energy that becomes distorted through the meanings given to us to rid us of the body's suffering. The child grounds her reading in her need of others to survive. The mother bases her socially informed reading in her observations of the infant's needs, reflected through her comfort or protest, pleasure or unpleasure, silence or crying. First reading through a basic, human, and affective capacity to make relations with other using the feeling power of our need for another is the primary way that the infant builds up the more sophisticated interpretive capacities for imagination and reason developed later in childhood.

By speaking to the primal bond, and at the same time, by resisting previous distinctions and (re)appropriations of motherhood and infancy, however difficult, feminist curriculum scholars might begin to look more closely at patriarchal psychosocial processes producing and reproducing common misrepresentative formations of maternal and infant subjectivity. In education, we define *curriculum* as the pedagogical project by which social objects are produced. However, we have yet to pay serious attention to examining how the mother's body, as our primary object upon which all other social texts are written and re-written, figures significantly in our body knowledge. Our phenomeno-logical and artistic expressions of embodiment, while approximating felt experience, can also defend against the truth of the body because when we write the body, when write of our body, we often foreclose the trouble we have thinking it. Those, artists and thinkers, who inhabit the affective domain of embodiment, who inhabit the insides of the flesh, are often estranged and startled by what they find. A curriculum of embodiment would support our children's and our own conflictual attempts to reconcile the unsightly feelings for and fact of our bodies with that of others. This affective reading curriculum would hold our unruly bodies gently, knowing that our bodies are both the source of and subaltern to self. Dominant representations of the body foreclose this struggle and in doing so fail to do the body justice. Our curricular knowledge is produced from the attempt and the failure to come to terms with the body always exceeding curricular thought. And if we have trouble representing our own body then it follows that represent-ing the (m)other's body is a project teeming with difficulty. The process by which the body comes to know and re-know self in relation to the other or objects forms our curriculum texts.

If feminist critiques of motherhood rethink the troubled role of women, as defined solely by the laws and guiding imperatives of all-too pervasive patriarchal, raced, heteronormative values, it overlooks how the child and the self risk being reconstituted not only by those same values but by the mother's secondary, and often overdetermined, interpretation (forced or voluntary) of those values according to her own societal and cultural norms imposed upon her within her own clan or family. As Peggy Kamuf (2000) insists, children become initiated in the 'family of man' by their constitution in cultural practices and norms through the voices of mothers, 'most often,' in the voices of mother's first reading to children (p. 19). Yet, the infant's 'first readings' of other and the world is undertheorized in feminism in favour of the mother's socially determined reading of the child. These secondary and cultur-ally conditioned readings forging 'adult' theories of woman's 'subjec-tivity,' 'agency,' 'identities,' and 'bodies,' more often than not, repeat, and sometimes with greater violence, patriarchal renderings of infancy. What would our curriculum be if we were to privilege our first infantile readings speaking the body's indeterminate 'truth' rather than socially certain, symbolic ones that silence the body and leave the body's affects wanting for expression?

Our dominant pedagogical process of misreading the infant's, the child's, the other's body continue to reproduce an unsustainable patriarchal curriculum bearing grave material effects and social inequities organizing human being and impacting upon sentient life. Consequently, it is my position that we might also think about how it is we are reading and writing our children through violating, legitimized structures of thought as imperative to personal, educational, or political interventions of feminist justice. While feminism has done much in the way of emancipating women from oppressive conditions of man-made existence, it fails, worldwide, to emancipate woman or her children from oppressive structures of thinking constituting maternity. If maternity, like culture, is on the move, it also moves and morphs according to particular constraints and conditions that seem invisible but compel us to accept doctrines and norms that often run counter to our deepest feelings and intuitions, where still reside some semblance of infantile human existence incoherently murmuring out the truth of human being.

Although my focus in this chapter is on learning to read the body of the child in relation to her mother's overdetermined responses, I want to make it clear that in learning to read our children otherwise I ask women not to forsake the mother for the sake of the child. Why must we choose, Jacqueline Rose (2003) might ask Audre Lorde (1984), between sacrificing our mothers/women and sacrificing our children? In asking us what we are doing when we put the sole burden of mother on women, Rose puts into tension, heteronormative theories and gender roles demanding the female mother be solely or even mainly responsible for the child's development. My argument in this chapter is not to shift theories of maternity from claiming woman's body to claiming responsibility for the body of child. From self-help books and instruction manuals on how to mother made by motherhood experts to the tireless and seemingly obsessive advising by mothers and mothers-in-law on what and how to 'do mommy,' mothers are constantly mothering their children with other feminine-inflecting patriarchal voices in their ears. A reconstituting of motherhood as a maternal environment, made of many, often competing, political, psychosocial, and cultural forces, can support mothers and/or primary caregivers to be, in Winnicott's (1953) words, 'good enough' in their individual practices with their children. Rearranging motherhood is not easily resolved by co-sharing the burden of child-rearing with men or by upholding the existence of queer or mixed-race families that disturb the Western heteronormative family narrative. Our modern, Western educational institutions of modern life will continue to strain to raise generations of children whose family structures belie that of the modern nuclear family, as long as the institution of motherhood remains bound to totalizing patriarchal, culture-hazing imperatives. Reconceptualizations of motherhood might take into its dominant account, as Spivak (1999) writes, the spectrum of lived experiences of motherhood and child care, giving to de-stable dominant embodiments of mother normatively instituted by and in the family of white man. A consideration of these lived experiences in relation to the other means that we are bound to consider the pedagogical practices of motherhood and family in other cultures or family arrangements, where mothering practices differ radically from and often put into question the gender roles and arrangements dominantly espoused by the values of the Western nuclear family.

In my own work, I resist conceiving the mother or the child as separate subjectivities, bodies, or even as a subject-position in and of itself. At the same time, in seeing the naming of 'mother' as a moment or an instance in the history of human relations as inevitable – and at the same time untenable – for an other-oriented maternity, I want to avoid mistaking the proximal, shuttling space of relation to and from the mother as the mother herself (Spivak, 2003). Jacqueline Rose (2003) writes, 'We try to limit the damage, we protect ourselves from the *felt* danger, by fleshing out our anxiety, giving that zone of anguish a name: femininity, non-language, body. But the name we give it before all others, the one we really hold answerable for it, is the mother' (pp. 158–159, emphasis added).

So, perhaps the anxiety, and not the name mother, or by consequence, woman, should be shared by all – mother, father, child, and society. Motherhood, then, is not a person nor tied to women's bodies but a curricular process that is felt in the transference circulating between the bodies of the infant and primary other(s) and constituted within the socializing processes that institute the infant's becoming human through making uneasy relations between affect and emotion, self and other, language and the social. Troubling maternity is a shared responsibility to and for, in Judith Butler's (2001) words, more 'just' readings of the infant's body. This just reading of the infant takes the plea of: 'Read me, hold me, but don't crush me, don't get too close. Above all, don't think you know, and I would want to add, don't expect to get it right' (Rose, 2003, p. 164).

The fact that we are born dependent on (m)others institutes an ethical demand in the maternal relation that cannot be ignored or reduced when supporting the child's being in a world of others that she did not create but with which she must contend. If the maternal is at once a relation and an environment, that mercifully holds the child's body, then our first readings of the dependent being we hold and represent are critical to how human beings, body, and relations materialize. These first readings hold the promise for the child's bringing newness to the world. They can also reorient how we think of education as of the mind leaving the body's complicated struggle to be heard out of our curricular and social justice imperatives.

Rich's (1981) exquisite suffering in facing those of her radically dependent children is not the sole domain of mothers. Teachers, helping professionals, and anyone who is charged with the difficult demand of having to care for the other's vulnerable, different, diseased, aging, dependent body are also faced with this suffering (Britzman, 2009). And yet, as helping professionals and artists, we have yet to create a social, curricular space that makes room to engage in conversations, learning, and creative acts that consider how the body is both the source of our greatest human achievements and failures. Feeling curriculum, curriculum that tends to the process by which each child learns to manage the affective excesses of the body in relation to those imagined in the body of (m)others might develop our capacity to rethink the maternal relation and the duty that curriculum has to lovingly serve the entry of the alien, fragile, and newly arrived creature into the often inhospitable territory of existential, human representation. Unseeing, babbling, with limited mobility, without definable recourse to fight or flight but teeming with unimaginable intelligence and mutability, we are born and will die in accordance with the mercy of others, a fleeting feeling that others will lovingly read and hold us without need for knowing, understanding, or mastering our traitorous, insatiable body's demands. Feeling curriculum might produce an education that supports the child's precarious entry and existence into the strangeness of having to reconcile the self to a life lived in a body indelibly read and worded by others.

Notes

1 I use *mother* to refer to mother as normatively conceived in the female form. Where I use *(m)other* I refer to the others that comprise the maternal environment, and they may or may not be women.

References

Arendt, H. (1993). *Between past and present*. New York: Penguin.

Britzman, D.P. (2009). Love's impression: A psychoanalytic contribution. *British Journal of Sociology of Education, 30* (6), 773–787.

Butler, J. (2001). Doing justice to someone: Sex reassignment and allegories of transexuality. *GLQ: A Journal of Lesbian and Gay Studies, 7* (4), 621–636.

Daly, Mary (1978*). Gyn/Ecology: The metaethics of radical feminism*. Boston, MA: Beacon Press.

Cixous, H. (1976). The laugh of the Medusa. Trans. K. Cohen & P. Cohen. *Signs: Journal of Women in Culture and Society, 1* (4), 875–893.

Coleman, D. (2009). *In bed with the Word: Reading, spirituality and cultural politics*. Edmonton: University of Alberta Press.

Derrida, J. (1976). *Of grammatology*. Trans. G. Spivak. Baltimore, MD: Johns Hopkins University Press.

Derrida, J. (1976/1995). Between brackets I. Trans. P. Kamuf. In E. Weber (Ed.), *Points . . . : Interviews, 1974–1994* (pp. 5–29). Stanford, CA: Stanford University Press.

Derrida, J. (1978a). Violence and metaphysics: An essay on the thought of Emmanuel Levinas. Trans. A. Bass. In *Writing and difference* (pp. 79–153). Chicago, IL: University of Chicago Press.

Derrida, Jacques. (1978b). The theater of cruelty and the closure of representation. Trans. A. Bass. In *Writing and Difference* (pp. 232–250). Chicago, IL: University of Chicago Press.

Derrida, J. (1989/1995). Eating well or the calculation of the subject. Trans. P. Conner & A. Ronell. In E. Weber (Ed.), *Points . . . : Interviews, 1974–1994* (pp. 255–287). Stanford, CA: Stanford University Press.

Derrida, J. (1995). Archive fever: A Freudian impression. Trans. E. Prenowitz. Chicago, IL: University of Chicago Press.

Derrida, J. (2007). Introduction. In T. Albrecht, G. Albert, & E. Rottenberg (Eds.), *Selected writings. Sarah Kofman* (pp. 1–36). Stanford, CA: Stanford University Press

Freud, S. (1999/2008). *The interpretation of dreams*. Trans. J. Crick. London: Oxford University Press.

Grumet, M.R. (1988). *Bitter milk: Women and teaching*. Amherst, MA: University of Massachusetts Press.

Kamuf, P. (2000). The ends of reading. [Electronic Version] Paper presented at the Book/Ends Conference, University of Alabama. Retrieved 29 January 2010, from http://www-rcf.usc.edu/kamuf/text.html.

Klein, M. (1928/1987). Early stages of the Oedipus conflict. In J. Mitchell (Ed.), *The selected Melanie Klein* (pp. 69–83). New York: Free Press.

Klein, M. (1935/1987). A contribution to the psychogenesis of manic-depressive states. In J. Mitchell (Ed.), *The selected Melanie Klein* (pp. 115–145). New York: Free Press.

Kofman, S. (1996). *Rue Ordener, Rue Labat.* Trans. A. Smock. Lincoln, NB: University of Nebraska Press.

Kristeva, J. (2001). *Melanie Klein.* New York: Columbia University Press.

Lévinas, E. (1969). *Totality and infinity: An essay on exteriority.* Trans. A. Lingis. Pittsburgh, PA: Duquesne University Press.

Lorde, A. (1984). *Sister outsider.* Berkeley, CA: Crossing Press.

Merleau-Ponty, M. (1962). *Phenomenology of perception.* Trans. C. Smith. New York: Humanities Press.

Mishra Tarc, A. (2007). *Literacy of the other: Making relations to language.* Unpublished manuscript.

Pinar, W. (1998). *Curriculum: Toward new identities.* New York: Garland.

Rich, A. (1981). *Of woman born: Motherhood as experience and institution.* London: Virago.

Rose, J. (2003). On knowledge and mothers: On the work of Christopher Bollas. In *On not being able to sleep: Psychoanalysis and the modern world* (pp. 149–166). Princeton, NJ: Princeton University Press.

Springgay, S., &Freedman, D. (2007). *Curriculum and the cultural body.* New York: Peter Lang.

Spivak, G. (1981) French feminism in an international frame. *Yale French Studies, 62,* 154–184.

Spivak, G. (1999). *A critique of postcolonial reason: Toward a history of the vanishing present.* Cambridge, MA: Harvard University Press

Spivak, G. (2003). *Death of a discipline: The Wellek Library lectures.* New York: Columbia University Press.

Winnicott, D. (1953). Transitional objects and transitional phenomena. *International Journal of Psychoanalysis, 34,* 89–97.

PART 4

Curricular Response

19 M/othering as Un(der)studied in Curriculum Studies: An Epilogue

ERIK MALEWSKI

> The lack of consensus on the significance of the maternal in education is very conspicuous, both in the public forum and in academia. An examination of contemporary discourse on the subject reveals responses ranging from complete rejection (often in the form of omission) to ambivalence, celebration, and radical reconstruction, depending upon who is speaking.
>
> – Kathleen Casey, 'Teacher as Mother'

In an ironic turn, the notion that subjects not only produce positions but also positions produce subjects has become 'commonplace' knowledge within curriculum studies. How the discourses of education collude to produce 'the vast map of normalcy' (Britzman, 1995, p. 152) regarding race, class, gender, and sexuality, however, endures in the present moment as unstudied and understudied curriculum. This edited collection, then, could not come at a more opportune time. With the resurgence of a 'strict father model' of teaching and learning, with its audit cultures and disciplining gazes, mothering curriculum functions as a much needed counter-force or alternate reading, a sort of 'intimate revolt' (Kristeva, 2002) towards other ways of thinking about becoming and learning-in-the-making. Yet, to study the subject of mothering after discomposing the subject and the demise of truth content – the effort to highlight in original truth a mobility, 'an instability that opens it to variant translations and interpretations' (Lather, 2000, p. 154) – might seem like a contradictory and, therefore, unreasonable thing to do. Why embrace the concept of mothering and risk perpetuating asymmetries in gender and class privilege present in both homes and schools to also read against it, to discompose it, and highlight its constructed character? What the authors of this collection do well is to engender complicated conversations within curriculum studies that illustrate how concepts such as mothering enable dialogue and action, while at the same time, they mark the very horizon of thought and deed. If there is a theme that runs through these essays, it is that in reading with and against the notion of mothering one might find the promise of a democracy yet-to-come.

Given their work on the curricular body and embodied experiences, we should not be surprised at Stephanie Springgay and Debra Freedman's latest collection focused on mothering, another dimension of embodied experience. Rather than dismiss mothering as a relic of a bygone era, they continue in this collection crafting and collecting compelling work that disrupts the search for essential qualities of the embodied mother and trouble commonplace ideas and notions of bodies, gender, performance, and educative experiences, this time bringing together authors who focus on notions of birthing, circumcision, mourning, and witnessing to homemaking, intimacy, and aggression. So common to conventional educational discourse focused on that one right strategy that – or individual (superman?) who – might save us, these editors bring together ideas and authors that challenge fabrications of individual self-presence separate from context, that a practice that happened over 'here' can be replicated over 'there,' and that testing and standards can relieve our 'fear of chaos in the classroom' and 'shame at being treated with paternalistic condescension' (Taubman, 2009, p. 128).

By conceptualizing motherhood at the intersection of processes so unique that they cannot be reduced to a single storyline and also so interrelated that they cannot be conceived of as disparate elements, the work included here confounds canonization. Refusing an addendum approach to reconceptualizing the field where mothering is one of a multitude of 'add ons' to the curricular core, Springgay and Freedman open sites in which to investigate how the narrative structures of education and the discourse of knowledge production are implicated in the creation of gendered, raced, classed, sexed, and variously abled subjects. Working spaces in-between and parallel – that is, working the unknown as a way of knowing and performativity alongside identity – they have assembled authors who problematize the notion of motherhood but also refuse to give up on mothering as a viable political, cultural, and economic project. Thinking messy over tidy, complexity over simplicity, and contamination over purity, Springgay and Freedman join their authors in asking readers to confront the recursive nature of curriculum issues such that the questions asked disrupt the very categories that make 'seminal texts' and paternal plot lines not only intelligible but commonplace, possibly the only thing imaginable.

The 'Good' Mother/'Bad' Mother: The Traffickers and Intractable Teachers of Education

> Bearing the credentials of a profession that claims the colors of motherhood and then systematically delivered the children over to the language, rules, and relations of the patriarchy, teachers understandably feel uneasy, mothers suspicious.
>
> – Madeleine Grumet, *Bitter Milk*

A forum for disciplining seemingly intractable teachers, producing teacher-selves who are calculable and self-regulating, what is before us in the age of data-driven instruction is a form of matricide, the refusal to grant mothers the status of subjects and knowers. Over a decade ago, Petra Munro (1998) described this as 'dutiful' mothers and daughters trafficking in the ideas of the father, securing his place as the originator (p. 272), and being rewarded as 'conduits' for patriarchy. Writing of the audit explosion that started in the 1980s and 1990s, Peter Taubman (2009) reminds us that the paternal lenses that frame education are not merely instilled from the outside by conservative government and business leaders, but promulgated by education scholars who wish to raise the professional standing of teachers, remove uncertainty from teaching, and recover from the shame associated with low status and low pay (i.e., recover from the 'feminization' of teaching). He writes of such trafficking as embedded in the gendered discourse of accountability and transferred from the scene of business to schooling by some of education's most esteemed scholars: 'Sounding like George Lakoff's (2004) "strict father" of the Right, Ratvich argued students "hunger for structure, discipline, and more rigorous standards" (1995, p. xiv). "Much of the movement for standards," Ratvich claimed aims, "to reestablish priorities by clarifying that the schools [are] responsible, first and foremost, for developing the intelligence of their students" (p. 5). Not, mind you, responsible for providing the conditions under which students can pursue

intellectual work but for the intellectual development of students'
(Taubman, 2009, p. 109).

Thinking of protection from the 'strict father,' thinking familial
knowing as the first form of knowing and, in this sense, re-membering
my own mother as central to my autobiography, mothering has offered
me a way to re-envision the future through reinterpreting the past. It offered me, in the language of Virginia Woolf, a 'room of my own,' away
from paternal discipline and order to create and invent out of emotion and intuition. By doing so, what has come to the surface in my
own thinking is an alternate way to read public education's incitement
towards extra-familial knowledge and aggression towards mothers
as our first teachers – an assumed, if implicit, rendition of education's
mechanism for reading the larger world. As a young boy, it was my
mother who helped me along my journey towards self-understanding
and, consequently, engendered in me a more hospitable disposition towards the other. As a young man coming to terms with his sexuality, it
was my mother who was my biggest advocate and protector, the one
who transgressed the private-public divide to become a social activist and change agent in the home and state and federal government,
spurred on by a sense that it was her duty to change the world in order
to protect her son from harm. Divided duty of home and public was
not distraction but the source of her knowing and becoming. You see,
mothers in my family have for generations held extraordinary power:
running households; working outside the home; taking care of the
emotional, spiritual, intellectual, and physical needs of both female and
male family and friends; and ensuring children and youth have relationships with their family and, therefore, know where they came from
and from whom they came. Knowing the network of relations among
which I grew up and now live allows me the safety to explore my subjectivity, to venture out into other places of learning, to re-turn to my
past to think it anew and, accordingly, to think my future differently. It
was these maternal forces that allowed me to move in excess of limits
on potentialities, movements, and directions, to 'restore to the learning self the experience and rich indeterminacy of the social (political)
body' (Ellsworth, 2004, p. 131). By this, I mean mothering engendered
embodied knowing and movement along passages between one form
of knowing and another, 'the qualitative transformation of self and of
self in relation to another' (p. 131).

Yet, in schooling, the experiences of mothers and mothering and,
indeed, the relationships between mothers and children as crucial,

valid sites of learning, knowing, and being were not made explicit. All around me – hidden in plain sight – mothering curriculum gave fellow students and myself sustenance in the form of textured insights about relationships, love, and living; a packed lunch; a loving touch; a bandage applied to a tender wound; an intellectual insight; and a listening ear. Rarely acknowledged and, when it was, attributed value as a vehicle for carrying out the ideas of the father, thus securing the position of males as creators, students are moved towards dismissive readings of motherly knowledge. As Jennifer Gilbert (2009) all too aptly notes, 'Reading allows one to imagine worlds beyond the confines of one's own ... But this venture out into the world acts as a violent repudiation of history' (p. 67), to which I add domestic history and knowing. The school curriculum pulled me from the study of both the pleasures and limitations of family life to a larger world that, for the most part, dismissed familial knowing. As in so many other situations, mothers became subjects of the school curriculum only when they aided and abetted paternal plot lines and public school experiences focused on control, individualization, and advancement.

Most recently, the predominantly female teaching force is caught in an unwinnable paradox: they are not to be trusted with the education of our children because they have failed to produce functioning citizens and workers in a global economy. Yet, they are also held to an unattainable ego ideal whereby the future is solely in the hands of our nation's teachers. This strange brew of celebration and demonization of teachers has its origins in the subjugation of mothering as a valid site of learning.

Engendering the Public-Private Split: The Maternal as the Organizer of the Paternal

Social arrangements in the modern West require of the mother that she deliver both male and female children to the world of the fathers, to the world of public authority and civic power.

– Jo Anne Pagano, 'Teaching Women'

Lest I make things sound too intentional, too planned, the silencing of mothers is not the result of official sanctions that deem maternal curriculum of little worth. There has never been a need for such unequivocal declarations ('mothers are not worthy'). Rather, such silences are woven into the very conditions that make public education possible. That is, 'public' education could not exist until familial, domestic ways of knowing and being were rendered non-knowledge (how would one test for it anyway?). Public/official knowledge had to be differentiated from private/informal knowledge and the character of that knowledge – intuitive, emotional, feeling, relational – as it was associated with domesticity, femininity, and motherhood – had to be rendered suspect and unreliable. Understudied and unstudied knowledge – and the fact that in 'present moments' maternal knowledge remains so – speaks to repression and the silencing of voices that nevertheless might speak if we just crafted the ears to hear, if we might intuit our being, and feel the vibrations of our hearing and doing.

Paul de Man described this phenomenon of understudied and unstudied histories using the visual terms of blindness and insight, 'where the necessary exclusion is the very organizer of whatever insights might be made and critical texts always turn back on the very things they denounce/renounce' (in Lather, 2007, p. vii). That mother's knowledge remains invisible among curriculum's objects is evident in all that constitutes schooling, never worthy enough of inclusion but always worthy enough 'as dutiful daughters [and mothers who] ensure the orderly transmission of property (knowledge) and title through the paternal line' (Munro, 1998, p. 272). This invisibility/hypervisibility is a painful and constant reminder that the curriculum field is predicated on gendered forms of subjugation, erasure, and blindness. This subjugation is not absence, however; it is the unknowable, unworthy, and non-knowledge that channels and programs paternal intelligibility.

Accordingly, the authors in this volume ascribe through their work that to do curriculum theorizing is to work the ruins of epistemological violence towards other ends. To state it another way, 'In human processes that are continuous across artificial categorical divides, such as the learning self in the making, all aspects of the process are available, including those that fall into the gaps between or circumscribe known meaning and identities' (Ellsworth, 2004, p. 129). Within such an understanding, power might be conceptualized as the actions and conditions that limit potential, direction, and movement. It is through the appropriation of the very expression of the unrealized and unthinkable. The limits of the motherly body and variation within a given situation or context might be understood as the limits of relationality. Paternal curriculum must operate as containers that direct or channel the potential and relational among and across cultural boundaries.

For oppression to occur, education must have the capacity to usurp matriarchal knowing and via a series of 'cultural membranes' express patriarchal potential. This has historically required teaching and learning to encourage mothers 'to distrust that power which rises from our deepest and non-rational knowledge' (Lorde, 1984, p. 53), to doubt or suppress those things that mothers do 'to make our lives and the lives of our children richer and more possible,' (p. 55) for expression to remain captured in pre-constructed cultural frameworks. The limits of new and different encounters and interactions might result from contemporary preoccupations with empiricism, behaviouralism, and capitalism that restrain the flow of ideas, thoughts, and bodies. By way of problematizing these dispositions towards knowledge production – the performative, feminist, narrativist approaches towards mothering that make up this collection – reveal that what might seem 'normal' systems of knowledge are actually contingencies.

According to Anne Winfield (2007), 'unexamined concepts such as "the past" are misleading and entrenched in specific dominant cultural approaches which seek to define the present by controlling what we think of the past' (p. 18). Her point is that curriculum subjects – the invention of public education in the image of white heterosexual middleclass males – were made possible by the invalidation, dismissal, and erasure of the other – in this case, the maternal self. The other acts as a frame, an organizer for channelling educational insights, and a device for evaluating knowledge for its worth. The appearance of unity, coherence, and order found in developmental theories, for example, does not have a direct relationship to the empirical world but necessitates the subjugation of contradiction, paradox, and disjuncture to give the illusion of causality and agreed-upon truths. The narratives of working-class mothers; lesbian, bisexual, transgendered, and intersexed mothers; differently abled mothers; international cross-cultural mothers; and mothers of colour as social bodies with potential in combining, interacting, and related in innumerable ways must be limited for the maintenance of developmental interpretative storylines. The authors of this collection, then, employ understudied and unstudied perspectives to trouble neat and tidy developmental theories focused on 'corrective' readings of mothering and 'appropriate' theories of motherhood.

The idea, of course, is not that developmental theories have no merit, but that absent the practice of reading with and against their claims in order to highlight partiality, investments, half-truths, and gender positioning – the sorts of ideas that emerge through successive processes of knowledge production and dissemination tend to subjugate and erase the other. The genderless, classless, raceless subject underwrites epistemological violence, channelling and particularizing mothering and parental roles, othering educative experiences and knowledge associated with the maternal body. A 'sheer sentimentality' about women bringing nurturing capacities to the schools, Grumet (1988) notes, 'it denied both the aspirations of the common school movement and the motives of those women who came to its classrooms in order to escape the horrifying isolation of domestic exile' (p. 56). Not only does Grumet's point speak to troubling knowledge and its romantic reinterpretation, it also speaks to the gendered character of everyday practices in contemporary schooling: that the individualized busy work of test preparation continues unabated, as does the assault on familial relationships, intersubjectivity, and home-knowledge, and domesticity cannot be disconnected from the othering of mothering. Re-membering requires modulating curricular variations by facilitating encounters between bodies (it should be noted it can regularize by disciplining or canonizing as well), thereby engendering new combinations and interactions with forces that are in excess of extant parameters of relationality. This work of relation and re-membering is taken up by the authors in this volume.

Aporias of Mothering: Discomposure and Recomposure in Curriculum Studies

The tension that marks this edited collection emerges from the need to offer an array of feasible alternate readings of mothering, from diverse races, ethnicities, regions, social classes, sexualities, gender identities, abilities, and so on, and concurrently discompose these categories and frameworks that essentialize mothering, that enable its subjugation and erasure. The authors of this collection work in what Derrida terms 'doubled writing,' forms of critique that are neither strictly inside nor strictly outside education, embracing a sort of fractal onto-epistemology; permutations link up, inflect relationalities, but nevertheless retain their uniqueness. Like a breath of fresh air with the resurgence of outcomes-based everything, these authors do well to avoid unifying theories and practices, ones so common in school curriculum scholarship, with the recognition that knowledge and being are complex and continually in the making. They are contradictory and partial but no more partial than in any of the range of gendered positions; these partial accounts seek to account for such complexity. To illustrate how reading with and against is both illogical and limiting, and nevertheless necessary, I briefly explain the analytical basis for each.

To write mothering into the curriculum has been the aim of prior curriculum studies scholars (see Grumet, 1988). This is important work and yet scholarship that adds the educational experiences of women and mothers, and other marginalized groups, as addendums, does little to discompose mainstream canonical or disciplinary models. That's where this text comes in. The issue that undergirds this collection 'is how to think when the generation of supplements so swells existing frameworks as to collapse canonical models under the weight of their own attempts to represent' (Malewski, 2010, pp. 518–519). This effort to undertake a compensatory history of mothering is necessary but it is not enough; it cannot displace everyday gendered educational practices that engender hierarchical differentiations and the public-private split that underwrites the very genesis of public schooling in so many nations.

As Casey (1990) explained over 20 years ago, while capturing the lived histories of teacher-mothers is essential work, diverse narratives of the maternal do not guarantee that the hierarchical relations of teaching or what counts as education will be problematized and discomposed. In short, the paternal approach to storytelling, as critiqued by Munro (1998), remains intact: manifest destiny, a metaphysics of presence, separation of animate from inanimate, and plot lines predicated on continuously unfolding tales of progress, growth, and development remain unquestioned. As a result, mothering, when maternal narratives are essentialized, retains the semblance of omnipresence, stories told by invisible narrators freed from the conditions that undergird intelligibility. Stated another way, such an approach to mothering risks that the empirical is all there is; the very categories that have blinded us to mothering curriculum remain undisputed.

So, what would it mean to think discomposure and recomposure differently? It would mean, in part, to think of it as a doubled movement that works the constitution of thinkable thoughts on mothering against the ways in which such thoughts limit the horizon of intelligibility and hence their discomposure. As this edited collection suggests, there is more work to be done on diverse representations of motherhood and issues of embodiment. Stories of educative experiences surrounding lesbian motherhood, transgendered mothering,

migration and childhood, performativity and family violence, breastfeeding and perception, 'ableism' and outlooks, and technology and
parenting must be told as forms of proliferation – multiplying alternative feasible readings of what it means to mother. In this sense, they
work as subaltern counter-texts, spinning off supplementary accounts
that fragment and discompose dominant narratives regarding motherhood and parenting. The perspectives shared here have implications for our public and private lives and the very terms by which
such a categorical divide has been created and maintained. This is a
political text.

Re-reading My Reading: Why This Text Is Un(der)studied Curriculum (on the Question of the Still and Yet Again in the Struggle for Discourse and Language)

In the introduction to the *Curriculum Studies Handbook: The Next Moment* (2009), which I edited, I claim that one of seven through-lines
that mark the collection involves understudied and unstudied histories. If asked, I would position this collection within that through-line,
although it is clear that all seven through-lines characterize this collection, from the infusion of theory and research from other fields to
reading historical work in the field differently. My reasons for positioning this collection within this through-line are multiple. As I read
through these 18 essays for the first time, I was at first taken aback
by the importance of the ideas contained in this text and the courage it takes to write personally about such intimate matters that range
from family violence and feelings of inadequacy to complications with
breastfeeding and questions of circumcision. As I reread the chapters
for themes and connections, I noticed a number of authors explored
the difficulty of the writing itself, of finding a language with which
to speak. That there remains, nearly 25 years after the publication of
Madeleine Grumet's *Bitter Milk: Women and Teaching*, limited discourse
and language to address the diverse experiences and perceptions,
performances and relationalities of mothers and mothering both surprised and troubled me. I asked myself, how can this be? How can it
be that decades after the reconceptualization of the curriculum field
and the infusion of feminist perspectives that curriculum scholars still
find that there is an absence of language and discourse that speaks to
educational experiences that range from birthing and breastfeeding to
transgendered parenting and family violence? This collection offers

a strategic function in providing nuanced ideas and perspectives on mothering to the curriculum field.

In her text, *Crusade for Justice: The Autobiography of Ida B. Wells* (1970), Wells speaks to her experiences with 'divided duty,' particularly the struggles she had raising four children and maintaining a commitment to end lynching and racial injustice. Splitting her time between her personal life and public commitments, Susan B. Anthony, among others, characterized Wells as 'distracted' and accused her of abandoning the movement to improve the lives of African Americans. Wells described at length how she felt pulled between the needs of her husband and children and civic engagement for social justice. If the work included in these chapters is an accurate indication, issues of divided duty remain a part of the mothering curriculum. Authors speak to the weight of cultural expectations that mothers be selfless and place the needs of their children first without remorse or regret. Speaking as both children of mothers and mothers of children, the authors challenge circumscribed identities for mothers, speaking to mothering as constituted by failures, regrets, ambivalences, multiplicities, half-truths, and unknowns. Leah Fowler wonders about the implications of mothering metaphors for supervising pre-service teachers. Aparna Mishra Tarc describes how patriarchy overwrites the mother-child relationship. Rebecca Lloyd and Karleen Pendelton Jiménez share narratives of breastfeeding and emergent knowledge through bodily experience. In each of these, becoming mother is neither a mere recovery of lived experience nor an issue of shifting or creating language. Rather, both approaches alone are problematic when we consider that what we know of mothering in the curriculum field comes to us through the scene of writing. These authors ask that we attend to the contours of the stories shared, the way mothering is presented as evidence of how mothering becomes thinkable through speech and writing.

Epitomized in Jake Burdick and Jonel Thaler's chapter on regimes of truth and parental consumption, images of the comfortable middle-class life made possible via commodity fetishism, authors in this collection speak of mothering as related to but also in excess of the marketplace and techno-rational discourse. Kathleen Gallagher speaks to the social structures, cultural scripts, and biology of lesbian motherhood. A mechanism for expending a different sort of capital, Nicolas Ng-A-Fook engages in memory work regarding the complicated and situational nature of oppression, re-collecting how he responded to racist comments by deploying class privilege. Debra Freedman describes her trials and tribulations associated with the religious tradition of male circumcision. Jennifer Eisenhauer analyses the discourse of international cross-cultural adoption.

In each of these essays, the authors are either critical of or ambivalent towards techno-rational thinking. There is anxiety and suspicion of developmental theories of latching and breastfeeding. Stories of adoption are analysed for their absences and constructions of parenting and the motivations for adopting a child that is not one's own. Learning-in-the-making and being and becoming eclipse stage theories or concerns over outcomes or best practices. Embodiment becomes a question of materiality – of touch, smell, sight, and sound in becoming that is not individualized and converted to numerical representation, but co-created in spaces between bodies. Authors, such as Heather Burns, explore memory by way of the shadows that obscure as much as they illuminate, an image not unlike de Man's (1983) notion of blindness and insight, which I explore earlier in this epilogue. For the authors of this collection, it is not enough to develop a techno-rational discourse of mothering. To borrow from Audre Lorde, such an attempt risks poor translations of the erotic into the pornographic. Rather, embodied, relational, affective, conjectural ways of thinking must be explored, created, and moved into the field of curriculum studies.

Against lovely texts as those that reinforce what we think we want to know in what we read, this collection evokes troubling, difficult knowledge. B. Stephen Carpenter II writes e-mails to a daughter not yet born into a world where he fears digital divides and 'digital substitution for interpersonal relationships of physical bodies,' particularly how it is she will be constructed in relation to the technology she uses. Using contemporary artwork to explore sensation and 'disgust in the maternal relationship,' Stephanie Springgay asks what it is about breast milk as the marriage of motherhood and sexuality that incites distaste. A doubled reading of transnational adoption as an act of both love and violence, Tara Goldstein speaks to the politics of parenthood and complications born of heteronormativity for a same-gender couple. Here the question becomes one of oscillation between ideal images of mothering and the maternal and ideas and thoughts that haunt us, that are difficult to think; as Heather Burns suggests, these difficult thoughts involve finding new meaning in mother-daughter relationships after loss, and as Diane Watt describes, in the exchange of the insanity and madness of public education for home schooling. Claudia

Malacrida asks what it means to be a mother in a world where mothering and ability are rarely thought together.

Thinking how to produce and learn out of stuck places in teaching and learning, the work contained herein asks educators to inquire into educative experiences and phenomena of studying but that they never think that they know what either is. For when educators think they are educators, this is precisely the moment they cease to be educators. This collection asks what it means to move on in spite of curriculum's fund of doubt, more humble and open, more determined if not hopeful, towards documenting becoming and theorizing experience.

My Hope: Birth Canals and Fallopian Tubes towards the As-of-Yet Unknown

I do think that women could make politics irrelevant by a kind of spontaneous cooperative action the likes of which we have never seen – which is so far from people's ideas of state structure or viable social structure that it seems to them like total anarchy – when what it really is, is very subtle forms of interrelation that do not follow some hierarchical pattern which is fundamentally patriarchal.

– Germaine Greer, *The Female Eunich*

My hope is that readers grapple with the implications of George Lakoff's (2004) caution regarding the invasive roots of surveillance in the image of the strict father, without regard for the field of study. To gain the capacity for reflexive teaching that allows educators to engage the complexities of relational onto-epistemological instructional practices towards more discomforting pedagogies demands troubling what Julie Maudlin implies in her exploration of discourse that equates educational transformation with penetration and control (male principle) rather than the capacity for absorption and conversion (female opening). As Springgay and Freedman describe in their introduction, theory on teaching and learning is beholden to language, to discourse that is indispensible to our knowing but contestable, a mechanism for practical change, but one that within schools has erased the maternal. A profound force in the history of the nation state, numerical conversion of lived experience has served as a mechanism in the theatre of influence in ways that map well onto the language and needs of educational policy makers. Mothering curriculum does not mean an end to the need and want of fathering, but incites a historical mapping, a troubling that renders all positions suspect, complicit, with the maternal and as potentially dangerous as the paternal. As Ugena Whitlock's work attests, because of the explicit intimacy of autobiography there is also the heightened risk of betrayal of trust. Refusing to situate the maternal as the good to the bad of the paternal, what would it mean for curriculum theorists to retain a mothering disposition while remaining ecstatically open to the paternal? Here the call is less for reconciliation or compromise, which all too often ends with dutiful mothers trafficking the ideas of fathers, but the need to be reflexive about disjunctive frames towards as-of-yet readings and interventions.

What would it mean, for example, to think mothering towards economics and funding shifts – economic analyses coupled with mothering curricula towards the sorts of justice and policy formations that Aliya Rahman called for in a 2010 *Journal of Curriculum Theorizing* conference session? Thinking of economics as a knowing practice that curriculum studies knows little about, she asks that we participate in the fields of business, to take up space within them, to reinvent them, to make them better. Transferred to the scene of mothering curriculum, Rahman might well be arguing for a shift from father-breadwinner to mother-purse strings. That is, she might be arguing for the move towards more livable, sustainable economic practices with an understanding of the monumental and contested history of the interrelationship of the material and resource allocation theories, a move towards a broadening of maternal democracy.

My hope is that readers grasp how this text speaks to the spectra of thinking in the ways identity categories structure and mark the excesses of our knowing. To examine the gendered and familial dimensions of our categories – disciplinary and otherwise – is to trouble scientific sterility in the house of hard science, the house of the father. To employ mothering subjectivities towards more fertile grounds for bearing witness, doubled and divided, relational theories of teaching and learning fruitful by way of hysterical onto-epistemologies might move us towards something other to the other of staid paternal plot lines and the tyranny of techno-rational lesson plans. Elsewhere I termed this sort of idea a commitment to curriculum-in-the-making (see Malewski, 2009), curriculum as the practice of symbolic re-representation and material re-distribution, a good tool to think with rather than the project of mastery in the house of the master. In excess of gender and the maternal as variables, this collection is about how gender and familial relations shape what is possible to name in thinking educative experiences. Key to this work, a marker of this text, are notions of assembling that provide non-reductionist frameworks for the troubled and troubling ways that various differences interrelate and shift across the contingencies of past, present, and future to shape the infinite aspects of our lives.

Finally, my hope is that readers will begin to think about questions of legitimate knowledge or the field's focus on (un)worthy knowledge. In her 1997 text, *Teaching Positions: Difference, Pedagogy, and the Power of Address,* Elizabeth Ellsworth speaks to the enabling and constraining effects of imagined audiences, the place of power in crafting feasible interpretations of events, and the ethical and political implications of our onto-epistemological choices. 'Performative pedagogy,' she asserts, 'strives not for Truth, but political and social response-ability, credibility, and usefulness-in-context, and in relation to its particular "audience" of students' (p. 162). Ellsworth's concern is that educational discourses frame teaching as a representational practice, legitimate to the extent it can strive to be truthful and accurate across time and context. Of course, Ellsworth's concern over what constitutes legitimate knowing echoes earlier work by Marianne Hirsch (1989), where she reads in the work of Virginia Woolf and Adrienne Rich a sort of wavering middle passage, a movement between a past that is no longer useful and a future that remains as-of-yet unknown, a sort of thinking back through our mothers to think differently of becoming as an act of survival.

Since Herbert Spencer published the essay, *What Knowledge Is of Most Worth?,* in 1884, legitimate knowing has been a problem with which to contend, not a solution to a long-standing concern. This is the situation across the theoretical clusters of curriculum studies, where questions of legitimacy are increasingly partial, contextual, and contested. Regardless of whether it is curriculum or pedagogy, how teaching and learning bodies establish themselves as such remains at issue. Taken as a contemporary montage of sensuality, resentment, emotion, sensation, symbiosis, intimacy, somaesthetics, and so on, this collection chronicles how meaning making takes place in political contexts. Springgay and Freedman's assertion is not merely that the conditions for thought cannot be separated from the conditions of credibility. The much more significant point woven throughout this collection is that the very measure of worth regarding what are good theories of teaching and learning, the very determination of worthy educative experiences, has shifted the terms for curriculum inquiry with crucial implications for faculty, graduate students, and teachers.

During the Curriculum and Pedagogy Conference panel focused on this collection, for example, co-editor Stephanie Springgay felt compelled to note the seriousness of this work on mothering prior to my paper in which I positioned the work within the field. I don't question the wisdom of such an assertion but, rather, ask if such an assertion would be necessary if this was a collection focused on effective assessment practices in curriculum development. What makes legitimacy thinkable? This collection is a necessary challenge to the dominance of logical positivism that underwrites the quantitative tradition and the focus on procedural mimetics by seeking to expand the curriculum field to include enfleshment, embodiment, and relationality. Regarding issues of legitimacy, there is much anxiety in the curriculum field surrounding influence, disciplinarity, and canonization. Yet, theories and practices that are grounded in the assumptions of empiricism are out of sorts in a field marked by onto-epistemological indeterminacy and multiplicity where being is underway and knowledge is contested. The result is a sort of discomposure or fraying at the borders that mark the field and proliferation of perspectives such that establishing legitimacy and worth becomes a 'limit question' with regard to curriculum studies, one that continuously returns to demand attention, a question that cannot be answered in any complete or absolute sense but, nevertheless, must be approached.

In summary, proliferation of potential framings within and in excess of mothering fractures the conditions by which to make claims to legitimacy, rendering suspect bounded theories of teaching and learning, and highlights the political and gendered dimensions of canonization. Rather, then, a formula for establishing a foothold in curriculum studies, this collection situates mothering as not just one of many issues in education, but as the crux of the issue, pointing towards the very origins of the field itself: paternal claims to authority regarding knowledge worthy enough to pass on to the next generation. Here the contestation between mothering as un(der)studied curriculum and pursuits of canonization as a transfer of property reaches an apex, illuminating the need for the reader to have an understanding of legitimacy and worth as far more than a disciplinary strategy to be solved by adding a series of 'me too' addendums to the canon.

Conclusion

Peter Hlebowitsh (2010) has asserted that a new centripetal force has arisen in curriculum studies where those who historically generated divergent scholarship against the historical orthodoxy of development have themselves turned towards the search for unifying ideas and principles. Interested in an 'uncomfortable synthesis,' as if the post has now passed, I see the interest in a 'common framework' that plays a 'policing role' as a resurgent anxiety having to do with generational influence and the loss of intellectual centres. The imposition of disciplinarity, with its attention to mapping the historical depth and breadth of the field and a canon of core texts, involves not only a rejection of the difference between what happens in the field and schools but also the ideas and concepts emerging out of post-discourses, ones that include mothering. Here a focus on mapping the history of the field is problematic, I think, for its failure to account for what remains unstudied and understudied in curriculum studies.

Against this centripetal force, this collection embraces multiple ways of going about curriculum studies on the way towards a less comfortable field where we are challenged to produce and learn out of our stuck places, and undecidability over responsibility, representation, and trust mark our theory and practice. Neither synthesis nor culture war of the maternal and paternal, this is about thinking gendered positions differently, a reappropriation of a familiar (familial?) binary script to engender alternate practices of teaching and learning as spaces of relational knowing and becoming.

In such spaces, Springgay and Freedman join their authors in a central task: what does it mean to think mothering when confronted with both the loss of legitimating metanarratives and, at the same time, the surfacing of new centripetal forces? Language as entanglement in complex, dynamic systems of practices, knowledge, and multiple kinds of power, this text is an urgent call for relational pedagogies among a thousand tiny curricula, to borrow from Britzman (2002, p. 94). Here what is 'shot through ... with the positivity of a knowledge' (Foucault, 2002, p. 214) is worked in, with, and across, giving rise to new pivot points of deauthorization and reauthorization in pursuit of patterns of course that open us to 'the irreducible heterogeneity of the other' (Lather, 2006, p. 52). Confronted with the issue of teaching in present moments, to study histories that never were towards futures that have not yet come, the challenge before us is to engender different curriculum histories and engender curriculum histories differently.

Curriculum faculty and graduate students can attend to such issues by moving into the undecidability, stuck places, and troubling knowledge of these essays as fruitful sites in which to engage the knowledge they need to become part of the transformation of curriculum history. The point, of course, is that by working across the disciplines within curriculum studies, faculty and students so prepared in the intersection of the maternal with cultural, ethical, and political questions will be able to traverse the ever-changing terrain of education far beyond prescriptive models of schooling and education. Foregrounding disjunctures, foiling breakdowns, thinking in excess of containment strategies and comfort texts, the aim of this collection is the proliferation of perspectives such that more useful and relational ways of teaching and learning will come into view.

References

Britzman, D. (1995). Is there a queer pedagogy? Or, stop reading straight. *Educational Theory, 45* (2), 151–165.

Britzman, D. (2002). The death of curriculum. In W.E. Doll & N. Gough (Eds.), *Curriculum visions* (pp. 92–101). New York: Peter Lang.

de Man, P. (1983). *Blindness and insight: Essays in the rhetoric of contemporary criticism* (2nd ed.). Minneapolis, MN: University of Minnesota Press.

Casey, K. (1990). Teacher as mother: Curriculum theorizing in the life histories of contemporary women teachers. *Cambridge Journal of Education, 20* (3), 301–321.

Ellsworth, E. (1997). *Teaching positions: Difference, pedagogy, and the power of address.* New York: Teachers College Press.

Ellsworth, E. (2004). *Places of learning: Media, architecture, pedagogy.* New York: Routledge.

Foucault, M. (2002). *Archeology of knowledge.* New York: Routledge.

Gilbert, J. (2009). Reading histories: Curriculum theory, psychoanalysis, and generational violence. In E. Malewski (Ed.), *Curriculum studies handbook: The next moment* (pp. 63–72). New York: Routledge.

Greer, G. (2001). *The female eunich.* New York: Farrar, Straus, & Giroux.

Grumet, M.R. (1988). *Bitter milk: Women and teaching.* Amherst, MA: University of Massachusetts Press.

Hirsch, M. (1989). *The mother/daughter plot: Narrative, psychoanalysis, feminism.* Bloomington, IN: Indiana University Press.

Hlebowitsh, P. (2010). Centripetal thinking in curriculum studies. *Curriculum Inquiry, 40* (4), 503–513.

Kristeva, J. (2002). *Intimate revolt: The powers and limits of psychoanalysis.* Trans. J. Herman. New York: Columbia University Press.

Lakoff, G. (2004). *Don't think of an elephant: Know your values and frame the debate.* White River Junction, VT: Chelsea Green Publishing.

Lather, P. (2000). Reading the image of Rigoberta Menchú: Undecidability and language lessons. *Qualitative Studies in Education, 13* (2), 153–162.

Lather, P. (2006). Paradigm proliferation as a good thing to think with: Teaching research in education as a wild profusion. *International Journal of Qualitative Studies in Education, 19* (1), 35–57.

Lather, P. (2007). *Getting lost: Feminist efforts toward a double(d) science.* Albany, NY: State University of New York Press.

Lorde, A. (1984). *Sister outsider.* Berkeley, CA: Crossing Press.

Malewski. E. (2009). Curriculum-in-the-making. *Journal of Curriculum Theorizing, 25* (3), 1–6.

Malewski, E. (2010). Proliferation as more and other to mutuality and synthesis within curriculum studies: A response to Hlebowitsh. *Curriculum Inquiry, 40*(4), 514–526.

Munro, P. (1998). Engendering curriculum history. In W. Pinar (Ed.), *Curriculum: Toward new identities* (pp. 263–294) New York: Garland.

Pagano, J. (1994). Teaching women. In L. Stone (Ed.), *The feminism reader* (pp. 252–277). New York: Routledge.

Rahman, A. (2010, October). *F-words, g-spots, and i-politics or beyond identity politics: Possibilities for global feminisms in education by women of color.* Paper presented at the annual meeting of the Journal of Curriculum Theorizing, Dayton, Ohio.

Spencer, H. (1884). *What knowledge is of most worth?* New York: J.B. Alden.

Taubman, P. (2009). *Teaching by numbers: Deconstructing the discourse of standards and accountability in education.* New York: Routledge.

Wells, I.B. (1970). *Crusade for justice: The autobiography of Ida B. Wells.* Edited by Alfreda Duster. Chicago, IL: University of Chicago Press.

Winfield, A.G. (2007). *Eugenics and education in America: Institutionalized racism and the implications of history, ideology, and memory.* New York: Peter Lang.

Contributors

Jake Burdick is a doctoral candidate in the Curriculum Studies Program at Arizona State University, where his research focuses largely on public sites of pedagogy and curriculum. He is the co-editor of *The Handbook of Public Pedagogy* and of *Complicated Conversations and Confirmed Commitments: Revitalizing Education for Democracy*. He has published scholarly writing in *Qualitative Inquiry, Curriculum Inquiry, Journal of Curriculum and Pedagogy,* and *The Sophist's Bane*, as well as creative non-fiction in the *Mississippi Review*. Currently, he is researching and writing a narrative study of the pedagogical roots of grassroots social justice activism.

B. Stephen Carpenter II is a professor of art education at Pennsylvania State University. His research is concerned with multilinear, interconnected, and interdisciplinary investigations of meaning and educational experiences as/through art education. Stephen Carpenter is the author or co-author of numerous book chapters and journal articles in art education, visual culture, and curriculum theory, and the co-author of *Interdisciplinary Approaches to Teaching Art in High School* (with Pamela G. Taylor, Christine Ballengee-Morris, and Billie Sessions) and co-editor of *Curriculum for a Progressive, Provocative, Poetic, and Public Pedagogy* (with Jennifer Milam, Stephanie Springgay, and Kris Sloan). He has served as the editor of *Art Education,* the journal of the National Art Education Association, and is currently the co-editor of the *Journal of Curriculum and Pedagogy*.

Jennifer Eisenhauer is an assistant professor of art education at Ohio State University and an affiliated faculty member in the Disability

Studies Program. Her research centres on an exploration of representations of disability in visual culture and, particularly, the cultural construction of understandings of mental health through both historical and contemporary representations. She has published book chapters and articles in journals such as *Studies in Art Education, Disability Studies Quarterly, Visual Arts Research, Journal of Cultural Research in Art Education,* and *Art Education.* Her artwork explores similar themes related to the representation of mental illness through multimedia installation and video. Jennifer Eisenhauer currently serves on the editorial board for *Studies in Art Education* and is on the review board for the *Review of Disability Studies.*

Debra Freedman is an instructor at the University of Guelph. Her research and teaching interests include curriculum theory, cultural studies, and teacher education. Her research foci with respect to curriculum studies include teacher identity and beliefs in relation to classroom practices, pedagogy, and curriculum, and the development of curriculum and pedagogical practices that sustain democratic communities. Debra Freedman is the co-editor, with Stephanie Springgay, of *Curriculum and the Cultural Body.* In her previous career, she was an associate professor of educational leadership at Pennsylvania State University.

Leah Fowler is an associate professor in the Faculty of Education at the University of Lethbridge, where she teaches undergraduates becoming teachers and experienced graduate student educators. Her book, *A Curriculum of Difficulty: Narrative Research in Education and the Practice of Teaching,* examines narrative inquiry, difficulty in teaching, teacher development (especially of experienced teachers), and curriculum studies. *Reading Canada: Teaching Fiction in Secondary Schools* (forthcoming, Oxford University Press, co-authored with W. Donawa), focuses on developing insight and empathy in young adults with great new Canadian authors. First Nations teacher education remains an abiding and central part of her work.

Caroline Fusco is an assistant professor in the Faculty of Physical Education and Health at the University of Toronto. She has published in the areas of sociology of physical activity and health; cultural geographies of children and youth's physical activity and health environments; post-structuralist and feminist theories of the body, gender, and sexuality; qualitative research methods; and equity and diversity studies in education. Her work appears in *Sport History Review, Preventive Medicine, International Review for the Sociology of Sport, Sociology of Sport Journal, Health and Place,* and the *Journal of Sport and Social Issues.* Former schoolteacher and international hockey player, and now professor – all eclipsed by being a parent!

Kathleen Gallagher is professor and Canada Research Chair in Theatre, Youth and Research in Urban Schools at the Ontario Institute for Studies in Education at the University of Toronto. She has published many books and articles on urban youth, school contexts, theatre, pedagogy, and gender, and she travels widely giving addresses and workshops for practitioners. Her books include *The Theatre of Urban: Youth and Schooling in Dangerous Times* and *Drama Education in the Lives of Girls: Imagining Possibilities.* Her edited collections include *The Methodological Dilemma: Creative, Critical and Collaborative Approaches to Qualitative Research* and *How Theatre Educates: Convergences and Counterpoints with Artists, Scholars, and Advocates.*

Tara Goldstein is a critical ethnographer, teacher educator, and playwright working in the Department of Curriculum, Teaching, and Learning at the Ontario Institute for Studies in Education at the University of Toronto. Her teaching and research interests include working towards equity in education, the schooling of immigrant adolescents in multilingual communities, schooling and sexuality, anti-homophobia education, performed ethnography, and research-informed theatre. These interests have all come together in her ten research-informed plays: *Hong Kong, Canada* (2001/2003); *Satellite Kids* (2003); *Snakes and Ladders* (2004/2010); *Alliance* (2004); *The Card* (2004); *Pound Predators* (2007); *Lost Daughter* (2008); *Zero Tolerance* (2008); *Harriet's House* (2010); and *Speaking Is a Political Act* (2010). Her latest project is a book entitled *Staging Harriet's House: Writing and Producing Research Informed Theatre* (forthcoming, Peter Lang).

Rebecca Lloyd is an assistant professor in the Faculty of Education with an interdisciplinary in education position, where she strives to further interdisciplinary understanding in health and health-related fitness pedagogy. Her background in professional ballet, human kinetics, sport psychology, and curriculum theory informs her motion-sensitive phenomenological approach to research. In collaboration with Stephen

Smith, Rebecca Lloyd has also developed a movement consciousness/ mindfulness specialization in curriculum theorizing that she typically relates to the process of becoming physically active and educated. In this chapter, however, she took a delightful turn from health and fitness to better understand ways of moving and being within a maternal and marital embrace.

Claudia Malacrida is a professor in sociology and university scholar (social sciences) at the University of Lethbridge. She publishes broadly on disability history, motherhood, and the social control of difference. Claudia Malacrida is the author of three books: *Mourning the Dreams: How Parents Create Meaning from Miscarriage, Stillbirth and Early Infant Death; Cold Comfort: Mothers, Professional Discourse, and ADD;* and *Sociology of the Body: A Reader.* Her research concerns mothering with disabilities in Canada and the United Kingdom, the history of eugenics and institutionalization in Alberta, Canada, and a critical analysis of institutional responses to children and families dealing with disabilities.

Erik Malewski is associate professor of curriculum studies at Purdue University. His research interests include post-structural approaches to curriculum theory, study abroad and internationalization, and media representations of youth and schooling. He recently published in *Curriculum Inquiry* and *Teachers College Record* and co-edited (with Nathalia Jaramillo) *Epistemologies of Ignorance in Education.*

Julie Garlen Maudlin is an assistant professor of early childhood education in the Department of Teaching and Learning at Georgia Southern University, where she works with doctoral students and teaches courses related to preschool to Grade 12 curriculum and instruction. Her research interests include cultural curriculum studies and connections between curriculum theory and educational practice. Her work has appeared in a number of edited collections, including, *Curriculum and the Cultural Body* (edited by Stephanie Springgay and Debra Freedman); *Kermit Culture: Critical Perspectives on Jim Henson's Muppets* (edited by Jennifer C. Garlen and Annisa Graham); and *Handbook of Public Pedagogy* (edited by Jenny Sandlin, Brian Schultz, and Jake Burdick). She is the co-editor of *Engaging the Possibilities and Complexities of Hope: Utterances of Curriculum and Pedagogy's Past, Present, and Future* (with Becky Stodghill and Ming Fang He). She lives in southeast

Georgia with her husband, Chris, and their three children, Taylor, James, and John.

Aparna Mishra Tarc is an assistant professor at the Faculty of Education, York University, Toronto. She teaches and carries out research in education, using literary and reading theory and resources. Her current scholarship theorizes the affective and/or aesthetic dimensions of human subject-formation through literature. Her articles appear in *Educational Theory, Educational Philosophy and Theory, Changing English, Letras y Letras,* and *Curriculum Inquiry.*

Nicholas Ng-A-Fook is an assistant professor of curriculum studies in the Faculty of Education at the University of Ottawa. As director of a Canadian Curriculum Theory Project, an associate member of the Making History/Faire Histoire Educational Research Unit, and Developing a Global Perspective for Educators organization, he continues to theorize his intellectual understandings of the field of curriculum studies as well as work towards building collaborative research partnerships with international and local indigenous communities. As such, he remains deeply indebted to colleagues, committed teacher-candidates, generous community partners, and the people who continue to support the work oriented to the future of social justice.

Karleen Pendleton Jiménez is a writer and assistant professor in the School of Education at Trent University. Her research focuses on the influences of sociocultural identities and communities on learning, broadly defined. Her recent publications include the essays 'Little White Children: Notes from a Chicana Dyke Dad' and 'Safe Walk Home: Cultural Literacy in the Regent Park Community,' and the co-edited collection (with Isabel Killoran) *'Unleashing the Unpopular': Talking about Sexual Orientation and Gender Diversity in Education.* She wrote the screenplay for the award-winning animation short *Tomboy,* based on her children's book *Are You a Boy or a Girl?* She is a stepparent of two teenagers, and gave birth to a daughter in July 2009.

Heather Pinedo-Burns is a former middle school English and preschool teacher. A doctoral candidate at Teachers College, Columbia University, her research interests include literacy, narrative inquiry, and aesthetics within qualitative research. She also instructs in-service graduate students at Pace University and Adelphi University.

Stephanie Springgay is an assistant professor in the Department of Curriculum, Teaching, and Learning at the Ontario Institute for Studies in Education at the University of Toronto. Her research focuses on embodiment and the senses in contemporary art and educational spaces, bringing together curriculum theory, aesthetics, and feminist pedagogy. She is the co-editor of *Curriculum and the Cultural Body* (with Debra Freedman) and the author of *Body Knowledge and Curriculum: Pedagogies of Touch in Youth and Visual Culture*. She has two children, Maurya and Liam.

Saskia Stille is a doctoral candidate in curriculum, teaching, and learning at the Ontario Institute for Studies in Education at the University of Toronto. Her research concerns the literacy development and engagement of multilingual children in urban schools, and provoking critical wonderings relating to textually mediated forms of identity and representation. In her methodology, she uses critical action research, working collaboratively with teachers and students to assist students to write creatively about their experiences and ideas using the full range of their bilingual cognitive tools. She is also a collaborator on the STEPs to English Language Proficiency project led by Jim Cummins and Eunice Jang at OISE/UT, exploring the validity, reliability, and fairness of a language assessment scale for English Language Learners in Kindergarten to Grade 12.

Jonel Thaller is a doctoral student in social work at Arizona State University, with an interest in women's sexual health and spirituality, as well as the prevention of violence against women. She has been published in the *Journal of Religion* and *Spirituality in Social Work* and has a forthcoming chapter about assessing fatal intimate partner violence in *Intimate Partner Violence: Domestic Abuse, Assault, and Spouse Battering*. She is currently working as a research assistant on a National Institute of Mental Health grant examining the efficacy of an Internet-based safety intervention for women living in abusive relationships. She is a mother of two and has experienced a hospital birth as well as a midwife-assisted home birth.

Diane Watt recently completed her doctoral dissertation in the Faculty of Education at the University of Ottawa, with a concentration in society, culture, and literacies. Her dissertation work draws from cultural studies, post-colonial theory, and feminist border epistemologies to open up the category 'Muslim woman.' She disrupts the mass media as curriculum by juxtaposing auto/ethno/graphic narratives with stories of the high schooling experiences of Muslim females and critical readings of images of Muslim women from the print media. She lived with her family in Pakistan, Syria, and Iran during the 1990s and spent fifteen years doing education other/wise with her two children outside of school. Her research interests include mothering and informal contexts of education, Muslim female identities, visual media literacy, and auto/ethno/graphic bricolage as decolonizing research. Her current work connects media and digital literacies with social justice issues.

Ugena Whitlock is an assistant professor of education and gender studies and associate coordinator of the Gender and Women's Studies Program at Kennesaw State University. She is secretary on the executive council of the American Association for the Advancement of Curriculum Studies. She is editor of the literacies section of the *Journal of Curriculum Theorizing* and is on the leadership team for the journal's annual Bergamo Conference. Her research interests include curriculum theory, queer theory, Southern studies, gender and sexuality, race, class, and popular culture. She is the author of *This Corner of Canaan: Curriculum Studies of Place and the Reconstruction of the South*.